ON THE EDGE OF EMPIRE

SUNY Series in Near Eastern Studies
Said Amir Arjomand, editor

ON THE EDGE OF EMPIRE

*Hadhramawt, Emigration, and the
Indian Ocean, 1880s–1930s*

Linda Boxberger

State University of New York Press

Published by
State University of New York Press, Albany

For information, address State University of New York Press,
90 State Street, Suite 700, Albany, NY 12207

Production by Dana Foote
Marketing by Patrick Durocher

Library of Congress Cataloging-in-Publication Data

Boxberger, Linda, 1951–
   On the edge of empire : Hadhramawt, emigration, and the Indian Ocean,
1880s–1930s / Linda Boxberger.
      p. cm — (SUNY series in Near Eastern studies)
   Includes bibliographical references and index.
   ISBN 0-7914-5217-4 (alk. paper) — ISBN 0-7914-5218-2 (pbk. : alk. paper)
      1. Hadhramawt (Yemen : Province)—History—19th century.   2. Hadhramawt
(Yemen : Province)—History—20th century.   3. Hadhramawt (Yemen : Province)—
Social life and customs—19th century.   4. Hadhramawt (Yemen : Province)—Social
life and customs—20th century.   I. Title.   II. Series.

DS247 .H37 B69 2002
953.3—dc21
                                                                              2001055141

10 9 8 7 6 5 4 3 2 1

To my mother and father

CONTENTS

PART FOUR
Politics, Power, and Conflict

ILLUSTRATIONS

PREFACE

Making History in Hadhramawt

The possibility of doing research in Hadhramawt opened up in May 1990, at the time of the long-awaited unification of the former Yemen Arab Republic (North Yemen) and the former People's Democratic Republic (South Yemen), into the Republic of Yemen. During the 1980s, when I lived and worked first in Kuwait and then in Sana'a', Y.A.R., I had tried to visit Hadhramawt as a tourist, but the P.D.R.Y. did not grant visas to Americans. As soon as I heard about the impending Yemeni unification, I started planning a research project in the social history of Hadhramawt, excited that I would finally have a chance to see this part of Yemen, which had previously been inaccessible to me.

After spending a month in Sana'a', my husband Awad and I made the three-day drive through rugged mountains and desert plains to the interior of Hadhramawt, arriving among the palm groves and tall mud-brick houses of the wadi for the first time together on December 31, 1992. We felt like pioneers. Since South Yemen's independence from the British in 1967, only a few Westerners had gained rather limited access for social research. Apart from a Soviet-Yemeni anthropological and archeological mission between 1986 and 1989, little research had been done by outsiders since that conducted by R. B. Serjeant in 1948 and 1949 and that by Abdalla Bujra in 1962 and 1963. At the same time, my preparatory research and a preliminary visit to Hadhramawt in the summer of 1991 had revealed the richness of the local source materials and the extensive work done by local scholars on their culture, history, and poetry. So we arrived in Hadhramawt, poised for adventure and bent on scholarship.

Our first surprise came when we found that there was no place to stay, as we were not the only ones seeking adventure in Hadhramawt. Because we arrived at the height of the European holiday season, the few small hotels and pensions in the three main towns of the interior wadi, Say'un, Tarim, and Shibam, were fully occupied with tourists. Numerous small groups of French and German "adventure tourists" had traveled across the desert in Landcruisers accompanied by beduin guides in order to view the splendid architecture and exotic sights of Hadhramawt for a day. For our first week in Hadhramawt, we pitched our tent on the windswept roof of a simple pension in Say'un as the tourists came and went below. After the previous night's tourists had left on their journeys, we used the facilities and drank the strong, sweet tea the innkeepers shared with us, before heading to work in the archives of the People's Museum, formerly the palace of the Kathiri sultanate. We

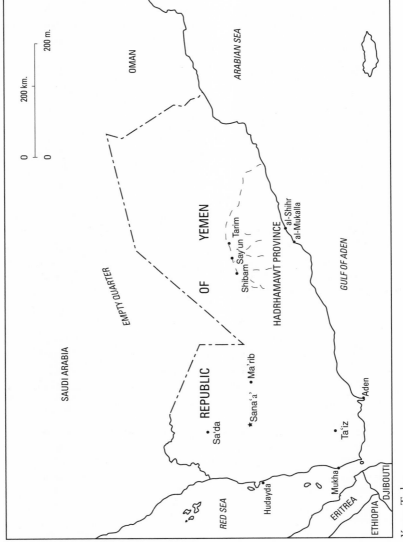

Yemen Today

had our own little round office in one of the corner watchtowers of this majestic white building, probably the largest mud-brick structure in existence.

While the museum director, 'Abd al-Qadir Muhammad al-Sabban, and the archivist, Muhammad 'Abd al-Qadir al-Sabban, were helpful to us, we found the documents opaque. We looked at personal documents, such as wills and deeds, dating from the late nineteenth and early twentieth century which, while not terribly old, were written in an archaic local terminology. We did not understand the terms and no one could explain them to us, although they recognized the language as "old words, having to do with 'this or that,' but no longer used."

But the most perplexing matter was that, aside from our mentors at the museum, hardly anyone would speak to us, beyond ordinary and distant pleasantries. Since my goal was to conduct in-depth interviews on cultural and historical topics with all kinds of people, this was most disconcerting. While we planned to spend the next year or so living in this community and getting to know it quite well, everyone ignored us and obviously considered us out of place. Even when people began to recognize us, the comments most frequently addressed to us were: "What, you two still here?" or "You haven't left yet?" Any trip to the airport to meet or see off visiting friends inspired the comment: "Ah, so you are leaving."

Even though accounts of such experiences are more than common in ethnographic literature, we had not anticipated these difficulties. We knew that Hadhramawt had been relatively isolated from outside intrusion for centuries, and that during the socialist period (1967–1990), foreign visitors were largely limited to Soviet development aid specialists who lived in their own compound and tourists who were shepherded past the sights with minimal contact with local people. But we did not expect it to be so difficult for us to find a niche in this society. Both Awad and I had lived and worked in North Yemen for years; we knew the language and the culture well and had valued our experiences living there. Originally from the Nubian region of Sudan, Awad is a Muslim and a native speaker of Arabic and is extremely skillful at getting along with different kinds of people, so he serves as a good cultural bridge for me, a non-Muslim Midwesterner.

We were stymied at our isolation. We had not realized the extent to which the peoples of Hadhramawt and other areas of the former South Yemen, while proudly part of the united Yemeni nation and state, retained separate regional cultures and identities. We knew that we were foreigners, but did not yet understand that our North Yemeni accents and ways marked us even further as "other," and seemed particularly peculiar since obviously neither of us was from North Yemen. The political, economic, and social stresses accompanying the unification of the two states not long before the Gulf War and the particular difficulties of the South's transition from socialism exacerbated the situation. It did not come as a surprise to us, when—at the end of our research experience, in spring 1994—the increasing political tension erupted into armed struggle.

But our immediate concern in the early days of the research was that it did not seem like anyone would be willing to talk to me about their culture and his-

tory. And certainly no one wanted to rent us a place to live, although we kept hearing about places that later turned out to be unavailable. People were naturally suspicious of my project and our purpose in coming there to live, which admittedly
was to nose around in their business (albeit for good ethnographic and historio-
graphic purposes). Months later, we learned that rumors had accompanied our arrival. An official source apparently had connected us with the bombing of an international hotel in Aden, which had taken place while we were en route from
Sana‘a’ to Hadhramawt. My bearded Sudanese husband and I were supposed to
embody an unholy alliance between international fundamentalist terrorism and
the Central Intelligence Agency! There had to be some explanation for an anomalous pair like us.

Our fortunes improved the day Awad went to a small car-parts shop where
he met the owner, ‘Abdallah Ba‘Atwa, who decided to ignore the unsavory rumors
associated with us and get to know us. He invited us to his house for our first home-
cooked meal in nearly a month, delicately seasoned rice and spicy boiled goat meat,
particularly savory as a result of the local practice of fattening the goats on alfalfa,
surplus onions, and ground date pits. Sated, we drank strong sweet tea brewed in
a samovar, while our host patiently answered our questions about the pre-1967 legal terminology used in the documents that we had been examining at the museum. Wise as well as knowledgeable, this self-educated businessman had long been
interested in the kind of social institutions, legal practices, and business dealings
that I was studying, and he had a remarkable memory. We were finally able to begin the long process of understanding this society and its past.

Through ‘Abdallah Ba’Atwa’s connections, we were eventually able to find a
place to live. We moved into the lovely Jawwas family “bungalow,” a small yet majestic three-story house set in a date-palm orchard near the family home. Built of
thick mud-brick walls covered with brilliant white slaked-lime plaster, its two main
rooms opened out onto loggias, terraces, and balconies framed by pillars and arched
colonnades. The tiny kitchen on the top floor opened onto a low-walled rooftop
terrace where we slept under the stars in hot weather. Between the ground-floor
guest room and our main sitting / sleeping room on the second floor, was the *jabiya,*
or “pool room.” Whenever water was pumped to irrigate the date palms, a strong
flow of fresh cold water circulated through the four-foot-deep bathing pool, remaining cool and still between waterings and providing the opportunity for a re-
freshing dip after a hot and tiring day. Following local practice, we had minimal furniture: a beautiful Baluchi carpet borrowed from the landlord for sitting and foam
pads for sleeping. Our household appliances included a refrigerator, a double gas
ring for cooking, plastic buckets and tubs for washing, and kerosene lamps for light
during the frequent power outages. Over the year and a half we lived there, we were
at times joined in our house by mosquitoes, flies, locusts, grasshoppers, bees, scor-
pions, and once by a poisonous snake. Despite these occasional unwelcome guests,
we loved our simple and beautiful living quarters, which provided us a cool and
quiet refuge from the heat, dust, noise—and sometimes hostility—of the streets.

As we settled in, we gradually met more people who were willing to help us with the research project. Despite an abundance of materials, the process was difficult. The time period that I was studying, the 1880s through the 1930s, was marked by social and political conflict. Even though I had delineated the time period of my study as ending around 1937, some of these conflicts and the suffering that they had caused had persisted for years after, manifesting themselves in new ways during the socialist and postsocialist eras. My historical research occasionally touched on topics associated with continuing pain and grief and with ongoing conflicts in the society. I tried as much as possible to avoid aligning myself with one faction or another in past and present conflicts. This was not easy, since the desire to enlist me, as an historian, on the side of one cause or another was one of the stronger factors motivating people to speak with me and assist me in my research in the first place.

Even though I was frequently rebuffed in my search for sources and interviews, as time passed more and more individuals expressed interest in my project and offered to help. Some of my fondest memories of Hadhramawt are of the cooperation and kindness of people who helped with the research. For example, when we interviewed a livestock broker in Shibam, he had a goat slaughtered. We sat on a rooftop terrace of his tall house during the dusk and early evening while he explained the workings of the market and the caravan trade to us. As we spoke, the goat roasted, and the interview ended with a feast. Another time, during an interview with a *munsib* (spiritual leader), he not only shared with us the grace of his warm and peaceful presence, he literally blessed my husband during the course of our discussion. During our last Ramadan in Hadhramawt, during the onset of war, we spent over a week in the beautiful seaside home of the Kasadi family in al-Hami. We pored over documents in our breezy top-floor apartment during the day, and feasted on delicious fresh fish, visited with the family and neighbors, and watched *America's Funniest Home Videos* on Yemeni TV during the night. The many positive experiences more than compensated for the difficult times: when people I hoped to interview saw me coming and politely excused themselves, abruptly remembered an urgent appointment elsewhere, or in one case, suddenly received psychic notification of a death in the family.

I hope that the book I eventually produced will be of benefit to its readers and that scholars and students learn from it about a complex and fascinating society and its history. But I especially hope that it will be of some interest and use to the people of Hadhramawt, from whom I have learned so much.

ACKNOWLEDGMENTS

A number of organizations and individuals helped make this study possible. A Fulbright-Hays Doctoral Dissertation Grant, a supplementary grant from the American Institute for Yemeni Studies, and a W. Gordon Whaley University Fellowship from The University of Texas at Austin funded the field research in Hadhramawt, Yemen, from December 1992 through April 1994. The Yemen Center for Research and Studies and the General Organization for Antiquities, Museums, and Manuscripts sponsored my residence and research in Yemen. During my stay in Hadhramawt, the local branches of the Ministry of Culture and Information, the Museums of Say'un and al-Mukalla, and the al-Ahqaf Libraries were generous in assisting me.

This work would not have been possible without the help and guidance that I received from people in Hadhramawt, to whom I express whole-hearted thanks and appreciation. My understanding of the history and culture of this society was guided by local scholars who have spent years doing research. Ja'far Muhammad al-Saqqaf and the late 'Abd al-Qadir Muhammad al-Saqqaf of Say'un, whom I met during a preresearch visit to Hadhramawt in 1991, encouraged and assisted me from the beginning. The late 'Abd al-Rahman 'Abdallah BaRaja generously shared his insights and his unpublished writings. 'Abd al-Rahman 'Abd al-Karim al-Mallahi shared his extensive knowledge of the coastal region, facilitated meetings for me, and served as a model of a conscientious scholar and a skillful and sensitive interviewer. He researched and created detailed historical maps that served as the base for the simplified English versions in this book. 'Ali Salim Bukayr, Ahmad 'Abd al-Qadir BaKathir, 'Abdallah Ahmad Mahrus, and Husayn Ahmad 'Aydid helped in many ways. All the individuals that I interviewed are acknowledged in the footnotes, but I must add my thanks for the insights that I gained through their sharing of their experiences with me.

From the new generation of scholars, 'Abd al-Rahman Hasan al-Saqqaf was very helpful; he and his family kindly shared documents and manuscripts of 'Abd al-Rahman b. Ubaydillah al-Saqqaf with me. Sanad Muhammad BaYa'shut was also of great help, sharing documents and books with me and setting up interviews. Husayn BaSalih, Sa'id Salih BaMakrid, Salih Ba'Amr, and 'Adil al-Kathiri all helped in multiple ways.

I also thank the friends whose kindness and encouragement helped me to endure the trials and travails of field research in a distant land. While space does not allow me to thank all who were hospitable, I wish to acknowledge: Shaykh Salim Muhammad Bin 'Ali Jabir, 'Umar Salim al-Kasadi, Hasan Ahmad al-'Amri,

Muhammad al-Hadi ʿAlaywa, and Saʿid Mubarak Shilshil and their families; our landlords and neighbors, the Muhammad ʿAbdallah Jawwas family; and the three generations of ladies of the household of the late Abu Bakr ʿAli al-Kaf. Finally, ʿAbdalla Salim BaʾAtwa deserves special gratitude for his great generosity, wise advice, staunch friendship, and for his stubborn refusal to let anyone or anything dissuade him from befriending us. I cannot thank him enough.

I also want to express appreciation to Engseng Ho and Thomas Pritzkat, who were doing research in Hadhramawt at the same time that I was. Although we seldom met, we had some good laughs when we did, and I was glad to know that I was not alone in my struggles to understand this complex society and its history.

While living in Hadhramawt, it was necessary to return every few months to the Yemeni capital, Sanaʿaʾ, to take care of administrative business. I must thank Claudia Cooper, Ursula Dreibholz, Cecelia Hite, Sabry and Andrea Saleem, and Dave van Hammen and Phyllis Crowell for hosting and sustaining us during those visits. I also thank Ann and Charles Wintheiser for their help at a difficult time. ʿAli Ahmad Saʿdallah and Hamid Qasim al-ʿAwadhi and their families also took good care of us in Sanaʿaʾ. Ahmad Muhammad al-Huwaysiq and his family generously hosted us en route when we took the desert road between Hadhramawt and Sanaʿaʾ. Several times we rode through the desert from Mareb to Sayʾun with the guides from the Sharif family; thanks to ʿAbdelkarim and Saʿid for making those journeys exciting and safe.

A year after I finished my field research in Yemen, I participated in the workshop, "Hadhramaut and the Hadhrami Diaspora, late 18th Century to c. 1967," held at the School for Oriental and African Studies, University of London, in April 1995. I thank the organizers, Ulrike Freitag and William Gervase Clarence-Smith, for creating the opportunity for scholars from all over the world to gather and share their interests in Hadhramis and Hadhrami emigration.

For their comments, criticisms, and advice, I thank Abraham Marcus, Denise Spellberg, Gail Minault, W. Roger Louis, Robert Fernea, and Renate Wise, and the three anonymous readers enlisted by State University of New York Press. Sultan Ghalib al-Quʾaitiʾs contributions to the political chapters were invaluable; I appreciate the time he spent answering my questions, relaying questions to Shaykh al-Nakhibi, and extensively commenting on the draft chapters.

For intellectual encouragement and human solidarity that helped me see this project through, I thank Elizabeth Warnock Fernea, Maria Ellis, Shelagh Weir, Leila Noman, Marta Colburn, Abubaker BaGader, Tariq al-Maashi, Diane Watts, ʿAlawi Hasan al-Saqqaf, John and Pinar VanderLippe, and Gwenn Okhrulik.

I am grateful to my late father and my mother, Carl and Irene Boxberger, and my aunt, Ruth Boxberger, for always having encouraged me to learn and to explore and for their unwavering support.

Finally, it gives me great pleasure to express my appreciation to my husband, Awad Abdelrahim Abdelgadir, for helping in every way, even though this project turned out to be far more difficult, complicated, and time-consuming than either of us had imagined. Thank you, Awad, for your unconditional support.

Note on transliteration and document references

I have used a simplified form of transliteration of Arabic terms, hoping to make the book accessible to a broad readership. For specialists, I have included an Arabic bibliography in full transliteration.

In document references, CO and FO prefixes refer to British Colonial Office and Foreign Office documents housed in the Public Record Office at Kew. Documents from the Say'un Museum collection are identified SMA, followed by section number and item number. Mukalla Museum documents are identified MMA, followed by item number. Privately held documents are identified by the Hijra date of the document, followed by the name of their owner.

INTRODUCTION

This is the story of an Islamic society of the Arabian Peninsula, part of a web of societies of the Indian Ocean littoral long connected through trade and emigration, at the time that European imperialism increasingly dominated the region. Between the 1880s and the 1930s, the Qu'ayti and the Kathiri sultanates of Hadhramawt were gradually incorporated into the Western imperial system. The two sultanates were established in the late nineteenth century, after a protracted struggle among a number of local rivals for power in this territory of southern Arabia. Their formal integration into the British Empire took place in stages. The Qu'ayti sultanate made a treaty of friendship with the British in 1882 and became a protectorate in 1888, while the Kathiri sultanate remained outside the imperial sphere until it was subsumed into the British-protected Qu'ayti state as a semi-autonomous entity in 1918. British protection had little direct impact on Hadhramawt: protectorate status meant that the sultanates could not independently enter relationships with other powers, but internal affairs remained in the hands of the sultanates. It was not until 1937, when the sultanates entered into an advisory agreement with the British and the resident advisor took up his post in the Qu'ayti capital, that the imperial power exerted direct influence within Hadhramawt. Yet during the decades preceding direct colonial intervention, Hadhramawt felt the impact of the European imperial transformation of the Indian Ocean region, largely through the mechanism of Hadhrami emigration.

Hadhramawt was isolated by desert and harsh barren mountains from the rest of the Arabian Peninsula, itself a backwater from the point of view of world politics and the world economy. But through its Arabian Sea ports, Hadhramawt was connected to the wider Indian Ocean region and its interlinking African, Arab, Persian, Indian, and East Asian networks of trade and migration. For centuries Hadhramis had left their poor and arid homeland to seek their fortunes throughout the Indian Ocean region from Zanzibar to the Indonesian archipelago, participating in the extensive trading networks of the region and also serving as religious leaders. These emigrants generally retained strong links with their homeland: they remitted money to their families in Hadhramawt; sent their foreign-born sons there to study; and many nurtured a deep nostalgia for the homeland, aspiring to return there to live out their final days.

By the 1880s, imperial technological developments in the region, such as the laying of telegraph cables and the expansion of steamship lines, greatly facilitated communications, travel, and the maintenance of connections between the Hadhrami emigrant communities in the Indian Ocean basin and their southern

Arabian homeland. While the European domination of trade supplanted the long-standing trading networks in the region, it also created new economic opportunities for Hadhrami emigrants. By the 1930s, an estimated one hundred thousand Hadhramis, perhaps 20 to 30 percent of the population, were outside of their homeland. Some of these emigrants labored for meager wages; a few amassed great fortunes.[1]

Emigrants who had benefited from the imperial transformation of the Indian Ocean region affected the political, economic, and social life of their homeland during this dynamic period, introducing new wealth, goods, fashions, and ideas to Hadhramawt. The Qu'ayti and Kathiri sultanates were created in the late nineteenth century by founders who had acquired wealth and power as leaders of the military forces of the Nizam of Hyderabad. After extended struggles for power in Hadhramawt among a number of players, these new ruling dynasties reshaped the political landscape, albeit employing time-honored methods of acquiring and maintaining power. After centuries of decentralized rule by local strongmen, Hadhramawt benefited from the consolidation of power and extension of state authority by these sultanates, which the Qu'ayti accomplished more successfully than the Kathiri. Both sultanates attempted to extend military, administrative, and legal authority within their territories, and to provide security for the populations, commerce, and travel. Both undertook public works, such as the building of town walls and fortifications that increased the security of their subjects and palaces and government buildings that asserted the legitimacy of the rulers. Thus they added visible physical symbols of their rule and authority at the same time that they extended and expanded their political and administrative control.

At the same time, other Hadhramis who had acquired wealth through emigration also made their mark on the homeland. Wealthy emigrants, particularly those with interests in trade and real estate in Singapore and the Dutch East Indies, built mosques, centers for religious study and practice, and schools. Besides financing the buildings, they supported their operations, and provided funding for religious leaders, teachers, and students. Through these acts of philanthropy, they revitalized religious practice in the homeland, fostered and rejuvenated religious education, and advanced secular education. These new educational institutions made it possible for more Hadhramis to have access to education than before, as did the funding of secular schools in the Qu'ayti sultanate.

The emigrants also spent money for private purposes: building palatial homes, importing luxury goods from Europe and Asia, and spending lavishly on hospitality. Private celebrations became an arena for display, with imported accoutrements replacing local ones and with imported styles of women's clothing and ornamentation becoming the fashion. The higher levels of hospitality and new fashions became the standard others tried to emulate. Reliance on imported goods for staples and necessities as well as for luxury items increased.

The political, social, and economic changes that took place during this period did not go uncontested. Rivals for power, backed by wealth gained through emigration, challenged the authority of the sultans. Civic reform associations, directed and funded by wealthy emigrants, demanded that the sultans allow them a role in governance. The religious and educational institutions created by emigrant wealth were beset by internal dissent and public debate as to the proper nature of religious practice and education. Even the new fashions became a subject for dispute. The civic reform associations attempted to limit the styles and materials of women's dresses and styles and quantities of jewelry, as well as displays of ostentation in entertaining and hospitality. The new materialism and conspicuous consumption were thought to threaten the social order, with wealth overpowering other measures of prestige. The need for general social reform and the need for reform of religious and educational institutions became subjects of public debate among the emigrant communities as well as in the homeland. Some of those calling for reform espoused the ideals of the Islamic modernists, Jamal al-Din al-Afghani, Muhammad 'Abdu, and Rashid Ridha, whose ideas were influential in the wider Muslim world, including the areas to which Hadhramis emigrated. Others decried the modernists, but agreeing with the need for change, advocated a return to the purer ways of an idealized past.

In the Hadhrami case, changes resulting from the dramatic Western imperial expansion of the nineteenth century were not imposed from outside. On the contrary, local rulers and leaders entered into relationships with the imperial powers in an effort to pursue their own advantage—sometimes voluntarily, sometimes impelled by a confluence of internal and external forces. Local people introduced material goods, fashions, and ideas that they had encountered in their experience abroad, selecting and importing that which they considered beneficial, a matter that turned out to be subject to differences of point of view and interpretation within the society.

The way that Hadhramis responded to the changes of this dramatic period resulted from the particular nature of their society. The political, economic, and social changes in Hadhramawt took place within a heterogeneous society. With some regional variations, Hadhrami society comprised a number of distinct identity groups, often referred to as social strata, which interacted in complex patterns determined by custom and considered to be part of an "age-old" order. These included religiously prestigious groups, arms-bearing tribes, townspeople, laborers, and slaves (the complexity of these groups is detailed in chapter 1). They held varying degrees and types of prestige and power and held different roles in political, religious, and community life. Members of less prestigious groups were not merely pawns in the hands of the powerful but acted as agents in pursuit of their individual and collective interests within the constraints determined by their position. Political power was a complicated affair, in which the sultans relied on different kinds of support from members of various social groups. During this period of change, rivalries flourished, alliances shifted, and boundaries of power were challenged. Religious prestige was a somewhat more straightforward matter, although the two religiously prestigious groups competed at times as well as cooperated. The revitalization of religious and educational institutions at this time, and the expansion of access to religious education—and education in general—to members of groups other than the religiously prestigious, led to the most heated debates and most implacable rifts in the society. These divisions created further discord at the political level at the same time that they thwarted many efforts toward social reform by civic organizations and by the sultans.

This account of Hadhrami society presents the experience of ordinary people in the everyday life of their communities, showing how they were affected by the changes sweeping the wider region, and how they incorporated change and adapted to it. At the same time, it takes into account the continuity of place, identity, custom, and social institutions that provided the background in which change took place. Hadhramawt was by no means transformed by its increasing connections with the outside world and the imperial powers. Old ways were not abandoned, but rather modified in their encounter with the new. Voices urging the maintenance of the ways of the ancestors debated with those voices espousing modernist reform.

Rather than looking at events in Hadhramawt simply from the point of view of its place in the European colonial enterprise, I depict the various points of view of different groups within the society.[2] The goal of presenting a multifaceted, polyphonic view of this complex society in a time of change shaped the methodology and sources employed. To elicit and portray the experience and point of view of diverse groups, including those whose concerns have often been ignored, it was necessary to employ a wide variety of types of sources, written and oral. For some aspects of Hadhrami history there exists a rich literature in print, although most of these works were produced in very limited quantities. Hadhrami scholars have written several general histories of Hadhramawt. In these works, the analysis of society and events varies according to the social identity and points of view of their authors.[3] Certain works of history produced under the auspices of the government of the People's Democratic Republic of Yemen, while influenced by the regime's and the author's political orientation, at the same time contain much valuable historical and cultural material.[4]

Besides these histories, Hadhramis produced other literary works that provide views of aspects of this society as perceived by its members. Several travel accounts by Hadhramis depicting journeys made during this time period have been published, including works by members of Hadhrami emigrant communities overseas who journeyed to their ancestral homeland and by Hadhramis in the homeland who travelled to areas previously unknown to them.[5]

Some collections of poetry contain material of social and historical significance. These include mimeographed pamphlets of "people's poetry" produced by the local branches of the Ministry of Culture and Information of the PDRY, as well as published collections of popular poetry. There are also a number of printed collections of the production of poets working within the formal tradition; more of these collections are found in manuscript in al-Ahqaf Library in

Tarim and in private libraries and family papers. Some of these collections include introductory and explanatory texts contextualizing the poems, furthering their utility to the social and historical researcher.[6]

Religious materials include, among a great many hagiographical works, biographies of spiritually prestigious individuals that illuminate religious education and practice. An increasing amount of this material is being privately printed by the descendants and adherents of these individuals; other manuscripts are being photocopied and distributed through local bookstores.[7] In published biographical collections that serve as essential research sources, the entries focus on the religious learning, teaching, and service of their subjects. Besides giving some details of individual lives, by enumerating the teachers and students of their subjects and their travels, they convey a sense of the extensive networks in which the elites of this society participated.[8] An increasing number of biographical collections of particular families are being privately printed.

Legal works indicate social, economic, and religious questions and problems that arose and the response to them by respected authorities. Since these works are intended as jurisprudential resources, most cases are presented in a timeless and depersonalized fashion, which limits their usefulness as social historical documents. This study utilizes collections of decisions by jurists active in its time period and a classic collection of juristic decisions compiled earlier in the nineteenth century. Many more such works of *fiqh,* Islamic jurisprudence, are available in manuscript at the al-Ahqaf Library.[9]

Debates on social and religious reform appear in printed polemics and articles and letters in periodicals published in the homeland, the Hadhrami emigrant communities overseas, and in the wider Muslim world. Of particular interest are *al-Tahdhib,* a handwritten journal circulated in Hadhramawt in 1930 and 1931, and *al-Rabita,* a journal published in Singapore in the 1920s. Hadhrami emigrants' correspondence appeared in the Egyptian Islamic modernist journal *al-Manar* throughout the period of its publication.

Recent works have been published which combine memoir and history, incorporating detail and analysis from participants in events. These include several works by former officials of the Qu'ayti state. Another "hybrid" work slated for publishing is *Badha'i' al-tabut* by 'Abd al-Rahman b. 'Ubaydillah al-Saqqaf, which combines an encyclopedic history of Hadhramawt with the memoirs and correspondence of its remarkable author, who communicated with many of the important figures of his time. The last Qu'ayti sultan, Sultan Ghalib al-Qu'aiti, deposed in 1968, has written published and unpublished works in Arabic and English on Hadhrami history. His extensive knowledge of the Qu'ayti sultanate derives from his personal experience of upbringing and rule, from his communications with its elder statesmen, and from his research using family and archival documents in Arabic, English, and Urdu.[10]

Primary documents such as official papers and correspondence are more numerous and varied than one might expect to find in the Arabian peninsula, although unfortunately both public and private collections are for the most part fragmentary. Some documents concerning local, regional, and international politics are available in the archives in the palaces of the erstwhile Kathiri and Quʻayti sultanates, particularly the former. Somewhat compensating for the unfortunate loss of most materials in the Quʻayti archives, the Kathiri archives include extensive correspondence received from the Quʻayti state and drafts of letters from the Kathiri to the Quʻayti state. The archives in the Sayʼun Museum, formerly the palace of the Kathiri sultanate, include: tribal agreements; Kathiri government proclamations and correspondence; financial records; and a collection of personal documents, such as wills, agricultural agreements, bills of sale, mortgages, pious endowments, and the like. The archives in the Mukalla Museum, in the palace of the former Quʻayti sultanate, contain holdings limited to a few tribal agreements and deeds of land purchases by the Quʻayti state. Personal legal documents, papers of prominent individuals, and records of reform organizations are held privately, usually by heirs among whom collections of documents are divided.[11]

Primary source material about Hadhramawt appears in English and European languages as well. *Le Hadhramout et les Colonies Arabes dans l'Archipel Indien* by L. W. C. van den Berg, an official of the Netherlands East Indies government, includes a section on Hadhramawt derived from the reports of informants of Hadhrami origin. It also includes a report on the Hadhrami communities in the East Indies in the early 1880s. Some travel accounts depict life in Hadhramawt as observed by Europeans. Although J. R. Wellsted visited the coast of Hadhramawt in the early nineteenth century and the Bents visited the coast and the interior at the end of the century, most travel accounts date from the 1930s, when Western travelers and colonial officials began to visit. Travelers Freya Stark and Daniel van der Meulen published books on their visits to Hadhramawt that contain much material of interest. Harold Ingrams and Doreen Ingrams both wrote official reports on Hadhramawt and both wrote memoirs of their years in Hadhramawt which reveal the depth of their understanding of the society and their high regard for its people.[12] European authors naturally present the material from their own points of view, which differ somewhat from the views originating within Hadhrami society.

Documents related to Hadhramawt and Hadhrami emigrant communities are found in British archives. These are found in the R / 20 series of Aden records in the India Office collection now in the British Library and the CO / 725 series of Colonial Office records in the Public Record Office at Kew. Concerns of Hadhrami emigrant communities appear in the British consular records of the countries hosting the emigrants; these are found in Foreign Office (FO) records in the Public Record Office. Since British records present Hadhrami concerns as a facet of British Empire and international relations, they are useful in contextualizing Hadhramawt within the wider sphere of European imperialism and European competition. They must be used judiciously, since internal Hadhrami matters are discussed in terms of their relationship to British interests even when the British interests were of little relevance to the Hadhramis involved. Since British officials were not physically present in Hadhramawt until the 1930s, official reports were derived largely from interviews and communications with Hadhramis in Aden and the various emigrant communities abroad. Pursuing their own interests, these informants tended to skew their presentation of matters in such a way that Hadhrami affairs appeared to have more to do with British interests than they actually did.

Despite the wide array of printed and handwritten materials available in Hadhramawt, they do not suffice to convey the point of view and experiences of various sectors of this society. Apart from religious notables, most people going about the everyday business of their lives left little mark in the written records. Yet the activities of farmers, camel herders, fishermen, sailors, and merchants were essential to the survival of the society and members of these groups were affected by social, political, and economic change. To elicit the stories of different tribal and occupational groups, one must turn to oral sources. Some poetry and lore of these groups has been collected by local scholars under the auspices of the local branches of the Ministry of Culture and Information of the PDRY and the Yemeni Writers' League, which printed a series of mimeographed pamphlets during the 1980s.[13] But in order to elicit the story of groups whose participation in their times has often been marginalized in historiography, it was necessary to conduct interviews with a wide range of people.

Investigating groups whose stories are not represented in print sources, a researcher comes to respect knowledge derived from collective human experience and the legitimacy of the oral media through which this knowledge is transmitted. Certain individuals are recognized as leaders by their tribal or occupational groups and are acknowledged by the larger community as experts in specialized areas. I conducted interviews with individuals, many retired but some still active, who were respected for their skills and leadership. Often born into a particular calling or position, they had become recognized as leaders through intelligence, ability, and communications skills combined with wisdom acquired through experience and training by their predecessors and elders. Besides knowing how to do their job, they had learned the lore and history of their group, which often included a timeless idealized past but also included notable events that had taken place in the time of their elders and predecessors. They used a variety of time markers to indicate chronology. These ranged from conventional markers like the world wars or the decades of the twentieth century, to Hadhrami-specific ones like the period of rule of a particular sultan or the period of public activity of a well-known figure, to more personal ones like the lifetime of an interviewee's parent or mentor or ancestor. Those interviewed were able to relate a wealth of material of particular concern to their group, including anecdotes, jokes, and popular poetry; some made references to printed works and manuscripts. Besides serving as sources of information about the past, these specialists offered their interpretations of the past.[14]

Some of the people interviewed were sea captains, sailors, fishermen, farmers, tribesmen and tribal leaders, craftsmen, boat builders, market brokers, merchants, soldiers, jurists, religious leaders, poets, and descendants of slaves. I relied on local scholars and friends to recommend people to be interviewed. They also helped persuade people to be interviewed, informing them about my interests and my work. In some cases, local scholars assisted in the interview process, as did my husband, who accompanied me in almost all meetings with men. Since the individuals I interviewed were elders respected for their expertise, knowledge, and leadership, they were often surrounded by visitors at the time of our meetings. This sometimes meant that several people participated in the interviews, which became collective processes ranging well beyond the research agendas that I had in mind.

Like written materials, the oral accounts of different groups sometimes contain contradictions. These often arise from conflicting points of view which led opposing sides both to declare that they gained "moral victory" from the same events or at least accomplished that which they had sought. One must pay attention to these subtexts in using oral accounts. Employing a wide variety of sources helps to sieve out misinformation, whether inadvertent or self-serving, in order that apparent contradictions may be resolved and conflicting viewpoints identified. But even misinformation can be valuable, embodying symbolic significance rather than factual accuracy. For example, one group of tribesmen told me that the (well-documented) shots fired by their fellow tribesmen at British Resident Advisor Harold Ingrams in the 1930s struck him and caused him to walk with a limp the rest of his life. Ingrams's limp was also well documented, but was actually the result of an injury previously incurred—in Europe during World War I. Although this tale is obviously counterfactual, it persists as a bit of tribal lore, with its own meaning in the context of the tribal history. In the late 1930s, Ingrams had ordered the bombing of this tribe's settlements—after repeated warnings—in retaliation for the tribe's continual raiding of caravan traffic through tribal territory. The tribe's account of their "wounding" of Ingrams may have served the function of "saving face," satisfying their obligation to have meted revenge for the bombing and enabling them to deal with him afterward without loss of honor.

As this instance indicates, events and the stories about them are imbued with a multiplicity of meanings, particularly in the case of a heterogeneous society like Hadhramawt, with its multiplicity of identity groups and interest groups. In order to convey the story of Hadhramawt during the dynamic period from the 1880s through the 1930s, this book will examine: the nature of Hadhrami identity in the homeland and the emigrant communities; the ordering of social and economic life in the towns and countryside along with changes taking place; the nature of social institutions, the ways that they were changing, and social debates resulting from change; and finally, an account of the conflicts and struggles over power that took place during this period of Hadhramawt's gradual incorporation into the structures of the Western imperial system.

PART ONE

Aspects of Social Identity in Hadramawt and Abroad

I
Identity in Hadhrami Society

Communities and Identities

Shared elements of heritage contribute to the notion of a community as envisioned by its members, thereby shaping individual identities. In the words of Benedict Anderson, "all communities larger than primordial villages of face-to-face contact (and perhaps even these) are imagined."[1] Membership in an "imagined community," or in a number of overlapping concentric communities, forms a meaningful background to an individual's experience. At the same time, identity encompasses multiple levels and tiers, with different aspects predominating in different contexts. It is constantly sustained by comparisons, and the aspects relevant to comparison vary according to geographical and social settings.[2]

People from different parts of Hadhramawt shared an attachment to a land and a heritage, while they also identified with smaller units—territory, town, quarter, neighborhood—associated with specific local cultural attributes and histories. A further aspect of Hadhrami identity was membership in one of the social groups into which the larger society was divided; this membership was acquired at birth. Social group membership affected a person's prospects in terms of marriage, education, occupation, and role in religious, economic, and political life. While different social groups comprised different types of subgroups, all were composed of families, and membership in a family was another important aspect of individual identity. Another aspect of identity, gender, transected the others. Gender determined important elements of a person's role in family and society and affected an individual's participation in education and in economic life; the boundaries of possibility varied among the different social groups.

Hadhramawt: The Land and Its People

The people of Hadhramawt shared a deep sense of attachment to a homeland with an ancient and honorable heritage. The term Hadhramawt, as used in this study, refers to the territory of the interior and coast of southern Arabia, which by the beginning of the twentieth century comprised the Qu'ayti and Kathiri sultanates. This territory included: its core, Wadi Hadhramawt, an enormous wadi or canyon lying south of the vast desert of the Empty Quarter of Arabia; smaller tributary

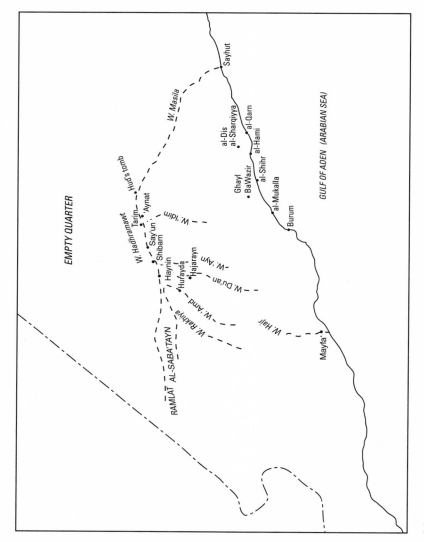

Map 1.1 Main towns and wadis of Hadhramawt

wadis running south from the main wadi; and the coast of the Gulf of Aden parallel to the main wadi, extending from Barum in the west to Masila in the east. The deep wadis or canyons cut through a barren high plateau, known as the *jawl*, which rose from the lowlands of the coast. While the towns and hamlets of the main wadi, smaller wadis, and coastal region all bore marks of geographic, cultural, and historical specificity, their inhabitants shared a strong sense of identification with an ancient land and participated in similar social institutions. Towns like Hurayda and 'Aynat, as autonomous city-states lay outside the boundaries of the two sultanates, although they too shared aspects of Hadhrami identity and social institutions.

The ports and agricultural communities of the coastal region were connected to the interior through several caravan routes that crossed the windswept *jawl* and then passed through the smaller wadis into Wadi Hadhramawt proper. The long and difficult caravan route westward to Sana'a', capital of Yemen, passed through the tongue of desert sands called Ramlat al-Sab'atayn before ascending the steep escarpments of the Yemeni highlands. Overland travel north and east of Wadi Hadhramawt led only to the most barren of deserts, while the overland route to Aden was obstructed by impassable mountains and rocky wastelands. The main connection between Hadhramawt and the rest of the world was through the ports of the Arabian Sea coast, which were linked by long-established sea trade routes to the ports of the Indian Ocean, Red Sea, and Persian Gulf. Hadhramawt had long-standing trade and cultural connections with the Red Sea and Swahili coasts and outlying islands of Africa, the east and west coasts of India, Ceylon, the East Indies, Singapore, and Malaya.

Wadi Hadhramawt, its tributaries, and the spring-watered oases of the coastal region contained fertile agricultural land remarkable in their surroundings of barren plateaus and harsh deserts. In the main wadi, permanently flowing water was found only in one part, the southeastern reach known as Wadi Masila. The western tributary of Wadi Hajr, known at its mouth as Wadi Mayfa', was watered by the only river in the Arabian peninsula flowing year round from source to mouth, making that wadi some of the most fertile land in the peninsula. Water flowed periodically through the other tributary wadis, including Wadi Sa'r, north of the main wadi, and Wadi 'Amd, Wadi Du'an, Wadi al-'Ayn, and Wadi 'Idim, south of the main wadi, particularly after summer rainfall in the mountains caused by the south-west monsoon. Wherever and whenever water flowed, Hadhrami agriculturalists employed spate irrigation techniques. Ground water was abundantly available throughout the wadi system, at shallower levels in the east. Both flood waters and ground water were used to irrigate date palms and fields of grain, fodder, and vegetables. In the coastal region, hot springs provided water for human consumption and for irrigation.

In the main wadi and its tributaries, most towns were built at the base of the almost vertical canyon walls, the tall mud-brick houses rising on the steep screeslopes at their base. The towns of Tarim and Say'un in the main wadi exemplified this pattern of siting, which offered the towns protection from the occasional flooding of the wadi and reserved the fertile silt of the wadi bottom for farming. There were a few exceptions to the pattern of towns lying at the base of the canyon walls. The towns of Wadi Hajr by necessity lay high on the steep walls of the wadi, since its permanently flowing river was swelled by the periodic floods that inundated the wadi bottom. Another exception to the general pattern was the remarkable city of Shibam in the main wadi. This walled city, an entrepôt of the Arabian caravan routes dating back to the frankincense trade of ancient times, stood on a tell in the middle of the wadi.

On the coastal plain, inland towns such as Ghayl BaWazir and al-Dis al-Sharqiyya were located near springs which provided water for the needs of the town and irrigation. Most of the port towns were located where natural harbors provided shelter for fishing boats and the sailing vessels of the Indian Ocean trade, although the historically important port town of al-Shihr faced the open sea from its site on an open plain. In the nineteenth century, al-Mukalla superseded al-Shihr in importance, probably because of its protected harbor and more defensible site: a narrow strip of land lying between the sea and the towering basalt mountains inland. The port of al-Shihr and the newer al-Mukalla were commonly referred to as *al-bandarayn,* an Arabized Persian word meaning "the two ports." Smaller ports included: Burum, lying west of al-Mukalla at the base of protective hills on a cape known as Ra's Burum, which provided the best anchorage along the entire coast during the southwest monsoon; al-Hami, east of al-Shihr, famous as the home of seafarers; and farther east, al-Qarn, a small port serving the inland town of al-Dis al-Sharqiyya.[3]

In the early 1880s, the population of the main wadi, tributaries, and coastal region was probably less than 150,000. By the mid-1930s, it may have been somewhat larger, perhaps as much as 170,000.[4] Most of the population was settled in the towns and agricultural hamlets of the wadi system, the ports, and the spring-fed agricultural towns of the coastal region, while a sparse population of tribal nomadic pastoralists was widely dispersed in the deserts and on barren plateau lands.

The inhabitants of the different parts of Hadhramawt shared the notion that the history of their homeland extended far back into the depths of time—a notion confirmed by legend, by scripture, and by ancient relics and ruins. They considered their land the home of the ancient people of 'Ad, who rejected the message of monotheism brought by the Prophet Hud a few generations after Noah's people had rejected monotheism. Like people in Noah's time, the people of 'Ad were destroyed by God for their arrogance and polytheism. The story of Hud and the people of 'Ad was recounted in the Qur'an, like the stories of the prophets of the Hebrew Bible and Jesus, as previous manifestations of the monotheistic message revealed to Muhammad. Medieval Islamic scholars located the land of the ancient people of 'Ad and the Prophet Hud in eastern Hadhramawt, consonant with local lore, which deemed an ancient sacred site there as the site of Hud's tomb and which attributed ancient remains throughout Hadhramawt to the time of 'Ad. People from all over Hadhramawt visited the tomb of Prophet Hud, in a ritual that confirmed their sharing of this ancient heritage.[5]

The legendary history of Hadhramawt reflected its past as the seat of an ancient civilization. It had been one of the southern Arabian kingdoms of the critical overland trade routes over which frankincense, spices, and luxury goods were transported by camel caravan in the centuries preceding the birth of Christ. At that time, Shibam was an entrepôt for frankincense and myrrh, the valuable resin gums produced in southern Arabia and used in the ancient Near East and Mediterranean world for religious rites, medicines, and mummification. The camel caravans also carried goods brought by sea from the east, including spices, silk, and precious stones and goods imported from Africa through the port of Aden, including ivory, gold, and exotic animal products.[6]

At the height of the incense trade in the centuries before the birth of Christ, dams and irrigation systems were maintained and a civilization based on trade and agriculture flourished in the interior of Hadhramawt. The coast of Hadhramawt was a link between the Indian Ocean sea trade and the Arabian overland caravans. An extensive trading system had existed in this region long before it was described in the Roman navigation guide, *The Periplus of the Erythraean Sea*, written in 50 to 60 C.E. Previously, the Indian Ocean sailing routes and the timing of the monsoon winds were known only to Arab and Indian seamen and traders, who also kept secret the places of origin of the precious luxury products in which they traded.

During the third century C.E., the trade diminished as the replacement of earlier religious practices by those of Christianity greatly lessened the demand for myrrh and frankincense at a time when the demand for other luxury goods was shrinking along with the Mediterranean economy as a whole. In addition, Roman shippers had begun to deal directly with India via the Red Sea, bypassing the Arabian caravan routes. Between the third and sixth centuries C.E., the irrigation systems fell into disrepair and the ancient civilizations of southern Arabia went into decline. After the dams and monumental architecture of the ancient civilization fell into ruins, the ample ground water of Hadhramawt continued to support a simple agricultural and pastoral economy. The people continued to participate in the trading systems of the Indian Ocean region, linked to the sea trade through the ports of the Hadhramawt coast.[7]

Another aspect of the heritage shared by Hadhramis was a history of participation in the Islamic community almost from its inception. The chronicles of early Islam record that in 630/631 C.E., known in Islamic historiography as the Year of the Delegations (*sanat al-wufud*), Wa'il b. Hajr led a delegation of the Hadhramawt tribes to the Hijaz. These tribal leaders proclaimed their belief in Islam and pledged the allegiance of their tribes to the Islamic community under Muhammad's leadership, as did similar delegations from Oman and Yemen. When some of the Arabs throughout the peninsula withdrew their allegiance from the Muslim community after the death of Muhammad, loyal Muslims from Hadhramawt helped put down the rebellions. Hadhramis were proud of their historic role

Figure 1.1 Shibam

in the establishment and spread of the early Islamic community throughout the Arabian Peninsula and beyond.[8]

Thus, people from Hadhramawt's main wadi, tributaries, and the associated coast shared aspects of identity and heritage. They were Arabs whose ancestors had participated in the establishment, success, and spread of Islam. According to both scripture and local lore, their homeland had been visited by prophets of the one true God, not long after the beginning of time. They were descendants of an ancient southern Arabian civilization that had left only traces of its former splendor. Since those ancient times, their ancestors had been connected to the trading networks of the Indian Ocean, Red Sea, and Gulf. While the different wadis and different towns of this land were each marked by particular local characteristics, they had at the same time many social, economic, and legal institutions in common. These common notions of homeland and heritage and shared "ways" shaped the identity of people from the different parts of this region.

Identity Groups in Hadhramawt

While people from disparate parts of Hadhramawt shared a common identity and heritage in many respects, the society was not at all homogeneous. Hadhrami society consisted of a number of different groups of people who largely married among themselves, shared a common array of occupational statuses, and bore tangible and intangible markers of group identification. Group identity, which affected an individual's possibilities in private and public life, was symbolically manifested in recognized signs, including: clothing, other body adornments, and weapons; the use of honorific titles; and physical positioning and movement, especially in ritual situations. This reflects the common tendency of identity to become embodied in symbolic expressions, "crystallizing" around recognized symbols and cues and sustaining itself by comparisons.[9]

Different groups varied in the prestige in which they were held within the society as a whole and at the same time standards of prestige and honor varied among groups. Because of the rather inflexible social boundaries and the variation in prestige among the different groups, Hadhramawt is often characterized as a highly stratified society. The important work on the social structure of Hadhramawt, *The Politics of Stratification* by Abdalla Bujra, emphasizes the hierarchical ordering of the different social groups by prestige. The Hadhrami scholar 'Abd al-Qadir Muhammad al-Sabban utilized a similar approach in his 'Adat wa taqalid bil-Ahqaf, employing both the traditional term for social group, *tabaqa,* denoting "layer" or "stratum," and the more modern sociological terminology, "*al-silm al-tarkibi lil-mujtama',*" literally, "the structural ladder of the society."[10] To order the layers by prestige ranking, al-Sabban relied primarily on the local practice of *kafa'a* (literally, "equality"), the standard by which women were prevented from marrying "down" into lower status social groups.[11]

While benefiting from the contributions of Bujra and al-Sabban, I approach
the social groups from a slightly different angle, taking into account the notion of
prestige, but at the same time emphasizing both the complexity within particular
groups and the intricate pattern of relations among groups. As anthropologist Sylvaine Camelin notes, there is no single "correct view" of this society: different communities have somewhat differing systems of values by which they define prestige;
relations within particular groups can be quite complex; and groups are linked to
each other in a variety of ways.[12] The relations, linkages, and cleavages are so complex that I try to consider the social system as a matrix or web rather than a hierarchy or "layer cake." This approach makes it easier to recognize the dynamics
within groups and the interactions between them, as well as to acknowledge the
more mutable groups that represent shared political, economic, and religious interests crossing the boundaries of the social groups.

Because of the lack of an alternate terminology, I employ the rather generic
terms "social groups" and, interchangeably, "identity groups," for the entities that
have often been referred to as "strata" or "levels." While the British Colonial official
Harold Ingrams used the term "classes" for the groups in his category system
(refining his usage by adding, "almost castes"), that term is not applicable because
of the imperfect correspondence of the social groups to economic classes in this society.[13] It would be inappropriate to redefine class as a purely social entity without
any economic implication, since the areas of disjuncture between social group and
economic class drive some of the critical events and profound conflicts in the history of this region. The term "kinship group" is too general; "occupational group"
is inaccurate; "tribe" is used for one particular category and cannot be applied to
the others. So for lack of a better term, I use "social group" and "identity group."

Sada
Mashayikh
Tribes, including:
{ Hadhrami tribes
{ Yafi'i, including:
{ ghurba'
{ tulud
Townspeople, including:
{ Qarwan
{ Masakin, including
al-huwik
Dhu'afa' (farmers, fishermen, builders)
'Abid (slaves)
Subiyan (found in particular areas)

Figure 1.2 Social System in Hadhramawt

It is important not to consider these groups as immutable, existing "since time out of mind."[14] The following analysis of the social system of Hadhramawt depends largely on sources from the late nineteenth and early twentieth century, in order to construct an outline of the system existing during that time. While this system displayed stability over the fifty-year period of this study, the meanings and importance of group identity would have varied somewhat from place to place and over time. These group categories existed before the 1880s, and have persisted— albeit in much attenuated form—until today, despite efforts in the socialist and postsocialist eras to officially eradicate the distinctions between social groups.

It is also important to remember that these social groups are merely components of a categorization system. They describe an idealized notional system shared among members of Hadhrami society, rather than a set of corporate entities. It may be useful to bear in mind the theoretical approach to social structures proposed by Anthony Giddens. According to his theory, people, in the context of their everyday lives, are social actors, acting in settings imbued with meanings that have been routinized and reproduced in time and space. In other words, groups are not historical actors, individuals are, at the same time that their actions are shaped by their group identity and group interests. Social structures are not determinants of individual action, but provide parameters in which a person finds meaning, makes choices, and takes action, and also provide parameters within which his or her actions are perceived.[15]

The ʿAlawi Sada: Descendants of the Prophet

The *sada* (sing. *sayyid*) of Hadhramawt claimed descent from the Prophet Muhammad through the Prophet's daughter Fatima and her husband, the Prophet's cousin, ʿAli b. Abi Talib, which afforded them a particular religious prestige and a high degree of influence within this society. While their origins thus lay in the Quraysh tribe of Mecca, they traced the advent of their lineage in Hadhramawt to the arrival of their ancestor, Sayyid Ahmad b. ʿIsa, known as "al-Muhajir," "the Emigrant." This ancestor and a band of compatriots had been living in southern Iraq, from which they traveled to Hadhramawt by way of Mecca and Medina in 929/930 C.E. (318 h). The Hadhrami *sada*, differentiating themselves from other descendants of the Prophet elsewhere, referred to themselves as the ʿAlawi *sada* or the ʿAlawiyin (colloquial plural of ʿAlawi), in reference to their ancestor Sayyid ʿAlawi b. ʿAbdallah b. Ahmad b. Isa, the grandson of al-Muhajir.[16]

Most of the *sada* did not carry arms, having given up the practice in the thirteenth century C.E. at the instigation of Sayyid Muhammad b. ʿAli b. Muhammad Sahib Mirbat, known as "al-Faqih al-Muqaddam." A few anomalous families of sada remained arms-bearers, including the family descended from al-Shaykh Abu Bakr Ibn Salim which was also anomalous in bearing the honorific Shaykh rather than Sayyid. The family of al-Shaykh Abu Bakr b. Salim included the prominent bayt (branch, literally "house") of al-Mihdhar, members of which served as primary political advisors and military commanders for the Qu'ayti sultans for generations.

Because of the significance of their belonging to the Prophet's lineage, the *sada* valued the keeping of genealogical records, to a degree notable even in a society generally quite conscious of lineage. Of all social groups, they were most adamant about maintaining *kafa'a*. Women from the *sada* did not marry men from outside the *sada*, although men from the *sada* sometimes married women from other groups, usually from the *mashayikh* (the religiously prestigious group not descended from the Prophet) and less often from the *qaba'il,* (the tribes). For the *sada,* the maintenance of *kafa'a* was more than a matter of family honor, it redounded to the eternal honor of *ahl al-bayt,* the Prophet's household and its descendants.

The *sada* avoided any sort of craft or manufacturing. Some avoided commerce to the point of not even setting foot in the local markets, although this group also included some of the wealthiest families of Hadhramawt with extensive business interests in the *mahjar* (the lands to which Hadhramis had emigrated), such as the al-Kaf and Bin Yahya families. Many of the *sada* followed religious professions, acting as *imams* (prayer leaders) of mosques, judges, jurisconsults, and religious teachers. They served as the administrators of *waqf* (pious endowment) properties. The descendants of individuals particularly renowned for their piety administered estates consisting of donations and bequests to their ancestor. The *sada* prided themselves on piety and the acquisition of religious education, even though many did not live up to the devout and scholarly image that was idealized among this group. Because of their religious prestige, they dominated the educational system, to which access was quite limited until the twentieth century. Many women from the *sada* also were recognized for their personal piety and religious knowledge, although women carried out their studies at home with family members rather than attending the schools and religious institutes.[17]

Certain families in this group held the hereditary position of *munsib,* or spiritual authority, a position which carried certain responsibilities, such as leading religious processions for holidays and ceremonial events, witnessing marriage contracts, and praying and reciting the Qur'an for the dead of the wider community. The *munsib* also received individuals who came seeking settlement of disputes or advice about personal problems. The families who served as spiritual authorities for the tribes also played important roles in mediation and negotiation for them. Bearing the standard of office, a *munsib* was able to move about among warring or feuding tribes without danger and his presence among them guaranteed a cease-fire.[18]

Sada were symbolically distinguished from other groups in a number of ways. They were the only people in Hadhramawt who merited being addressed by the honorifics "Sayyid" (literally, "Master") o r "Habib" (literally "Beloved," signifying "Beloved of God") for men and "Sharifa," "Habiba," or less commonly "Sayyida" for women. They received gestures of respect from the rest of the population in recognition of their descent from the Prophet. These gestures included the method of greeting, in which their hands were kissed, a practice known as *taq-bil.* This hand kissing was performed even when the recipient was a child or a person without any special distinction in terms of religious knowledge or piety, in recognition of the nobility of the bloodline rather than the merits of the particular individual.[19]

Convention dictated that when any person entered a roomful of people, he or she ascertained whether there were *sada* present, and greeted them first. If unsure, the individual might ask if there was a *sayyid* or a *sharifa* present in order to greet them first, kissing or "sniffing" the hand (the equivalent to a kiss of greeting) of the *sayyid* or *sharifa.* After greeting the *sada,* the entrant then greeted the others present, shaking the hand, kissing the hand, sniffing the hand, or sniffing the head of each one, depending on his or her relationship with them.

Ceremonial protocols also manifested the inherited spiritual prestige of the *sada.* In some mosques, particularly in Tarim, the *sada* comprised the front rows of worshippers. In religious processions, they led. In collective celebrations, the *sada* made the first entrances. In recitation of the names of the dead on behalf of whose spirits prayers were addressed, the names of the *sada* were recited first. After the death of respected spiritual leaders, their graves were marked with tombs that became the site of visits by people seeking to feel closer to God in the presence of the pious departed one. Among the burial sites of highly respected *sada* of earlier times that received visits during the time period of this study were those of al-Faqih al-Muqaddam in Tarim, and Sayyid Ahmad b. Zayn al-Hibshi in Hawtat al-Hibshi, east of Shibam.[20]

Men from the *sada* were distinguishable by their dress, although women of the *sada* wore loose dresses similar to those worn by most women, knee length in front and trailing on the ground in back. *Sada* men wore a belted *futa,* saronglike garment, like men of other groups did, but theirs were longer, approaching ankle length. They wore tucked-in shirts, which they covered with long, cream-colored cloth coats open at the front. On their heads they wore stiff cylindrical cloth caps decorated with embroidery with a head cloth (*'imama*) wrapped around. Over one shoulder, they loosely draped a long brightly colored woolen shawl. No member of another group might wear these particular clothing items.[21]

The *sada* justified their differentiation from others and the systematized paying of respect to them, employing accounts that the Prophet had promised to intervene on Judgment Day on behalf of four kinds of people: those who were generous to his descendants; those who provided his descendants with their needs; those who helped them; and those who were well disposed to them in spirit and in word. Thus the common folk were to be persuaded that preferential treatment of the *sada* was encouraged by their religion, correct behavior according to the *sunna* (the model of the Prophet's life) that would lead to rewards in the afterlife.[22]

In the nineteenth and twentieth centuries, some members of the *sada* continued to put forth justifications for their special treatment. In a well-known collection of *fatawa* (legal opinions), the prominent jurist 'Abd al-Rahman b. Muham-

Figure 1.3 The tomb of Ahmed b. 'Isa, ancestor of the Hadhrami *sada*

mad al-Mashhur addressed the matter of the special status of the *sada* in Hadhra-mawt. He asserted that "the descendants of the Prophet were the most favored of people, and the descendants of 'Alawi the most favored of them all" because of their religious learning and practice, their high moral standing, their blessedness, and their piety. In response to a question as to the correctness of the practice of kissing the hands of *sada*, he asserted that it was correct according to Shafi'i authorities. He argued that since the performance of *taqbil* was carried out by members of other so-cial groups even if the *sayyid* was a child or an ignorant person, it was clear that the gesture was directed not toward the individual but toward the Prophet's bloodline and the grace associated with this earthly link to the sacred.[23]

In the early twentieth century, Sayyid 'Alawi b. 'Abd al-Rahman al-Mash-hur wrote a *risala* (treatise) entitled "al-Burhan wa al-dalil wa idhah al-sabil li-man yunkar al-taqbil" or "Proof and evidence and clarification of the way for those that deny [the legitimacy of] *taqbil*." While the treatise was not dated, the author men-tioned that the practice of *taqbil* was contested in 1911 by members of the Kathiri and Yafi'i tribes, giving no further particulars. He pointed out that legal authori-ties approved the kissing of the black stone at the Ka'aba, kissing the face of a re-turned traveler, and kissing the face of a deceased person. In addition, he gave ex-amples from the *sunna*: Muhammad kissed his daughter and his grandsons; the delegations of Arab tribes which met with Muhammad kissed him in greeting; and other examples of kissing within the early Muslim community. In another work, an explication of a poem he had written justifying *taqbil*, al-Mashhur included ac-counts from the life of the Prophet in which Muhammad urged believers to treat his descendants with special respect and benevolence.[24]

The Hadhrami *sada* also called on external authorities to assist them in jus-tifying their position. In 1932, Imam Yahya of Yemen affixed his seal and certification to a genealogical tree illustrating the descent of the 'Alawiyin from the Prophet's family. While the Imam held no political authority over Hadhramawt, he too was a descendant of the Prophet, like a number of other leaders in the Ara-bian peninsula, including Sharif Husayn of Mecca, and the rulers of Mar'ib, Bay-han, and the 'Asir.[25]

Although many Hadhramis held the *sada* in special respect because of their heritage and their access to religious power and position, the continual production of works justifying their position of social and religious prestige suggests concern about opposition to their special position in their homeland. Differing stances were held with respect to the 'Alawi *sada* in other parts of the Arabian peninsula. 'Alawi *sada* of Hadhrami origin were respected as Islamic scholars and jurists in the holy cities of the Hijaz.[26] At the same time in the nearby Najd, the Wahhabi movement was ideologically opposed to the notion of the *sada* enjoying a particular status. The Wahhabis also objected to the combination of mystical practices, use of eso-teric symbols, veneration of pious ancestors, and the centering of popular worship practices around a revered pious figure that characterized the religious belief and practice of the 'Alawi *sada*.[27]

Finally, it must be emphasized that while *sada* enjoyed social prestige and had access to religious occupations not available to all, their prestige did not necessarily equate to wealth. Some *sada* families controlled extensive estates that had been donated and bequeathed in the name of ancestors revered for their piety. In addition, certain families had acquired great wealth through trading and real estate interests in the East Indies. Still, many of the *sada* were not wealthy, as was illustrated in the will of one wealthy *sayyid,* who included among his charitable bequests a large sum for needy *sada* as well as another sum for needy members of other groups.[28]

The Mashayikh: *Local Families of Religious Renown*

The *mashayikh* were another unarmed group holding religious prestige. This group was respected by the public, but on the whole were considered second in prestige to the *sada* as a result of that group's special connection with the Prophet's lineage. This group predated the *sada* as religious authorities in Hadhramawt, and some of the *mashayikh* claimed that *taqbil* and the honorific "Habib" had been their due before the arrival of the *sada* in Hadhramawt. Men from this group were addressed with the honorific "Shaykh" and women were addressed as "Shaykha," in a usage distinct from the use of the term *shaykh* for a tribal leader or religious teacher.

The *mashayikh* families included among their ancestors individuals who had been renowned during their lifetimes for their piety and spiritual authority. In some cases, tombs of *mashayikh* pious ancestors received ritual visits.[29] These included an annual visit to the Ba'Abbad tombs in Shibam and both annual and informal visits to the tomb of the renowned pious woman, al-Shaykha Sultana al-Zubaydi.[30] The Ba'Abbad family served as the guardians of the important *ziyara* or ritual visit to the tomb of the Prophet Hud, an ancient practice of great importance to the inhabitants of Hadhramawt and Mahra.[31]

Mashayikh had a long and proud history in religious activity, in the Sufi tradition as practiced in Hadhramawt and in scholarship and jurisprudence. Several Hadhrami *mashayikh* appeared in the fifteenth-century biographical collection of prominent Yemeni Sufis, including members of the 'Amudi, BaWazir, and Ba'Abbad families. Many prominent jurists throughout Hadhrami history had been from the *mashayikh.*[32]

At times spiritual authorities from the *sada* appeared to have competed with authorities from *mashayikh* for the loyalty of the populace. Although the *sada* had an advantage because of the respect granted their descent, they did not automatically supersede the *mashayikh*. Sometimes spiritual leaders from the *sada* eclipsed the authority of earlier leaders from the *mashayikh,* while at times they co-opted *mashayikh* authority, so that popular rituals and popular loyalties incorporated both *sada* and *mashayikh*. An example of this "competition" was when the eighteenth-century Sufi leader Sayyid 'Abdallah b. 'Alawi al-Haddad sent two of his students from the *sada* as "missionaries" to Shibam and environs to revitalize religion and they superceded the local authority of the Ba'Abbad. In Shibam the authority of the Ba'Abbad was incorporated into that of the authority of the Bin Sumayt family of *sada,* while in the countryside a new settlement was founded in which spiritual authority was held entirely by a branch of the al-Hibshi family of *sada.*[33]

Despite the *sada* claim to superior authority, *mashayikh* maintained their status as religious specialists. Women as well as men of this group received a religious education, although women carried out their studies at home with male family members rather than attending the schools and religious institutes. While some members of this group were landowners and businessmen, most made their living through the employment of their learning. They taught jurisprudence and served as spiritual guides in the mystical tradition practiced in Hadhramawt. They worked as administrators for *waqf* properties and as jurists. They also professionally provided services of a spiritual nature such as reciting the Qur'an on behalf of the spirits of the dead. As specialists in religious occupations, they worked closely alongside the *sada* and in certain respects formed a common interest group.[34] When social and religious reform became subjects of contention in the twentieth century, *mashayikh* participated on both sides of the debate, with some advocating reform and even adoption of Islamic modernist ideals, while others took the more conservative stance of advocating preservation of Hadhramawt's particular traditions.[35]

Like particular families of *sada,* certain *mashayikh* families served as spiritual authorities to the tribes. Some tribes looked both to a *munsib* from the *sada* and to a *mashayikh* family for spiritual authority and political intermediation. Some tribe members, particularly *badu* (roaming pastoralists), preferred to turn to *mashayikh* as their spiritual mentors, legal authorities, and political intermediaries. They expressed this preference with the saying, "A *shaykh* is a *shaykh,* but a *sayyid*— what sort is that?" (*al-shaykh shaykh, wa al-sayyid, ish min tahisha?*) Some authorities among the *mashayikh* had specialized knowledge of *'urf* (customary tribal law) as well as of *shari'a* (Islamic law), which enhanced their appeal among the tribes, who in many cases favored their customary tribal practices over the *shari'a.*[36]

Tribes (Qaba'il): *Settled Tribes and* Badu

The tribes of Hadhramawt traced their descent from a distant ancestor known as Qahtan, the ancestor of the tribes of southern Arabia, differentiating themselves from the northern Arabian tribes that traced their descent from 'Adnan. (The *sada* derived from 'Adnan, as descendants of the Prophet, who was from the northern Arabian Quraysh tribe.) The tribes, whose men bore arms, defined themselves by the right to their tribal name and by authority over their tribal land, the latter being the primary cause of disputes within this group and between tribes and the governments of the sultanates. Tribal identity and affiliations were described in terms of lineage, and blood linkages were expected to provide solidarity and mutual support, although reality frequently differed from that ideal. As in other tribal areas, genealogical links often reflected political alliances as much as blood relationship.[37] In addition to the manipulation of genealogy, relations among tribes were governed by negotiated written agreements, which included: the *hilf* or alliance for mutual security and benefit; the *sulh* or temporary peace agreement during which conflicts might be resolved; and the *hudna* or cease-fire, in the case of active warfare. These were negotiated, authorized, and witnessed by those spiritual authorities from the *sada* or *mashayikh* recognized by the participating tribes. Through alliances and agreements the tribes were able to extend both their networks of support and the physical territories accessible to them. Travel through tribal territories was restricted, with individuals or caravans passing through having to be accompanied by a *siyar* or tribal guide who guaranteed their security. A *siyar* could guarantee security within his own tribal territory and that of tribes with which his was associated through a *hilf.*

Honor (*sharaf*), highly important among this group, was associated with the role of arms bearer and the ability to defend one's self, family, and cohort, and to protect those in a dependent position. When a tribesman said to another person "*inta fi wajhi*" meaning "you are in my face," or indicated the same by simply touching his face and pulling his index finger down his cheek, he was responsible for that person's safety even to the point of giving up his own life in defense of the other. The primacy of honor also resulted in blood feuds. When a tribesman was killed, a relative of the deceased was obligated to kill a family member of the killer in order to maintain the family honor. If the revenge was not carried out, the responsibility was inherited.[38]

The armed status of members of this group was immediately apparent. Boys began bearing daggers at the age of two and rifles when they reached "the age of reason" at seven to twelve years of age. Adults wore white, indigo-dyed, or striped *futas* belted with decorated scabbards holding a curved dagger, sometimes with a straight knife tucked behind. Those who carried muzzle loaders wore leather pouches or horns for powder on their belts; those with modern rifles wore cartridge belts.[39] Women did not bear arms. They were protected by their position in their families, so except in times of conflict they were safe in their tribal territory. Their protected position allowed them to move about rather freely for extended periods, alone or in groups of two or three women as they herded their goats and sheep.[40]

Even though the women and men of most tribes raised livestock, the majority were not seasonal nomads. Most were settled, their members living in small settlements of homes found outside the towns and villages, in the agricultural areas and rangelands within their territories. A few farmed their tribal lands or had it farmed by tenant farmers or dependent "client" tribes. Poorer families from this group lived in tiny rough huts of branches and thatch. More prosperous ones lived in mud-brick houses that ranged from simple one-roomed houses without windows to huge, multistoried, mud-brick homes with windows, rooftop terraces, and turrets. These imposing and highly defensible houses called *husun* (literally "forts," sing. *husn*) were popular with tribal families who had prospered as overseas emigrants. As particular families and clans flourished, they began to identify their interests more with the towns and their elites while maintaining their tribal identity.[41]

Although some settled tribes farmed their own lands, most avoided agriculture as well as any sort of manufacturing, preferring to make their living through their capacity as arms bearers. Neither men nor women of this group participated in religious education beyond learning the fundamentals of belief and practice. At the same time, they respected and depended on the spiritual authority of the particular leaders from the *sada* or *mashayikh* recognized by their tribe. Prosperous men and women from the settled tribes showed their piety and compensated for their lack of formal religious training by bequeathing money for charity and for acts of piety such as Qur'anic recitation.[42]

Some tribes and subtribes, known as *badu,* were primarily pastoralists living in remote areas, spending most of their time outdoors. Some *badu* moved seasonally from place to place in search of water and food for their animals. Others lived in simple isolated kin-based communities deep within their tribal territory and far from the cities, towns, and agricultural villages that formed the cores of the Kathiri and Qu'ayti sultanates. They gained their livelihood by raising livestock, conducting the camel caravan trade between cities, and collecting tolls from caravans that passed through their territory in exchange for right of passage and pasturage. They also levied duties on production by settled populations within the territory they considered under their authority. These included: portions of grain and dates from the harvests; duties on the boats harboring in small ports; and measures of fresh or dried fish. They considered these duties to be their right in exchange for providing security, protecting the property from theft. Their insistence on the collection of these duties eventually brought them into conflict with state authorities.[43]

The *badu,* considered uncivilized, were deplored and shunned by settled folk of other groups. Their participation in trade and dealings with towns were mediated by specialized individuals such as the *dallal al-suq* (market brokers, sing. *dillal*) in order that they be kept separate from ordinary town life. At the same time, within the category of *qaba'il,* the boundary between settled and *badu* was somewhat permeable. Settled tribes all considered themselves to have derived from *badu* ancestry. The process of "settling" was an ongoing one, with *badu* moving closer to towns and cities or taking up agriculture and settling into villages. Still, the process was not irreversible; times of hardship could cause recently settled tribesmen to return to the *badu* lifestyle.

One reason for the disparagement of the *badu* as uncivilized was their utilization of *'urf,* their particular tribal standards and practices, rather than adherence to the standards embodied in the *shari'a.* Since land was collectively held, the *badu* followed different standards for inheritance of the right to use land or the right to "protect" territory rather than the system of inheritance prescribed in the Qur'an. *Badu* women did not follow the same standards of modesty as settled women. Heavily adorned, they traveled about freely with their flocks, which was

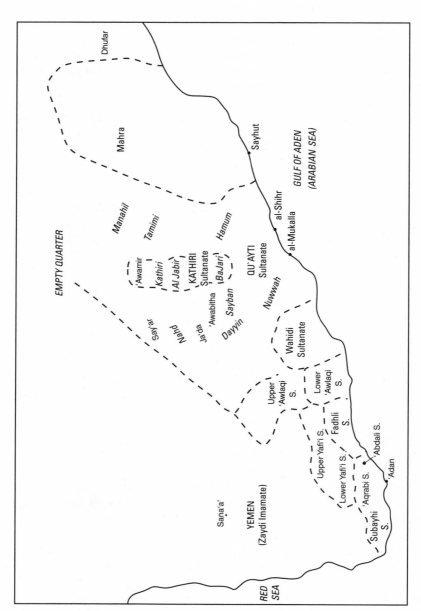

Map 1.2 Sultanates and Shaykdoms of Southern Arabia and Hadhrami tribes, c. 1930s

deemed unseemly behavior for women of other groups. It was understood that *badu* had different standards for the behavior of unmarried women.[44]

Badu men and women both were distinguishable by their appearance, which was noted by Western travellers in the 1890s and the 1930s. *Badu* men covered their skin with indigo mixed with oil, for protection from sun, wind, and cold. This coating, burnished by the constant sun and wind, gave their skin a dark plum-colored gloss. They lined their eyes with kohl. They wore their hair long, with a band of cloth tied around their head. Their clothes were of sturdy indigo-dyed cloth, a fringed piece wrapped around their waist like a short sarong and another twisted around their waist as a belt or draped across their chest for protection from the cold. They wore belts with daggers and carried muskets or rifles. They wore silver armbands just above the elbow, silver rings and amulets with garnet stones, and bands of wool tied around their legs just below the knees.

Badu women wore the same style of dress that townswomen and settled tribeswomen wore, except that those of the *badu* women were made of special sturdy indigo-dyed cloth that had been pounded to a high luster. They wore a cloth of lighter weight and texture to cover their head and hair. In some areas, they went bare faced, in others they wore stiff indigo-dyed masks with narrow eye slits.[45]

Badu women wore more decorations than others, even apart from festive occasions. They wore large amounts of jewelry, including: silver rings and pendants set with carnelian, garnet, and agate, and pieces of animal horn; heavy silver belts; bracelets; and anklets that tinkled and clanked as they walked. Those who could not afford silver wore jewelry of brass and iron. Like women of other groups, they wore numerous massive earrings arrayed around their earlobes, but only *badu* women wore rings in their left nostril as well. Each tribe had specific styles of jewelry items that men were required to furnish their brides. The amount of jewelry these women received at the time of their marriage recognized the substantial property in the form of personal flocks that they took into the marriage.

The women did not use indigo like the men, but stained their skin yellow with *wars,* a powdered herb similar to turmeric. Unlike settled women, who applied *wars* for the forty days after a childbirth or miscarriage, they used it all the time for protection from the elements. They decorated their faces with contrasting patterns of blue, black, green, or red. They shaved their eyebrows, painting a solid contrasting line across, as well as lining their eyes with kohl. For *badu* women, reducing the amount and splendor of their ornaments and decorations was an important part of the process of "settling."[46]

All the tribes, settled and *badu,* identified themselves with land they considered under their authority (*sulta*). The territory controlled by the Shanafir association, which included the Al Kathiri, Al Jabir, and Al 'Awamir tribes and the smaller BaJari tribe, corresponded to the territory of the Kathiri sultanate. The Shanafir was not a confederation (*zay*), since the tribes within it were affiliated but not united under the authority of a paramount *shaykh.* While the Kathiri sultan ruled his domains with the support of the Shanafir, he was not paramount leader of a tribal confederation.[47] The territory of the Qu'ayti sultanate comprised the following tribal groups: the Bani Zuna, including the powerful Al Tamim tribe; the Sayban; the Nahid; the 'Awabitha; the Say'ar; the Dayyin of Wadi Du'an; the Nuwwah of Wadi Hajr; and the Hamum, a large confederation whose tribes were almost entirely *badu*.[48]

The Kathiri and Qu'ayti sultans made two types of political agreements with the tribes: one in which the tribe agreed to support the Sultan and respond to his call at any time; the other in which the tribe agreed to cooperate in matters of mutual interest. The sultans paid a subsidy to the tribal leader in both types of agreement. When there was any question of loyalty, the governments held hostages from the tribe. The sultanates reimbursed the tribe for the hostages, paid monthly maintenance for them, and made arrangements for exchanges of hostages.[49]

The Yafi'i comprised a discrete subgroup of the Hadhrami tribes, with an identity distinct from all other tribes, settled or *badu*. In some areas, the Yafi'i were referred to generically as *'asakir,* soldiers, reflecting their historical role serving as military forces and leaders. They had originated in the mountainous Yaf' region just east of the lands controlled by tribes loyal to the Zaydi Imam of Yemen. Large numbers of Yafi'is emigrated as a result of periodic drought and famine in their rugged and marginally productive homeland, which also suffered from continual incursions by the powerful Zaydi tribes to their west. There were two categories of Yafi'i in Hadhramawt; the *tulud* (sing. *tild*) and the *ghurba'* (sing. *ghurab*). The *tulud* were of Yafi'i ancestry, but born in Hadhramawt. Some of the *tulud* had been connected with Hadhramawt since the sixteenth century when the most powerful ruler of the first Kathiri dynasty, Sultan Badr "Abu Tuwayriq" al-Kathiri had brought in Yafi'i tribesmen to serve as his military forces, granting estates to the tribal leaders. The Yafi'i provided security over the countryside, with different tribes and subtribes holding responsibility for particular areas. As the power of later generations of the first Kathiri dynasty diminished, the Yafi'i consolidated their power over the localities they controlled, becoming semiautonomous local strongmen. Those Yafi'i stayed, joined periodically by new emigrants from their homeland.[50] The *ghurba'* were newcomers to Hadhramawt who came to serve in the armed forces of the Qu'ayti state either as regular soldiers or as irregular forces settled in different locations around the sultanate. Some of the *ghurba'* came to Hadhramawt directly from Yaf' and others via service in the armed forces of the Nizam of Hyderabad led by the Qu'ayti *jama'dar* (commanding officer). Some of these soldiers stayed in Hadhramawt, marrying a woman of the *tulud* and fathering children who within a generation or two were considered *tulud*.[51]

While the Yafi'i formed a distinct identity group, they were not a single tribe. They were divided into three tribal groups, called *makatib* (sing. *maktab*), al-Zubi, al-Mawsata, and Bani Qasid, each of which comprised several tribes. All the Yafi'i tribes looked to Al Shaykh Abu Bakr b. Salim, an armed branch of the *sada*, as their spiritual authority. Although several players in the nineteenth-century struggles for power over Hadhramawt were of Yafi'i origin, all the Yafi'i tribes ultimately ended up supporting their kinsmen, the Qu'ayti.[52] Despite their external origin, the Yafi'i were recognized as a powerful group within Hadhramawt because of their heritage of local political power and their critical support for the Qu'ayti sultanate. The degree of power they held was sometimes resented by members of other groups.[53]

Townspeople: Masakin *and* Qarwan, *or* Hadhar

Most of the inhabitants of towns and villages of Hadhramawt were merchants and craftsmen who did not bear arms or have a tribal identity and did not claim ancestry of any particular religious prestige. They were referred to as *masakin* or "inhabitants," from the verb *sakana*, "to dwell." In this usage *masakin* did not mean "poor" (as it does in standard Arabic); members of this group ranged from people making a simple livelihood to wealthy families. *Qarar* or *qarwan* (sing. *qarwi*) was a term used for townspeople of substantial business interests which distinguished them from the craftsmen, providers of services, laborers, and vendors in the public marketplace, whose occupations were considered of lower status. The term may indicate a transitional category of townspeople who had become "upwardly mobile" through occupational status, wealth, and acquisition of education.[54] In the coastal region, the more inclusive term *hadhar* (literally "civilized") was used rather than *masakin* and *qarwan*. *Hadhar* referred to merchants, craftsmen, service providers, farmers, and fishermen (the latter two occupational groups formed distinct subgroups, included in the following section).[55]

Most artisans and skilled craftsmen were trained in their occupations by fathers and uncles, who passed on skills, tools, and workshops through the generations. Similarly, merchants of the *suq* (market) passed down not only their shop or niche in the marketplace but also the skills and knowledge required by their particular trade. Boys from these groups usually acquired minimal religious education in Qur'anic schools, while training for their life work and source of livelihood took place on the job. Girls usually received only the basic fundamentals of religious training in the requirements of ablutions, prayer, and fasting.[56]

The clothing of townspeople varied according to local styles and according to the prosperity of the wearer, as was noted by the Bents in the 1890s. Men wore the *futa* and a head wrap. Women wore square-necked dresses, cut wide and shaped like a large rectangle, the width of which stretched from fingertip to fingertip with the arms extended. These dresses were knee length in front and trailed the ground in back. The fabric in women's dresses varied in quality depending on the economic situation of their family. Women who could afford it wore dresses of fine cloth imported from India or Asia, decorated with embroidery, beads, and spangles, with different towns having their own particular styles of ornamentation that changed over time, as fashions do. Women from the craftsmen's and service providers' families wore dresses of the same shape as those of women from more prosperous families, but made from heavy cotton locally dyed with indigo.[57]

A few families in the marketplace held hereditary positions of responsibility as intermediaries between tribes and town. These general brokers, the *dallal al-suq,* took care of the buying and selling for *badu* and saw to all their needs when they came to the market. In times of conflict they aided in negotiations between tribes or between tribes and government. These brokers were considered of low social status as *ahl al-suq* or "market people," sometimes contemptuously referred to by others as *kilab al-suq,* "market dogs." They were tainted by their association with the least prestigious public aspect of the marketplace, and by their hosting of the "uncivilized" *badu.* At the same time, they played a significant role in mediation and had a similar function in tribal negotiations to that of highly respected spiritual authorities of the *sada* and *mashayikh.* Like those spiritual authorities, the *dallal al-suq* could travel freely in tribal territory without fear of molestation or need for a tribal guide (*siyar*).[58]

Market people, artisans, laborers, and providers of services played a visible and important role in their communities, dominating the social institution known as the "quarter system." While the actual neighborhoods of the towns consisted of a mixture of the different social groups, the quarters were characterized and defined by the activities of these groups, called *ahl al-hara* or *ahl al-hafa,* both meaning "people of the quarter," or *al-huwik* (literally "weavers"), meaning artisans. There was a high degree of solidarity among the *ahl al-hara* within a given quarter and a high degree of competition between quarters. They performed in dance and po-etry competitions at times of public celebrations. Those families from this group that provided social and personal services jealously guarded their right to perform services, for pay, to all the inhabitants of their quarter.

The *ahl al-hara* of each quarter were responsible for emergency services in that quarter: putting out fires, rescuing people trapped in a collapsed house, or ex-tricating a person who had fallen down a well. When an emergency took place, the cry went out for *ahl al-hara* to respond. They carried loads too heavy for one per-son to carry and removed the corpses of camels or donkeys who died within the town walls. Members of this group prepared and served the food for feasts in honor of weddings, births, and deaths. They served throughout ceremonial occasions. They prepared and accompanied the bride and groom during all the stages of the wedding, and played drums, sang, and danced during those portions of the cele-bration. When a death took place, they announced it, prepared the body, carried the bier, and dug the graves. The leader of each quarter, *muqaddam al-hara,* as-signed the task of assisting in these events to specific families within this social group; he was responsible for seeing that the paid duties were properly organized and fairly distributed. The *muqaddam* was a member of this group, which chose him in respect for his wisdom and experience.[59]

Farmers, Builders, and Fishermen (dhu'afa')

People who worked in earth or clay, such as farmers, builders, brick makers, potters, and pounders of lime plaster were part of an unarmed group often referred to as *dhu'afa'* (literally, weak). While they can be considered a subgroup of the *masakin* or *hadhar,* these occupational groups shared characteristics and experiences that differentiated them from the urban artisans, market people, and service providers.[60]

This group was low in the hierarchy of marriageability. The men could not marry women from any other group. Men from the *'abid* (slaves) might marry women from the *dhu'afa',* but men from the *dhu'afa'* could not marry women from the *'abid.*[61] The association of these working people with the earth had a negative connotation; they were identified with soil, straw, and dung, but not with the ownership of land. Some people addressed farmers by calling "*Ya fugish,*" meaning "Hey, clod." Landowners were known as *ahl al-'ardh,* "people of the land," or *ahl al-mawala,* "people of property," while the laborers who dug the wells, constructed the irrigation channels, and tilled the land were known as *ahl al-'awala,* or "people who break up and work the earth."[62]

The life experience of this group was marked by hard labor and a marginal social and economic status. Neither men nor women had the opportunity to acquire even rudimentary education. Farmers' contractual agreements with landowners included the labor of the farmers' entire families, with women and children having certain specific tasks. These women not only worked in the fields in their gender-specific tasks such as cutting alfalfa, they labored alongside men and beasts in the endless back-breaking job of raising water for irrigation. In their homes, women wove from palm leaves the baskets that contained and protected dates on the branch and mats used for various purposes. Women from this group also served as water carriers in the towns, carrying water from wells or cisterns in goatskin bags. They slung the heavy bags from one shoulder so that the weight was supported by their hip. Women of this group experienced little leisure in their lives and had little time to rest even before and after childbirth, because family survival depended on their labor.

Farmers, their lives dominated by hard labor and poverty, lived and dressed simply and without adornment. They lived in small square windowless mud-brick houses roofed with mud and palm fronds, just high enough to stand up in, which meant the doors were so low that a person had to stoop to enter. These houses consisted of one or two rooms with dimensions of perhaps ten by six feet. In some areas, farmers wore clothes made from indigo-dyed cloth like that worn by the *badu;* in other areas their clothes were made from the coarse unbleached canvas known as *amrikani,* an imported cotton cloth that had probably replaced locally woven cloth of camel or goat hair. They wore a saronglike garment (*mahzima* or *kara,* a type of *futa*) alone or with a light shapeless cotton shirt (*mazdra*) and a head cloth. Some farmers added a *nas'a,* a rustic version of a money belt which was a woven camel-skin belt with an attached drawstring bag made from the skin of bull's testicles. Women of this group wore plain squarish indigo-dyed dresses (*birkala*), which were shorter in front than back. They wore a head cloth and some women wore indigo-dyed face coverings although most left their faces bare. For work in the fields or in the towns, they often wore wide-brimmed peaked straw hats.[63]

In the coastal region of Hadhramawt, farmers and fishermen were part of the larger group called *hadhar,* which included merchants and craftsmen. But at the same time, farmers and fishermen constituted two discrete groups that intermarried among themselves and followed their hereditary occupations. Although one group's work involved the earth and the other's involved the sea, these hereditary occupational groups shared similar social and economic experiences. Both farmers and fishermen spent their lives in hard labor for little gain, struggling to eke out bare survival for their families. Both were socially stigmatized to some degree and did not attend celebrations or feasts held by members of other groups. In the coastal towns, fishermen were forbidden from entering certain areas and were excluded from others' wedding or birth celebrations and public holiday festivities, which they had to watch from a distance.

Both farmers and fishermen were vulnerable to the greater power of other groups. Most fishermen were chronically indebted to boat owners, as farmers were indebted to landowners, and the state of indebtedness was a family affair. When a farmer or fisherman died, his family inherited his contractual obligations and his debts. Rather than inheriting a house, the heirs usually inherited the mortgage on the family home, with the house deed being held by the creditor. The farmers and fishermen were also often indebted to the merchants who purchased their production and they usually had to sell their produce for low prices.

Farmers' harvests and fishermen's catch were subject to the imposts of the *badu,* who regularly collected tributes of grain (*kayla*), dates (*shiraha*), and fish (*juduh*). Occasionally *badu* demands on farmers or fishermen were higher, sometimes because the *badu* were in dire need, at other times because they wanted to challenge the authority of the state. In more secure areas, farmers had to contribute similar payments to the arms bearers responsible for their protection, usually soldiers or tribal supporters of the state who either leased or were awarded the duty of providing security with its concomitant measure of the harvest or catch.[64]

Slaves ('abid): *Soldiers of the Sultanates*

Slaves (*'abid*) of African origin constituted a distinct identity group in Hadhramawt. Before 1863, the Hadhrami ports of al-Mukalla and al-Shihr had been the two principal slave ports of southern Arabia, with slaves being brought from Zanzibar and from the Somalian coast. In that year, the rulers of al-Mukalla and al-Shihr concluded treaties with the British abolishing the import and export of slaves within their territories, which the Qu'ayti extended in an 1873 treaty after he came into power. The rulers supported the prohibition of slave trading and enforced compliance.[65]

But even though slaves were no longer imported by the 1880s, the African slaves who had earlier been imported and their descendants were still around. These slaves were by no means the least powerful nor the least independent people in their society. Most served in the regular military forces of the Qu'ayti and

Kathiri sultanates; they were known as the *hashiya*. Women of their families were household servants in the palaces. The *hashiya* were provided with housing, clothing, and salaries. They were able to rise to the highest ranks of the administration, frequently serving as provincial governors and town magistrates. When British colonial official Harold Ingrams arrived in Hadhramawt on his 1934 visit, the governor of Shibam province was a slave, as was the magistrate of al-Mukalla, the Qu'ayti capital.[66]

Another way in which the sultans provided members of the *hashiya* with livelihood was granting them the responsibility to provide security in exchange for portions of the production of dates (*shiraha*) and grain (*kayla*) in particular areas. In some places this led to slaves becoming semiautonomous authorities, as happened with a group of slaves of the Kathiri state in Ghayl Bin Yamin in the early twentieth century.[67]

A few slaves were owned by private families. Some slaves owned by members of the Kasadi family, which had once ruled a portion of the coast, were household servants, others served as trusted retainers in the capacity of business managers, acting as legal agents for women as well as men and as executors of estates. These slaves were inherited, although individuals often bequeathed in wills that their slaves be freed.[68]

Although the Kathiri state declared in a 1913 declaration to the rebellious *hashiya* of Ghayl Bin Yamin that slaves could not sell property, slaves did own property. They bought and sold it, and passed it on to their children. They acted both as buyers and sellers in the Hadhrami practice of sale of custody of property (*al-bay' 'ala sabil al-'uhda*), in which individuals sold temporary usage rights to their property in exchange for a temporary payment of cash.[69]

Service in the state military forces and administration not only provided a comfortable standard of living with greater economic security than was available to many in this society, it gave the *hashiya* some influence and prestige. Their armed status afforded them a measure of power and of honor, but while they were armed like tribesmen, they were not members of a tribe. Enslavement had severed them from their original tribal identities, ancestors, and heritage, which resulted in a degree of social stigmatization. The *'abid* compensated for their loss by identifying with one or the other of two tribes of their own, the Bahri and the Nubi. Neither the Bahri or the Nubi tribe was identified with a particular place or tribe in Africa, although it is tempting to speculate that the Bahri had been traded and transported through Zanzibar and the Nubi through Sudan. While they had been separated from their African tribal identity, the *'abid* valued their heritage in Hadhramawt, keeping track of their lineages and visiting the graves of their ancestors.[70]

The Qu'ayti and Kathiri complied with the international ban on the slave trade and there were no slave markets in the ports, towns, or hinterlands of the Kathiri or Qu'ayti sultanates. Still, a few unfortunate slaves were bought in the lawless zones outside Qu'ayti jurisdiction and smuggled in. Some of these were formerly free persons from the region of Abyan (northeast of Aden) who had surrendered themselves into slavery to escape starvation during the famines that regularly plagued their homeland. Occasionally a returning traveler managed to evade the port authorities and brought in a slave acquired in India or Timor.[71]

Subiyan: *Socially Excluded Workers*

A group known as the *subiyan* was distinguished by its low social status and limited occupational opportunity. The name derives from the plural of the word *sabi,* meaning "lad" or "houseboy." This group was not found in the towns of the main wadi in the interior. They were found in their homeland of Wadi Hajr, in Wadi 'Amd, and in the coastal cities to which they migrated in search of work. The *subiyan* were believed to be of Ethiopian origin, but had long been resident in Wadi Hajr, where they served as agricultural labor and household servants of the resident tribes and *mashayikh*. Local tribal lore related that in earlier centuries, the Hajr tribes were so busy fighting each other that agricultural production declined. Needing someone to cultivate, they brought in landless laborers, descendants of Abraha's invasion of Yemen, which had taken place in the year of the Prophet's birth.

The *subiyan* were clients of the tribes of Hajr, with each tribe protecting its own group of *subiyan*. Each family of *subiyan* "belonged to" or "was attached to" (*tabi' li*) a tribal family and carried its name. Besides cultivating the farms of Hajr and doing all labor related to agriculture, the *subiyan* provided social services in weddings, deaths, and burials for the group to which they belonged. Thus in the rural environment of Hajr, this group of agricultural laborers provided for the tribe to which they were attached the social services which in the towns of Hadhramawt were provided by the *ahl al-hara* for pay. The clientage or subordinate relationship of a family of *subiyan* to a tribal family lasted for generations, with the tribal families considering this hierarchy of dominance simply a part of the natural order of things.[72]

There was no social mobility in Hajr for members of the *subiyan* group, who were locked into their responsibilities to the tribes and families to which they were attached. Sometimes they left Wadi Hajr in search of opportunity, in which case they ended up living in shanty towns like that outside the town wall of al-Mukalla, doing menial labor such as cleaning the streets and toilets. They lived separately from the mixed neighborhoods and quarters, and members of other groups avoided eating with them.[73]

Communities and Cleavages

Hadhrami society was divided by cleavages not corresponding to the divisions between social groups. For example, the distinction between *badu* and settled extended far beyond the *qaba'il* social group. While the *badu* were a subgroup within the *qaba'il* or tribes, the settled population included all other social groups as well as the settled tribal people. The distinction between *badu* and settled marked an important cleavage in this society, a division that shaped the physical structure of towns and villages, the organization of the marketplace and transportation system, and the relation between ruler and subjects.

The distinction between armed and unarmed also crossed the boundaries of identity groups. Arms bearers included a few anomalous families of *sada,* all of the *qaba'il* or tribes, and slaves. The distinction between armed and unarmed, particularly during times of insecurity, was critical in the shaping of relations between rulers and subjects. The ruler was obligated to provide security for unarmed subjects, while he depended on the armed groups for support and maintenance of local security.

Another critical cleavage within the society was unrelated to the identity groups. Returned emigrants and their foreign-born offspring had experiences and held attitudes different from those who were born and lived out their lives within the walls of the wadis. In addition, families with members in the overseas emigrant communities had access to money and goods from abroad while other families had to rely on the local economy.

Finally, it must be emphasized that the various social groups were not corporate bodies and did not act as such. People from the different social groups lived in the same neighborhoods and participated in the same social and ritual events, albeit playing different roles according to group status. And in the contests for power that took place during this time period, the groups that jockeyed for power consisted of temporary alliances of members of different social groups that identified themselves with a common interest. In matters of power and politics, most conflicts took place among such interest groups, rather than between the identity groups per se.

2

Hadhrami Emigration and the *Mahjar*

Emigration and Identity

Hadhrami identity was shaped by the widespread practice of emigration, which profoundly affected Hadhrami culture. At any given time, part of the population of Hadhramawt has lived in the *balad,* the homeland, while another part has been abroad, dispersed among the different overseas communities collectively known as the *mahjar,* or place of emigration. The culture of Hadhramawt and the Hadhrami communities abroad has been shaped by the process of emigration, the return of emigrants, and the maintenance of connections among the emigrant communities and the homeland. The factors causing emigration, the experience of the emigrants, and the degree to which Hadhrami identity was maintained among emigrants and their descendants have all varied depending on the time period, the social group from which the emigrants originated, and the host society they entered. At the same time, the process led to the development of a "culture of emigration" shared by Hadhramis.[1]

This culture of emigration included core values that enabled the Hadhrami emigrants to survive and succeed economically and socially in their host societies, at the same time that they maintained, to one degree or another, their Hadhrami identity. It combined social adaptability and mercantile skills with a strong identification with the southern Arabian homeland and a strong affection for it, which precluded total assimilation for most, although not all, emigrants. These cultural characteristics were instrumental in the dynamic period of the late nineteenth and early twentieth century, when Hadhrami emigrants and returned emigrants attempted to effect social change in the homeland at the same time that deeply embedded cultural conservatism created resistance to change among residents of the homeland and of the *mahjar.*

The Tradition of Emigration

Hadhramis traveled in the Indian Ocean region for many centuries before the nineteenth. Traveling on the Arab-Indian trading routes, they settled first in port cities and later ventured inland, sometimes as individuals and sometimes as communities. They found economic niches in international trade and in small trading on the local level. They often intermarried with local women, which assisted them in developing links with the local communities. Their status as Arabs from the Arabian Peninsula and in the case of the *sada,* as descendants of the Prophet, endowed them with a degree of religious prestige within the Muslim communities to which they emigrated. They functioned within interlinking networks of trade, kinship, and religion.[2]

With nineteenth-century imperial economic development in the region and concomitant advances in transportation and communication, emigration from Hadhramawt flourished. Imperial expansion in the Indian Ocean region created niche opportunities that were exploited by the existing trading networks. At the same time, the rapid expansion of steam lines and telegraph lines throughout the region enhanced travel and communications among the Hadhrami emigrant communities, the trading networks, and between the emigrant communities and the homeland.

At the same time that advances in communications and transportation and economic opportunities in the region were increasing, various problems within Hadhramawt encouraged emigration. The natural environment was harsh and parsimonious. Agriculture was difficult and unproductive due to the extreme heat of the long summers and the cold winter winds. Rainfall was sparse and unreliable, and lifting underground water took a great toll of human and animal energy. The meager crops were vulnerable to the depredations of birds and insects. The wadi increasingly relied on imported food to feed its population and money from outside to pay for that food.

In the nineteenth century, political instability in Hadhramawt caused emigration to increase. The struggles for power that preceded the establishment of the Qu'ayti and Kathiri states created generalized insecurity detrimental to agriculture and other forms of productive activity. Intertribal fighting and tribal rebellions continued sporadically into the early twentieth century. Tribal fighting led to blood debts, in which any males from the tribe guilty of a killing were liable to being killed at the age of fifteen. Many individuals emigrated to escape the fighting; others emigrated to make money to help their tribe finance its participation in the fighting.[3]

The primary purpose of most emigrants was to earn money for their families. Poor people emigrated to the nearby Red Sea and East African port cities, where they sought money for the survival of their families through any work including manual labor. Emigrants from wealthier families were able to travel further to the Dutch East Indies and Singapore, where they found more lucrative and more prestigious possibilities. While Hadhramis were proud of the influence of their emigrant ancestors in the spread of Islam in the Indian Ocean, proselytizing zeal was not a primary motivating factor for the emigrants of the late nineteenth and early twentieth century. Some emigrants found their livelihood as religious teachers and prayer leaders within their own communities or among the indigenous people, but most came for the employment opportunity rather than missionary activity.[4]

Most Hadhramis who emigrated eventually intended to return to the homeland permanently. They used their earnings to support their family at home, to acquire property in the homeland, and to provide for a comfortable retirement there. Athough some emigrants ended up abandoning their homeland, most aspired to return after prospering from the business opportunities available in the *mahjar*. They felt responsible for their families at home. It was strongly believed that an individual's income should contribute to the prosperity of the entire family, and neglect of family obligations incurred social censure within the emigrant communities.[5] The proverb *"mal ma huwa fi baladik, la lak wa la li-waladik,"* literally, "money that is not in your homeland, is not yours or your sons," indicated the feeling prevalent among emigrants that for the security of one's family and its future, it was necessary to own property in the homeland.[6] Even many emigrants who did not return to their homeland invested in property there, as a family "safety net."

In the 1930s, perhaps 20 to 30 percent of the population of Hadhramawt (around 100,000 out of about 260,000) lived outside. Most emigrants stayed in touch with the homeland, sending messages and remittances home by means of traveling Hadhramis. In 1934, the British colonial official Harold Ingrams estimated the total remittances entering Hadhramawt from all over the *mahjar* at 630,000 pounds sterling annually. Some Hadhramis abroad amassed huge fortunes, such as that belonging to the al-Kaf family, which owned property in Singapore worth two million pounds sterling and a similar amount in Java. Other emigrants traveled abroad, worked for a year or two, and returned with a few hundred *riyal*s (the silver Maria Teresa *thaler*s used as currency in the Arabian peninsula).[7]

Homeland and Mahjar

To the Hadhrami, the world was divided into two parts: the *balad* or homeland, and the *mahjar* or sphere of emigration. Those who emigrated to East Africa and India were able to make return visits to the homeland more easily and more often than those who emigrated to the East Indies, since Arab sailing vessels made annual trading voyages between India, Arabia, and East Africa. Before the steam lines were established in the Indian Ocean, the sailing voyage to the East Indies was more time consuming, requiring stops en route to wait almost a year for the monsoon winds. Before steam travel, many who emigrated to the East Indies settled there permanently. Even after steam travel made it easier for emigrants to the East Indies to return to the homeland for family or business reasons, they made fewer and longer return trips than the emigrants to East Africa due to the length and expense of the journey.

Women rarely emigrated, although occasionally poor women from the *masakin* and *dhu'afa'* traveled with their husbands to East Africa, where both lived and worked for a year or two. Most emigrants went abroad without their wives. Many who settled in the *mahjar* eventually married two wives: one in the homeland, usually a relative, and one in the *mahjar*, either an indigenous woman or a woman of mixed blood from the Hadhrami expatriate community, who might also be a relative. They considered children born in the *mahjar* (*muwalladin* colloquial plural, sing. *muwallad*), as Hadhrami and tried to send their sons back to the homeland to learn the language and customs and to marry there. It was considered best for young boys to return to the homeland for this cultural training at the age of seven if possible, in order that the culture of the child's birthplace not override that of the homeland. In the *mahjar*, they married their daughters to other Hadhrami emigrants or to *muwalladin*, with a preference for the former as being more "Hadhrami," more culturally pure.

For the most part, Hadhramis lived together in the *mahjar*. Although individuals and small groups in search of new business opportunities continually branched out and away from the close-knit Hadhrami communities in port or other major cities, as soon as they met a degree of commercial success they tended to be joined by other members of their family or tribe. As a result, in many Hadhrami emigrant communities the majority of the inhabitants were from the same part of Hadhramawt, since new emigrants gravitated toward locations where they could expect to find kin or compatriots who would help them get acculturated and find employment. People from al-Mukalla and al-Shihr on the Hadhramawt coast tended to emigrate to India, to the Malabar coast and Hyderabad, as well as the islands and towns of the East African coast. People from Wadi Du'an gravitated toward the Hadhrami communities of Aden, Jedda, Suakin, and Cairo. In the 1880s, many of the Hadhrami emigrants in the East Indies came from the interior, between the cities of Shibam and Tarim. These included *sada* and tribesmen, including Kathiri, Tamimi, and Yafi'i. Later arrivals included emigrants from Wadi 'Amd and tribesmen from the western reaches of the wadi. Although in the nineteenth century few *badu* emigrated, by the 1930s this group had also taken up emigration.[8]

Leaving the Homeland for the Mahjar

Emigration evoked a mixture of emotions and attitudes. The emigrant, with his experience and his earnings from the *mahjar*, was considered sophisticated and successful; at the same time, leaving the homeland was considered painful. The contrasting viewpoints can be seen in common proverbs. The proverbs "*al-ghurba kurba*" or "being far from home is a torment," and "*al-gharib a'ma*," or "a stranger in a strange land is a blind person," illustrate the pain of leaving one's home and the difficulty of coping in a foreign environment. But "*al-sa'ir ta'ir wa al-jalis hajar*" or "a traveler is like a bird, while he who stays behind is like a stone" illustrates the pride associated with the exposure and activity available to emigrants in the larger world of the *mahjar*.[9]

Young men usually emigrated at the age of twelve to fourteen, when they were considered ready to leave the protection of home and family life and the comfort of life among women and make their own way in the world. Immediately they began having to acquire the survival skills of their "culture of emigration." Young men from wealthy families did not have a much easier time than did those from poor families, as even the sons of the prosperous were expected to become hardened and experienced through the struggle to survive in a harsh world. An emigrant youth from a family with extensive business interests abroad usually did not start out in the family business; instead he worked at low-level jobs in other people's shops and businesses, living on his earnings in austere conditions. In this way, each generation of a trading family learned business from the bottom up, and learned the value of hard work, as expressed in the proverb *"ghubar al-'amal wa la za'fran al-batala,"* or "the dust from hard work is better than the perfume of leisure." They also learned self-reliance, a quality much valued by their society, as illustrated by the proverb *"kulin yijmir 'ala qarsihi,"* or "everyone lights charcoal for his own loaf," meaning that each person has to work toward his own benefit. They were expected to apply themselves to work even though it might not be easy or pleasant, in accordance with the proverb *"law lak muslaha fi dubr al-himar, dukhilha ila al-kursu'."* That is, "if there is benefit to you in the ass of a donkey, stick your hand in it up to the wrist," meaning "you can bear to do even unpleasant tasks, if you will benefit from them."[10] Through the experience of leaving his homeland in search of livelihood in an unknown land, the young emigrant was enculturated in the values of his society, learning the necessity of hard work and self-reliance through the exigencies of the emigrant experience.

Emigrants from the interior experienced their first "foreign" culture on the journey to the coast, traveling with the caravans led by the *badu.* Emigrants who left the wadi in the early 1920s remembered marvelling at the bread baked from dough laid directly on embers, and other strange ways of the *badu* with their long hair and indigo-dyed skins. When they arrived at the coast, young men from the interior experienced the awesome sight of the sea and saw the bustle of the port towns, crowded with travellers and full of goods and activity, quite different from the sedate towns of the interior. While some young men headed to a specific destination to join family members, many did not yet know their final destination. They would talk to sailors and returned emigrants in the harbor and coffeehouses of al-Shihr or al-Mukalla to learn which ports of the Indian Ocean might offer the best opportunity for young newcomers. While some had their onward fare provided them, many spent a year or more working in the port cities to earn their onward fare.[11]

Those who traveled by sea faced a difficult passage on rough water on sailing ships with all passengers riding together on the open deck. Those who traveled by steam ship did not travel in luxury. It was extremely rare for any Hadhrami to travel even second class; this was observed by van den Berg in the 1880s and continued to be the case in the twentieth century.[12] In the 1920s, when the East Indies was a far more promising destination for emigrants than East Africa, some emigrants with little money traveled by sail or foot to Jedda. There they were sometimes able to cheaply purchase the return portion of the round-trip tickets of pilgrims from the East Indies who had died while performing the Hajj. One emigrant remembered his attempt in 1922 to purchase the return ticket of a deceased pilgrim from Jedda to Singapore. After the port police thwarted the purchase, he stowed away with the help of ticket-holding friends.[13]

When the emigrants arrived at their destination, they saw familiar faces. When ships arrived in the ports of the *mahjar*, each was met by Hadhramis looking out for arriving kinsmen or compatriots and mail or news from home. The veteran emigrants assisted and advised the newcomers, helping them find work and lodging. A common beginning job for a newcomer was guarding a shop owned by an earlier immigrant; he got a small stipend and a place to sleep until he found a more active and lucrative job.[14]

A few emigrants arrived without contacts from the homeland. This was the fate of some of the *badu*, who did not take up emigration until the twentieth century. Australian sailor Alan Villiers reported the arrival of Hadhrami *badu* emigrants in Mombasa in 1938 as a poignant sight. Badu, knowing nothing except that in the *mahjar* people found their fortunes, wandered around the city, their bodies covered with indigo and their hair with ghee, "staring at the strange sights as if unable to comprehend them."[15]

Attitudes toward Homeland and Mahjar

A remarkable feature about their "culture of emigration" was the ability of Hadhramis to maintain their sense of identity with their homeland and affection for it at the same time that they were able to adapt to their adopted homelands in the *mahjar* and thrive in them. The emigrants fostered a strong sense of nostalgia for their homeland, the birthplace and burial place of their ancestors (both literal and spiritual), and tried to instill this nostalgia for the homeland in their foreign-born descendants as well. Even many emigrants who chose to live out their lives in their adopted homelands maintained an idealized image of Hadhramawt and the moral purity of the way of life there.

The emigrants pined for the remembered beauty of their homeland, even those living in the lush East Indies islands. A poem written by a Hadhrami emigrant in the East Indies expressed the pain of his homesickness. Regretting that it had been his fate to have traveled from his blessed homeland, the poet lauded its abundance of grain and fruit, likening the millet to pearls, and savoring the memory of the flavor of its melons. Another emigrant poet lauded the wadi's marvelous abundance of date palms, recording the names and attributes of more than seventy varieties of dates and praising their value as food and medicine. Such poetic motifs said more about the nostalgia of the emigrants than about their homeland. While its wadis and oases certainly provided a spectacular contrast to the surrounding deserts of the Arabian peninsula, Hadhramawt had long experienced low agricultural productivity and frequent famines, a reality far different from the poetry of abundance.[16] Hadhramis were not always successful at convincing others in the *mahjar* of the bounty of their homeland. Early in the twentieth century, Sharif 'Abdallah of Mecca derided Hadhramis whose wealth was gained outside for their inordinate praise of their homeland when in fact the land and the people living there were in a miserable condition. (He predicted that the ultimate result would be foreign occupation of Hadhramawt).[17]

Hadhrami literary production also extolled the homeland for its moral purity, contrasting it with the temptations and corruptions of the outside world, as anthropologist Eng Seng Ho has pointed out. In works examined by Ho, the austere pure homeland was the abode of pious and worthy spiritual teachers, living and dead, who provided an anchor to the Hadhramis' ancestral and religious roots. The outside world, on the other hand, was a corrupt place where the quest for material wealth led to the abandonment of ancestry and religion.[18]

The idealization of the homeland served to foster the ties of the emigrants with Hadhramawt and created solidarity among the widely spread Hadhrami emigrant communities in the Indian Ocean and Red Sea region. In Hadhramawt, this idealization of the homeland and its purity was manifested in a high degree of cultural conservatism, with frequent appeals to an age-old essentially Hadhrami way of doing things and a nostalgia for an imagined uncorrupted past, before the introductions of innovations from the outside world. In the wadi, returned emigrants and the foreign-born offspring of emigrants were subjected to strict censure for any behavior that departed from local norms. The idealized notion of Hadhramawt's "purer past" was also used as a weapon against Hadhrami proponents of social reform, many of whom were either returned emigrants or *muwalladin*.[19]

An Overview of the Hadhrami Communities of the Mahjar

The Hadhrami Communities of East Africa

Africa's Swahili coast was linked to the coast of Hadhramawt by the seasonal sailing routes over which exotic animal products and hardwoods were carried from Africa to the Middle East since long before the inception of Islam. Hadhrami sailors and traders had visited and probably settled in East African ports for centuries. Between the thirteenth and the eighteenth centuries, a series of individuals from the *sada* arrived in various ports and towns of the Swahili coast and its islands, where they served as religious authorities and often as advisors to local rulers seeking to enhance their Islamic legitimacy. They often became well known and even revered by the local population, whom they impressed by performing miracles and magic. While the religious prestige and role of the *sada* made them the most visible of the Hadhramis in East Africa, all of the social groups were represented, with large numbers of Hadhramis of modest origin taking advantage of economic opportunities in East Africa in the nineteenth and twentieth centuries.[20]

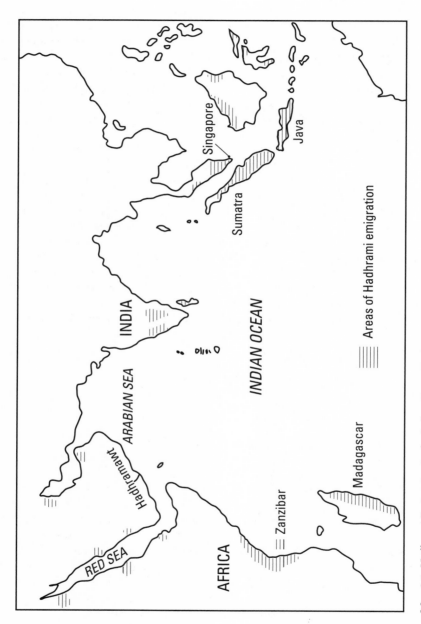

Map 2.1 Hadhrami Emigration in the Indian Ocean Region

The Hadhrami communities in East Africa were a minority in a larger Arab population. Many Arabs of Omani origin were settled in the cities of the East African coast, which were ruled by the Sultan of Musqat. Sailors and traders from Kuwait and Oman made regular seasonal visits, some staying for years. In addition, a large proportion of the Swahili population, who were mainly of mixed Arab and African blood, considered themselves to be Arab on cultural and religious grounds. As Sunni Muslims, the Hadhramis had their own mosques and burial grounds, separate from those of the Omanis, who were 'Ibadhis and Shi'is. The Hadhramis had good relations with the other Arabs and with the Africans.[21]

While some Hadhramis settled there for the long term, most did not consider East Africa home, but as a place to trade or to labor for a year or a few years and make money to return.[22] Because the fare for the sailing voyage to East Africa was so much cheaper than fares for steam travel to the East Indies, more of these emigrants were poor, with many performing manual labor or menial tasks. In the port cities, they worked as stevedores and porters, water carriers, and coffee sellers. Outside of the port cities they were cultivators and small traders or peddlers.

During the nineteenth century, the Hadhrami communities prospered. Some families in Mombasa and Zanzibar were well-to-do, owning houses and clove and coconut plantations. Others benefited from the abundance of stevedore's work, which they monopolized in Zanzibar and Mombasa. The prohibition of slavery in 1890 decimated the plantation economy, since cultivation had been carried out by slave labor. By the 1920s and 1930s, the situation of Hadhrami laborers became more difficult. African labor was taking over the stevedore trade, and motor trucks and piped water were taking business from the water carriers. These straitened circumstances and the competition among different emigrant groups for shrinking opportunities may explain Hadhrami participation in disputes among different Indian and Arab ethnic groups in Zanzibar in the 1920s, an exception to the Hadhramis' normally positive relations with their neighbors.

Hadhramis were active in commerce, dealing in dried fish and shark, baskets and mats. They dealt in goods brought in by the Arab sailing vessels on their seasonal journeys, which included: ghee, salt, Hamumi tobacco, cotton goods, sugar, honey, henna, dates, and Somalian livestock. They were active in the meat trade between Zanzibar and the mainland. Many peddled in rural areas and most aspired to own a small shop.

The Hadhramis, known locally as either Hadhramis or Shihris depending on their place of origin, did not mix much with others. They eschewed public entertainment, not going dancing, to bars, or to coffee shops. Among temporary residents, short-term marriages with local women were common. Permanent residents either married local women or married within their community. Into the 1930s, the youth of this community showed less inclination to Western clothes and ways than did the African and other Arab youth.

In the 1930s, British officials estimated the permanently settled Hadhrami population of Zanzibar at about six hundred, not counting the large numbers who came for only two or three years nor the sailors and traders who spent the spring and summer there. The 1924 census of the Zanzibar protectorate recorded a Hadhrami population of almost twenty-five hundred and that of 1931 nearly twenty-eight hundred, but these figures were inflated by the timing and method of the count, which resulted in the inclusion of seasonal inhabitants. The estimate of the Hadhrami population of Mombasa at that time was around five thousand and Lamu, fifteen hundred. The coastal towns of mainland Tanganyika territory included between two and three thousand Hadhramis. The Comoros islands and Madagascar also had Hadhrami residents.[23]

The Hadhrami Communities of the Red Sea Region

The Hadhrami community in Egypt dated to the 1880s, when several families settled in Cairo, where they traded in Yemeni coffee, incense, Syrian soap, and other goods. This was a prosperous community which owned significant property in Cairo, numbering around five hundred in the 1930s. In Sudan, Hadhramis were settled mainly in the ports of the Red Sea coast including Port Sudan and Suakin, with total numbers near 750. Only a handful of families lived in Khartoum and Omdurman and a few Hadhramis, including a number of bachelors, were scattered in remote outposts in the interior. Most were shopkeepers or shop assistants. About half were permanently settled while the other half spent a few years in Sudan and then returned home or alternated between a few years in Sudan and a year at home. They were frugal and sent most of their profits home. Colonial officials assessed them as insular, quiet and law abiding, with a local reputation for stinginess.[24]

Hadhramis had long connections with the Hijaz. They traveled to Mecca and Medina on the Hajj and members of the *'ulama'* (Islamic scholars) from the *sada* and the *mashayikh* spent time there as students, teachers, and jurists, as Snouck Hurgronje observed in 1890.[25] A large proportion of the merchants of Mecca were from Hadhramawt, large merchants who were settled there for the long term, and smaller merchants who alternated between keeping their shops and visiting the homeland while relatives tended the shop. Hadhramis were involved in trade and owned real estate in Jedda as well. A British official estimated that in the 1930s the Hadhrami population was about five thousand, which was a great reduction from previous times, since the international economic downturn had severely affected the merchants serving the pilgrim trade of the Hijaz.

While all Hadhramis were British-protected persons after 1918, those in the Hijaz often preferred to downplay that status. In the early 1930s, the Saudi Arabian government began to demand that resident foreigners be able to present documentary proof of nationality, or else choose between adopting Hijazi nationality and leaving the country. Even though the British consulate in Jedda began to issue passports to Hadhramis who wished them, the situation presented a dilemma for the Hadhramis who feared the hostility of the Saudis and also feared for the security of their property in Hadhramawt if they were identified with the imperial power. Some

Hadhramis in the Hijaz acquired passports from the British consulate, while others kept passports issued them by the British consulates of Batavia and other cities of the *mahjar*. Still others, particularly the large merchants with substantial real estate, took Hijazi nationality. The decisions were made by individuals and individual families, so many extended families of Hadhramis were split, with some members Saudi Arabian nationals and others British-protected persons.[26]

Hadhramis in India

The trade routes and network connecting the coasts of India with the coast of Hadhramawt detailed in the first-century Roman navigation guide *The Periplus of the Erythraean Sea* had existed long before the Romans became involved in the trade. After the advent of Islam, the cultural links between Hadhramawt and India increased, as a network of religious leaders and scholars supplemented that of trade.

At the time of Ibn Battuta's visit to the Malabar coast of India in the fourteenth century, he noted a prominent Arabian Muslim merchant community, although he did not specifically mention Hadhramis. The fact that the Malabar coast has long adhered to the Shafiʻi *madhhab* (school of legal thought) suggests the religious influence of Hadhramis. In the eighteenth century, members of two Hadhrami *sayyid* families arrived in Kerala to serve as religious teachers and authorities in religious law. The Hadhrami *sada* were respected by local Muslims because of their linguistic ability in Arabic, the language of scripture, their knowledge of religious scholarship, and their descent from the Prophet. In the nineteenth century, followers of a member of one of these families participated in civil rebellion and communal violence. [27]

In addition to the religious leaders, Hadhramis and other southern Arabian tribesmen came to India as soldiers, particularly from the middle of the nineteenth century. At that time, following the decline of the Mughal empire, local Indian leaders competed among themselves for territory and power. In these struggles for power, the Indian leaders soon began to employ, alongside European mercenaries, the services of tribesmen from southern Arabia. The skill in marksmanship and swift raiding that they had developed in intertribal feuding in their homeland were well suited to the needs of the rival Indian leaders, who rewarded the leaders of their Arab forces with estates.

In Hyderabad, southern Arabian troops formed the backbone of the Nizam's army from the beginning of the nineteenth century, and their leaders, known as *jamaʻdars*, amassed great fortunes. Some of these leaders branched out into moneylending, a profession in which it was advantageous to be backed by force of arms. By 1849 five thousand Arabs served in the Nizam's army. The *jamaʻdars* and their troops followed the Nizam in his support of the British in the Indian Mutiny of 1857. They retained power, wealth, and an important role in the Nizam's service even after reforms of the 1870s and 1880s brought them more firmly under state control. Some of these military leaders, notably the founders of the Kathiri and the

Qu'ayti sultanates, used their fortunes to acquire power in their homeland.[28] In the 1930s, according to Qu'ayti authorities, the troops of the Nizam of Hyderabad numbered five to six thousand men, of whom between two and three thousand were Yafi'is, mostly with Hadhrami connections and members of tribes including the Nuwwah, Ja'da, and Say'ar.[29] These tribesmen who went to India as mercenary soldiers followed the general Hadhrami pattern of bachelor emigration. While powerful and wealthy *jama'dars* married Indian women, we know little of the family life of the common soldiers or of their pattern of movements between Yaf', Hadhramawt, and India.

The Hadhrami Communities in the Dutch East Indies, Singapore, and the Straits

Hadhramis had probably been traveling to the eastern reaches of the Indian Ocean region as participants in the Arab and Indian trading networks since before the tenth century C.E. Muslims from India and Arabia flourished in trade in this region during the sixteenth century and were well established in the ports when the Dutch East India Company arrived at the end of the sixteenth century. The Arab population increased at the beginning of the nineteenth century, and again later in the century when steam lines were established.[30]

Information about the Hadhrami communities in the East Indies appeared in the 1880s in a report to the Dutch government on the Arab population, which was primarily Hadhrami, of the Dutch and British colonies of the region. According to the report by van den Berg, a Dutch colonial official, the Arab population had recently grown significantly as a result of the steam lines which by 1870 connected Arabia with the ports of the Dutch East Indies and the British-administered Straits of Malacca and Singapore. Van den Berg's figures indicated the Arab population of the entire region in the mid-1880s as around twenty-two thousand, most of whom were either Hadhrami emigrants or their foreign-born offspring. This figure did not include indigenous women married to Hadhramis.[31]

Emigration continued high in the late nineteenth and early twentieth century. In the 1930s, Dutch colonial official L. de Vries gave the Hadhrami population of the Dutch East Indies in 1900 as twenty-seven thousand, in 1920 as around forty-five thousand, and in 1930 as over seventy thousand. He estimated the Hadhrami community in Singapore in the mid-1930s at 580, a decrease from previous years since the worldwide economic depression had hit Singapore harder than the surrounding region.[32]

The Hadhrami population represented most of the social groups from Hadhramawt, although not evenly distributed. Van den Berg mentioned that the Hadhrami community of Batavia, the port of entry to the Dutch East Indies, included few *sada,* while that of Surabaya on the other hand included a large proportion of *sada.* A new Hadhrami community of van den Berg's time was composed primarily of members of the Nahd, Kathiri, and Yafi'i tribes. Some communities, including that of Surabaya were prosperous; others were poor, living in surroundings van den Berg described as squalid.

In the early nineteenth century, Hadhramis had prospered in navigation and the sea trade, both local and long distance. With the advent of steam travel, most of those communities that had depended on sailing went into decline, although in some areas Hadhrami sailing ships filled niche markets in shipping. They carried livestock between islands and served small islands and ports lacking steam service. They were able to spend several weeks in each port buying and selling, which enabled them to profit from routes that were unprofitable for steam ships, which stopped only for a few hours. But even this coasting trade died out in the early twentieth century.

After sailing ceased to be profitable, the most important source of livelihood for the Hadhrami emigrants was small-scale commerce and petty trading. Few had storefront establishments; most traded from storerooms in their homes or traveled out into rural areas peddling. They sold goods on credit and also loaned cash to the indigenous population, filling a gap left by the Dutch banking system. A few merchants handled the export trade to Arabia, sending spices and textiles to Aden, Hadhramawt, the Red Sea, and the Persian Gulf. Hadhrami merchants owned four British-flagged steam ships, which engaged in the lucrative business of carrying pilgrims to the Hajj. In Singapore, Hadhramis traded in cloth and also owned impressive amounts of real estate, including houses, hotels, and whole streets of shops.[33]

Hadhrami communities were able to maintain many of the values held dear in their homeland. They did not use or sell alcohol or opium. Even the poorest families did not resort to the prostitution of the young women, unlike the poor of the indigenous population. Most lived simply and frugally, sending money regularly to their families in Hadhramawt. Their quiet conservatism was agreeable to the colonial authorities. Van den Berg depicted them as conservative, moral, and self-sufficient. At the same time, he made the critical comments that some were excessively parsimonious, to the detriment of their business and personal affairs, and that they had few scruples with regard to making money. De Vries gave a positive assessment in his report of 1934, describing the Hadhrami emigrants as conservative, law abiding, and respectful to their host countries. Even Snouck Hurgronje, who described Hadhramawt and its people in the most scathing terms (regardless of not having been there), opined in 1916 that under a strong European government like that of the Dutch East Indies, Hadhramis were quiet and industrious subjects who adapted well to life in the modern colonial world.[34]

At the same time, the Hadhramis in the Dutch East Indies were subject to a high degree of regulation by colonial authorities. Along with Chinese and Indians, Arabs were classified as Foreign Orientals (in Dutch, *vreemde oosterlingen*), a category distinct both from Europeans and the indigenous people. From 1866 onward, they were obliged to reside in specific Arab quarters, each of which had a head selected by the colonial authorities. In order to travel within the country, they were forced to apply for permission, which was granted in dated passes for specific routes. The Hadhramis resented the quarter and pass systems, particularly because both systems made it more difficult for them to pursue their usual livelihoods in trade. This, of course, was the justification for the systems in the first place, with the colonial authorities claiming that the restrictions on the immigrants were to protect the supposedly naive indigenous population from being taken advantage of by swindlers. Paradoxically, at the same time that the quarter and pass systems were being implemented, immigration policy became freer. After 1866, conditions for immigration of Arabs were relaxed, a situation which endured until the early twentieth century. Largely due to the influence of Snouck Hurgronje, who opposed the quarter and pass systems but advocated a ban on Hadhrami immigration, the number of Arabs allowed to enter the country between 1912 and 1919 was strictly limited. Protests by the Arab community, the nascent indigenous nationalist movement, and the British, who after 1918 considered all Hadhramis to be British-protected persons, influenced the colonial government to rescind the exclusionary policy in 1919.[35]

While the Hadhramis on the whole enjoyed positive relations with the indigenous population and with the colonial authorities, the community experienced a certain degree of internal conflict. Tension existed between the emigrants born in Hadhramawt and their offspring and descendants born in the *mahjar*, the *muwalladin*. Since virtually no Hadhrami women emigrated, the emigrants married indigenous women or women of mixed Hadhrami and indigenous blood. The children of the emigrants grew up in a household speaking the local language, and their Arabic was often weak or even nonexistent. Immersed in the culture and language of their surroundings, the *muwalladin* tended to assimilate to the local culture, to the consternation of their fathers. Many followed the cultural ideal of sending their foreign-born sons to the homeland at the age of seven to learn the language and culture, but not all were able to do so. The Hadhramawt-born emigrants were more comfortable around others like themselves than they were around the more assimilated *muwalladin*. They tended to choose other emigrants from the homeland to marry their daughters or for employment in their businesses, which was resented by the *muwalladin*.

In addition, tensions existed among members of the different social groups due to the persistence of notions of the relative prestige of the groups, which often were not consonant with the personal status of individuals and particular families in the *mahjar*. In the 1880s, van den Berg thought that the disparity between social groups was less in the East Indies than in the homeland, since tribe members became more sophisticated and acquired more religious knowledge, while the *sada* enjoyed a less prestigious status. Even so, he observed that some *sada* resented the fact that members of groups of low prestige in Hadhramawt had amassed wealth and developed local social stature in the East Indies. Not surprisingly, that resentment was reciprocated. Lines of authority were blurred as well, since the

Dutch government at times appointed non-*sayyid* individuals as heads of local Hadhrami quarters and communities.[36] Problems persisted and increased in the following decades, reaching a state of crisis in the 1920s. Ironically, the efforts of the Hadhrami community of the East Indies to address one problem, the increasing assimilation of the foreign-born generations, ended up exacerbating the other problem, tensions between members of different social groups.

Conflict in the Mahjar: *Benevolent Associations and Rival Ideologies*

Early in the twentieth century, the Hadhramis of the East Indies responded to the social tensions resulting from the increasing alienation of the *muwalladin* from the language and culture of their fathers by forming associations that attempted to implement new educational institutions to serve their community. Unfortunately, the organizations and institutions that they created succumbed to the other tension in the community noted by van den Berg already in the 1880s. This was the resentment by certain members of the *sada* of the success and local prestige achieved by members of groups deemed of low prestige in the homeland and the concomitant unwillingness of those individuals to continue the traditional deference to the *sada*. The desire of some of the *sada* to maintain their entitlement to special prestige proved incompatible with the goal of raising the social, moral, and educational standard of the community as a whole. Efforts to meet the common goal of providing good Arabic language and religious education to the community's youth foundered as a result. Some subsequent efforts at organizing for community development and education failed due to the rift in the community. Successful organizing efforts tended to result in increasing factionalization of the community. Despite numerous attempts at reconciliation and attempts at intermediation by *sada* and non-*sada* alike, the community became polarized. Hadhrami visitors to the East Indies deplored the rift that had split the community, feeling that everyone was either blindly on one side or the other, or simply confused by the situation.[37]

Islamic modernist ideology as promulgated by Muhammad 'Abdu and Rashid Ridha supported the general notion of the equality of all Muslims and of merit as a function of religious knowledge and piety. This ideal of spiritual equality implicitly denied a special spiritual status or role to the *sada,* which was felt as a challenge to their authority by traditionalists among the Hadhrami *sada*. An indication of the influence of this movement in the East Indies among the local Muslims and some Hadhramis (including some *sada*) was indicated by their correspondence on a wide variety of topics with the influential Egyptian journal *al-Manar* through the duration of its publication from 1898 to 1936. Modernist literature had circulated in the East Indies even earlier than that: copies of Jamal al-Din al-Afghani's journal, *al-'Urwa al-Wuthqa,* had circulated in the East Indies, smuggled in despite its having been banned by Dutch authorities.[38]

Jam'iyat Khayr (Charitable League)

In Batavia in 1903, a small group of *sada* from the Bin Shihab and al-Mash-hur families organized to promote education in the Hadhrami community. They submitted a request to the Dutch government to form Jam'iyat Khayr, a league in-tended to better the situation of the Hadhrami community as a whole, with a specific mandate to provide Arabic Islamic education in modern schools for Hadhrami youth. The organization was chartered in 1905. The leadership of the league, wealthy businessmen and property owners, included prominent non-*sada* as well as *sada*. The Jam'iyat Khayr elementary school opened that same year, with local teachers. The Hadhrami community was pleased with the improvement in the level of linguistic and religious knowledge and in 1911 the administration de-cided to bring teachers in from outside. They wrote to two Hadhrami scholars in Mecca, who sent three qualified teachers to Batavia. Arriving in 1912, their leader was the teacher Shaykh Ahmad Muhammad al-Surkatti, a respected Dongalawi Sudanese scholar who had been studying and teaching in the Hijaz for about fifteen years. The Jam'iyat Khayr was delighted with his character, knowledge, and teach-ing ability and with the accomplishments of the students of Jam'iyat Khayr school. When the school held a public meeting after examinations in the summer of 1914, local and Hadhrami students gave speeches in classical Arabic. While most Hadhramis were impressed and delighted with the student performances, a few of the more conservative *sada* complained privately about the spectacle of students from backgrounds of low prestige in Hadhramawt standing before a crowd speak-ing of religion in classical Arabic. This group feared that Islamic learning as they knew it was being undermined; they were already worried about the use of illus-trated texts, the study of subjects other than religion in the school, and an emphasis on comprehension rather than learning by rote.

Shaykh Ahmad al-Surkatti soon further outraged that conservative element. During the school holidays of 1913, he traveled to Solo, and in a reception at the home of the leader of the Hadhrami community, his host 'Awadh b. Muhammad Bin Sunkar asked his opinion as to the permissibility of a *sharifa* marrying a non-*sayyid*. This issue was under discussion because of the case of a Hadhrami *sayyid*'s orphaned daughter, who was living with a Chinese man on a remote island. When the Hadhrami community became concerned with the girl's case, it transpired that none of the *sada* wanted to marry the girl, but they rejected the possibility of her marrying a non-*sayyid* Hadhrami. Al-Surkatti rendered his opinion: according to the *shari'a*, the marriage was permissible as long as the bride and her guardian con-sented to it, the *mahr* (bridal money) was set, and two witnesses were in atten-dance. The news of al-Surkatti's statement preceded his return to Jakarta, where his opponents had stirred up the *sada* against him for his perceived challenge to their strict adherence to the *kafa'a* standards for marriages and their emphasis on their bloodlines and heritage. As a result of the animosity, al-Surkatti resigned his position as Jam'iyat Khayr school headmaster.[39]

This climactic incident in al-Surkatti's career recapitulated an earlier ideological contest over *kafa'a*. In 1905 in Singapore, a *sharifa* had married an Indian man of questionable lineage. Some religious authorities declared the marriage invalid, angering the family and provoking debate. A Hadhrami wrote to the journal *al-Manar* inquiring as to the validity of the marriage. Rashid Ridha responded with a *fatwa* (legal opinion) deeming the marriage permissible. Sayyid 'Umar b. Salim al-'Attas issued a *fatwa* in response. Part of his argument on *kafa'a* analogized the relationship between *sada* and non-*sada* to slave and master. He also explained that the marriage of a *sharifa* to a non-*sayyid* was not only contrary to *kafa'a,* it would be an affront to the Prophet. Rashid Ridha issued a lengthy reply, arguing that the criteria for permissibility of a woman's marriage were: the religion of the husband; his status as slave or free; his character; the husband's ability to support a wife; and the permission of the bride's guardian. Using the Qur'an, *hadith* (accounts of the life of the Prophet and his companions), and scholarly opinions, he argued that all Muslims were equal and that nobility was determined by deeds, religious knowledge, and piety, rather than by descent.[40]

In 1915, a year after al-Surkatti resigned from the Jam'iyat Khayr school, at the request of his non-*sada* Hadhrami supporters, he issued an extensive *fatwa* using the Qur'an and hadith to repudiate the *sada* argument for *kafa'a*, with an argument similar to Rashid Ridha's earlier one. The hostility many of the *sada* held toward him increased. An example of their antipathy was demonstrated by the well-known poet Sayyid Abu Bakr b. 'Abd al-Rahman Bin Shihab in a poem responding to the *fatwa*. The poem called al-Surkatti "Ibn Sinar" ("son of Sinar," al-Surkatti's homeland in Sudan), and asked him if he or the devil had written the *fatwa*, saying that al-Surkatti had too little learning to offer opinions. The poem stated that the descendants of the Prophet about whose ways al-Surkatti was offering judgment were fine and noble, while the people of Sinar were black with big noses.[41]

Jam'iyat al-Islah wa al-Irshad (Reform and Guidance League)

Before al-Surkatti returned to Hijaz, another league was quickly formed by Hadhramis who respected al-Surkatti's contribution to the education of their youth. Led by 'Umar b. Yusuf Manqush, a group of wealthy businessmen supported the creation of a new school, which opened in fall 1914 under al-Surkatti's direction. The supporters were primarily non-*sada*, although a few *sada* actively supported the school and organization in its early years. Enrollment for the new school quickly filled with students who transferred from the Jam'iyat Khayr school and new students, Hadhrami and local.

The charter of Jam'iyat al-Islah wa al-Irshad, henceforth called simply Irshad, stated its goals. Like Jam'iyat Khayr, it was a charitable organization that would focus on establishing: schools; hostels for orphans, widows, and handicapped; clubs and public libraries. It also aimed to support publishing, lectures, and educational delegations. The only controversial article in its charter was the fifth, which stated that while any adult male Muslim had the right to join the association, no member of the 'Alawi *sada* could be on the board of directors. This article reflected the circumstances of the organization's inception and the fear of *sayyid* interference. It was also a response to the *sayyid* claim that no organization could succeed without *sayyid* guidance. The exclusionary article did not deter some members of the *sada* from participating in the organization in its early years. Al-Surkatti played a critical role as advisor and his contacts with indigenous Muslim leaders and reform organizations fostered a high degree of outside support for the fledgling association. At the same time, it experienced opposition not only from some of the *sada* but also from leaders of local mystical groups that performed rites at the tombs of particularly revered Hadhrami *sada* of earlier times.[42]

Despite opposition, the organization grew rapidly and gained in influence. By 1931 it had twenty-four branches with eight hundred registered members, which included many members of the indigenous population as well as Hadhramis. A women's movement called Nahdat al-Mu'minat (Awakening of the Female Believers), which had begun in Pekalongan the previous year, held its Saturday night lectures for women in the local Irshad school. That movement, which also opened multiple branches around the islands, by 1938 had its own congress. It formally became the women's section of Irshad in 1939.[43]

At the same time, Irshad continued to antagonize the 'Alawis. The 1928 Irshad conference rescinded the prohibition of any member of the 'Alawi *sada* from serving on the board of directors, although by that time there were only a handful of *sada* associated with the organization in any way. The animosity increased after the 1931 Irshad conference passed a controversial resolution, proclaiming that the honorific "Sayyid" should not be limited to the 'Alawis, but rather be used for everyone, equivalent to the Indo-Malay honorific "Tuan." The 'Alawis responded to that and other challenges by establishing their own organization.[44]

Al-Rabita al-'Alawiyya (The 'Alawi Brotherhood)

This organization, closely associated with Jam'iyat Khayr, was established in Batavia in 1927 and branches quickly spread among the *sada* of the East Indies and Singapore. It was founded to solidify 'Alawi identity and pride and spread knowledge of the 'Alawi heritage among that community, particularly among the *muwalladin* of the *mahjar* who were felt to be in danger of slipping away from their heritage because of the attractions of assimilation. The charter of the organization was printed and sold and also was printed in the first issue of the first volume of the organization's journal, *al-Rabita*. The first article of the charter stated the necessity for unity and solidarity among the Hadhramis. While this group considered themselves to have a special status, they perceived themselves as unifiers and considered supporters of Irshad as the ones dividing and disrupting their society.

The charter defined the organization as a charitable one devoted to social welfare and to the spread of knowledge of Islam and the Arabic language. It had the goal of raising moral standards and resisting moral corruption and to encourage correct behavior and was not organized to oppose governmental control. These goals, with their expressions of concern about moral development, education, and care of orphans did not differ from those of earlier organizations, including Irshad. Only the fourth article focused on the 'Alawi heritage, advocating that the *sada* ascertain the accurate genealogies of all their far-flung members. The last part of the charter expressed aspirations for the further moral development of all members of all sectors of Hadhrami society, albeit organized according to the social group categories that Irshad was trying to overcome.[45]

The organization had its first conference in Batavia in September 1929, which featured a speech by Sayyid 'Alawi b. Tahir al-Haddad, later Mufti of Johore, who was a central figure inspiring the movement. Shortly after that conference, membership numbers rose to thirteen hundred. Sayyid 'Alawi b. Tahir's speech, which was printed in *al-Rabita,* likened the members of the organization to the foundation of a house, necessary for the community as a whole to stand strong. He emphasized the importance of the spiritual power of the 'Alawis, which had lasted for eleven centuries during which political powers came and went, in promoting reform and public good and the moral and material advancement of the people of Hadhramawt. Like the charter, he associated strengthening the ties among 'Alawis with strengthening Hadhramawt in general; that is, he presented 'Alawis as a force for unity against divisiveness. This speech, like other lectures and writings by Sayyid 'Alawi b. Tahir, focused on heritage and history of the 'Alawis and the necessity for the new generations to connect with their heritage.[46]

In the first two years of publication, *al-Rabita* devoted the majority of its pages to "pro-Alawi" rather than "anti-Irshad" material. These included administrative details such as: membership lists; records of meetings; treasury reports; news of schools, branches, and delegations travelling to speak in areas without branches. They included texts of lectures by Sayyid 'Alawi b. Tahir on 'Alawi heritage, Islamic and Hadhrami history; he delivered these lectures twice a month in Batavia. Subjects of other articles included: the early history of the 'Alawis in India, the East Indies, the Comoros Islands, and China; the Hadhrami dialect; and the history of Tarim. A practical question of transmitting heritage in this *mahjar* community was raised several times: how to strengthen ties between fathers and sons.[47]

A particularly interesting article, or rather collection of notes on varied topics, appeared under the pseudonym "lam" (the letter l), entitled "Khawatir saniha wa ara' nasiha" (Auspicious ideas and advisable views). It included a bit which attributed the encouragement of women's education to one of the revered pious ancestors of the *sada,* and portrayed Hadhramawt in that time as blessed with the spirit of learning permeating the households. Another portion of this piece suggested a critical attitude toward the *sada* in Hadhramawt. The author suggested that the *sada* in Tarim and Say'un were in danger on two sides, moral and material. Moral danger resulted from the confusion causing people to leave the path of their rightly guided ancestors. Material danger resulted from the *sada* having developed an aversion to agriculture and business that had not originally been part of their heritage. He criticized the *sada* for sitting idly, subsisting on rents from the *mahjar,* and living in luxury until expenses finally forced them to lose their property and to have to emigrate.[48]

The journal also included a handful of articles directly criticizing Irshad and its activities. A note questioned the article in the Irshad charter forbidding 'Alawi membership of Irshad's board of directors. Another brief article questioned why copies of their journal were lost in the post between Aden and Hadhramawt, suggesting deliberate interference by Irshad sympathizers.[49]

The organization distributed another publication that directly responded to Irshad, a sixty-three-page proclamation entitled *Haqa'iq* (*Truths*), implying a response to lies. This work, issued in May 1931, was a response to the Irshad conference earlier that year. al-Rabita al-'Alawiyya responded to several points: the Irshad depiction of their beliefs with respect to *kafa'a* and the importance of their heritage; the prohibition of *sada* from the board of directors of Irshad (although according to Irshad sources, that had been rescinded in the conference of 1928); and the conference resolution that the honorific "Sayyid" should not be limited to the 'Alawis, but rather be used for everyone. The proclamation referred to the use of the honorific "Sayyid" for other than the 'Alawi *sada* as an attack, even a rape. As a cap to the counterarguments on that issue, the proclamation included citations from Western Orientalists, including van den Berg and Hirsch, and encyclopedias, documenting the Hadhrami usage of the honorific "Sayyid" specifically for the 'Alawi *sada.*[50]

Members of al-Rabita al-'Alawiyya were active in lobbying on behalf of this cause. After the Irshad congress of 1931, when Irshad members began to refer to everyone as "Sayyid," they requested that honorific on their own travel documents and other official papers, which followed the usage common in most of the Arab world. The *sada* responded with alacrity, appealing to the Dutch government to take an official stance on the use of the honorific "Sayyid" and restrict it only to the 'Alawi *sada.* At the same time, they wrote to the Aden government, pointing out that the kind of equality urged by Irshad was not only inimical to Islam but tantamount to Bolshevism. They requested that the British consul in Batavia be sent to the Dutch government to explain their case and let them know the harm that might come from Hadhramis who were non-*sada* referring to themselves as such. Sayyid 'Alawi b. Tahir al-Haddad contacted the British consul in Batavia presenting the argument. There is no sign that the British consul followed their advice. He had been embroiled in the same issue the previous year and tried to avoid coming down on either side of the issue. In early 1933, the Dutch government also declined to intervene, but suggested an alternative to the *sada:* that they might distinguish themselves from others by using the appellation al-'Alawi after their family name.[51]

Organizations: Unity, Reform, and Rifts

In Solo in 1912, a group of prominent Hadhramis from various traditional social groups formed al-Jamʿiya al-ʿArabiyya al-Islamiyya (Arabic Islamic League) and opened a school. In later years the supporters of the school became so polarized along Irshad-ʿAlawi lines that they were no longer able to operate the school. They managed to agree enough to follow the suggestion of Sayyid ʿAbdallah b. Salim al-ʿAttas to turn the school over to the Dutch government, who ran it as a Dutch-Arabic school, following the standard Dutch elementary curriculum.[52]

In Solo in 1919, an extensive group of Hadhramis from all social groups met to form an organization called al-Wahda al-ʿArabiyya (Arab Unity) to attempt to unite the community toward common goals, such as establishing an Indonesian language newspaper discussing Arab affairs. This organization soon fell apart because of ʿAlawi objection to Ahmad Surkatti's participation.[53]

Another organization with the same name, al-Wahda al-ʿArabiyya, also focused on education and community improvement, was founded by Shaykh Muhammad ʿAbdallah al-ʿAmudi in the late 1920s. Like many Hadhramis who lived in remote areas, al-ʿAmudi had studied in Dutch schools; unlike most who were educated in Dutch, he also had a good grounding in the Arabic language. Despite high interest in the organization, it failed within a few years from lack of unity resulting in part from ʿAlawi opposition. Its founder then started a different organization, Wahdat Mawalid al-ʿArab al-Indunisiyin (Unity of the Indonesian-born Arabs), to further the educational, social, and financial status of the *muwalladin,* which met with greater success.[54]

The Yafiʿi tribes formed an association, al-Jamʿiya al-Yafiʿiyya (The Yafiʿi League), in the mid-1920s to try to further the situation of their compatriots in the homeland and the *mahjar.* One of the main purposes of this organization was to present the case of Irshad to their kinsman, the Quʿayti sultan and his strongly anti-Irshad *wazir* (chief minister), Sayyid Husayn b. Hamid al-Mihdhar.[55]

Members of the Kathiri tribe, prominent and wealthy members of the Hadhrami communities of the East Indies and Singapore, had been strong and active supporters of Irshad, although they had sometimes been accused of attempting to take over the leadership of that organization. In 1933, they formed an organization—al-Jamʿiya al-Kathiriyya (The Kathiri League)—which aspired to have a positive influence on their homeland by influencing the government and intervening with the feuding tribes. They created a school in Batavia, where they had the greatest presence, but in other locations their children continued to attend Irshad schools. Some other Irshad members deplored what they called a resort to tribalism and racism, knowing that there had been conflicts between Kathiri and Yafiʿi Irshad members. Some activist *sada* tried to take advantage of the situation by emphasizing the long-standing close relations between the *sada* and the Kathiri sultans. Some of the Kathiri were drawn to the ʿAlawi cause, although most retained their Irshad loyalties.[56]

Attempts to Settle the Rift

In 1927 and 1928, two well-known poets and scholars traveled from Hadhramawt to the East Indies to try to reconcile the divided Hadhrami population there. While both had the respect of the *mahjar* communities, neither was able to succeed. In 1927, 'Ali Ahmad BaKathir returned to Java, his birthplace, where he attempted to ameliorate the conflict between Irshad and the 'Alawis. An adherent of the Islamic modernist ideals espoused by Egypt's Muhammad 'Abdu, BaKathir supported the ideological foundation of the Irshad movement, but strongly opposed the aggressive anti-*sayyid* stance and tactics adopted by many of its supporters. He also appreciated the interest of educated and progressive members of the *sada* in efforts toward the betterment of the moral and educational standards of all. His efforts met with failure and he returned to Say'un.[57]

Another poet and scholar, the respected but controversial Sayyid 'Abd al-Rahman b. 'Ubaydillah al-Saqqaf, traveled to Java in 1927/1928 (1346 h.) to try to settle the rift between the two factions. He met with partisans of both sides, and particularly urged his 'Alawi kin to forgive past wounds and come to an accommodation with Irshad supporters. His pleas for fairness and his equanimity toward what his kinsmen portrayed as Irshad insults to the 'Alawi heritage and the special spiritual status of the *sada* angered the 'Alawi supporters. He made speeches in Batavia and Surabaya stressing that for hundreds of years *sada* and non-*sada* had peacefully coexisted. He urged compromise and pointed out that God had advised Muslims to support each other and unite against their enemies, the Hadhrami community of the East Indies were perversely uniting against each other. Although both factions initially dealt with him in good faith, ultimately his efforts failed and he left Java without managing to achieve any sort of reconciliation. While neither side was ready to make peace with the other, he was particularly disappointed with the 'Alawi faction, perhaps because of his identification with that community and his wish to have influence on his peers.[58] Despite the efforts of these two and others to reconcile the conflict, the rift in the community was exacerbated at around this same time. The heightened tension accompanied 'Alawi domination of what was supposed to be a general Hadhrami reform conference, the Singapore Conference of 1928.[59]

Pride, Polarization, and Violence

Both Irshad and al-Rabita al-'Alawiyya expanded their branches and built schools in the late 1920s and 1930s. With the emphasis on heritage that it provided in its lectures, printed works, and schools, al-Rabita al-'Alawiyya met a need of the *sada* community of the *mahjar*. This community felt threated from within by the increasing alienation of its youth from their special heritage, and from without by the burgeoning Irshad movement which appeared to denigrate that heritage.

The Irshad provided the youth of the other groups with opportunities for education that had not been available to their fathers. They responded zealously both to the education and to the notion of the equality of all Muslims. After studying, many taught in Irshad schools proliferating throughout the islands and traveled to isolated communities to spread the message. Nearly seventy years later, one student of al-Surkatti remembered his excitement at having access to bound volumes of *al-Manar* in the school library. Another staunch Irshad supporter remembered proselytizing door to door as he traveled through the rural hinterlands of Sumatra and Sarawak peddling cloth.[60]

But while each faction benefited from its own institutions, the rift between the factions deepened. An increasing number of acts of intimidation and violence took place. The worst incident took place in January 1933, in al-Nur Mosque in Bandoso in eastern Java, during the *tarawih* prayer, the special nighttime prayers performed during Ramadan. According to a Singapore Arabic-language newspaper, a small group including six Irshad supporters were lined up for prayers that were just about to begin, when a crowd of around fifty *sada* who did not normally pray at that particular mosque entered. They pushed themselves between Irshad congregants and the Imam. Told to move to the back, they replied that the others should move to the back, that the front rows were rightfully theirs. A fracas ensued, in which two of the 'Alawi *sada* were killed and nine wounded, and all six Irshad supporters were wounded. The mosque was littered with rocks, knives, and sticks afterward, with the newspaper attributing the former weapon to the *sada* and the latter ones to Irshad.[61]

Concern about the Spread of Irshad Influence in Hadhramawt

The 'Alawi *sada* vigorously attempted to keep Irshad influence from reaching from the East Indies into the homeland. During World War I, influential members of the Hadhrami *sada* community of the Netherlands East Indies had cooperated with the British in countering German propaganda among the Muslims of the East Indies, for which the British held them in high regard. At least one *sayyid* used this influence to prejudice the British consul against supporters of Irshad, by depicting them as anti-British and even "Bolshevist." Stressing the *sada* support of the British-favored Sharif Husayn of Mecca as the new Caliph of the Muslims, they played on British fears of a pan-Islamic movement that might challenge British imperial power in Africa and Asia. As a result, travel documents were denied to Irshad supporters who wished to return to their homeland, creating hardship for them and their families. It was only in late 1920 and early 1921 that J. Crosby, the new British consul in Batavia, became aware that reports of one *sayyid* informant were affecting the ability of numerous non-*sayyid* individuals, suspected of sympathizing with Irshad, to travel to their homeland. On further examination, he concluded that they posed little threat to British influence there, contrary to the reports of the informant. His concerns were confirmed when he learned that Sharif

Husayn of Mecca had been contacted by some of the Hadhrami *sada* from Java, who had requested that Irshad sympathizers not be granted permission to travel to Hijaz to perform the Hajj. Crosby studied the problem, notified the Foreign Office, and rectified the situation regarding travel passes issued from his office as soon as he received permission to do so.[62]

At the same time, the Hadhrami *sada* in the Netherlands East Indies who actively opposed the Irshad movement were in close communication with the *wazir* of the Qu'ayti government. The *wazir,* Sayyid Husayn b. Hamid al-Mihdhar, regularly disparaged Irshad to the Qu'ayti. He also encouraged Sayyid 'Umar b. Ahmad BaSurra, the governor of Wadi Du'an, the ancestral seat of the al-Mihdhar family, to persecute the families of Irshad members unless word was sent that they had withdrawn from the organization. Al-Mihdhar also tried to use the traditional spiritual influence of his heritage as a member of the Shaykh Abu Bakr b. Salim family to pressure the Yafi'i in the East Indies to abandon their support of Irshad.

Some Irshad members whose families had been threatened by BaSurra wrote a letter of protest to the Qu'ayti sultan in 1919, to no avail. In 1919 the Qu'ayti and Kathiri sultans sent a proclamation to their subjects in the East Indies, claiming that the British had ordered them to ban their subjects from joining Irshad. In 1920 they sent another proclamation with the same message but a considerably more threatening tone.[63]

The Irshad movement did not manifest itself in the homeland, although in the 1930s there was a great deal of concern about potential Irshad influence in Hadhramawt. During her journey to Hadhramawt, British traveller Freya Stark noticed people talking about it. Correspondence on the topic circulated among an influential group: the wealthy and influential member of the Kathiri tribe, Salim b. Ja'far Bin Talib; the Kathiri sultan; Sayyid Abu Bakr b. Shaykh al-Kaf and his brother Sayyid 'Abd al-Rahman b. Shaykh; the *wazir* Sayyid Abu Bakr b. Husayn al-Mihdhar; and members of al-Rabita al-'Alawiyya. All agreed that Hadhramawt must remain free of Irshad influence. Efforts to thwart Irshad presence in the homeland succeeded at this time, but the ideas and ideals of Islamic modernism still became part of the debate over social change.[64]

Emigration and Change

The widespread experience of emigration shaped the culture of the Hadhramis in the homeland and in the *mahjar* and had an impact on the identity of Hadhramis at home as well as abroad. The different areas to which Hadhramis emigrated had specific histories of emigration, each drawing a somewhat different set of emigrants and each having its own particular characteristics. The most tumultuous history was that of the communities of the Dutch East Indies, due to the degree of assimilation of their offspring, and tension over the disjuncture of the traditional group system with the realities of their existence in their adopted land. The challenges to the traditional system led to a cleft in the emigrant community that had reflections and reverberations in other emigrant communities and the homeland. Despite all efforts to insulate the homeland from the influence of the Irshad movement, the high degree of connection between the homeland and the *mahjar* fostered the development of reformist ideology, critique, and debates in the homeland. These ideological contests affected the development of social, religious, and educational institutions, and became sources of political conflict as well.

Influences from the *mahjar* affected life in the homeland to a notable degree during the late nineteenth and twentieth century. Emigrants, returnees, and emigrant remittances effected political, social, economic, and material changes in the wadi, not without some resistance. Even though social and economic institutions ordering the society remained remarkably stable, life in town and countryside was beginning to change. Both social change and the perceived lack of social change became matters of ideological contestation and public debate.

PART TWO

The Ordering of Life in Town and Country

3
Urban and Rural Life in the Interior

The interior of Hadhramawt was rather isolated, with the harsh and barren desert plateau known as the *jawl* separating the interior from the coastal region that was linked by sea with the societies of the Indian Ocean littoral. Despite the physical barrier of the *jawl,* the population of the interior maintained connections with the Indian Ocean world through the emigrant communities and through the Hadhrami coastal towns. At the time of the foundations of the Qu'ayti and Kathiri states in the late nineteenth century, highly developed social and economic institutions ordered life in town and country. This system of ordering remained stable, even as the towns changed physically as a result of new manifestations of political authority and new infusions of wealth derived from emigration.

Towns: Organization and Institutions

The main wadi of the interior, or Wadi Hadhramawt proper, comprised three main towns: Say'un, Tarim, and Shibam. Say'un and Tarim along with the outlying villages and their immediate hinterlands, constituted the Kathiri sultanate, Say'un being its capital. Shibam, the main market center of the interior, became an outlying commercial and administrative center within the Qu'ayti sultanate. Say'un and Tarim both were organized into a quarter system, which ordered the neighborhoods and their inhabitants and systematized relations between the different social groups. Shibam differed from other towns of the interior and coast in lacking such a quarter system. Shibam, as a market town, exemplified another ordering system prevalent in Hadhramawt, the organization of the markets, which accomodated the economic and social interdependence of the settled populations in towns and countryside and the often-reviled *badu* of the barren hinterlands.

Say'un, Kathiri Sultanate Capital, and Its Quarter System

Say'un had been the capital of the first Kathiri state from its inception in the early fifteenth century through its loss of power at the beginning of the eighteenth. Subsequently, Say'un was an agricultural town at the center of one "mini-state" (*duwayla*) among many in the area until Ghalib b. Muhsin al-Kathiri established the second Kathiri state in the name of the Al 'Abdallah branch of the Kathiri in the 1850s and 1860s. In the latter decades of the nineteenth century, Say'un ex-

Figure 3.1 Say'un town gate

perienced renewed economic and infrastructural development as the political center of the modern Kathiri sultanate. At the same time it developed as a spiritual
center, largely due to the activity of the pious and charismatic Sayyid 'Ali Muhammad al-Hibshi and the benefactors from the *mahjar* whose endowments helped establish new religious institutions. The population of Say'un was probably between
twelve thousand and fifteen thousand during the late nineteenth and early twentieth century.[1] Like most towns and villages in Wadi Hadhramawt and its tributaries, Say'un was built against the cliff side that bounded the wadi. It lay against
the southward cliffs, at the point where a watercourse emptied onto the floor of
the main wadi.

The town wall of Say'un had originally been built by the most powerful ruler
of the first Kathiri state, Badr b. 'Abdallah al-Kathiri, known as "Abu Tuwayriq,"
in the sixteenth century. Two substantial forts stood at the foothills of the cliff side,
overlooking the oldest part of the town. Forts stood where the town wall met the
cliff side, and at strategic points along the wall, with a cluster of forts guarding the
exit of the watercourse. Each large gate or *sidda* (sometimes called *bawaba*), was
fortified, with all fortifications manned by the *hashiya,* slave soldiers of the sultan.

The most imposing structure in the town was the Kathiri sultan's palace, on
a high, flat-topped hill which had been the site of a Kathiri government building
as early as 1411. In 1873, the second sultan of the modern Kathiri dynasty, al-
Mansur b. Ghalib constructed a majestic mud-brick palace there, a five-story structure twenty-five meters high. The thick walls of the huge mud-brick structure
sloped inward as they rose between four round corner watchtowers. Inside, the
palace consisted of small rooms, labyrinthine passages, and multiple stairways. The
sultan's family and members of the *hashiya* families who worked as servants lived
there. A wall surrounded the palace and a small mosque, the garrison and stables
for the *hashiya,* and the palace well. Outside the wall, private homes and shops were
built up the side of the hill. In 1926, Sultan 'Ali b. Mansur al-Kathiri renovated
the palace. He had the exterior coated with *nura,* fired gypsum plaster. He built a
reception room with sixteen columns supporting the ceiling. He built a main gate
and cleared the buildings from outside the wall, creating a public square. These al-
terations gave the palace a grander and more monumental appearance. A second,
smaller palace called "Muhsin palace" stood nearby. Muhsin b. Ghalib, the younger
brother of Sultan al-Mansur b. Ghalib held court there until 1916, when rule over
the Kathiri domains was divided and rule of Tarim was granted to Sultan Muhsin
and his descendants.[2]

Another nearby public building was the congregational mosque. Scattered
around the town were numerous mosques, including one dating from the sixteenth
century known as Masjid bint al-Shaykh, "the mosque of the *shaykh*'s daughter,"
since it had been endowed by Ruqaya bint 'Uthman al-'Amudi, a devout woman
from a prominent *mashayikh* family.

Across from the sultan's palace was the market, Suq al-Qasbal, a cluster of
small shops. The Say'un market primarily served the town and nearby hamlets.

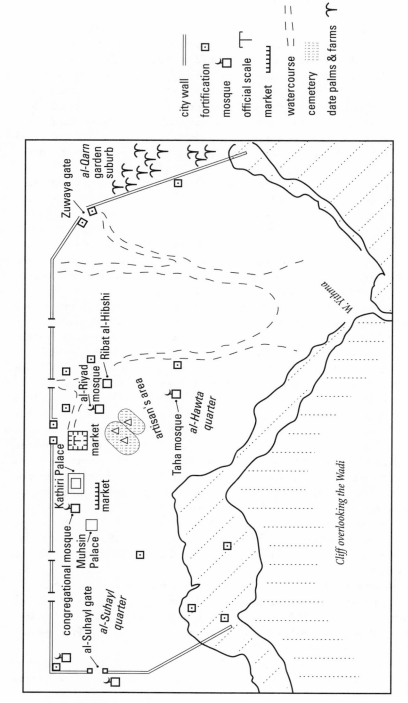

Map 3.1 Say'un, c. 1920s

city wall
fortification
mosque
official scale
market
watercourse
cemetery
date palms & farms

Zuwaya gate

al-Qarn garden suburb

Ribat al-Hibshi

al-Riyad mosque

market

artisan's area

Taha mosque

al-Hawta quarter

Kathiri Palace

congregational mosque

Muhsin Palace

market

al-Suhayl gate

al-Suhayl quarter

W. Yibhna

Cliff overlooking the Wadi

Most goods came to Qasbal market from Shibam, including: imported foodstuffs and cloth from al-Mukalla, tobacco from Ghayl BaWazir, coffee from Yaf', and some goods from Yemen. Locally produced goods included cloth, silver, knives, and agricultural tools. The larger merchants did much of their business on credit, providing the families of emigrants with everything they needed, including spending money. The emigrants periodically reimbursed the merchants by sending the equivalent value of imported goods from the *mahjar*. Another market, Suq al-Hanzal, sold preserved fish products and locally produced foodstuffs. The *qubban* or large official scale was located there, for the authoritative weighing of bulk goods. Disputes in the market were taken to the *hakim al-suq* (market arbitrator).[3]

Say'un's main gate, largest forts, palaces, markets, graveyards, and wells were clustered in a small area. Nearby stood a complex of buildings forming the spiritual center, which grew in the late nineteenth century under the leadership of Sayyid 'Ali Muhammad al-Hibshi. Between 1876 and 1880, with the endowments of supporters in the *mahjar,* he constructed the Riyadh mosque, and a new institute of learning and worship, the *ribat,* near the town center. After his death in 1915, his tomb nearby became an additional site of religious observation.[4]

Say'un's mud-brick houses were three or four stories high, the walls covered with fired gypsum plaster, *nura,* to the extent that the owner could afford. At the minimum, *nura* was applied to rooftops and around door and window openings, to protect the structure from rain. A house was constructed around a central pillar called *'urus al-riqad,* or "bridegroom of the stairs," around which the main staircase rotated. An open space surrounding the central pillar allowed fresh air and sunlight to enter the rooms. Houses of the wealthy included a large ground floor reception room called *Umm arba'a,* or "mother of four," because four pillars supported the ceiling. An extensive system of pillars, beams, and crossbeams supported the roofs of the rooms. During the 1920s and 1930s, wealthy families began to build elaborate facades on their houses, including porches and balconies behind stately rows of stone columns topped with capitals. Another style innovation of that time was the enlargement of windows and the doorways leading onto balconies and rooftop terraces. Windows were expensive, since the frames, lattices, and shutters were carved from a special strong hard red acacia wood.

The interiors of the larger houses were divided into two parts, each with a separate stairway, allowing the family to receive men and women as guests while respecting the privacy of the women. The separate sections were not permanently designated for men or women, rather the usage of the space was flexible and followed convenience. In the absence of guests, men and women were not usually separated in the home, although strategically placed curtains hung temporarily between the pillars of a sitting room served to separate women from the gaze of "unrelated" family members, such as a brother-in-law. Except for the kitchen, water closet, and storage rooms, rooms did not have permanently designated uses. At different times, the large pillared rooms might be used as reception rooms for guests, family living and working space, and at night for sleeping. They were used as

dining areas for family meals and for feasts for guests on holidays and special occasions. Furnishings were simple, even in the large houses of prosperous families.
The family sat on carpets. Seating cushions were not normally used, although a
family might have a few pillows to offer elderly or honored guests. Thin cotton-
stuffed mats were rolled out for sleeping and put away during the day. Round mats
woven from strips of palm leaves were laid out on the floor for meals and stored in
the pantry when not in use. Coffee and tea services, the most elaborate goods in
the household, were stored in shelved niches in the thick walls. Houses included
partially walled rooftop terraces on which families passed the evenings and slept
during warm weather. The ground floor included the kitchen, grinding stones, and
clay bread ovens as well as storage rooms for grain and dates. Some homes had
chicken cages suspended outside kitchen windows and families sometimes kept a
goat or sheep in the lower level of the houses.[5]

Outside the western town wall lay the well-watered and fertile orchards of
al-Qarn. In the late nineteenth century, as a result of increased political stability
and prosperity, al-Qarn gradually transformed from a rural agricultural area outside the Say'un walls to a "garden suburb." Wealthy families, mainly those who
had prospered in the East Indies, began to build stately homes (*qusur*, literally
"palaces," sing. *qasr*) among the date palms on their agricultural properties. These
homes benefited from the spaciousness, privacy, and breeziness of their bucolic sites
and water from their own wells. Additional privacy was provided by high mud
walls around the homes and their orchards and fields. These fashionable suburban
homes included decorative elements from the East Indies and contained goods imported from India, the East Indies, and Europe. When electric pumps began to be
imported in the 1920s and 1930s, homes began to include an indoor bathing pool.
When irrigation water was pumped, it first circulated into a pool in a room on the
perimeter of the house before passing into an aqueduct carrying it to the date palms
and fields. This provided the family with an opportunity for a cooling dip during
the heat of the day.

Neighborhoods included a mixture of inhabitants from different social
groups, including slaves, some of whom had homes in town. While several areas
of town had names, there were only two true quarters, al-Suhayl in the densely
populated eastern third of the town and al-Hawta in the west. The dividing line
between the two quarters passed through the square between the two palaces, with
the main palace in al-Hawta quarter and Muhsin Palace in al-Suhayl quarter.

Say'un had perhaps the greatest rivalry between the quarters of any town in
Hadhramawt. At times of celebration, the two quarters competed formally in extemporaneous poetry composition and in dancing. Their rivalry was manifested
outside these formal situations, when members of one quarter were considered by
the other to have "crossed the line" into their territory and thus merited attack by
fists, clubs, or even knives. The rivalry was so severe that the only time that *al-
huwik* from al-Suhayl could enter Say'un as a group through the town's main gate

in al-Hawta quarter was during the ceremonial return from the *ziyara,* ritual visit, to the tomb of Prophet Hud.

For ordinary purposes such as attending Friday prayers or visiting relatives, individuals might cross the dividing line between quarters. But when emergencies or celebrations took place in one quarter, *al-huwik* from the other could not appear there without risk. There were only a few exceptions; for example, a member of *al-huwik* might attend the funeral or wedding of a relative in the other quarter. In such a case, the members of the quarter where the event took place closely watched the "outsider" to see that he or she did not participate in the provision of services or interfere with them in any way. He or she could not even sing or dance at a wedding of a relative in the other quarter.

An exception was also made for Sultan Muhsin, who until 1916 lived in his palace in al-Suhayl quarter. He sometimes requested to employ service providers from the main palace in al-Hawta, which required the consent of the leaders of the quarters. The agreement reached was that service providers from al-Hawta could cook for Sultan Muhsin but could not serve the food. The cooks from al-Hawta were so afraid that the servers from al-Suhayl would sabotage their food that they sealed the door of the kitchen so that the servers could not enter and made a window through which to pass the food.

The sultans, while subject to the system of service providers, mediated in disputes between the quarters that their leaders were unable to resolve. Deaths, particularly sudden ones, were more often the cause of disputes than the more predictable celebrations of weddings and births, which allowed more time for settlement of potential conflicts. It was particularly tricky when a person happened to die in the quarter other than the one in which he or she lived. In the course of funeral observations, the body of a man was taken from the home to the mosque for prayers and recitation of the Qur'an. Since a large number of the mosques in Say'un, including the oldest and most renowned, were located in al-Hawta, disputes often arose after a death took place in al-Suhayl if the family of the deceased were fond of a mosque in al-Hawta. In one case, after a person in al-Suhayl died, the family insisted on having the body taken to the Taha mosque in al-Hawta. The service providers from al-Suhayl set out bearing the bier, accompanied by *hashiya,* which they had requested to insure their safe passage to the Taha mosque. At the boundary between the quarters they found other *hashiya* accompanying the service providers of al-Hawta, who demanded that the corpse be handed over at the dividing line.

In another case, a merchant from al-Hawta bought a sesame seed oil press from a seller in al-Suhayl. When the merchant sent his men from al-Hawta to get it, *al-huwik* of al-Suhayl would not allow them to cross the line into their quarter. The leader of the *al-huwik* of al-Hawta appealed to the sultan, who ordered that a team from al-Suhayl should carry the press to the boundary, where the team from al-Hawta might receive it and take it to the merchant's premises.[6]

Even within the quarters, disputes took place over the right to provide services. They were settled with the assistance of the leaders of the quarters, through the forging of intricate agreements. For example, a 1911 agreement specified the distribution of payments for individual services performed by the men and women of some families that worked together serving in wedding celebrations or feasts. It included details such as the cash equivalent of the groom's old clothes given to the person who handed the groom the soap, towel, and perfume as he bathed in preparation for his wedding night—half a *riyal.* It also specified who received the head of the sheep butchered for the feast.[7]

While to the society at large providing social services was associated with low social status, providing social services gave these specialized families the opportunity to make a living and support their households. Competition that had long existed among providers of social services was exacerbated as the wealth in the community increased. Those needing services, unable to freely choose their providers or to negotiate fees, sometimes felt like victims before the quarter system, its power, and the consequent conflicts.[8]

Tarim: Holy Town (Graveyard of the Martyrs to Islam)

The town of Tarim claimed special prestige as a spiritual center, the home of the remains of blessed ancestors and their living descendants. The basis for its status lay in the critical cusp of Islamic history at the time of the death of the Prophet. When Arabs throughout the peninsula responded to their acknowledged leader's death by withdrawing their allegiance from Islam and the Muslim community, the people of Tarim remained faithful and supported the Caliph Abu Bakr in the *ridda* wars, the Muslims' struggle against apostasy. One of the battles was fought just outside Tarim, at al-Najir, and its martyrs were buried in the town. Tarim was blessed for this faithfulness; it was said that its inhabitants would be favored on Judgment Day, taken directly to paradise by the hand of Abu Bakr. The town was the home of a great number of *sada,* and had been the birthplace of many of the revered figures whose tombs stood elsewhere in Hadhramawt and beyond, besides the notable ones in the Tarim cemetery.[9]

Tarim enjoyed a renaissance of sorts in the 1880s after several decades of decline. Despite the town's holy status, its population had decreased and its buildings had fallen into ruins in the middle of the nineteenth century. The struggles for power among rival strongmen and tribal leaders of the 1860s and 1870s created insecurity and chaos in Tarim. Unarmed *sada* and agriculturalists had little defense against the depredations of warring armed groups; some left the town and moved to less vulnerable villages. In 1877, some *sada* managed to forge an agreement by which the Kathiri and Qu'ayti leaders agreed not to compete over Tarim in their power struggles. At the same time, they appealed for funds to their compatriots in the *mahjar* in order to pay ten thousand *riyals* to eject a Yafi'i strongman and his forces from the town.[10] The accommodation, or stalemate, reached by the Qu'ayti and Al 'Abdallah Kathiri at the end of the 1870s made possible Tarim's revitalization. The population was estimated at ten thousand at the beginning of the 1880s and at twelve thousand at the start of the 1930s.[11]

Tarim lay under the cliff of the wadi. The exposed perimeter of the town was surrounded by a mud-brick wall dating from the sixteenth century, with regular guard towers manned by slave soldiers. In 1925, the wall was reinforced and a substantial guard tower was built by the reform league then governing Tarim in lieu of its nominal Kathiri ruler. Many farms and date orchards were found within the town walls. Outside the walls lay the suburbs of 'Aydid and Damoon.

Inside the main gate lay the famed walled cemeteries of Tarim. Nearest the town wall was the most famous, Zanbal, said to be the resting place of ten thousand of the *awliya'*, those close to God. Buried there were the martyrs of the *ridda* wars, including companions of the Prophet. In addition, many generations of *sada,* some with whitewashed domes raised over their tombs, and *'ulama'* from the *mashayikh* were buried there, among the graves of ordinary folk. The people of Tarim made regular visits to these tombs. Across the road lay the cemetery of Furayt, and that of Akdar, which contained a unique tomb. A *saqifa*, a flat-roofed pillared cube-shaped shelter, covered the grave of the spiritual patron of the farmers, the fifteenth-century poet of agriculture and water raising, Sa'd b. 'Ali Madhhaj, known as Sa'd al-Suwayni; the nickname al-Suwayni was the diminutive for the person who raised water (*sani*). Farmers frequently visited the grave and considered it a favorable site from which to pray, since Sa'd al-Suwayni, a farmer, had been close to God through religious learning and initiation into spiritual practice. The many anecdotes about Sa'd al-Suwayni included some about supernatural rivalries between him and his contemporary, Sayyid Abu Bakr b. 'Abdallah al-'Aydarus, during their lives and continuing even after their deaths, when Sa'd al-Suwayni lay in his tomb in Akdar and Sayyid Abu Bakr b. 'Abdallah al-'Aydarus lay in a tomb in Aden.[12]

Near the three graveyards stood several mosques and Zawiyat BaFadhl, a center for Sufi teaching and practice. They were overlooked by the ruins of an ancient fort, called al-Rinad, which dated to the time of the pre-Islamic incense trade. This ruined fort was reconstructed in 1931 by Sultan Muhammad b. Muhsin al-Kathiri in an attempt to symbolize the renewal of the town's ancient glory under his rule.

Northeast of the cemeteries stood the living center of the town, including the congregational mosque and the *ribat* or Sufi center, the construction of which was begun in 1886 with funding of wealthy families from the *mahjar*. Its large building included rooms for study circles and devotional practices and boarding facilities for students. Numerous historic mosques stood throughout the town, commemorating the beloved spiritual leaders of the past, such as: Sayyid 'Umar "al-Mihdhar," and Sayyid Abu Bakr "al-Sakran" (late fourteenth and early fifteenth century), the sons of 'Abd al-Rahman b. Muhammad al-Saqqaf; and Sayyid 'Abdallah b. 'Alawi al-Haddad (late seventeenth and early eighteenth century). With

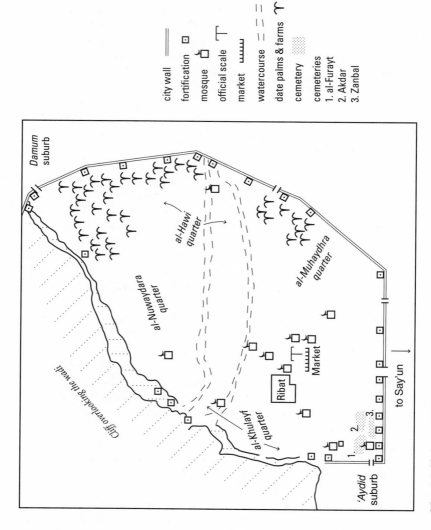

Map 3.2 Tarim, c. 1920s

city wall
fortification
mosque
official scale
market
watercourse
date palms & farms
cemetery
cemeteries
1. al-Furayt
2. Akdar
3. Zanbal

Damum suburb

al-Nuwaydara quarter

al-Hawi quarter

al-Muhaydhra quarter

al-Khulayf quarter

Cliff overlooking the wadi

Ribat

Market

'Aydid suburb

to Say'un

Tarim's new prosperity, old mosques were renovated; in 1914, al-Mihdhar Mosque was rebuilt with Indian and Southeast Asian decorative elements and a 175-foot-tall minaret was added. New mosques were constructed at the benefaction of prosperous emigrants. One of the wealthy Hadhramis of Batavia, Sayyid Ahmad b. Muhammad Bin Shihab, endowed two mosques, one with the income of land and palm trees worth more than ten thousand riyals, and the other with the income of several houses in Batavia worth more than fifteen thousand *guilders*.[13]

Near the palace of Sultan Muhsin b. Ghalib al-Kathiri, who left Say'un to become semiautonomous ruler of Tarim after 1916, stood the market. At the market entrance stood the *qubban,* the large standard scale. The market sold the production of local silversmiths and weavers; preserved fish products from the coast; and rice, spices, tea, and cloth from India and Java. Goods were brought from al-Shihr by caravan on the eastern route, through the territory of the Hamum and the Al Jabir.

Tarim, like Say'un, was organized in a quarter system characterized by competition among the artisans, workers, and providers of services. As in Say'un, the providers of services were fiercely protective of their territories, and conflicts arose, especially when people died outside their own neighborhoods. It sometimes happened that a corpse lay on its bier in the street while service providers from rival quarters came to blows. Tarim, with its sizable and prominent population of *sada,* included among the service providers a specialized group, the black-scarfed Khuddam al-Saqqaf (literally, "the servers of the Saqqaf," named after the Saqqaf mosque), who provided special services in rites of passage of the *sada.* They accompanied *sada* during processions, such as that from the bride's to the groom's house on the wedding night, playing drums, flute, and chanting. After the death of a *sayyid,* they accompanied the bier from the home to the mosque and from the mosque to the cemetery, performing special chants, along with the young students from the Qur'anic schools, who left their studies to take part.[14]

The skilled workmen of Tarim displayed a degree of collective organization and solidarity, although they did not have formal guilds. The boom in construction of religious buildings and majestic homes begun in the 1880s had led to regular employment and a degree of prosperity among the builders and artisans. During the early 1930s, the wealthy families, supported by the Kathiri sultan, attempted to reduce the wages of the builders by half. Some of the builders left town for the village of Thibi, a stronghold of the Tamimi tribe, while others remained in Tarim but refused to work in the building trades. Eventually their employers, stranded in the midst of their building projects, relented and the daily wage was restored.[15]

The houses of Tarim were typically three and four stories high, built of mud brick. They included distinctive design elements, including walls and door frames decorated with designs and written inscriptions such as phrases from the Qur'an. Designs modeled from smooth shiny gypsum plaster decorated ceilings and alcoves. In the late nineteenth and early twentieth century, the families that had acquired wealth in Singapore and Java, such as the prosperous al-'Aydarus, Bin Sahl, al-Kaf, and Bin Yahya families of *sada,* began to compete in the construction of larger, grander houses, which retained older decorative elements while incorporating new design elements of Indian and Southeast Asian origin. New pastel color schemes of lime green, pink, blue, and yellow further embellished the decorations of ceilings, walls, and doorways.

These splendid new homes were built along the sides of the watercourses and in the suburb of 'Aydid. These locations allowed the breeze to flow through freely and afforded ample room for the large homes and complexes of homes as well as enough space for the increasingly elaborate facades of the houses to be viewed in full splendor. These homes had their own wells in the courtyard, rather than relying on water carriers as in the denser quarters of town. The courtyards had enormous gates, large enough to allow entry to a camel loaded with goods, enabling the wealthy families to fill their homes with imported goods and housewares from South Asia, the East Indies, and Europe. Among the most popular European furniture items were elaborately decorative mirrors from Vienna and glass-fronted cabinetry in which silver and china tea services and crystal were displayed. While these luxury household items were brought into the homes by camel, the courtyard gates also allowed entrance of automobiles. By the 1930s, there were several automobiles in Tarim and a few in the other towns and the tributary wadis, all having been carried disassembled over the *jawl* by camel caravan and reassembled in the interior.[16]

Shibam, Market Center

Shibam, a walled town of majestic tower houses, was a market town of great antiquity; its importance as a commercial center dated to pre-Islamic times, when it was a staging point on the incense trail before the beginning of the Common Era. As a destination for caravan traffic from Yemen in the west and from the coast via both eastern and western routes, it was the primary entrepôt for the interior of Hadhramawt, serving the *badu* as well as the town and villages of the Qu'ayti and Kathiri territories. This town, the object of military confrontation among rivals for power in the mid-nineteenth century, prospered from the greater stability of the late nineteenth and early twentieth century. The population may not have been as low as the 1886 estimate of two thousand, nor as high as the 1931 estimate of eight thousand, but it certainly increased during those decades due to the stability and prosperity that accompanied the town's incorporation into the Qu'ayti sultanate.[17]

Shibam was unique among the towns of the main and tributary wadis of Hadhramawt in standing in the center of the wadi rather than being built at the base of the cliffs. Completely encircled by a thick mud town wall, its tall tower houses stood on a high tell in the middle of orchards and fields served by a complex system of irrigation canals, which by the late nineteenth century had deteriorated seriously. Fortified guardhouses stood at each of the four corners of the wall, manned by the *hashiya* of the Qu'ayti sultan. Since Shibam was built at the narrowest point of the wadi, anyone passing the town was within firing range. Brass cannons originally belonging to the East India Company pointed toward the Kathiri domains. The tall main gate, which was closed every night, was large enough to allow camel caravans to enter and unload inside the town walls. The streets of the town were narrow, so the tall houses shaded pedestrians from the harsh sunlight except at noon.

The Qu'ayti governor of Shibam, who enjoyed a high degree of autonomy, occupied an immense palace in an open square inside the main gate, where another palace was constructed in 1920. Near the center of town stood the congregational mosque, believed to have been built by the Abbasid caliph Harun al-Rashid in the tenth century (although archaeological evidence suggests an earlier construction). Nearby was a square around which was a large market consisting of booths and small shops, with the *qubban* standing in an area where bulk goods were traded.

The main well providing the town's drinking water was located outside the town wall. Water carriers delivered water to the houses: women carried goatskin water bags slung over a shoulder and men loaded larger bags on to donkeys. Donkeys also carried better water from across the wadi. Near the well stood workshops for the manufacture of indigo dye. Nearby, workers soaked palm leaves and pounded them to separate the fibers for use in making palm-fiber rope. Farther from the town walls stood dung-fueled kilns in which limestone was fired to make *nura*, a critical element for the preservation of the tall mud-brick houses. Outside the kilns, rows of workers facing each other alternated in pounding the fired stones into a fine powder, keeping their rhythm by chanting lines of poetry. Between the workshops and the farms were expanses of land where mud bricks were formed and dried in the sun. Also outside the town walls stood a cluster of the simple houses of the workers in these industries.

The most notable feature of the town was the impressive appearance of its densely built mud-brick houses, ranging from five to eight stories, the tallest standing almost a hundred feet high. The number of stories depended on the height of the land on which the houses stood, as local regulations required a uniform height in order that no house overlook the rooftops of surrounding houses, in the interest of the modesty of the inhabitants. Highly decorated heavy carved wooden doors with intricate wooden locks opened onto the narrow paved streets, while windows consisting of finely carved wooden lattices allowed light and air to enter the rooms while protecting privacy. The upper floors had overhangs which allowed a person inside to look down to the street below or even drop a basket on a rope to pass small items up or down. Ropes stretched between the upper floors of neighboring houses so people could pass items such as sugar or tea back and forth. The bottom floor of the house included: housing for sheep or goats kept for milk; storage for

Figure 3.2 Well outside Shibam town wall

grain and firewood; pottery water jugs with the household water supply; and grind-stones and bread ovens. Homes were fortified, and had a trenchlike cellar where people could go for protection; a few houses had wells inside for emergency use.

While all houses were built according to a similar plan, there were differences in usage according to the occupation of the owner. Homes of merchants and brokers included storage rooms for wholesale goods and associated reception rooms that served as offices for negotiations with customers. Reception rooms in the lower floors of the homes of the *dallal al-suq,* market brokers, housed tribesmen who came to the town on business and storerooms held goods left in the brokers' trust. The home of the *munsib,* from the Bin Sumayt family, included a vast reception room with six wooden pillars and a *qibla* (recess in the wall indicating the direction of Mecca) as in a mosque. Men gathered there after the sunset prayer for Sufi devotional practices, and seekers of knowledge came to study. Although a few members of families of religious prestige, including the Ba'Abbad family of *mashayikh* and the Bin Sumayt family of *sada,* lived in Shibam, the majority of the population was involved in the market and wholesale trade, crafts, or building. There was no system of quarters with corresponding organization of providers of social services as found in other towns. The town consisted of neighborhoods, each centered on a square, but they were not competitive entities.

Across from the ancient town, the garden suburb of al-Suhayl had grown up at the base of the southern cliff of the wadi. During the late nineteenth and early twentieth centuries, wealthy individuals increasingly moved from the crowded town to the more verdant setting of al-Suhayl, where tall homes and Indian-style bungalows with ornate pastel plaster decorations were surrounded by spacious courtyards containing orchards and gardens. Homes here had their own wells and, after the 1920s, petrol water pumps raised water that circulated through outdoor bathing pools before irrigating the gardens. Families with wealth from the *mahjar,* such as the La'jam and al-Tawi families, built these new elegant villas and furnished them with imported conveniences and luxury items.[18]

A notable feature of Shibam was its ubiquitous trade. The market was not found in a single location: goods were sold from booths and stalls in two town squares, nearby storerooms, and from the lower floors of houses of merchants throughout the town. Caravans of as many as two hundred camels arrived constantly all winter, to unload within the town walls for security. Caravans from the coast unloaded in the palace square just inside the town gate. The goods they carried—preserved fish, rice, tea, spices, and cloth—were received by the agents of the coastal merchants and sold in an open-air market which also sold local goods, such as livestock, wood, charcoal, and palm leaves used as cooking fuel. Caravans from the west, from Sana'a', Ma'rib, Bayhan, and Yaf', unloaded in the town center. From San'a' they brought yellow and white sorghum, millet, wheat, ghee, sesame oil, almonds, and raisins. From the desert region around Ma'rib, caravans brought sturdy black goat-hair rugs and camels for meat and breeding. From Yaf' they brought coffee and coffee husks (*qishr*). Other caravans traveled from the arid

Figure 3.3 Congregational mosque, Shibam

western part of wadi Hadhramawt bearing charcoal, hides, and wood. Caravans traveling through Shabwa brought loads of salt.

The wholesale merchants bought goods from the caravans from the tribesmen in charge of transport, with the mediation of the market brokers. The camels were unloaded and sack weights were checked on the massive scale (*qubban*), known as the *qunfan*. The tribesmen settled down at the side of the square, drank coffee provided by their broker, and began to prepare food. While they waited, the broker oversaw the weighing and carried out negotiations for their goods with the local merchants. When the transactions were completed, the broker gave the tribesmen a freshly slaughtered goat or two and their money. After eating, they chanted and sang as they prepared their camels for the return journey. If they needed to stay in town, they stayed in reception rooms in the lower floors of the houses of their broker, who also purchased for them items such as cloth, silver, and flour. If they were not able to get an acceptable price for all their goods, they left unsold goods in the storehouses of the broker, who would sell the goods for them later.

All tribesmen, those associated with the caravans and both *badu* and settled tribesmen from the area who came to town to trade, were under the authority of designated brokers. These brokers were from families that had held this responsibility for centuries, including the Al Ham, Al Nusayr, and Al Qufayl. Each tribe had a written agreement with a specific broker, while the brokers were responsible for several tribes. The brokers knew their tribes' genealogy, history, internal and external relations, and *'urf* or customary law. Along with the responsibility to handle their commercial transactions, the brokers held the authority to censure, which caused the tribes to fear them as well as respect and trust them. If a tribesman had committed a shameful act (*'ayb*) such as killing without justification, failing to safeguard someone under his protection, or failing to revenge an offense against his tribe, the broker would refuse to handle market transactions for him and his kin. He would do so in a dramatic fashion that intensified the potency of the censure. In one case, a broker refused to shake hands with an offending tribesman, saying that he had performed his ablutions and was on his way to pray, implying that he did not want the touch of the miscreant to destroy his state of ritual purity. In another, the broker refused to sell a goat for an offender, saying that no one wanted to buy a black goat, even though the goat was actually white and in any case, people often bought black goats. Censures often employed the same themes: that the offending tribesmen and their goods were dirty, or that their goods were black instead of white, reflecting the stain on their tribal honor (figuratively, the blackness of their heart). After public humiliation by the broker, the tribe had to provide restitution for their misdeed before they were allowed once again to buy or sell in the market.

The market broker families were not from groups considered prestigious by the larger society; they did not hold the religious prestige of the *sada* or *mashayikh*, nor the honor of the armed tribesmen. But they were trusted by the townsmen who relied on them to ensure the stability of market operations by acting as cul-

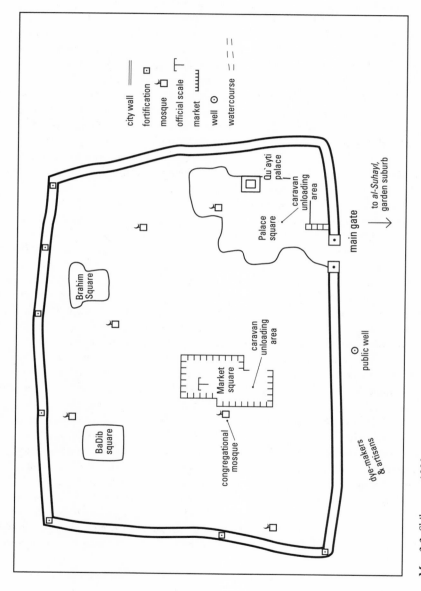

Legend:

- city wall
- fortification
- mosque
- official scale
- market
- well
- watercourse

Labels:

Qu'ayti palace

caravan unloading area

Palace square

Brahim Square

BaDib square

congregational mosque

Market square

caravan unloading area

public well

dye-makers & artisans

main gate

to *al-Suhayl*, garden suburb

Map 3.3 Shibam, c. 1920s

tural intermediaries as well as commercial brokers between the tribesmen and the urban marketplace. The tribesmen looked to the market brokers for political as well as commercial intermediation: they mediated and witnessed cease-fires and treaties of alliance between tribes. Like the *munsib*s from the *sada* and *mashayikh* who held hereditary positions as spiritual authorities and political intermediaries for the different tribes, the market broker could travel through tribal territories without danger or the need for a tribal guide (*siyar*). Even when Qu'ayti authorities set up a blockade to prevent goods from reaching the Kathiri territory during World War I, the brokers took goods from Shibam to Say'un.

The market brokers received commissions from their transactions on behalf of the tribesmen as well as earning from their wholesale dealings in goods and retail sales of livestock. If they ran into financial difficulties, they might sell or mortgage the responsibility for one of their tribes to another member of one of the hereditary market broker families. This was a source of shame, and the broker selling or mortgaging a tribe would avoid telling them, leaving the matter for the purchasing broker. The families who held these positions had conflicts among themselves as to their rights. During most of the late nineteenth and early twentieth centuries, the Ham and Nusayr families were in conflict over which held responsibility for certain tribes. Responsibility had been transferred from one family to another and then had been passed from father to son as an inheritance and the two families disputed whether the original transaction had been a mortgage or a sale.

People other than tribesmen carried out their own transactions in the market. In the case of conflicts over prices or other negotiations, the *hakim al-suq* mediated. He had no office; he spent his days sitting in different places around the market and observing. As a representative of the Qu'ayti state, he had the power to issue warrants to summon parties in a dispute to appear before him. While the warrant itself might simply be a piece of paper or a stone, when presented in his name, the individuals were obligated to appear. In the case of intractable problems, the aggrieved party took his complaint to the *qadhi*, judge of the *shari'a* court. The Qu'ayti sultan levied a tax on all goods and animals sold in the market, which the merchants paid to an agent of the state. The town gates were guarded at all times by the sultan's *hashiya*, who recorded all goods brought into town and took a surety (*'urbun*), often a dagger or other weapon, from any *badu* or other tribesmen entering with goods for sale. When they left, the guards checked to see what had been sold, collected the government impost, and returned the surety. The Yafi'i tribesmen living in the area were exempt from taxation, in exchange for their commitment to serve in the forces of the Qu'ayti sultan whenever necessary.[19]

The Countryside: The Agricultural System

The mainstay of the economy of the interior, apart from remittances from emigrants, was agriculture. Agricultural production followed a long-standing system that was standardized by custom and contract. The complexity of the traditional ordering of the agricultural economy in Hadhramawt can be seen in the detailed terminology relating to the ownership and usage of land and in the detailed contracts governing the responsibilities of landowners and agricultural laborers. Even though mechanized water raising and plantation agriculture had become widespread in the larger Indian Ocean region, only a few attempts were made to introduce any innovation in agriculture in the interior of Hadhramawt during this time period. Water was raised by an inefficient technology that exhausted the agricultural laborers and their animals, and farm workers received only a meager and insecure livelihood from their efforts. Social critics deplored the fact that agricultural productivity was declining rather than prospering, increasing the pressure toward emigration, rather than increasing the prosperity of the homeland. But their criticisms went unheeded.

Land and Water

Land in Hadhramawt was classified according to usage and mode of watering. A large cultivated area of land with wells and palm trees, which we might call an oasis, was a *hima*. An area of cultivated land that lacked wells and depended entirely on flood water (*sayl*) irrigation was known as *nashr*. An individual plot of land was called a *dhubr*, *khita*, or *mutayra*, depending on size. An individual clump of palm trees, containing one to five plants, was called a *hufra* (literally, "hole"). Often fields, clumps of palms, and sometimes even individual palms were identified by given names.[20]

Land normally irrigated by wells also used flood water when it was available, depending on local rainfall and on the more frequent rainfall high above the wadi on the *jawl* plateau. When *sayl* waters arrived in the wadi, farmers went out to tend the distribution channels, by lantern light if it was night.[21]

Distribution of the *sayl* waters was highly regulated; the *wala* or right to use *sayl* waters was legally attached to plots of land and was bought, sold, or rented along with the land. The *sayl* water was identified with its point of origin in the cliffs above; this upland origin of floodwater was called the *musqi*. As floodwater tumbled down the cliff sides toward the fields, each of its naturally occurring branches was known as a *saqiya* (pl. *sawaqi*). Near the fields, the watercourses were engineered to distribute the water in equal shares to different parcels of land. It was forbidden to tamper with the simple stone structures that regulated the amount of water flowing to particular fields. According to local lore, irrigation channels were so skillfully engineered that if someone dropped twenty-four sticks into water flowing through a channel which ultimately distributed water to twenty-four shareholders, each end user would receive the same number of sticks as he had shares.[22]

The *saqiya*, or irrigation waters contained in the smaller channels, were specified as part of the property, along with palms and other plants growing there, irrigation channels, and boundary walls. Landholders, as shareholders in floodwater rights, collectively paid for repair and maintenance of the distribution system, each paying according to the number of shares held, that is according to the amount of land owned. A landowner or farmer, appointed as the *kharras,* annually assessed the productivity of each stand of palm trees to set the amount owed toward the maintenance of the boundaries and channels distributing the *sayl* waters.

Any tampering with the water distribution system was extremely serious. In case of disputes that shareholders failed to settle themselves, the traditional arbiter was the *khayyal.* The *khayyal,* a member of a family holding authority on irrigation issues, met with the disputing parties, studied the problem, and made a decision, which was the final word on the issue.[23] The *shari'a* court also handled disputes over water. The judgment in a 1901 case was decided on the principle that landowners did not have the right to alter the *sayl* flow or interfere with the established channel system. A landowner might not develop additional fields if those would divert water flow from adjacent landowners.[24]

The most highly developed flood-water irrigation distribution system was around Shibam. The *mawza'* or distribution dam west of Shibam diverted the *sayl* from the town and distributed the waters to surrounding farmlands. Although Shibam in ancient times had been served by a larger dam and more extensive irrigation system, the dam standing in the nineteenth century was still the largest in the wadi, over a kilometer long. As emigration increased in the late nineteenth century, maintenance of the dam was neglected, and the structure deteriorated, receiving its last major renovation in 1911/1912.[25]

Because of the shortage of rain in the region, most farmland relied on ground-water irrigation. Water flowed into the open irrigation channels watering the fields from a pool filled with water raised from a well (*bi'r,* locally pronounced *bir*). The importance of the wells was indicated by the practice of naming farms after them, with farms having their own names (distinct from the names of the owners), such as Bir Bin Mahdi, Bir al-Shams, and Bir BaWa'il. Maintaining the watering schedule, particularly for palm trees, was the most difficult, time-consuming, and back-breaking aspect of agricultural labor. The process of raising water, called *sinawa* after the apparatus employed, was powered by animal and human energy. The quantity of water raised by this labor-intensive method varied greatly, with an average around four hundred gallons per hour.[26] The *sinawa* consisted of a wooden frame built over a stone-lined well approached by a long sloping path. The frame supported a pulley, a grooved wheel over which ran a rope which at one end was connected to a skin container and at the other end was yoked to the lifters, animal or human or both. As the lifters descended the slope, the skin container of water was lifted to the top of the well and tipped over to flow into the reservoir. In Shibam and the western wadi, male camels and bulls were usually used to lift water, since the ground water was deep and the fields were large. Elsewhere, cows and donkeys were used; donkeys were always paired with human lifters. Humans backed down the slope as they lifted water, with the rope attached to a belt slung around their hips to bring the strength of their back into the task. Humans always worked either in teams with animals or in two pairs.[27]

A song sung by farmers laboring to raise water, attributed to Sa'd al-Suwayni, counseled the water lifters to appreciate their hard lot and not to envy emigrants, who paid for their prosperity by facing unknown dangers.

> O Water lifters, do not envy the emigrants
> We saw from the boards and rope (wooden sailing vessel)
> Between me and death seven hand spans (the height of a sailboat)
> Envy only him who stays home
> And settles for a mere clenched fistful of dates.[28]

The rhythm of the *sinawa* songs helped the workers to maintain the rhythm of their labor and to coordinate their movements. The task seemed endless; it took a full day of working at the *sinawa* to water a single *hij*, the amount of land that could be plowed in one day by a pair of bulls (also called a *hij*).[29]

Agreements between Landowners and Laborers

Agricultural agreements, called *mufakhadha, mukhabara,* or *mukhala'a,* were made between the landowner (*tibin,* meaning owner of means of production) and two or three farmers who worked together, equipped with tools and farm animals and a team of family members to help. The agreements were between landowners and the farmers' families, as the arduous work of cultivation, irrigation, and harvest required the labor of many, and if a farmer died, his family had to carry out the contract. Women had gender-specific tasks such as cutting alfalfa and clearing away dry palm fronds, and contributed to general labor such as lifting water. While occasionally an agreement relegated duties to specific family members, including the women, usually tasks were assigned collectively.[30]

Some farmers lacked tools and animals, sometimes because they had had to sell them to repay debts to landowners. These individuals provided day labor, working for a daily ration, which was usually a pound and a half of grain but in bad times might be merely a handful of dates. They performed tasks that were the responsibility of the landowner, such as maintaining boundary walls.

Some laborers, called *baqqar,* specialized in plowing. They would do the plowing for a landowner who owned bulls in exchange for daily rations of a pound and a half of grain and the opportunity to use the landowner's bulls to work other people's land for a daily wage.

Sometimes farmers were able to make an agreement, called *sani,* to lift water for a prosperous landowner in exchange for a fixed wage, often a pound and a half of grain and three pounds of dates daily. The farmer then had no share of the production, farmers considered the *sani* agreement desirable, since their work was limited to a single task, their livelihood was secure, and they did not have to worry about debt.[31]

Some agricultural labor was in the hands of tribe members. In the rain-fed farming in areas of fields (called *qawf*) owned by tribes on the *jawl*, the labor was done by weaker tribes that had fallen into client status and labored in exchange for their livelihood and the "protection" of the stronger tribes.[32]

Security of fields and crops was controlled by armed groups, either local tribesmen or semiautonomous representatives of the government, usually powerful Yafiʿi families or *hashiya*. Holders of the *shiraha* (the right and responsibility to provide security) received a tenth of the produce of the palm trees. The holding of the *shiraha* for land was a matter of public record; the market brokers knew who was responsible for protecting what property and notified the public of any changes. During times of security, the holder of the *shiraha* was able to protect the property simply by reputation; at times when crops were vulnerable, guards were posted in *kuts* (small fortified towers), from which they would fire to call their fellow tribesmen in the case of interference.[33]

Crops, and Work

Agricultural seasons were measured by the stellar (solar) calendar rather than the lunar-based Islamic calendar. Summer sorghum was planted in early March; red and green millet in July; winter sorghum in mid-July; alfalfa in early October; and wheat in mid-October. In addition to the grain, stalks were a valuable part of the crop as they were used for fodder. Other crops grown were pearl millet, melons, pumpkins, sesame, and henna.

The labor required for annual crops began with turning over the land in each plot to expose the soil to sun and wind, then turning it again, and fertilizing it. Plowing was done by the *baqqar* and his pair of oxen. After plowing, the clods of earth were further broken by women using hand tools. Both women and men then worked in the process of smoothing and leveling the soil, pulling a flat board across the fields. Animal manure was the most common fertilizer, with human excrement cleared from household toilet pits favored as the best fertilizer (an opinion still held by many today).[34]

A great deal of labor went into raising the water for the annual crops. For example, for the four-month season of wheat production, each plot was flooded six inches deep, once in the first month (one *awad*), twice in each of the next two months, and in the last month once every eight days. Summer and winter sorghum both required fewer waterings.

Women cleared weeds, for which they used a hand tool with a curved, serrated blade, which they also used for harvesting and chopping alfalfa. They worked collectively, singing and chanting as they worked. While the crops were maturing, they had to be guarded from birds. The youth of the farmer's family took turns mounted on a platform in the field, watching for birds and chasing them away by flinging stones from a sling.[35]

The harvest was known as *hisad,* or *sirab.* Men and women worked together harvesting with hand tools, singing and chanting. The high spirits of harvest time were expressed in a chant in which the men sang, "*Ya bint 'amm, min hawashi ba-mut,*" or "O daughter of my uncle, I am dying from your love." The women answered in chorus, "*La mutit banalqi 'alayk tabut*" or "Don't die or we'll put you in a coffin."[36]

The responsibilities of the landowner to the farmer in his employ and of the farmer to the landowner followed local custom and the obligations were formalized by legal contract.[37] In the case of the development of land without a known owner, the person granted development rights by the sultan made an agreement with a farmer in which the farmer had the opportunity to gain one third of the land. Only through managing to complete the extended arduous labor of creating a new farm did a farmer have the chance to acquire land of his own. Few succeeded in doing so.

The landowner's responsibility was to have the well dug and lined and to pay for palm shoots. The farmer was responsible for fertilizing, plowing, building field boundaries and irrigation channels, planting the palms and watering them for the fifteen years to maturity, and doing all necessary maintenance. The farmer and the owner each kept portions of the field crops, while the farmer kept any dates harvested before the trees reached maturity. It was rare for farmers to acquire their third of the land, as they often had to sell their share to the owner for subsistence even if they managed to maintain and water the farm for fifteen years.[38]

When planting new stands of palms on land already developed, a farmer was able to acquire one-third of the production of the palm trees after maturity, although not the land on which they stood. Again, it was common for farmers to mortgage or sell their right to the share, or simply lose it by failing to keep up with the watering. Still some farmers managed to retain their right to future production until the division after the palms matured.[39]

The landowner was responsible for the maintenance of the well and the *sinawa* apparatus, and he paid for fertilizer. He gave the farmer a cash payment once or twice a year, and regularly advanced money to the farmer, to be repaid either at the time of the grain harvests or after the palm trees matured.

The farmer was responsible for maintenance tasks and irrigation of the palms—a heavy burden. The usual irrigation pattern was four waterings a month for the first five years after planting, three a month for the second five years, and two a month for the third five years, or until the trees reached maturity. Contracts sometimes specified that if the farmer fell short in his watering duties, he lost his future share of the production immediately. Less onerous agreements specified that if he missed three waterings, the agreement was nullified, while if he missed two, the landowners would contract out the watering, deducting the charge from the farmer's pay.[40]

If the farmer failed to keep up with his obligations, he lost his right to a third of the future production. Because irrigation was so difficult, requiring continual hard labor of several people and animals, it was common for farmers to lose their stake in the palms and move on to day labor or annual labor. The landowner then hired others to irrigate the dates. These farmers received cash, most of the crops grown around the date palms, and a portion of the date harvest, but had no claim on the future harvest of the palms.[41]

After the palm trees reached maturity, they still needed watering twice a month. The farmer was responsible for irrigation, for pollination, and for thinning the early fruit. The landowners paid for the woven palm-fiber baskets, made by women from the farming families in their homes, that were placed around each bunch of growing fruit for protection from birds and fruit bats. When the dates were ripe, the landowner paid for the harvest and for the dates to be processed, cleaned, pitted, and packed into large clay jars.[42]

Fields without palm trees were often leased to farmers for a fixed amount of the harvest. The rent consisted of an amount from each harvest—summer sorghum, wheat, and winter sorghum. This type of agreement held risks for farmers, since the same amount was owed to the landowner regardless of the actual production. If crops were lost due to pests, disease, or inclement weather, the farmer still owed the fixed payment. Sometimes an agricultural agreement took into account the fact that crops might be lost, in which case the amount of rent would be renegotiated. But too often, the burden of the risk lay on the farmer.[43]

Farmer Debt

Agricultural agreements often included loans and advances from the landowner to the farmer, which were also sometimes recorded in separate documents. Indebtedness was prevalent among farmers, who often borrowed from the landowner at the outset of an agreement in order to buy the animals they needed to work the land and raise water. At other times, they had to borrow to pay for their expenses and for the subsistence of their families. A landowner particularly liked to have a proficient farmer with a healthy, hardworking family in his debt, so that he was guaranteed the benefit of their services in the future. In exchange for cash loans, the farmers' property, including working farm animals, shares in the future date harvests, and their houses, often ended up in the hands of the landowners. While interest was not recorded in the contract, some landowners charged 10 percent; that is, a farmer who borrowed twenty *riyals* had to pay back twenty-two.[44]

A typical case of farmer debt can be seen in an 1896 agricultural agreement between a landowner and three farmers who were brothers. The agreement for watering and tending palms was made for a period of six years, with the specification that the farmers might continue working the property after that, if the landowner agreed. At the time of the agreement, the landowner advanced the farmers 360 pounds of grain until the next harvest. He also loaned them twenty *riyals*. As security, the landowner held custody of the farmers' two cows, and any livestock, crops, or palms they owned. Only a month later the farmers borrowed ten more *riyals*.[45]

In agreements to tend and water newly planted palms, in which the farmer was to receive a third of the palm production after the trees reached maturity, the farmer often immediately mortgaged his share of one-third of future production.[46] For example, in an 1895 agreement, a landowner managing farms owned by his family and neighbors advanced a farmer twenty-four *riyals* in exchange for the farmer's right to a third of future date production. If the farmer maintained his duties until the time of the division of the mature palms, he was to repay the landowner the twenty-four *riyals* and give him one palm tree. At the same time, the landowner and farmer made another agreement for the cultivation of grains and alfalfa, in which the landowner advanced the farmer additional money. In later years, the farmer continued to borrow against future harvests from the landowner and another creditor; the farmer and landowner were continually in dispute during this period. Within ten years of the original agreement, the farmer had sold his third of future date production to the landowner.[47]

The songs and poetry of the farmers warned of the problem of indebtedness. A poem attributed to Sa'ad al-Suwayni cautioned:

> I told you to be careful when you are farming
> Don't be in debt to those whose water you are raising.[48]

In a poem by Sa'id b. Salim b. 'Ubaydillah, known as "Nuna," the farmer narrator deplored the losses of farm production to birds, insect pests, and to the government in taxes, which consumed almost half of his production while he was deeply in debt. In this poem, debt was an affliction that ate at the farmer's well-being the way locusts and worms consumed his crops.[49] Another poem by the poet known as "al-Mu'allim 'Abd al-Haq" played on the similarity of the word "mortgage" (*rahn*) to the word "hostage" (*rahin*), suggesting that the farmer who had to borrow against the coming harvest became the hostage of his employers.[50]

Modern Methods of Farming and a Reformist Critique

Even though agriculture was dominated by traditional methods, some Hadhramis began to attempt agricultural modernization. Sultan Ghalib b. 'Awadh al-Qu'ayti displayed interest in modernization of agriculture by requesting the services of a British agricultural expert and financing the investigative mission to al-Mukalla and environs by M. M. Heald in 1919.[51]

But in the interior, most interest in agricultural improvement originated among private citizens, particularly those who had emigrated to India and Southeast Asia. The first they tried to improve was the difficult task of raising water. As early as 1882/1883, a landowner of Say'un from the *mashayikh* family of BaSalama imported a mechanical hand pump from Indonesia, which received a great amount of public attention. The experiment failed, which drew a commensurate amount of attention, including the composition of verses mocking those who had attempted to import this innovation.

Two years later, a *sayyid* emigrant to India recruited partners in Hadhramawt to implement a tube-well project in Wadi Ja'ima, for which he imported a large amount of pipe. When the well was dug, although it was quite deep, it did not suit hydrological conditions, and the water failed to flow. The pipe was then left abandoned at the site.

Nearly twenty years later in 1902/1903, a *sayyid* from Tarim purchased the pipes that had been abandoned in Wadi Ja'ima and transported them by camel to Say'un to construct a new irrigation project, using a pressurizing pump. Unfortunately, the design of the pump was flawed and the project failed.

In another early attempt to import technology successfully used elsewhere, a partnership implemented a project in Maryama that used a device similar to the Persian water wheel, in which camels revolved around the wheel, lifting the water to the surface in clay pots. This water wheel irrigated profitably productive fields for more than two years, but ultimately failed as the exertion was too great for the camels.[52]

In 1905/1906, Sayyid Hud b. Ahmad al-Saqqaf promoted a project among investors from Say'un that ultimately imported a pump with a gasoline engine, a tractor, an electrical generator, and an old Ford motorcar. A Japanese engineer from Singapore was brought to set up and maintain the machinery; he spent three years in Say'un. Later one of the farmers involved in the project took over maintenance and repairs, and his sons followed him in this new field. More gasoline engines were imported, and people continued to experiment with importing simple mechanical technologies that were an improvement over the *sinawa* and its backbreaking labor. In 1911, a hand-powered pump was installed in Wadi Sirr, and another in 1922.[53]

In 1921/1922, a large partnership, named Hadiyat al-Watan, formed to develop an immense plot of farmland north of Maryama. This ambitious project included the planting of seven hundred palm shoots. The shoots were planted and British water pumps were installed for their irrigation. Unfortunately, the pump broke down for lack of maintenance. Rather than hiring someone skilled in repair and maintenance of machinery, the members of the partnership despaired of the project and ultimately withdrew, leaving the plants to the people of the village of Maryama to water with the *sinawa*.

The social critic 'Ali Ahmad BaKathir claimed that the cause of the demise of this ambitious project had been the lack of solidarity and trust among the partners. He asserted that the project had been plagued from the beginning with poor financial decisions and that partnership funds had been spent wastefully, with partners deducting personal expenses from project funds.

Following sounder financial principles, a successful agricultural development partnership called Sharikat al-Khayr was established by some of the *sada* of

Say'un and Tarim, including the al-Kaf family. In 1930, the *qadhi* of Say'un, Shaykh 'Abd al-Rahman BaRaja, headed another partnership that faced problems. First the project encountered a lack of sufficient water. Then the partnership was swindled by an unscrupulous Egyptian. Still, this partnership weathered the challenges and moved its operations to another farm with an ample supply of water. It was hoped that success of this partnership, despite its setbacks, would encourage more Hadhrami investment in agriculture.

In his writings, 'Ali Ahmad BaKathir deplored the fact that the importance of agriculture to Hadhramawt was not recognized and that agriculture there was not advancing as it was elsewhere. Asserting that the land was fertile and had been highly productive in the past, he blamed the current low productivity on lack of interest from the landowners. He accused them of failing even to tend the palm trees left them by their ancestors, much less apply themselves to the expansion and development of agriculture.

BaKathir traced the decay of agriculture in the wadi to the mid-nineteenth century, when Hadhramawt continued using traditional methods of irrigation while other places began using pumps and new systems. Quoting a visitor to Hadhramawt, he asserted that the land had the potential to become a paradise on earth if the farmers were properly supported. He encouraged landowners to experiment with crops being grown on Java and elsewhere. He pointed out that true prosperity relied on local production, not on the foreign imports proliferating in the wadi. BaKathir analyzed the failures and successes of attempts at mechanization and for investment in modern agriculture.[54] His first appeal was ignored and in later years he wrote further, arguing the necessity of technical and financial assistance for agricultural development. He called for the development of dams and more efficient irrigation systems, the improvement of seed and animal breeding, and the establishment of a system of credit for farmers to alleviate their persistent problems with indebtedness.[55] This call to action was not heeded until after the tragic famine of the 1940s in which over ten thousand people died.[56]

Change in Town and Country in the Interior

Despite their isolation, the towns of the interior experienced changes during the late nineteenth and early twentieth century. This resulted from the stability afforded by the establishment of Qu'ayti and Kathiri rule over their respective territories and also from the growing wealth coming from the overseas Hadhrami communities, particularly those of the East Indies. The towns grew and so did the markets. As the governments of the sultanates extended their presence, Say'un, Tarim, and Shibam each eventually acquired a palace of its ruling dynasty, as well as reinforced town walls and garrisoned fortifications. As wealth derived from the emigrant communities grew, prosperous families built private "palaces" inside the towns and in new garden suburbs, while prosperous tribesmen built private "forts" outside the towns. Wealthy emigrants also funded the buildings that housed new religious and educational institutions in Say'un and Tarim. The countryside saw less change, as only a handful of innovators attempted to develop and modernize agriculture through mechanical means of water raising. Relations between landowners, farmers, and other laborers continued to be regulated by custom and contract, according to a system of long duration. Even in the more dynamic towns, traditional systems of ordering the market and the provision of social services also remained in place. This led to increasing tension between the old ways of ordering society and the new institutions and fashions introduced by wealthy emigrants.

4
Urban and Rural Life on the Coast and Its Hinterland

The coastal region of Hadhramawt differed from the interior in critical ways. Because of its connection to the outside world by sea, the coast had a more diverse and livelier economy and a more cosmopolitan population and the pace of change was more rapid. The late nineteenth and early twentieth centuries were a particularly dynamic time for the coastal region, as steam shipping and the telegraph transformed transportation and communications in the Indian Ocean basin. The stability resulting from the establishment of the Qu'ayti sultanate led to a greater degree of development than the coast had previously experienced, in the towns and in agricultural areas. At the same time, as in the interior, traditional systems continued to order social and economic relations in town and countryside.

Towns: Organization and Institutions

The main ports, al-Mukalla and al-Shihr, provided the link between the interior of Hadhramawt and the outside world. While al-Shihr had been an important Arabian Sea port for centuries, al-Mukalla had been a small fishing village before it was raised in prominence by the Qu'ayti rulers. The gradual eclipse of al-Shihr by al-Mukalla was accelerated in 1915, when the Qu'ayti sultan moved his capital from al-Shihr to al-Mukalla. These coastal towns had systems of organization similar to those of the interior, with the quarter system regulating social services in the neighborhoods and the market and brokers mediating among settled populations and badu, and these systems continued to operate even in the face of growth and change.

Al-Mukalla, Capital of the Qu'ayti Sultanate

Probably because of its superior harbor and greater defensibility, al-Mukalla began to supersede al-Shihr in importance in the late nineteenth century. Unlike al-Shihr, where goods were offloaded from ships in the open sea, al-Mukalla had a sheltered harbor in which ships were able to dock, except during the southwest monsoon, when they harbored at Ras Burum. In addition, the strategic position of al-Mukalla was superior, since the city was sheltered between the sea and rugged cliffs, unlike al-Shihr, which sat by the sea on an open plain, making al-Mukalla much easier to defend. After the Qu'ayti moved his capital from al-Shihr to al-Mukalla in 1915, the city thrived, developing into the commercial as well as the political heart of the Qu'ayti sultanate.

The town of al-Mukalla grew to be one of the most important ports of Southern Arabia, second only to that of Aden. The stability brought by Qu'ayti rule allowed business to flourish; the Qu'ayti sultan encouraged business, organizing and regulating the port and the caravan trade. The commercial houses handling imports and exports benefitted both from this stability and from the expansion of trade throughout the region. The town grew significantly during this period. During Kasadi rule, before the boom of the late nineteenth century, the town wall enclosed a tongue of land protruding into the sea and its immediate hinterland below the cliff wall. During Qu'ayti rule, this tongue became increasingly devoted to commercial activity and the population expanded westward into the narrow strip of land between the cliffs and the sea. This new part of town was protected by a wall beside a watercourse forming a tidal inlet that prevented access by land from the west.

The new wall's fortified main gate was closed in times of insecurity, such as tribal raiding in the hinterlands, but the town's primary defense was its position between the rugged cliffs and the sea, with a series of fortified watchtowers standing along the clifftop, overlooking the sea. During Qu'ayti rule, five new fortified watchtowers were built on the cliffs, in addition to the two already standing. A string of forts and watchtowers was built alongside the channel bringing the city's water supply from its inland source. During times of security the watchtowers stood empty.[1]

The population of al-Mukalla during this period grew from perhaps six thousand in the 1880s to more than fifteen thousand in the 1930s.[2] Population estimates varied widely; as in any Hadhrami town, it would have been difficult to know how many people lived in each house, due to the privacy in which family life was held, and in addition, the population of this trading center was constantly in flux. At any time, part of many households was either abroad or at sea. Also, the population rose and fell, like that of any port city, with the influx and egress of travelers in transit. Traditional Indian Ocean transport and trade depended on the seasonal pattern of the monsoon, with the timing of the winds and thus the timing of sailing ship arrivals and departures varying somewhat from year to year. Thus, at certain times of year, the population was swelled by travelers from the interior waiting for the winds for their onward passage. For young men who worked on the coast to earn their onward fare, a practice common even among prosperous families, their sojourn in al-Mukalla might last as long as a year or two. At times when ships were docked, the population would include sailors and ships' passengers temporarily on shore. While steamships only stopped briefly on their scheduled routes, sailing ships lingered in port waiting for customers for cargo, for a better purchase price, or for passengers.

The population also increased during the periodic famines suffered in the interior. People fled from the interior to the greater abundance of the coast, with its springs, spring-fed agriculture, greater supply of imported foodstuffs, and profusion of fresh and dried fish. In addition, for centuries Somalians had sailed to refuge on the coast of Southern Arabia during periodic droughts and famines in the Horn of Africa. They often remained for several years in al-Mukalla, where they worked as porters until conditions improved at home.[3]

The densely populated tongue of land that had once contained the entire city remained the heart of the city's commercial activity. This old part of the city included a cemetery, the market, and the port, as well as the crowded poor quarter known as Hafat al-'Abid, literally "Slaves' quarter." At the point of the tongue was the neighborhood known as Hafat al-Bilad, literally "Homeland quarter," which included homes of merchants, commercial warehouses, the simple housing of Somalian porters, and the ruins of the fort of the Kasadi Naqib who had once ruled al-Mukalla. The palace and high court buildings of the Kasadi became the administrative offices and the law court of the Qu'ayti sultanate. Near these government buildings was the prison, which held tribal hostages as well as criminals.[4]

The busy port and customs office lay near ship-building yards, where ships were also repaired and maintained and sails were sewn. The small shops and tea stalls of the retail market lined the road from the port, with some shops selling imported goods while others sold goods produced on premise or in nearby artisanal workshops.[5]

In addition to locally produced cloth and clothing, shops sold cloth imported from India and the East Indies; by the 1930s, cloth and clothing from Japan were found in abundance. Other imported goods sold were spices and tea from the East Indies and Ceylon, coffee and coffee husks from Yaf', rice and sugar from India, kerosene, and matches.[6] Locally produced goods included sesame oil, Hamumi tobacco from Ghayl BaWazir, sorghum and other grains, and fruits and vegetables.

Between the market and the cliff were the houses of the quarter known as Hafat al-Hara, literally "Quarter quarter," which also included the new part of the town, called Bara' al-Sidda.[7] Bara' al-Sidda, with the newest and finest houses, became the home for the more prosperous segment of society in this booming port town. Stretching parallel to the sea front and away from the activity of the port, market, and artisanal workshops, this area was less densely populated and less bustling than the older part of town. It was quieter, cleaner, and breezier.

In 1925, Sultan 'Umar built a new palace on the sea front at the western end of Bara' al-Sidda, not far inside the main town gate. This grand building included spacious reception halls, decorative woodwork inside and out, and unique architectural features including seaward balconies. It was splendidly equipped with fittings and furniture imported from Europe and India. The rest of the beach front was open, leaving a roadway along the seaside from the main city gate to the entrance of the market in the old city. Goods were carried from the port and whole-

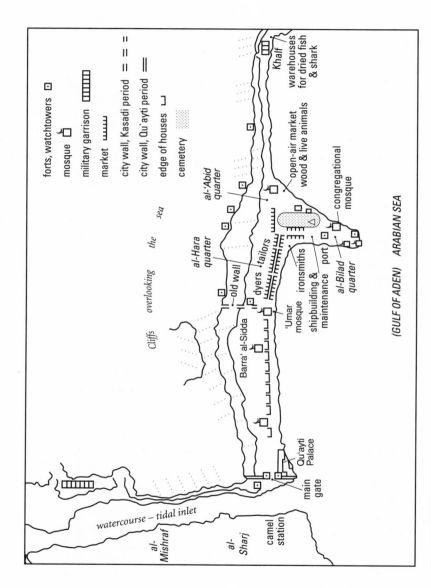

Map 4.1 Al-Mukalla, late 1920s

forts, watchtowers ⊡

mosque

military garrison ⬚⬚⬚⬚⬚

market ⎍⎍⎍⎍⎍

city wall, Kasadi period = = =

city wall, Qu'ayti period =

edge of houses ⌐

cemetery

al-Mishraf

al-Sharj

watercourse – tidal inlet

camel station

main gate

Qu'ayti Palace

Barra' al-Sidda

old wall

al-Hara quarter

'Umar mosque

dyers tailors

ironsmiths

shipbuilding & maintenance

port

al-Bilad quarter

al-'Abid quarter

open-air market wood & live animals

congregational mosque

Khalf

warehouses for dried fish & shark

Cliffs overlooking the sea

(GULF OF ADEN) ARABIAN SEA

sale warehouses of the old city to the camel caravan staging site across the tidal inlet outside the city wall.

The homes in the new part of town were tall, to catch the sea breeze and to
maximize the limited space available between cliff and sea. They were built of limestone blocks, except at the top, where rooftop terraces were walled by latticework
patterns of bricks to provide the optimal combination of privacy and breeze. The
small windows of the houses had wooden shutters. Like other coastal cities of the
Gulf of Aden, Red Sea, and the Gulf, the houses included decorative woodwork
rare elsewhere on the Arabian Peninsula. The homes of the big merchant families
were decorated by shutters, doors, pillars, capitals, and beams carved from hardwoods imported from the Swahili and Malabar coasts. The wooden decorative elements were echoed in elaborate designs carved in the plaster walls around windows and wall niches. Otherwise, home furnishings were simple, consisting
primarily of carpets and tea and coffee services.

As the new part of the city developed, some merchant families located their
commercial houses there, although their warehouses were still located in the old
city near the port and the retail market. The commercial houses looked like residential houses, but functioned as nodes in the matrix of agencies forming the far-
flung Hadhrami trading networks. The ground floors of these buildings were for
storage of dry goods and upper floors included reception rooms and offices used
by the merchants and their agents, clerks, and messengers.

Not all of the population lived in the striking tall white houses of al-Mukalla,
although the merchants and artisans who formed the backbone of the city's economy did. The poorer classes, such as porters and laborers lived in crude huts constructed of branches, woven palm-fiber mats, and thatch. These were clustered inland on the irregular hilly ground just at the base of the cliffs. Somalians lived in
similar housing near the port. The simplest of housing was located across the tidal
inlet outside the town gate, in an area called al-Sharj, where the *subiyan* lived. As
al-Mukalla grew, increasing numbers of *subiyan* left their lives of agricultural labor
and servitude in Wadi Hajr and moved there, where they performed the most menial tasks of the port and town. They carried wood from the market to homes for
kitchen use, brought skins of water from the city's wells and cisterns, and also
cleaned out the refuse chambers of the tall houses' "long-drop" toilets.[8]

The camel station was near al-Sharj, and when the seasonal winds brought
heavy shipping activity to the port, hundreds of camels stood outside the town
wall, waiting to be loaded with goods. The camelmen stayed in this area as well,
living in the open air. They slept in their clothing on the ground, and baked bread
and prepared food and coffee on open fires. The *badu* of the western hinterlands
controlled the caravan trade from al-Mukalla to the western wadis, Hajr, 'Amd,
and Du'an, and to Shibam via Du'an. They sold animals and animal products in
al-Mukalla, and bought cloth, weapons, and grain. An important link in the provision of essential and luxury goods to the interior, the camel park was a busy place.

In the 1930s it was estimated that more than fifty thousand camels were loaded in this park to travel to the interior annually.

Simple industries stood outside the town. In al-Sharj stood camel-powered sesame oil presses. East of the old town, *nura* (lime plaster) was produced, fired in kilns and pounded for hours by hand. All over Hadhramawt it was used to seal walls, here it was also used in the construction and maintenance of ships, as holds were sealed with a mixture of fish oil and lime plaster.[9] In the late 1920s, Sultan 'Umar moved all fish processing outside town, to a narrow strip of land below the cliffs east of the city, in order to improve the aesthetics of his capital.[10]

Of all Hadhrami towns, al-Mukalla had the most dynamic economy, the largest numbers of visitors, and grew most in the late nineteenth and early twentieth centuries; it was the most cosmopolitan. Families running the commercial houses originated from Du'an and al-Shihr; agents and employees of the great commercial houses came from Kathiri territory. Tribesmen from all over western Hadhramawt and from the interior came to the market. Somalians regularly came on trading voyages, staying long enough to sell their cargo of sheep and gum resins. There was also a small population of Banyans, or Hindu merchants from India. Banyan merchants had been active in the ports of the Arab-Africa trade since the mid-eighteenth century, and were prominent in both trade and money lending in al-Mukalla.[11]

As Qu'ayti capital, al-Mukalla was the first to benefit from the social and technological advances that the sultans introduced to their domain. When Harold Ingrams visited al-Mukalla in the 1930s, he was impressed that the town had piped-in water from a good source, that an Indian doctor held a clinic in the old city, and that there were three government schools, one of which taught English.[12]

Al-Shihr, Eastern Port and Commercial Center

Unlike the cliff-ringed al-Mukalla, al-Shihr sprawled on an open plain. In contrast to the tall stone houses of al-Mukalla and the tall mud-brick houses of the interior, the houses were low: two-story limestone block houses with rooftop terraces and courtyards. Although al-Shihr had been Hadhramawt's most important port town for centuries, during the nineteenth century its importance declined significantly. While the population of al-Shihr at the time of its attack had been significantly higher in earlier centuries, by the 1880s the population was around twelve thousand, twice that of al-Mukalla at the time. The population shrank rapidly in the following decades, while that of al-Mukalla grew. In the 1890s, western visitors to al-Shihr already noted its decline and referred to it as "a detestable place by the sea."[13] In the 1930s, another visitor said of the newly renovated city wall, "the garment is too large for what it has to cover and a half-dead town is pining away within the walls."[14] By then, the population had shrunk further, perhaps as low as six thousand, although since al-Shihr was a port city with a high seasonal transient population, the population was probably larger at times.[15]

The problem of al-Shihr's vulnerable site was more easily remedied than its lack of a sheltered harbor. The town had been the object of competition between rival Hadrami strongmen in the nineteenth century, but from 1876 onward al-Shihr was securely in the hands of the Qu'ayti sultanate and became its first capital. Still, the security of the town was vulnerable to two threats. The first was the desire of the Kathiri sultan in Say'un to have a port giving access to the Indian Ocean and the outside world. The second was the threat of the Hamum tribe in al-Shihr's hinterlands, who resisted the interference of the Qu'ayti in what they considered their domains. The Qu'ayti ruler met those challenges by fortifying al-Shihr.

After Ghalib b. Muhsin al-Kathiri, aided by the Hamum, attempted to take al-Shihr from the Qu'ayti in 1867, 'Abdallah b. 'Umar al-Qu'ayti began to construct a fortified wall around the town, the construction of which took twenty years. He also moved people from the outskirts of town inside the walls to assure their defensibility. The fortified wall was the city's most dramatic feature, extending from the beach into the surf, with watchtowers standing in the sea on each side of town. Four round watchtowers jutted from the wall on land, and fortifications were built into the wall, in which members of the elite security force of the Qu'ayti *hashiya* lived. Each fortress was known by the family name of the *hashiya* who occupied it. These fortifications transformed the lives of the people of al-Shihr, who previously had been forced to flee to the shelter of smaller outlying communities when their city came under attack.[16]

The town's drinking water came from increasingly brackish wells until the second decade of the twentieth century, when the Qu'ayti government constructed a piped-in water system. Water was piped from springs in Tubbala five miles inland and held in a cistern. The government brought the water to the cistern, protecting the aqueduct with a parallel chain of fortified watchtowers. Private carriers took the water to homes in skins or jerry cans.

The port of al-Shihr served as the principal port for the Kathiri sultanate and was used by the tribes of Mahra as well. Ships approached from the open sea, anchored in open roadsteads, and were offloaded into smaller sailing vessels, which were offloaded on the beach. Merchants receiving cargo sold some goods wholesale from the beach, some goods were taken to the camel park to be loaded on caravans to the interior, and some were warehoused in al-Shihr for later sale. Caravans from al-Shihr took the eastern routes to the interior, which were shorter and faster than the western routes from al-Mukalla. The caravan trade was divided among the different branches of the Hamum tribe, so the routes functioned only during times of good relations between the Qu'ayti state and the tribe. The first automobile road in Hadramawt, constructed in the 1930s by the al-Kaf family, linked al-Shihr to Tarim. It drew a great deal of opposition from the Hamum, threatened by the loss of the carrying trade.

Two Qu'ayti customs buildings stood on the sea front, an area of intense activity. When ships were being unloaded, the beach was lined with sacks, bales, and tins and was crowded with merchants and porters. In the town center, the market

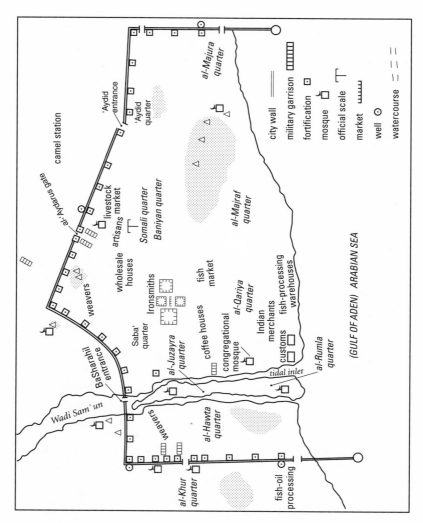

Map 4.2 Al-Shihr, c. 1920s

camel station

'Aydid entrance

al-Aydarus gate

al-Majura quarter

'Aydid quarter

livestock market

artisans market

wholesale houses

Somali quarter

Baniyan quarter

al-Majraf quarter

weavers

Ironsmiths

fish market

Saba' quarter

al-Juzayra quarter

coffee houses

congregational mosque

al-Qariya quarter

Indian merchants

fish-processing warehouses

customs

al-Rumla quarter

BaSharahil entrance

Wadi Sam`un

weavers

al-Hawta quarter

tidal inlet

(GULF OF ADEN) ARABIAN SEA

al-Khur quarter

fish-oil processing

city wall

military garrison

fortification

mosque

official scale

market

well

watercourse

consisted of clustered shops, workshops, coffee shops, and restaurants. Shops carried imported rice, spices, kerosene, and cloth and local fresh and preserved fish, dates, and sweets. In the neighborhoods were numerous artisinal workshops, more than in any other Hadhrami town. Indigo dyers, weavers, and silversmiths produced goods for tribes nearby and in the interior as well as for townspeople in al-Shihr. Inside the al-'Aydarus gate was the live animal market, where market brokers sold sheep and goats for the *badu* and used the proceeds to buy cloth and silver jewelry for them.[17]

Near the market were the areas where foreigners lived: the Banyan quarter and the Somalian quarter. While these were called quarters, they were not part of the competitive system that characterized the quarters inhabited by local people. The service providers, tradesmen, and workers of the quarters of al-Shihr were almost as competitive as those of Say'un. Late in the nineteenth century, a rivalry between two quarters led to a fracas with knives in which seven people died.[18] The quarter known as al-Hawta, once the home of wealthy merchants and Islamic scholars and jurists, by the late nineteenth century had a population of artisans and merchants. An island in the middle of Wadi Samun consisted of two quarters. The quarters followed a pattern: fishermen lived in poor homes in the seaward quarters, while the inland quarters included artisans, builders, ship owners, and merchants. In Harat al-Qariya (literally "Village quarter"), fishermen lived among porters and the former slave soldiers of the previous rulers, the Bin Birayk, who had been settled there by the Qu'ayti. The inland quarters north of the market consisted of a densely populated mixture of residential houses, commercial houses, and workshops of weavers, indigo dyers, and silversmiths.

The *sada* of al-Shihr lived inland, many in the newest quarter, al-Majura. This part of town, distant from the busy market and the fish-processing warehouses, included grand homes, including those of the Shaykh Abu Bakr b. Salim and 'Attas families and that of the Bin Birayk.[19] Also in this area was a center for Sufi study and practice. In the far northeastern corner, just inside the city walls, stood al-Bagh, a large building surrounded by a walled courtyard and gardens belonging to the Qu'ayti Sultan, who turned it over to al-Shihr's first civil school, Madrasat Makarim al-Akhlaq (School of Noble Character Traits), which opened in December 1918.[20]

A single quarter lying outside the city walls included the homes of fishermen and tanks for the extraction of fish oil. Outside al-'Aydarus gate was the busy camel park where caravans were loaded for the eastern routes to the interior, including Tarim. In the 1930s more than thirty thousand camels were loaded there annually. Overlooked by a garrison of Qu'ayti soldiers, this area was where visiting *badu* stayed, in the open air. East of the city wall was an area, in the distant past a horse market, where some *badu* had settled, living in rough houses made of branches and palm leaves.[21]

Even in its decline, al-Shihr had a cosmopolitan population. The town was nicknamed "Mother of Orphans," which referred to its willingness to take in strangers and aid wayfarers in need. The foreign population, Banyan merchants and Somalian laborers and traders, were mainly bachelors. Because of the city's defensive needs, there were a great number of soldiers stationed around town: slave soldiers and Yafi'i irregulars, *tulud* and *ghurba'*. Because of the large number of bachelors, soldiers, emigrants en route to the *mahjar,* seamen, and transient merchants, al-Shihr—unlike most Hadhrami towns—had hostels, restaurants, and coffee shops where men met, socialized, and exchanged news.[22]

Livelihoods of the Coastal Towns

The economy of al-Mukalla and al-Shihr and the smaller towns of the Hadhramawt coast relied on the sea: the predominant industries were boat building, fishing, and fish processing. Sailors and merchants participated in the sail-borne coasting trade of the western Indian Ocean that persisted alongside the European steamship lines. The markets of the two ports included goods imported from throughout the Indian Ocean region, some of which were locally purchased and some carried to the interior by caravan. While increasing quantities and varieties of imported goods were brought to the coast and carried to the interior on long-standing trade and caravan routes, the local economy retained its traditional livelihoods, based on fishing, trade, and transportation of goods.

Boat-Building

Hardwood for boat building was imported from the Malabar coast of India. The boat-building industry was in the hands of specific families; as in other trades, the skills of the craft were passed from generation to generation within the family. The boat builders of the Hadhramawt coast built: small fishing boats; small cargo carriers (*za'ima,* sing. *za'im*) used for unloading the larger ships and carrying cargo and passengers into port; and the large cargo ships (*sanabiq,* sing. *sanbuk,* also called *sa'iya*) that sailed between the East African coast, Arabia, and India.[23]

The most frequently built boats were the small sewn wooden boats used in the local fishing industry. A master boat builder (*mu'allim*) supervised the framing and the early construction and then moved on to another job, while less highly skilled and lower-paid builders finished the work. The longitudinal spine (*hayrab*) of the boat was cut first, and the ribs were tied into it. Hand-sawn planks were laid over the ribs and the planks were sewed together with rope made from palm fronds. On the sides of the boats single vertical stitches joined the planks, while the center spine of the boat was cross-stitched. Interior joints were filled with wood and palm fibers and stitched over with palm-frond rope, which local people braided and sold to the boat makers. Fishermen rather than boat builders did the sewing since their labor was cheaper. The boat was put in the sun, so that the wood dried and contracted and the planks pulled away from each other before the boat was sealed. The buyer for whom the new boat was constructed contracted ahead to have fish oil made, and when the wood was dry, the fish oil was used to seal the boat inside and out. It took about forty days to build a fishing boat and make it seaworthy. The construction of a cargo vessel followed the same pattern as that of a fishing boat, although they were nailed rather than sewn. Building a large *sanbuk* required the labor of fourteen builders and apprentices working under a master builder.

After the wooden structure was finished, sailors fitted the sails and ropes. The inside of the boat was coated with fish oil. Outside, the wood was protected with grease made from finely pounded lime plaster mixed with boiled animal fat. This protective coating had to be renewed regularly; boats carried it with them on their voyages, and it was available at stopping points along the coast. Every three or four months, sailors took their vessel out of the water at any place with a convenient landfall, for renovation.[24]

Fishing

The fishing industry was one of the most important aspects of the coastal economy. Fresh fish and preserved fish products were the staple food on the coast and preserved fish products were shipped to the interior and to overseas markets in the Indian Ocean region.

The small sewn fishing boats, powered by oars and a single square sail, were efficient, moving easily in the lightest of winds. Each year, agreements were drawn up between the boat owner (*tibin*) and individual fishermen, who were free agents. A master fisherman (*rubban*) was hired as the head of crew for each boat; he hired the fishermen, who worked for shares of the catch.

The master fisherman served as captain, navigator, and overseer of the crew. He reached his position by knowing the areas with the richest fishing potential, such as underwater hills and coral reefs. The *rubban* directed the crew where to row, while he held the rope that gathered together the edges of the submerged fishnet. When the net moved with fish, divers collected the net. The fishing boats went out in the mornings and stayed as long as the men had the strength to work, which depended on wind and weather conditions.

Sometimes, fishermen took their catch directly to the fish-processing plant and wholesale warehouse. The fish broker paid them a day or two after they brought in their catch. The fishermen complained that the brokers formed a cartel and fixed prices, but the brokers were able to ignore their complaints, since the fishermen had few options for selling such a highly perishable product. Sometimes they took the catch directly to the retail market, in which case they did not receive money until after the fish sold. In either case, the fishermen's take was meager. Like agricultural laborers, many were chronically indebted to fish wholesalers or boat owners who held mortgages on the fishermen's homes as collateral for loans. The fish wholesalers and boat owners were keen to make loans to the most skillful master fishermen in order to bind them into a long-term contractual relationship, even though fishing agreements were renegotiated annually.[25]

The life of a fisherman was difficult and precarious. The work was physically taxing, especially for divers, and the sea was dangerous, particularly in early summer when waves were high. The fishermen formed a mutually supportive community, living in the same area of town and socializing among themselves. While they experienced a degree of social exclusion by other groups, they benefited from the high degree of internal solidarity that resulted. Whenever a fishing boat was delayed at sea or missing, all the other boats would go out and search until they found the fishermen, dead or alive.[26]

Fish Processing and the Fish Trade

Seven types of processed fish were produced for local consumption and export. Salt fish (*malah*) was consumed locally, stored as a hedge against lean times, sold to *badu* and agriculturalists in the immediate hinterlands of the coast, and substantial quantities were exported. Salted dried fish (*baghaziz*) and dried shark (*lakhm*) were exported by sea and shipped by camel caravan to the interior. Dried fish chunks (*hanid*) were consumed locally and sent to the interior. Dried sardines (*wazif*) were used as camel feed in the carrying trade, and some was eaten by humans, although it was considered to be the poorest of foods. Fish oil (*sifa*) was used in the boat-building industry and carried on sailing ships. Fish meal, a by-product of fish-oil production, was sold as manure in agricultural areas near the coast.[27]

Simple plants for fish processing and preservation were owned by fish brokers, whose wholesale trade was passed from father to son. *Malah* was made from large and medium-sized fish such as tuna and swordfish. It kept well for years. Workers cleaned and split the fish, salted them, and placed chunks in large plaster-lined stone or metal containers that were airtight after the lid was sealed with mud. Rocks were placed on top of large pieces of fish, which were left to cure for forty days. *Baghaziz* was made from sardines (*'ayd*) that were gutted, opened, salted, and dried in the open air for one day in the sun and for five to ten days in the shade. Hanid were made from large fish chopped into large chunks that were salted, pierced with sticks, and put into a clay oven over wood embers. The dried fish was taken out half-cooked, dried in the sun, and then stored. Dried shark was made by salting large lengthwise segments of the shark and drying them in the sun. *Wazif* were produced from *'ayd* caught before mid-September, when the fish begin to get fatty. The fish were simply spread on the ground to dry for a few days, then stored in sacks. Fish oil, a more valuable product than *wazif*, was made (from the fatty sardines caught mid-September to January) in stone troughs located outside town, because of the smell.[28]

Sailing vessels from Oman and Kuwait sometimes brought fish drying on their decks. They sold them to the wholesalers, who completed the processing, and the ships used the proceeds of the sale to buy imported sugar and rice to sell on their onward journey or back home.

The broker sold fish products locally, shipped them to the interior by camel caravan or shipped them to overseas markets on the vessels that stopped at al-Shihr and al-Mukalla on their trading journeys. For shipping fish products to the interior, ten or fifteen camels at a time were loaded, each camel carrying four hundred pounds. Sometimes brokers would charter a ship to take dried shark and salt fish to Mombasa and Zanzibar. There they bartered their preserved fish products for coffee, sorghum, maize, coconut oil, and brown sugar. They sent dried shark to Aden, which had a port exclusively for this product. Other fish products were shipped to more distant locations, some as far as Ceylon, where a Yemeni trader had a warehouse in which he received fish products, shipping tea back in exchange.[29]

Seafaring and Trade

Even after steam ships began stopping at al-Mukalla and al-Shihr in the 1870s, traditional wooden sailing vessels continued to carry cargo and passengers on seasonal voyages from Hadhramawt to the East African coast, the Gulf, and India's Malabar coast. In the age of steam, sailing vessels no longer made the long voyage to Southeast Asia: Hadhramis going to the East Indies traveled by sail to Aden, and then onward by steam ship to Singapore.[30]

The traditional sailing vessels of the Indian Ocean traveled a seasonal route determined by the monsoons. While many of these ships came from India and the Gulf, many crews came from the Hadhramawt coast, particularly from al-Hami. Seafaring was the lifeblood of al-Hami and its sailors were well known throughout the Indian Ocean. The ships they sailed came into the ports of Hadhramawt in late April or May from the East African ports of Zanzibar, Mombasa, and Berbera. During the rough seas and unreliable winds of June, July, and August, the sailors stayed ashore with their families and maintained and repaired ships.[31]

After maintenance, one group of ships sailed out in the middle of August when the seas became smoother, heading for Musqat and the Gulf or India. A second group sailed eastward in September heading to Musqat by way of Salala on the coast of Dhufar.[32] These voyages were usually speculative business ventures involving numerous transactions at different ports. The ships earned money in two ways: by carrying cargo consigned by merchants and by buying and selling their own goods. The owner of a cargo vessel hired the *nakhuda*, who was both captain and business manager for the journey. The *nakhuda* then hired his crew, giving each sailor a small payment in advance. Sailors sometimes used that money to buy goods to sell during the trip.[33]

After hiring the crew, the nakhuda went to traders to see if they wanted to move goods anywhere along the sailing route. They gave him *riyals* in white canvas bags, with between a thousand and two thousand *riyals* filling a ship with goods in the 1920s. Large merchants gave orders for purchases and sales at specific points

Figure 4.1 Al-Mukalla from the sea

along the journey, and some had agents in the various ports to handle their transactions. Small merchants would invest in the journey for a share in the profits, giving money to the *nakhuda* to manage it. He put the bags of money under his bed, usually in an ornately carved wooden trunk from India.[34]

The crew of a sailing vessel carrying two hundred fifty tons might consist of twenty-five sailors. Like many other livelihoods, sailing was a hereditary calling. Knowledge of navigation was handed down from father to son, grandfather to grandson, or uncle to nephew. No matter how prominent his background, a youth always started out at the bottom, usually as a cook or food server, and worked up through the positions of ordinary seaman, apprentice helmsman, and helmsman, to *nakhuda*.[35] Some benefited from training that began before their apprenticeship. A young boy from a sea-faring family learned the directions, distances, and difficult spots on the sea routes from his seniors, who drilled him on the information even before he went to sea. Knowledge was also passed along in writing. A *nakhuda* recorded details of the sea route and navigational tables and used the manuscript to teach those learning the routes from him, such as his helmsman or clerk. After he retired from the sea, he used it to teach people who came to his house. When he died, he left the record to his heirs.[36]

The wooden vessels sailed day and night, using a compass and the stars for navigation. Only the *nakhuda*, his assistant, the helmsmen, and the clerk had beds, cots under a shade in the helm. The other sailors, as well as passengers, spent day and night on the open deck. Goods were carried below. The sailors fished while traveling, and ate fish, rice, bread, and dates. When the boat ran out of water, part of the crew took goat-skin bags and metal barrels in the small boat to the shore, usually a journey of hours. They also collected or bought cooking wood while ashore.

Depending on the weather and sea conditions, sailing was often a perilous business. Particularly dangerous spots included Saffariyat in the straits near Bab al-Mandab and Salama wa Binatiha (Salama and her daughters), an island surrounded by rocks near Hormuz. If a sailor was swept off the deck in severe conditions, he often had to be left behind. In one case, when a sailor fell overboard in a storm while using the shipboard toilet (a small box hanging over the side of the ship), the crew, which included his relatives, could see him floating in the box among the waves. But the ship was too unwieldy to turn around in the rough seas and they were not able to launch the small boat in such conditions.

When the ships left the Hadhrami coast, they carried a load of Hadhramawt's few export products. For the eastward journey, these included: salt; sheet quartz; small amounts of frankincense and myrrh; fish oil; dry sardines; dried shrimp; and a kind of clay used to wash clothes. For the westward journey, the cargo included preserved fish products; salt, and sesame oil bound to Africa; and fish products and shark fin headed to Aden for reexport. Because Hadhramawt produced relatively little, the sheet quartz was a convenient export. It brought little money but was easy to acquire and provided ballast until more lucrative cargoes could be loaded. Indian artisans bought it for use in decorative inlay work.[37]

Ships that sailed in August, the early voyage of the season, traveled into the
Gulf to Basra, a center for the date trade dominated by Kuwaiti merchants. In
Basra, Kuwaiti or Adeni merchants might hire the Hadhrami-crewed ships to carry
Basra dates into the Indian Ocean for sale. Otherwise, the *nakhuda* invested in
dates for sale on the onward journey.

Ships that sailed from Hadhramawt in September, the second voyage of the
season, stopped in Salala, where they bought ghee, coconuts, and frankincense
(products that had been carried on these routes for centuries) to sell in Musqat.
Rather than sailing into the Gulf, they bought Basra dates in Musqat. They returned to sell the dates in the ports of southern Arabia; if they had not sold them
by the time they reached Aden, they took them on to Somalia, Mombasa, and
Zanzibar.[38] Some ships were hired in Musqat by Omani or Indian merchants to
carry dried dates to Bombay. Then they traveled to Malabar, where they bought
wood for shipbuilding and house construction, coconut fiber rope used for rigging
sails and for sewing fishing boats, rice, spices, and cloth.

An unusual cargo was corpses, which only Hadhrami crews were willing to
carry. Musqat had a large Shi'i population, and the Shi'i liked to bury their dead at
Najaf, so that they could receive the spiritual benefit of resting in the holy ground
where the martyred 'Ali was buried. Hadhrami ships carried the bodies from Musqat
to Basra, where relatives collected them and took them to Najaf for burial. The heat
caused the corpses to smell bad even though they had been drained of their body
fluids, so no other ships would carry them. The Hadhramis did so in order to benefit
from the fare for the corpse, which was half that for a live passenger.[39]

Sometimes the ships stayed in the ports for days or weeks, waiting to buy
goods or waiting for the arrival of consigned cargo. Sailors seldom deserted, since
they were not paid until the end of the journey. Because a *nakhuda* was considered
prosperous and marriageable, the women of the ports took note of him, covering
themselves and behaving modestly in his presence. But women paid little attention to the ordinary sailors, considered poor and inconsequential. In Shi'i areas of
the Gulf, a sailor occasionally engaged in the local practice of a "temporary" (*mut'a*)
marriage, even though this practice was not sanctioned by the Shafi'i *madhhab*
prevalent in Hadhramawt. In East Africa, the sailors ate and socialized with the local population and some sailors consorted with local women.[40]

The *nakhuda* stayed in a facility provided by the agent of the boat owner or
by the large merchants. He met with different agents there and carried out transactions concerning the ship's cargo. Passengers who were engaged in private trading voyages went into port to buy and sell goods. The sailors went into port to ped-
dle their own merchandise. This became more difficult after World War I, when
the imperial powers took greater control of ports and customs.[41]

Sailors made small investments in goods to sell in the ports, following the
traditional adage "*zuqul bi-'ayd ya'tik hut*" or "throw in a little fish as bait, and
it will bring you a whale."[42] Sailors from al-Hami remembered carrying products
to sell in Basra during the 1920s and 1930s. They took: incense; frankincense;

woven palm-frond fans, baskets, and hand-brooms; crocheted caps; pottery incense burners; a special kind of clay used as soap; and *mur aswad*, a resin-based medicinal mixture which also gave protection against the evil eye. Each day in port, the sailors took their goods, by-passing the market to go into the palm groves of the countryside. They walked along calling out *"tin Jawi, tin Jawi"* (the washing clay, called Javanese clay); "Abu Mismar" (cloves); *"'alush, 'alush"* (incense); and *"mur makki, mur makki"* ("Meccan" resin). Although the resin came from Hadhramawt or Mahra, associating it with Mecca made the item more attractive, because of the spiritual benefit associated with the holy site. Women came out of their homes and traded dates for the peddlers' goods. A sailor who peddled actively could end up with five or six sacks of the best Basra dates to carry home and sell for a good sum.[43]

Sailors received their official wage at the journey's end, when the income and expenses were calculated and the profits apportioned. Ship expenses were paid by the boat owner, but voyage expenses, including food, customs, and port charges, were divided between the boat owner and the crew, who strove to keep expenses low. They consumed a simple diet and went ashore themselves to supply the ship. They did their own repairs and maintenance. They made minimal port expenditures: the wooden ships stayed at anchor out in the harbors and used little in the way of port facilities and services, landing goods in their own small boats. After World War I, when ports instituted immigration controls and health fees, the sailors tried as much as possible simply to bribe the officials rather than pay the fees.[44]

In the end, the profitability of a voyage was dependent on the fortune of the markets and on the skills of the *nakhuda*. A successful *nakhuda* enjoyed a level of prosperity, but the sailors were usually pressed to maintain a livelihood for their families. In the off season, they repaired and maintained ships and went inland to help with the date harvest.[45]

In al-Hami, the families of the seafarers eagerly awaited the return of the ships. In the final days of the season, ships were often delayed by irregular wind patterns or treacherous currents, which caused anxiety for the waiting families. Every year at the end of the season, the women and children of the sailors' families gathered in the evenings on the beach, laid rugs and mats on the ground looking out to sea, and sang and danced and drummed until late. They recited verses beseeching God to bring the ships and sailors safely home.

On ships that were delayed on their way home, the sailors also gathered in the evenings to play drums and sing and pray for a safe journey's end. For the sailors these rituals served a dual purpose: they provided the reassurance of prayer and a diversion for sailors impatient to return home. At the end of the season, the dried flowers from Musqat that the sailors bought as gifts for the women at home began to powerfully spread their fragrance on the ships. The women claimed that the scent of the flowers announced a vessel's arrival, preceding it by a day.[46]

The sailing ships arrived in groups. Each would fire a gun while approaching, to announce its arrival. Small boats went out to greet the sailors at the same time that the ship lowered its small boat to carry goods and passengers to shore. The women waited on shore wearing new clothes, decorated and ornamented to look their best. Goods and passengers came in together on the small boats. Import-export agents claimed spots on the beach, where they had porters bring the goods consigned to them as they were offloaded. Trade began immediately, with brokers offering goods for sale on the beach.

The Caravan Trade from Coast to the Interior

Every year the *badu* came with their camels to the ports to carry goods to the interior. In winter, there might be hundreds of camels waiting at the caravan station outside the town walls. The merchants of the interior had transport agents on the coast, who purchased goods and hired the camel caravans to carry them to the interior.

The camel drivers of each tribe were represented in the carrying trade by one of the tribe's members, called the *fassal,* who solicited the merchants for transport business. He did not bargain, as prices were fixed, but he arranged the shipping agreements and guaranteed delivery, for which he received a commission from both sides, called "coffee money." His importance lay in his reputation, as he was known and trusted among both camelmen and merchants. He was responsible for delivery of the cargo, "*bi-wajhihi*" ("on his face" or on his honor); his personal and tribal integrity was at stake. He mediated in case anything was lost, stolen, or damaged. If a camel driver ran away with his load, or otherwise failed to deliver, no camel driver from his tribe was allowed to load until the miscreant had been brought to justice.[47]

The market broker, since he was responsible for relations between *badu* and town, oversaw the business dealings between the *badu* carriers and the merchants. When *badu* arrived with their camels, the market broker went to the camel station, where he drank coffee with the *badu* and ascertained how many camels they had and what kind of loads they wanted to carry. He also came to the loading sites to check the weights of sacks after packing. [48]

After the goods were weighed, the camel driver received half his pay in advance; he received the rest on delivery. Sacks were weighed on arrival and the camel driver was responsible for the difference if it exceeded the allowance for loss in transit. The sacks were marked with symbols identifying the receiving merchants so that illiterate porters were able to identify their loads.

A sensitive cargo was money, *riyals*. White canvas bags of the large silver coins were packed in sacks of rice or sugar. Sometimes, the placement of the money was known only to the market broker, the tribe's agent, and the worker who packed and sewed the sacks. Some merchants sending money would put a mark on each sack that had money in it and pay the camel driver extra to guard it. Other less trusting merchants did not tell anyone and just slipped the money into sacks of rice, cloth, or other goods.

A letter, informing merchants in the interior that the caravan was en route, was carried by the courier (*mukattib*) who made the trip to the interior by foot in two days (as opposed to the usual eight days) with mail and messages. On the road, each caravan was accompanied by a leader who was responsible for the security of the load. The tribes took routes within their own territory and that of allies, to avoid having to pay for protection from a *siyar,* or tribal guard. Caravans usually took seven to eight days to make the trip, although some weeks longer, since payment did not depend on speed of delivery. If the goods were damaged by rain or other causes outside the camel driver's control, the market broker interceded to solve the problem.[49]

The powerful Hamum tribe, which controlled the caravan routes from al-Mukalla and al-Shihr to Du'an and Hadhramawt, opposed the introduction of wheeled transport of goods that began during the 1930s with the construction of the al-Kaf road from al-Shihr to Tarim. Along with interior tribes such as the Al Jabir, they repeatedly disrupted road construction and travel. The camel caravan trade was one of their few sources of livelihood, and even the tribesmen not actively involved in carrying benefited by extracting fees for pasturage and protection from passing caravans. In the end, the government regulated the carrying trade and required merchants to use camels as well as truck transport. After 1937, for every truckload of goods carried, the merchants had to hire thirty camels to carry the same amount. The market broker registered the loads and oversaw the hiring of camel transport by the merchants.[50]

Agricultural Communities of the Coastal Region

The agricultural system in most coastal region farming communities, such as Ghayl BaWazir and al-Hami, resembled the system of the interior in its organization of relations between landowner and farmer. Wadi Hajr differed in having a system of serfdom in which client families were attached to the land-owning families. In the coastal region, systems of apportioning and distributing irrigation water differed from the system prevalent in the interior, with its dependence on wells. Ghayl BaWazir and al-Hami and other agricultural communities benefited from abundant spring water, while Wadi Hajr enjoyed permanently flowing water.

Ghayl BaWazir

The small town of Ghayl BaWazir was a productive center of spring-irrigated agriculture, producing grain, vegetables, fruit, dates, and Hamumi tobacco. Incorporated in the Qu'ayti state from its inception, this agricultural oasis benefited from the development of the port of al-Mukalla and the security of the transportation route from Ghayl BaWazir to the port fostered by Qu'ayti rule.

This had been a watering spot for camel caravans before the founding of the town early in the fourteenth century by Shaykh 'Abd al- Rahim b. 'Umar BaWazir.[51] In the nineteenth century, the BaWazir and Ba'Amir families owned most of the land. At the same time, the 'Awabitha tribe considered Ghayl BaWazir to be part of their territory, so they collected levies for the security of agricultural production (*shiraha*).

During the nineteenth century struggles for power, Ghayl BaWazir had been for a time in the hands of the 'Awlaqi *jama'dar,* but it was taken by 'Awadh b. 'Umar al-Qu'ayti in 1876 and was thenceforth incorporated into the Qu'ayti state. Taxes on production and export of Hamumi tobacco provided a source of revenue for the Qu'ayti state, which also owned large tracts of land leased out for annual rents.[52]

Without direct involvement of imperial powers or their agricultural experts, highly organized plantations had been developed for the production of tobacco. According to local lore, Hamumi tobacco seeds were brought to Ghayl BaWazir from India in the eighteenth century, and at first tobacco was grown for local use. After the British occupation of Aden in 1859, Ghayl BaWazir began producing greater amounts of tobacco for export to Aden. Sultan 'Umar encouraged production and during his time (1921–1935), tobacco began to be exported to Yemen and Egypt. During this period, a local agriculturist succeeded in selectively breeding the tobacco plants to increase yields. In 1936, the total annual value of the crop was 500,000 Indian rupees, with the Qu'ayti receiving 120,000 for rents and duties and the cultivators a profit of 80,000, the cost of production being 300,000.[53] This tobacco was used primarily in pipes and water pipes.

Some land in Ghayl BaWazir was owned by local families who hired tenant farmers, but much of the land was the property of the state. Wealthy merchants, such as BaSharahil and BuSaba'a of al-Shihr, leased tracts from the state, which they rented to the farmers of Ghayl BaWazir. A tax (*'ashur*) was paid to the government on production of tobacco and a further impost (*rusum*) was levied on that exported. In addition, date producers paid a portion of the harvest to the neighboring tribes or to the sultan's soldiers for protection.

The farmers received one-fourth of production and the owners or lease-holders three-fourths. In the case of tobacco, the farmers had to sell their portion of the crop to the landowner or leaseholder for whom they worked. As elsewhere, farmer debt was common and landowners liked to keep good farmers in debt. Even with the whole family working in the fields, farmers often died in debt to the owners, who could then take everything from the family except their house.

The high degree of organization of agriculture in Ghayl BaWazir was made possible by the abundant springs found there. The springs flowed into large cisterns (*ma'yan*), from which a network of channels carried the water to the fields, which each received a prescribed amount of water on schedule.[54] Plants were grown from seed at a nursery field and then transplanted. The plants were fertilized three times, with guano, dried fish, and dung. After harvest, the whole tobacco plants were dried in the sun and packed into bales. The bales were carried to al-

Mukalla by camel caravan, until motor transport replaced the caravans in the late 1920s.

The valuable farms of Ghayl BaWazir and its tall mud-brick homes were enclosed within a massive wall with a fortified gate, always kept closed. The population was not large; in the 1930s it was probably between six and seven thousand. The population included farmers, a few private landholders, and a few artisans.[55] In order to enjoy the lush and fertile atmosphere of this oasis, in the 1920s Sultan 'Umar built a summer palace or rest house, a wooden villa of Indian design with a long reflecting pool in front, the whole shaded by fruit trees.[56]

Al-Hami

The small coastal town of al-Hami thrived on a mixed economy based on spring-fed agriculture, fishing, and seafaring. Its homes and farms sheltered by a semicircular ring of fortified watchtowers, al-Hami had no town wall. Each watchtower housed guards, four in times of security, six in times of unrest. To alert the townspeople of danger, they blew a warning blast on a horn made from a cow horn or conch shell.[57]

The Kasadi family, of Yafi'i *tulud* extraction, which had ruled al-Mukalla from 1703 until the Qu'ayti takeover in 1876, had its home base in al-Hami, where part of the family remained after the Kasadi ruler and his entourage went into exile in Zanzibar. Even after the Qu'ayti state superseded the authority of the Kasadi Naqib, the branches of the Kasadi family remaining in al-Hami retained local authority and prestige. Often, the position of governor of al-Hami was held by a member of the Kasadi family, so their unofficial status was reinforced by an official status under the Qu'ayti state.

Most of the population lived near the seaside. Standing side by side like rowhouses, the houses were narrow and deep, designed to maximize the number of homes receiving the sea breeze. Every house had on the bottom floor a long narrow sitting room, which was four meters wide, the width of the house, and about thirty meters deep, with a courtyard inside the front wall. The second story of these mud-brick houses included a rooftop terrace. The grandest homes of al-Hami, those of the Kasadi family, were constructed of white limestone and stood three or four stories tall. As in other towns of the Red Sea and Indian Ocean coasts, the better houses included ornate pillars and doors carved from Indian and African hardwoods and elaborate designs molded in plaster. In keeping with al-Hami's seafaring tradition, a wooden interior pillar was called *sariya,* after the mast of a sailing ship. The houses of the Yafi'i *tulud* included a feature not found in the homes of others, an upper-story room extending beyond the streetside facade of the lower story, incorporating viewing ports and gun holes, one pointing straight down over the entrance. Since al-Hami was blessed with fresh water only a few meters underground, houses often had a well in the rear courtyard and a shaft allowing water to be raised to the upper story.

The town was organized by quarters, although since al-Hami was a small town, the quarters were not as competitive as those of larger towns. As in the larger towns, quarters and neighborhoods included a mixed population, with people identified as being from the armed groups, the Yafi'i and other tribal landowners or the Yafi'i civil guards; sailors; fishermen; or farmers. The market was small, since the population relied on the market and workshops of nearby al-Shihr. Local industry was limited to fish processing and the production of fish oil for ship maintenance.[58]

The town had no natural harbor; as in al-Shihr, vessels had to anchor in the open sea and goods and passengers were brought to shore by small boats. Although larger vessels summered in the harbor at al-Burum, west of al-Mukalla, small sailing ships spent the summer in al-Hami. They were pulled onto the shore at the end of the sailing season and a half-mile stretch of beach would fill with ships being repaired and maintained. Many were owned by prominent Hadhrami businessmen from outside al-Hami, such as the BuSab'a of al-Mukalla, BaSharahil of al-Shihr, and the BaZara'a of Aden, originally from Du'an.

Despite al-Hami's lack of a natural harbor, the town was a stopping point for many passing vessels, which stopped to replenish their water supply from the spring-fed cisterns, one of the most abundant sources of fresh water on the southern Arabian coast. Sailors from passing caravans of sailing vessels came to shore in small boats to fill goatskin water bags and buckets.[59]

The numerous springs and artesian wells also fostered a high level of agricultural development. Each farm unit consisting of a spring or springs with irrigation channels and flood-irrigated fields, was known as a *ma'yan*. The productive farms were irrigated by thirteen springs of varying temperatures and mineral content. The waters of the smaller hot springs collected and cooled in cisterns, each of which supplied a network of irrigation channels serving fields of fodder, grain, vegetables, fruit, and date and coconut palms. The largest spring, al-Rawdha, had no cistern but flowed into an aqueduct extending almost the breadth of town. Each field included an allotment of water corresponding to its size.

Agreements between farmers and tenants were arranged by shares. A common arrangement was that production was divided in thirds, one-third going to the landowner, one-third to the farmer, and one-third paying for fertilizer and seed. In some cases, a well-established farmer who could provide his own seed agreed to supply seed and fertilizer for one-half of production, with the landowner receiving the other half.[60]

Some of the land in al-Hami, including the extensive farms watered by al-Rawdha spring, was owned by the Qu'ayti state, which had appropriated it from the Kasadi Naqib after he failed to pay his large debt to the Qu'ayti. Farmers rented land and irrigation water from the state, from private owners, or in the case of *waqf* land, from the mosque, for a payment of half of the harvest. The farmers of al-Hami paid the *kayla*, or protection payment, to three clans of the Hamum tribe. This impost, traditionally levied by the Hamum, had been sanctioned by the

Kasadi ruler. Although the Qu'ayti government at first tried to end it, in the time of Sultan 'Umar the right to *kayla* was restored to the Hamum. Some farmers considered the payment as simple extortion, while others felt that it was reasonable, given the productivity of the farms of al-Hami and the poverty of the Hamumi tribesmen.[61]

Wadi Hajr

With the only permanently flowing river on the Arabian Peninsula, Hajr was blessed with a particularly productive agricultural system. Containing more than a million palm trees as well as fields of fodder and grain, Wadi Hajr benefited from abundant springs, artesian wells, and the continual flow of the Hajr River. Few farms had to resort to the *sinawa* for the raising of water.

Agricultural labor in Hajr was performed by *subiyan,* each family of which was attached to a tribal or *mashayikh* family, serving in their households and laboring on their lands. The *subiyan* lived along the sides of the wadi above the flood line, in simple houses of mud brick with roofs of palm leaves and mud, with some poorer families living in rough huts of branches and sticks. Daily, they descended the steep slope to work in fields in the lower part of the wadi. The wadi bottom, while productive agriculturally, was unhealthy, as malaria was rife and in many places standing water was contaminated.

There were also slaves (*'abid*) in Hajr. Like *subiyan,* each family of slaves was attached to a tribal group, with the slaves considered under the protection of their tribe and dependent on it. But they enjoyed a higher social status than the *subiyan,* since slaves carried arms and fought alongside the tribesmen. Although some members of slave families worked as household servants in Hajr, they generally did not participate in agricultural labor.

Most of the landowners of Hajr were tribesmen. By far the largest tribal group was the Nuwwah, who owned perhaps 80 to 90 percent of the land, while the remainder was in the hands of the Kinda. Land was also held by a prominent family of *mashayikh*, the BaRas, who were greatly respected by the tribes. A member of the BaRas family served as spiritual leader or *munsib* to the Nuwwah, and the tribe looked to senior members of the BaRas family for counsel and mediation. The Nuwwah revered the memory of one of the BaRas ancestors by participating, along with the Saybani tribe of Du'an, in an annual ritual visit to a BaRas tomb in Saybani territory.

The tribes and the BaRas of Hajr were absentee landlords. Their stone houses stood high up in the mountains above the sides of the wadi, where the climate was drier and healthier, and they had rain-fed cisterns for water. They seldom descended into the wadi except to check on their lands and crops.

Families of cultivators, as mentioned above, were usually attached to landowning families over generations. The in-kind payment of the cultivators was determined by local custom and expressed in legal agreements. The landowners' greatest interest in the property was date palm production. The farmer who planted, tended, and pollinated palms got half of the harvest, while the owner got half. When a farmer who planted and tended palm trees died, his agreement with the landowner continued with his sons.[62]

The tribes of Hajr were amenable to Qu'ayti rule and loyal, after a short-lived resistance to Qu'ayti incorporation of their territory in 1899/1900. Still, they evaded Qu'ayti customs duties whenever possible, facilitated by their distance from al-Mukalla and their proximity to the ports of B'ir 'Ali and BalHaf in Wahidi territory. Few caravans came to Hajr from al-Mukalla, where the camel park was strictly supervised by Qu'ayti government agents; most came from the Wahidi ports of B'ir 'Ali and BalHaf, which did not impose customs duties. Thus Wadi Hajr, while under Qu'ayti rule, possessed a certain degree of autonomy.[63]

Change in Town and Country on the Coast

The port towns, entrepôts for imported goods and staging points on the journeys of emigrants, had a cosmopolitan nature compared to the insular character of the interior towns and had a seasonal fluctuation in population which depended on the monsoon winds and on steamship schedules. They differed from the interior towns in having public gathering places such as the cafes where travelers, seamen, and merchants exchanged information.

Like the towns of the interior, the towns of the coast saw significant development in the late nineteenth and early twentieth centuries, with the construction of palaces, fortifications, governmental and religious buildings, and large private homes. They also experienced growth in activity of ports, markets, and caravans, although al-Shihr declined relative to al-Mukalla. The coastal region, with its abundant springs and greater productivity, experienced more agricultural development than the interior, particularly under Qu'ayti rule. While plantation production of tobacco had previously been established, the Qu'ayti rulers further developed the system and incorporated its profits into state revenues. At the same time, traditional systems ordering water allocation, tenancy agreements, and relations between land owners and agricultural laborers persisted.

While the systems ordering life in town and country remained in place as the towns grew, changes during this time period—the influx of wealth and imported goods from abroad, and the development of new religious and educational institutions—did not take place without creating friction. Social institutions such as the celebrations of rites of passage and religious education and religious practice became arenas for contestation among social critics.

PART THREE

Social Institutions and the Emergence of Social Criticism

Rites of Passage, Ceremonies, and Social Critique

In Hadhramawt, the celebrations of rites of passage were shared rituals that connected the lives of individuals and families with their community, combining religious elements with expressions of social standing and offerings of hospitality. These ceremonies functioned as enactments of social station of the participating families as well as benchmarks in the lives of individuals. They marked changes of status in the lives of individuals and families, and thereby were part of private life. At the same time, relatives, friends, and neighbors participated in these celebrations or observed them, so they were also a part of public life, particularly in the case of celebrations involving processions. For women, gatherings associated with these ceremonies were an important aspect of their public life, providing the opportunity to socialize and interact with numerous women beyond those of their households and neighborhoods. Many of the elements of these celebrations are not unique to Hadhramawt or even to the Arabian peninsula, although particular elaborations of these elements are characteristic of Hadhramawt during the period in question.[1]

In the late nineteenth and early twentieth century, the increase in imported goods and fashions led to changes in the observances of these ceremonies, pioneered by those families that had acquired fortunes in the *mahjar* and imitated by those less wealthy. The rising standards of hospitality, increasing splendor of women's dress and ornamentation, and increasing requirements to employ professional attendants began to make it difficult for many families to carry out these celebrations in the style they felt was expected of them. Criticisms of these innovations in "tradition" were expressed by the government, by civic reform organizations, and by the new print media. The government and the reform groups attempted to ban the new customs and fashions, with little success.

Rites of Passage: Enactments of Social Station and Social Roles

The events of an individual's life—birth, coming of age, marriage, procreation, and death, and in the case of men, emigration and return—were marked by observations involving the individual's extended family and the larger community. The ceremonies reinforced the status of the individual and family as members of an identity group, which also reinforced the system as a whole. Different groups had particular roles to play, with associated standards of behavior. In their idealized form, these rituals embodied a set of shared "models and metaphors" relating events in the life of an individual and a family to the larger society.[2] While practice varied in different locales, among different families, and according to particular circumstances, the following presents an idealized notion of the rite-of-passage rituals practiced in the early twentieth century, at the time that customs thought to be "age-old" were being modified by changing fashions derived from the increase in emigrant wealth.

Birth

The production and rearing of children was considered the duty and most important accomplishment of women, and the purpose and culmination of married life. Since women married young, they also began having children young, often in the early teen years. Among married women whose husbands were present or who returned to the homeland frequently, the pregnancy rate was high, although pregnancies frequently ended in miscarriage, particularly among very young women. Still it was not unusual for a woman whose husband was around to give birth every year or year and a half. Even though many infants and young children died, many families had from four to ten or more children survive.

Ideally, a woman pregnant with her first child returned to her father's home for her pregnancy and birth. For later pregnancies, she might return to her father's home or not. The husband paid his wife's family for her maintenance while she stayed with them. This stipend included payments for attendants and the hospitality required after a birth; by the 1920s that could be as much as ten *riyals*. The situation was different for pregnant women among the *dhu'afa'*, farmers and builders. These women remained in the husband's family's home until the birth and went to their father's home only for the confinement period afterward, which was shorter than that of other women. Women agriculturalists often continued working in the fields until they went into labor and returned not long after giving birth.[3]

Among other social groups, the expectant mother did not go out of the house during pregnancy. As the birth approached, her mother or another female relative stayed by her side. Sometimes a *munaffisa*, a local woman from *al-huwik* specialized in midwifery, was called in to attend the birth. The newborn was usually laid on a mat woven of palm leaf fibers while the call to prayer was recited in its ear, a religious requirement. Sometimes, the afterbirth was put in a container with ashes and a man from *al-huwik* buried it, to protect the spirit of the newborn from envy and evil. This service had to be performed by a specialist, who was paid for the service.

While the birth of a healthy baby to a well mother was always a cause for celebration, the birth of a boy was usually more joyfully received and announced than that of a girl, as an additional male member was considered a greater asset to the family. Great care had to be taken to protect a boy baby from the evil eye—a supernatural manifestation of human envy, by concealing him from the gaze of on-lookers and by providing him with an amulet containing verses from the Qur'an. The manner in which a birth was announced depended on the social group into which the child was born, whether it was a boy or girl, and whether it was the first boy or a later child. The birth of the first boy was the occasion most celebrated. Births were usually announced by women's ululations and the sending out of a messenger or messengers to inform other family members and other households. The birth of a boy in the sultan's family was greeted with drumming and weapons fire, and in the case of the first born, the firing of the palace cannons. The birth of a boy among the *sada* also might be announced with drumming and weapons fire. Among the arms-bearing groups, tribes and slaves, the birth of a boy was also an-nounced with weapons fire.[4]

After a birth, the new mother was to rest for forty days. Women of the *dhu'afa'* spent a shorter period at rest than other women did, twenty rather than forty days, due to the need for their contribution in the struggle for economic sur-vival. Women with several previous children or other responsibilities sometimes cut the rest period short, but whenever possible, other women in the family took over the duties of the mother so that she could have the full forty days. Prosperous families had the midwife stay and tend the mother and infant during the forty days. She took care of the baby and massaged the mother with oil, rubbing her skin with turmeric and *wars,* for purification and strength. She received new clothes and cash for her services; the price increased in the early twentieth century until reform groups limited it. Ideally, the new mother had only to recover her strength and nurse her infant. Even the latter task was occasionally done by other nursing moth-ers, who were quick to feed a crying infant. In tightly knit communities this prac-tice sometimes led to problems in arranging marriages, as people who had nursed from the same woman were considered siblings of a sort.[5]

A celebration called *al-shamma,* attended by large numbers of women, took place on the seventh day after the birth. Women visited in the afternoon. The new mother rested on a mattress in the far corner of the reception room, reclining on cushions and pillows with her female relatives next to her. A hired attendant fanned her continuously. This service was necessary for all social groups, and women of *al-huwik* specialized as attendants for particular social groups. The visitors greeted the new mother by kissing the top of her head or quickly sniffing the air just above her head, congratulated her and inquired after her well-being. Amenities for guests included the passing around of incense and freshly roasted coffee beans and the serving of coffee. In pairs, guests danced briefly in honor of the new mother and infant.

The family also privately celebrated the naming of the newborn on the sev-enth day, called naming day (*yawm al-tasmiyya*). Among the *sada,* an elderly fam-ily member, male or female, said the Fatiha (the opening chapter of the Qur'an) on behalf of the child, announcing its new name and reciting its paternal lineage all the way back to the Prophet. Among other groups, a respected member of the *sada* or *mashayikh* came to recite the Fatiha and bless the infant. The father's family held a feast in honor of the naming day. For the naming of a girl, this might be served to family members only, while for the naming of a boy, it was served to larger numbers of guests, depending on the wealth and station of the family.[6]

The end of a new mother's confinement was another occasion for celebration. The husband and his family brought gifts such as coffee, sugar, and cloves to the family of the wife. Accompanied by an attendant who carried the gift, the husband's family requested the wife's return and set the date for the celebration known as the *wufa'*. The new mother was groomed for her return, her hair braided and her hands and feet decorated with henna. Her family provided her with a new dress and when there was enough money, traded her silver or gold jewelry in for new pieces in later styles. The husband collected his wife and baby and took them, accompanied by an attendant, to his home where his family waited to receive them. On her arrival, the threshold of the house was prepared to protect mother and child from evil and envy. Depending on the family's wealth, the new mother would step onto the threshold over the blood of a freshly slaughtered sheep, freshly broken eggs, or poured sesame oil. The wife presented her husband and his family with presents of cakes baked by the women of her family. These included *al-khamir*, a cake baked of fermented dough of wheat or sorghum flour. Early in the twentieth century, *ka'k* and *kawiya*, lighter and fancier types of cake made with sugar, oil, and eggs, became the fashion for these gifts. The husband's family hosted the wife's family for a feast in honor of the homecoming and in the late afternoon, the husband's family hosted a *zilla*, a celebration which all women of the area were free to attend. The *zilla* took place outside, often in a temporary courtyard devised in an alley, street, or square. Women drummers and singers from *al-huwik* performed while guests danced in pairs in honor of the new mother's return. Some women performed the *na'ish*, whipping their long hair from side to side by sharp snaps of the neck. To cap the festivity, the new mother danced, showing off her new dress.[7]

Markers of Maturity

Families of modest means circumcised their baby boys on *yawm al-tasmiyya*, the naming day seven days after birth, so that the circumcision was celebrated along with the naming. In other cases, people circumcised their sons at the age of seven or eleven, occasioning additional celebrations. Circumcisions were performed by a specialist, the *khittan*, who inherited the right to provide this service and was confirmed in the position by the local spiritual leader, either the munsib or another spiritual authority.

On the day of his circumcision, a boy was usually taken to the house of relatives where the *khittan* and the boy's relatives and neighbors awaited him. The boy was distracted so that he would not see the circumciser's blade. The procedure was carried out swiftly and local medicines such as sesame oil, turmeric, and *wars* were applied to the wound. The newly circumcised boy was accompanied by an attendant while he and his relatives and neighbors walked in procession to his home. The women waiting at the boy's house ululated to greet the arrival of the procession. The boy was propped up on cushions and pillows in the courtyard or a reception room where guests came to congratulate him and his parents. The guests gave gifts of money, called *tarh* (literally "tossing") to the boy. Donors and recipients kept track of *tarh* gifts, since families were bound by reciprocal obligations. The boy's family hosted a feast to which they invited relatives, neighbors, and respected members of the religiously prestigious groups.

Among the *badu*, the circumcision ceremony differed from that of the settled groups. Several branches of a tribe would gather for a collective ceremony in which a number of boys were circumcised. Members of neighboring tribes were invited and the event created a cease-fire among tribal groups that ordinarily might be in antagonistic relations. The father put some of the family's flock in the name of his son and other relatives presented gifts of livestock or money.[8]

Among the settled populations, a girl's entrance into maturity took place before puberty, often at the age of ten, eleven, or twelve, when she adopted the standards of modesty expected of a mature unmarried girl. This point was marked by the girl's donning of the *hijab*, outer covering garments which protected her modesty. Thereafter, she could not see or be seen by any men, even those living in the same house, except for her father, grandfather, or brothers. She could not even be seen by married women from other households. From this time until her marriage, the girl was known as *bint al-bayt*, or "girl of the house." She was expected to remain at home, not able to move between households as freely as younger girls nor yet able to socialize among married women. When she attended events such as weddings or feasts, she was confined to the company of other unmarried girls and not allowed to speak or mix with married women. She remained fully covered by the *hijab* even indoors so that married women from outside her household could not see her. In the time until she married and entered the social life of married women, she was expected to devote herself to learning to manage a household.

The custom of seclusion of unmarried girls was prevalent among all settled social groups except the *dhu'afa'*, whose need for the labor of all family members precluded the isolation of the unmarried girls. It created hardship for those women of the sada who remained single later into maturity as a result of the limited availability of suitable marriage partners, since they experienced an extended period of social "invisibility" and social limitation. The *badu* did not observe the custom. *Badu* girls and young women were visible and mobile, since they were responsible for the grazing of sheep and goats, including flocks of their own.[9]

Marriage and Weddings

Since secluding and covering unmarried girls purported to prevent competition for the most attractive young girls as marriage partners, women seeking marriage partners for sons or nephews assessed girls' marriage potential during their childhood. The gap between childhood and marriage was not long, as many girls married not long after puberty, often at the age of twelve or thirteen. Boys often married at an equally early age, although some delayed until the age of seventeen or eighteen, or if they emigrated in the meantime, until even later in life.

The search for a marriage partner took place within a sharply delineated field. Most people looking for a spouse for their sons and daughters preferred someone close, a relative or someone whose parents were associated with the family. The widespread preference for paternal cousin bonds was expressed in a number of proverbs such as "*nar al-qarib wa la jinnat al-gharib,*" or "the hell-fire of a relative is better than the paradise of a stranger."[10] In such a match, the families of the couple shared not only a common lineage, but also common values and lifestyles and inherited property was retained within the extended family. Despite the prevalence of this ideal, in fact most people did not marry paternal cousins. People did usually marry within the extended family, or a cluster of families who tended to intermarry. The emphasis on a shared background between marriage partners furthered the strong social ideal of "permanent" marriage. Divorce, while permissible in Islam, was highly discouraged in this society and was not common. Nor was it common for a man to have more than one wife within Hadhramawt, although many emigrants had a wife and children in the homeland and another family in the *mahjar,* particularly those who emigrated to Southeast Asia.

The first stage of marriage negotiations between families took place through an indirect approach. A woman from a family with a boy or girl of marriageable age would visit the family with a suitable potential partner and inquire. After the subject of marriage was brought into the open, the guardians of the boy and girl met to formalize the engagement and set the wedding date. Assisted by an intermediary, they agreed on the trousseau and the bridal money (*mahr*) which the groom's family would provide. The girl was not informed of the matter. Neither bride nor groom had the right to refuse to participate in a marriage arranged by their parents. They met on the wedding day, although they may have had some contact as children.

After the agreement on engagement, the groom's family gathered the trousseau. The *mahr* consisted of cash, to provide security for the bride in case of divorce, abandonment, or widowhood. Different families and tribes had customary standards for the *mahr,* the amount of which did not correspond to the prestige of the social group or the wealth of the family. The entire sum was not always paid, although the husband then legally owed it to his wife. The trousseau consisted of dresses, cloth, and household goods. During the early twentieth century, the standard for the trousseau was raised. Dresses, cloth, and pillows and cushions were expected to be fine silks and embroidered materials and the household goods became increasingly elaborate, including copper and brass utensils and imported coffee and tea services of silver and china. After the goods were presented to the bride's family, the engagement was announced and members of the community went to congratulate the bride's family and view the displayed trousseau.[11]

The wedding festivities were initiated with the setting up of coffee and tea services and everything needed to provide hospitality. Among *sada* and *mashayikh*, relatives presented gifts of sheep as *tarh* to the father of the groom; among other groups, relatives contributed cash. Women danced, sang, and ululated at a party in the groom's house while the feasts were prepared. This day was called *yawm al-mubaraka*, or day of congratulations, except in Tarim, where it was called *yawm ka'da*.

The next day was called *yawm al-dahina*, day of anointing, since an anointing ceremony took place after the afternoon prayers. Earlier that afternoon there was a public procession and performance (*'aradh*) by the *ahl al-hara* if the wedding families were from particular groups. If the families were from the Sultan's family, the *sada*, or *mashayikh*, *ahl al-hara* performed in their honor. They also performed when the marriage took place within their own group. In the *'aradh*, the wedding families and notable guests gathered in an open area on the outskirts of town or in a square. The musicians, drummers, and flute players who accompanied wedding processions met the *ahl al-hara* and to the accompaniment of the musicians, they sang, drummed, and performed assertive line dances, stepping, whirling, and beating staffs rhythmically on the ground as they processed through the streets to the house of the groom.

That evening, festivities took place at both the bride's and groom's houses. The party for the groom, called *al-dahina* (anointing) or *al-mariya*, took place in an open space lit with lamps fueled with kerosene, or in the case of poorer families, lamps fueled with locally produced sesame oil. In the 1920s, lamps fueled by pressurized white gas, called *kahraban*, became popular among those who could afford them. Cushions were put down for elderly and honored guests near a throne of cushions on which the groom sat with his feet propped up to be anointed with oil, perfume, and henna. The rest of the crowd sat or stood, surrounding the clearing where men took turns dancing in pairs.

Details of the *dahina* varied depending on the social group of the groom. The *dahina* of members of the arms-bearing groups included weapons fire. Particular kinds of drums and flutes were played for ceremonies of *sada*, *mashayikh*, and *qaba'il*. Men of the *qaba'il*, the *'abid*, and the *dhu'afa'* performed characteristic dances for grooms from their group. The *dahina* of the *masakin* included performance of the *'idda*, a line dance in which the dancers bore a stick and small shield, before the house of the leader of their town quarter.[12] At the same time as the *dahina*, festivities called *al-hika'*, which included the *qabdha* or "seizure" of the bride, took place at the home of the bride. Married women guests gathered with the bride-to-be, who was attended by a woman specialist called *al-kubara*. Other attendants sat on either side of the bride, fanned her, and tended incense burners. If the bride was from the *sada*, the attendants also invoked praise of the Prophet and his descendants. During the festivities, the mother of the bride suddenly threw a green cloth over her, confining and covering her body, saying "we join you in marriage to so and so," which was the girl's first overt news of the marriage and the identity of the groom. While the women in the room drummed and ululated, the bride cried or pretended to do so. Absence of crying would have indicated that the bride was eager to marry, a shameful situation, but the women did not expect the girl to be genuinely alarmed about the situation. They were satisfied to hear feigned sobs, since the onlookers and the girl herself considered marriage to be the fruition of her girlhood and a step to the higher status of married woman and eventually mother. In some places, the *qabdha* was called *rabut* or "joining," after the announcement that the girl would be joined with the groom. Later the women prepared the bride for the upcoming wedding night, decorating her hands and feet with henna. Women from *al-huwik* specialized in bridal preparation washed and oiled the bride's hair and braided it into numerous fine plaits.[13]

The following day, known as *al-ghussa*, included the *'aqd*, the signing of the contract, and the men's procession known as the *harawa*. The women gathered to present gifts to the bride. Women ululated and the band drummed and sang as women danced in pairs. Some women did the *na'ish* dance in which they flipped their long hair from side to side. Finally the bride sat on a round eating mat of woven palm leaves called a *tifal* while the women danced around her and flipped their hair above her head. In the 1920s, prosperous families replaced the *tifal* on which the bride sat with imported silk cushions.[14]

Later in the day was the *harawa*, or procession of the groom and his entourage to the bride's house for the signing of the contract. More than any other part of the wedding, this was a public event. When the groom was from a prominent family, the procession drew large crowds of participants. Even when the groom came from modest circumstances, the procession drew the attention of bystanders from the streets and homes and businesses along the route.

A *harawa* for a member of the sultan's family or a *munsib*'s family was a special public event in which various groups took part. The procession moved to the beat of drums and followed a raised standard. The groom rode a horse or, after the import of motorcars in the 1930s, might ride in a car. On each side of the groom an attendant wafted incense from a burner. Behind the groom and guests from the religiously prestigious groups, the *qaba'il* processed in their tribal groups, each chanting the *zamil* or poem with which they accompanied processions. Behind the tribesmen, the *'abid* followed, chanting their *zamil* to the accompaniment of drums and the *mizmar*, the short flute. Behind them, the *ahl al-hara* performed their processional line dance, singing, chanting, and pounding the ground with their staffs as they moved.

For other *sada* families, the *harawa* was distinguished by the groom's riding a horse or riding in a car and by the presence of several attendants fanning the groom and wafting incense along the path. A special musical group accompanied the *harawa* of *sada*, playing drums and the long flute, singing and chanting in praise of the Prophet and his descendants. In Tarim, these musicians came from a select group of the *ahl al-hara* known as Khuddam al-Saqqaf, who wore a distinctive style of black headcloth. The *'udhba* or groom's wedding garb for the *sada* included a cap with a tassel on the side and encircling scarf with a tail hanging down the back, and a green scarf draped around the back of the neck and hanging down the chest. The splendor of these processions was enhanced by the number of *rijal al-din,* men of religion, in attendance at the front of the procession, distinguishable by their long white coats and white turbans. Some religious leaders walked at the front of the procession in every wedding, even that of the humblest members of the populace, but in weddings of the *sada* their numbers were greatest.[15]

The *harawa* of the *mashayikh* was simpler and quieter than the *harawa* of other groups, but maintained its own air of stately splendor, with the groom walking at the front of the crowd with an attendant. The *harawa* of the *qaba'il* included rifle fire. An attendant and a few *rijal al-din* walked with the groom, with the tribesmen following, chanting and firing their weapons as they processed. The *harawa* of the *'abid* also began with rifle fire and included chanting and the sound of drums and *mizmar.* The groom, accompanied by an attendant, wore the wedding garb characteristic of this group and carried a staff. Among the *masakin,* the *harawa* proceeded as a noisy celebration, with *ahl al-hara* performing their line dance behind the groom and his attendant. Among the *dhu'afa',* the crowd chanted as they walked, with lines of men pounding the ground with staffs to provide the beat for the chanting.[16]

At the house of the bride, the groom, his family, and the religious notables entered the house, where the groom and the father or guardian of the bride signed the contract sealing the marriage. After the signing, the family of the bride served a feast. That evening there was another procession, *al-zafaf,* which accompanied the bride to the groom's house for *laylat al-dukhla,* "night of entering." This procession was similar among social groups. First women surrounded the bride, singing and drumming, later the unmarried girls visited the bride. In the evening, the married women gathered in a courtyard or temporary courtyard fashioned outside the bride's house to sing and dance. Sometimes a female poet from the bride's family, or one hired for the occasion, presented a poem of praise (*khayb'an*) to the bride and her family. This event was called *al-musamara* (literally, "chatting") and women passed the evening and most of the night relaxing and chatting, with the bride waiting inside. Toward the middle of the night, the women of the groom's family and their guests joined the bride's family and their guests. Shortly afterward, the groom was taken among the collected women and placed on a seat in front of them. Since the groom would not have been among so many unrelated women since he was a small child, he found it intimidating to be separated from the men and surrounded by perfume, incense, and a mass of women who were assessing him, discussing him, and periodically emitting high, shrill ululations.

After that, the groom met inside with the bride and her mother and presented the bride's mother with gifts, called *shuna.* The crowds of women guests massed outside for the *zafaf,* the procession of the covered bride and groom from her house to his. This procession was similar for all, except that a bride from the *sada* might ride a horse or be carried in a litter. Other than that, differences depended on wealth rather than social group, with wealthier families able to light the procession with pressure gas lamps, more modest families using kerosene lamps, and the poor having to use sesame oil lamps. This procession was dominated by women, who sang, chanted, and ululated as they moved along, the men following.

When the procession reached the specially prepared room at the groom's house, the women accompanied the bride and groom inside to congratulate them. When the couple was finally left alone near dawn, the women remained outside, ululating periodically. The groom was expected to be patient in his approach to the bride. This was symbolically expressed in his first duty, which was to remove her veil and the elaborate array of bracelets, necklaces, earrings, rings, ceremonial head-piece, and silver belts she was wearing and arrange them in a case. This society did not emphasize a quick consummation of the marriage. The young men knew the proverb "*al-hurma maniha, ma dhabiha.*" Literally, "a wife is for milking, not for slaughter," this signified that the marriage existed as a long-term partnership for the purpose of raising offspring. The groom was to be conscious of that, rather than considering the occasion as an opportunity to satisfy physical desire.[17]

The following morning, guests gathered for another celebration, the *subha*, in which they congratulated the bride and groom and their families. Prosperous families began to set the standard of hosting a feast for this occasion. Later there was a women's party called a *zilla*, which was open to all. Women came to this event to congratulate the bride, who sat in all her finery, until she danced among the guests for her first time as a married woman. The celebrations continued even after the end of the wedding. In the week following the wedding, the bride's family hosted feasts, called *khutra* in the interior and *tuhzira*, among other names, on the coast.[18]

Death

The final collective ceremony in the life of an individual took place after death. The observations after a death included three elements: the preparation and disposition of the body, ritual observances on behalf of the soul, and the settling of the affairs and property of the deceased. In the case of this most profound of transitions, the public ceremonies were essentially the same for all social groups, with some variation according to the prominence and wealth of the individual who had died. Most people left a will that included instructions for their funeral. All adults were encouraged to write a will and most did so at the time of their father's death. The will always began with the testimony of faith, and included a summation of Islamic belief, particularly with regard to the Judgement Day and the afterlife. It included instructions for preparing the body for burial, carrying out the necessary religious observances, paying the providers of services, and offering hospitality to those who attended.[19] Some people hesitated to take cognizance of their mortality, as indicated by a Hadhrami proverb which counseled "*al-wasa ma taqta' 'amr*" or "writing a will does not shorten your life span."[20]

When a person died, a companion whispered the *shahada* (the Muslim profession of faith, "There is no god but God, and Muhammad is the Messenger of

God") in his or her ear in order that the deceased person be accompanied by the testimony of faith through the passage to the afterlife. Immediately after a death, the family began to pray and recite the Qur'an, particularly the chapter Ya Sin, on behalf of the deceased, and to take care of practical matters. Neighbors often learned of the death by hearing the wails and cries of the women of the family and came to join in the prayers and recitation. While it was common for women to wail and cry after a death in the family, some opposed such outpourings of grief on the grounds that it suggested lack of acceptance of God's will. Some specified in their wills that the family not cry or wail, but pray and recite the Qur'an.

Someone from the family went to the muqaddam of their urban quarter or village to report the death. The *muqaddam* arranged for providers of services who specialized in the tasks of announcing the death, washing and laying out the body, carrying the body on a wooden bier to the mosque (if the deceased was a man) and to the cemetery, digging the grave, and filling it. After notifying the *muqaddam,* the family members bought the materials for the service provider to use in preparing the body, the winding sheet (*kafan*), and coffee to serve to the reciters of the Qur'an and guests.[21]

The service provider washed the body in the home, following Islamic law and local custom. Sometimes the will specified that the washing be supervised by a member of the *'ulama'* or other agents of the deceased. A man washed men's bodies and a woman washed women's. The requirement of women's modesty continued even after death, when the women's private parts were covered during washing by a piece of cloth cut from her winding sheet. The service provider washed the body, closed the eyes, applied preserving substances, and wrapped the body in the winding-sheet. For a man the shroud, a length of white cloth folded into thirds, was wrapped around the body three times and tied, and for a woman the shroud material was cut and sewn into a shapeless dress, head cover, and face cover. The body was washed with *ghussa,* the dried powdered leaves of the acacia tree, and rubbed with ground camphor. Some wills delineated the preparation of the body in great detail, while others merely stated that the body be handled appropriately to the social and economic status of the deceased. The will of a prosperous tribeswoman stated that her body be handled "*bi-amthaliha halan wa malan,*" that is, "as those like her in station and wealth."[22]

Social status and wealth made little difference in the handling of the body except for the amount of preserving materials and incense used. The critical part of the washing process was the same for all: the body was washed in a way corresponding to the *wudhu'* or ritual cleansing done before prayer, so that the deceased entered the afterlife in a state of ritual purity. Some people kept a winding cloth stored in a chest in preparation for their deaths, a prudent act in a place where recurrent famine could result in a shortage of the cloth preferred for shrouds, leaving only jute sack cloth.[23]

Family members also arranged observations on behalf of the soul of the deceased. When a death took place at night or late in the day, the burial did not take place until the following day, and relatives, neighbors, and community members recited the Qur'an throughout the night in the presence of the body. Just as the muqaddam was notified of a death in order to organize the service providers, the *munsib* or other spiritual leader was notified to guide the Qur'an recitation and spiritual observances.[24]

During the day, the body of a man was taken to the neighborhood mosque for further recitation of the Qur'an and then from the mosque to the cemetery, where recitation continued. After a *sayyid* died, the mourners accompanying the body as it was carried to the mosque and from the mosque to the graveyard performed a special chant to commemorate the death of a descendant of the Prophet. In Tarim, the Khuddam al-Saqqaf accompanied the funeral processions of *sada* with chanting, joined by students from the religious institutions.

When a public figure such as a sultan or a respected religious leader died, his body was taken to the *jami'* or congregational mosque, where crowds came to pay their last respects. In these cases, the streets through which the body was carried and the square next to the *jami'* resounded with prayers and devotions performed on behalf of the dead. In the case of spiritual leaders, crowds gathered around the bier in order to receive *baraka,* blessings, through proximity to the pious one whose spirit was believed to be in the presence of God while his body was among them. When the body of a person of spiritual authority was carried through the streets, people attempted to approach God symbolically through contact with the bier. While professional pallbearers were hired to carry the body as usual, mourners joined in, rotating in and out of position, taking turns shouldering the bier momentarily as it made its passage accompanied by throngs of mourners.[25]

Continuous recitation of the Qur'an over the deceased person comforted the mourners and was thought to ease the passage of the soul. For men's funeral observations, recitation of the Qur'an took place at the home, in the mosque, at the head of the grave during burial, and over the grave after burial. The body of a woman was laid out at home and the Qur'an was recited there and at the grave during and after burial. The recitation of the Qur'an was done in sections, each of which was called a *khatma* or *sharwa,* and continued over three or four days. The reciters were given refreshments and money, except for the *munsib,* who recited without pay as part of his duty as community spiritual leader. The reciters were not a specialized professional group like the body washers and gravediggers, but were neighbors of the deceased and members of the community. Most were from the *sada* and *mashayikh,* since they had access to religious education. The family of the deceased served coffee to the reciters, and the prosperous provided for them to be sprinkled with rose water and wafted with smoke from incense. Those who could afford it also bequeathed a meal of rice and goat meat to the reciters and other mourners. Some people left instructions in their wills for particular individuals to recite the Qur'an after their death.[26]

The proper observation of a funeral involved significant expenses for embalming materials, service providers, and hospitality.[27] At the same time, this society included many people who were poor and died in debt. Services for poor people were paid for by *waqf* funds, the income produced by properties left as pious donations. In the market town of Shibam, the money for poor people's burial services was endowed by commerce, through the fees paid for use of the massive scale (*qubban*) in the city center on which sacks were weighed for the wholesale trade. For the poor, these charitable funds paid for the service providers and Qur'an reciters, minimal amounts of embalming materials, and coffee for guests.[28]

Prosperous individuals often left bequests for alms to be distributed to the poor during funeral observations. The poor collected allotments of cash, grain, or dates, and invoked mercy on the spirit of the deceased. People from different social groups made such bequests, with the sultans making particularly generous ones, commensurate with their public role in society.[29] Besides bequeathing alms, some people bequeathed additional observances such as special recitations, acts of charity, and acts performed for the benefit of their spirit. The latter were known as *wahba* or *wahbat thawab*, pious acts done by the living for the benefit of the spirit of the departed. Many who bequeathed additional observances were wealthy, but not all, and some wealthy people did not bequeath such acts.

Sultan al-Mansur b. Ghalib al-Kathiri, ruler of the Kathiri state, provided a spectacular example of extra bequests. He bequeathed that twelve hundred pounds of dates be distributed on the day of his burial, along with one thousand eighty pounds of grain. He left seven hundred *riyals* as an endowment to purchase date palms, the production of which would pay people to recite a section of the Qur'an daily over his grave. An additional seven hundred *riyals* endowed palm trees, the proceeds of which would pay people to recite four *ashraf*, that is, two chapters of the Qur'an, Ya Sin and Tabarak, at the graves of his father, mother, wife, and daughter. He left six hundred *riyals* to hire someone to do the Hajj and visit the Prophet's tomb, greet the Prophet and ask forgiveness on the Sultan's behalf, and to butcher a sheep at 'Id al-Adhha every year for twenty-five years for him. He left money for someone to recite the *shahada* seventy thousand times for his sake, and to say "*subhan Allah*" (Praise God) five thousand times. He left money for sections of the Qur'an to be recited for the benefit of his soul during Ramadhan, paying three *riyals* for each. He also paid for someone to pray five times a day on his behalf for a year after his death.

The Sultan left money for alms as well: ninety pounds of wheat and rice, one hundred pounds of dates, and five hundred *riyals* to be distributed among the poor each day for the last ten days of Ramadhan. Ninety pounds of sorghum, wheat, and rice were to be distributed in the Hajj month and also in the month of Rajab. Every Friday, six pounds of grain and five pounds of dates were to be distributed as alms to the very poor. In a revision of the will, the Sultan added provision for a fund so that a poor family would receive five *riyals* upon the birth of a child, and a poor man or woman would receive seven *riyals* at the time of marriage. This fund also provided a riyal for a poor woman at Ramadhan and two *riyals* for a poor man. The Sultan died in 1929 while on the Hajj, and people re-

member to this day both the grace of his death at 'Arafat and the generosity of his
bequests to his subjects.[30]

Sultan al-Mansur's contemporary, the wealthy Sayyid Muhammad b.
Husayn al-Saqqaf, endowed a number of charitable acts and forgave the debts he
held. He ordered the return to his debtors of the custody of two houses he held
and the return of brass, silver, and gold items he held as security for loans. He endowed one pious act to be done for the benefit of his soul, forgiving the debt owed
him by brothers on the condition that they recite sections of the Qur'an on behalf
of his soul, according to a prior agreement.[31]

People from all social groups often endowed charitable acts and pious acts
to be done on behalf of their departed spirits, although not on such a grand scale
as Sultan al-Mansur. *Sada* and *mashayikh* did so, but prosperous men and women
from the *qaba'il* in particular endowed those acts as an expression of piety and perhaps as a means of compensation for the fact that those of their station typically
did not participate in religious study or extensive spiritual practice.[32] People from
the humbler groups also endowed charitable acts when they could afford to do so.
For example, in 1911 a farmer bequeathed the income from three clusters of palm
trees to pay for recitation of the Qur'an over his grave.[33]

At the same time that the body was prepared for burial and rites were performed on behalf of the soul of the deceased, the process of distribution of his or
her property was implemented. Immediately after a death, the executor of the estate was notified and as soon as possible he met with the family and took possession of legal papers belonging to the deceased and keys to trunks and storage
rooms. He also read the will to the assembled family. In accordance with the Shafi'i
tradition of Islamic jurisprudence, the bulk of the estate was distributed to heirs
according to the formula laid out in the Qur'an, a complicated process which in
some cases required the services of legal experts specialized in the division and distribution of estates (*qisma*). But one third of the estate could be distributed according to the wishes of the deceased as indicated in the will. These discretionary
bequests included charitable contributions and gifts of money, land, houses, clothing, furniture, utensils, weapons, or jewelry to individuals.[34]

A special case of charitable act was that of the manumission of a slave upon
the death of his owner. A person who wished to bequeath in his will the freeing of
a loyal slave faced the dilemma that doing so at the time of death removed part of
the property from his estate. The problem was solved by a practical device allowed
by Shafi'i law as interpreted and elaborated in Hadhramawt. For example, some
members of the Kasadi family had inherited personal slaves who often served their
owners in the role of business manager. They left instructions in their wills for manumission, stating that the slave be freed before the owner's death "by a day." This
"retroactive manumission," taking place upon the death of the owner, freed the
slave without compromising the integrity of the estate.[35]

The disposition of the estate broke the last of an individual's ties to the material world. After a death, the living continued a period of mourning that varied

depending on circumstances. After the death of a man, following the *shari'a*, his wife was isolated during a period called the *'idda*. This period of isolation lasted four months and ten days for a woman of childbearing age and forty days for a woman past childbearing age. During this time, the woman wore no adornments, perfume, or cosmetics, stayed hidden from everyone except her closest relatives, and refrained even from looking at herself in the mirror. Each Friday, the other women in her family as well as neighbors came to offer prayers for mercy on the deceased and to recite portions of the Qur'an. For a period of as much as a year, the family might observe a period of mourning by limiting festivities and display at celebrations of other events within the family such as weddings or births.[36]

The observances of a death were similar for the different groups, except that the death of a person of spiritual prestige offered the mourners a special opportunity to feel near God even as they grieved. Because of charitable endowments for the purpose, the poor had access to the same essential services as the rich. As in other observances, the families of the wealthy offered greater hospitality to their guests by holding feasts for the mourners. Excessive public displays associated with the death of spiritually prestigious persons and the holding of feasts as part of the funeral observations drew the attention of social reformers who criticized the increasing ostentation of the celebrations marking births and weddings.

Increasing Display in Celebrations of Rites of Passage

During the late nineteenth century, the increase in wealth from the *mahjar* and the increasing availability of imported goods altered the social meaning of these celebrations of rites of passage. They more and more became displays of family wealth, in which families that had prospered in the *mahjar* set the standard. The public nature of the celebrations meant that standards of expectation were raised among the society as a whole, even though there were many who benefited little from the new prosperity.

Expectations were raised on a number of levels. The number of separate parties included in the observation of a wedding or a birth increased. At the same time, the standard for hospitality at the parties was raised. Even at large receptions, it became necessary to serve refreshments, which increasingly included imported tea and novelties such as European-style cakes and cookies made with finely ground flour and white sugar. The number of feasts that had to be served as part of a celebration grew, as did the range of guests who had to be served refreshments or meals. More service providers were hired to function as attendants and performers. Within the family celebrating, more gifts were required, with the gifts being displayed to guests. Within the otherwise austere home furnishings, silk cushions and pillows and elaborate tea services were displayed at the celebrations. In addition, there was a veritable "arms race" in women's dresses and ornamentation. New styles of jewelry and clothing of fine fabrics, influenced by East Indies and European fashions, were introduced by the wealthy families and imitated by others.

Since the celebrations of rites of passage normally consisted of a number of different parties and gatherings, women guests had the opportunity to don new outfits several times during an event. Regardless of social group or wealth, people tried at great cost to keep up with the new standards being set.[37]

Criticism of Social Practice and Ostentation

Not surprisingly, criticism arose of the tendency toward increasing display in the celebrations of rites of passage, and the problem of ostentation in hospitality and public display in general. Since the celebration of rites of passage was an essential part of every family's participation in the larger social order, increasing pressure to use imported fashions placed a burden on those families without access to wealth and goods from the *mahjar*. This problem was addressed on several levels, with the sultanates and reform-minded civic organizations attempting to regulate social display, and with concerned individuals attempting to increase public awareness of the problem through articles in the new print media. This criticism condemned ostentation as a breach of moral behavior and a transgression against society. Since women's dress and ornamentation and the showing of the trousseau and other gifts figured significantly as opportunities for displays of opulence, the morality of women's modesty was incorporated into the critiques.

State and Civil Attempts to Regulate Social Display

In the early twentieth century, the impulse to social reform was manifested by attempts to impose standards of behavior through what might be called "sumptuary regulations." Reformers considered the increasing materialism and ostentation displayed by the wealthy and imitated at all levels of the society to be a matter of public concern. Attempts to prohibit or to limit behaviors felt detrimental to the society were initiated by different groups of citizens concerned about the negative social effects of ostentation and competition in social and material display. On the urging of concerned subjects, the sultan promulgated official proclamations prohibiting or limiting ostentation. Although the authority of the state was brought to bear, it was difficult to regulate private behavior, even when it was related to celebrations of rites of passage, which included events of a public nature.

Continual revisions of the sultan's proclamations indicated the degree to which his subjects continually evaded or subverted the regulations. Wedding celebrations consisted of several parts lasting over several days including "after parties" in the week following the wedding. When the sultan forbade serving food or tea during the ceremony, people adapted by serving it at a different time or by sending gifts of food to in-laws in lieu of a feast. Similarly, since women's fashions were elaborate and constantly changing, people adapted to prohibitions of fashion by introducing new clothing and jewelry styles after old ones were prohibited, thus accelerating the competition.

In 1923, the Kathiri sultan issued a proclamation of sumptuary regulations at the urging of influential subjects inclined toward social reform, who had compiled a list of customs that needed to be prohibited for the good of the society. The sultan ordered obedience of the prohibitions because of the social evil caused by those customs. Competition in the ostentatious display of material wealth forced men to migrate in search of fortune and caused the homeland to suffer the lack of the emigrants' contribution to society at the same time that their wives and children suffered the absence of their husbands and fathers.

The proclamation stated that competition among women with respect to clothing decorated with embroidery, cowry shells, and jewels had become excessive. As a corrective measure, twenty-eight articles detailed the prohibition or limitation of various types of ostentation in dress, display, and celebrations. These included the prohibition of the wearing of clothing made of silk and other delicate fabrics and of clothing decorated with beads and other adornments. Wearing silk was prohibited at all events except for certain specified parts of a wedding celebration; the wearing of certain types of jewelry was similarly limited. Silk and jewelry were allowed for the bride during her wedding celebration, for a woman whose husband had just returned from abroad, or for a woman who was celebrating having given birth. All precious stones including diamonds were prohibited, although imitation stones were acceptable, and any new style or innovation in jewelry was prohibited. This proclamation specifically prohibited the wearing of a "Javan" style blouse called a *til*, which sometimes had gold decorations, and of other decorated types of clothing of Asian origin. The wearing of ankle bracelets was forbidden, although an exception was allowed for the bride during certain portions of the wedding celebration. Women were prohibited from wearing anything "flashy" in the streets; their under-trousers were to be white or match the color of the dress. There was a limitation on the number and types of tea-making devices and cups that a bride could bring to her marriage. Silk cushions, decorated pillows, and silk handbags were prohibited. Certain portions of the wedding celebrations were limited to women and specified male relatives. Welcoming parties for returned emigrants were limited to one party after arrival, with no parties preceding the emigrant's return. Similarly, celebrations of a birth were limited to the third day after a birth only and not to be held on other days. There was to be no celebratory luncheon feast on either the day of birth or the third day. Feasts were prohibited as observations of deaths as well. Drumming was prohibited in women's gatherings other than wedding celebrations. The proclamation extended beyond matters of ostentation and display in ceremonies by forbidding women to go out for the nighttime prayers in Ramadhan, directly addressing and limiting women's public behavior outside the sphere of ceremonies and parties. The proclamation allowed women to wear what they already had until the middle of the following month. It challenged those who failed to abide by its strictures as contributing to the misery of the poor.[38]

A dialectic of sorts developed. Individuals advised the sultan of customs that he should prohibit, because previous prohibitions of them had been ignored or because previous prohibitions had resulted in the development of new customs and fashions, requiring new regulations. In some cases when prohibitions of practices failed, it was later attempted merely to limit them. Thus the sultan had to issue periodic revisions of these regulations.

In 1931, one of the *sada* wrote to the sultan advising some revisions of prohibited customs. He recommended that silk be allowed in dresses in limited yardage, although the til should be forbidden in any fabric. For the bride's "throne," only one cushion should be allowed, and no silk pillows. Jewelry and implements for coffee and tea service were also limited. This individual's suggestions indicated a connection between women's ostentation and their sexuality. He stated that women might wear any type of prohibited finery, including gold belts, when they were at home alone with their husband. He recommended that henna decorations of women's hands and feet be prohibited, claiming that they encouraged illicit sexuality. He also recommended the prohibition of events in which unrelated men and women mixed.[39]

In 1933, the sultan issued a new proclamation prohibiting ostentation in celebrations, apparel, and jewelry. This proclamation forbade giving the bride tea equipment. It also prohibited any display of the clothing and household items she took into the marriage, even among the bride's or the groom's families. Serving lunch on the third day of the wedding celebration was limited to women only; and serving tea and supper on the first and second days of the wedding was forbidden. A week after the wedding, serving lunch was permitted only to the immediate relatives of bride and groom and serving supper was permitted only to the couple and their parents. It was prohibited for women to wear glittering dresses or veils or dresses with gold yokes. A number of jewelry items were prohibited and value limitations were placed on other items. Silver necklaces, ropes, bracelets, and ankle bracelets were limited in weight to the value of a *riyal.* Any new styles of jewelry were prohibited.

Articles specifically addressing the *masakin* or lower-status social groups dealt primarily with expenditures related to marriage. In the case of a virgin bride, her trousseau was limited to thirty *riyals* in cash and ten *riyals* worth of goods, while the *mahr* was limited to six *riyals.* In the case of a previously married woman, the trousseau was limited to twenty *riyals* cash and four of goods, while the *mahr* was again six *riyals.* Celebrations on the third day of the wedding were forbidden and supper on that day was limited to women of the family. Expensive silk dresses were prohibited.[40]

Less than a year later, the sultan set out another set of prohibitions, superseding earlier ones. It specified the portions of the wedding ceremony at which feasts were permissible and limited the guests for different events to specific family members. It forbade tea service on the first and second days of the wedding celebration. The communal wedding procession was prohibited, as was display of the trousseau. All gifts were forbidden and gifts of clothing from the groom to the bride were limited to her wedding apparel. Stricter limitations were placed on jewelry. Limitations were set on marriage-related expenditures, although those for the masakin were relaxed somewhat.[41] Revisions of the limitations on marriage expenses were necessary because people resisted them. The imposition of limits on the trousseau provided by the bride's family and on the bride price from the groom's family was perceived as an affront, a devaluation of the worth of the bride and by extension the honor of the families. Copies of these proclamations were sent to respected members of the community, who were responsible for seeing that people knew of them and followed them. The proclamations were also posted publicly in the marketplace, where names of those who disobeyed the regulations were also posted.[42]

Some sets of regulations were created specifically for particular social groups. In 1931, the Kathiri sultan proclaimed a set of regulations concerning dress and wedding ceremonies for slaves. As in other social groups, competition had developed in the arenas of wedding celebration and women's clothing among this group, not surprising since members of this group held high positions in the military and the administration. But since members of this group did not emigrate and so lacked access to money and goods from the *mahjar,* such competition was particularly onerous for them and perhaps also for those under their authority. The proclamation stated that marriages among slaves were voluntary. Money donations and all other gifts were prohibited. The *zilla,* third day of the wedding celebration, and gatherings the week after the wedding were prohibited. Decorated clothing was prohibited, with specific mention of the Javan *til,* and any innovation in clothing for women of this social group was prohibited.[43]

In 1936, the Kathiri sultan found it necessary to issue another proclamation regulating the marriage customs of the *'abid* group. This proclamation was approved and signed by eight individuals, leaders among the *'abid,* on behalf of themselves, their families, and all connected with them. Articles limited the amount of the trousseau for brides from this group to nineteen *riyals.* The feast on the third day of the wedding was allowed but guests were limited to fifty and the total expenditures were limited to twenty-five *riyals.* For a previously married bride, the trousseau was limited to eight *riyals* and the feast was limited to twenty-five guests with an expenditure of twelve *riyals.* While total expenditures were limited to twenty *riyals,* additional expenditures were allowed for: the mother of the bride; the bride's professional attendant; the musicians who performed during the procession; and the camel-attendant for the procession. The total number of service providers for the *harawa* or procession from the bride's to the groom's house, including camel attendants and musicians, was limited to ten for the wedding of a virgin and five for the wedding of a previously married woman. It was forbidden to have additional parties after the wedding celebration. Serving coffee or cookies was forbidden, as were gifts. Silk dresses in styles favored by this group (*zaytun* and *'anab*) were prohibited. Women guests were allowed only one dress for the wedding celebrations and bringing a carrying case with additional dresses for different parts of the celebration was forbidden. The custom of guests giving money during the dancing was prohibited. Particular styles of silver jewelry were prohibited, while others were allowed.[44]

In addition to advising the sultan regarding proclamations regulating consumption and prohibiting ostentation, organizations of reform-minded subjects produced their own proclamations and regulations that they expected the public to obey. In Tarim, the reform organization Jam'iyat al-Haqq focused its attention on public morality from its inception in late 1915. Early discussions considered excessive public display in times of celebration and also times of mourning. In several sessions the committee discussed appropriate behavior during funerals. They mandated that condolence visits should be limited to one day and restricted to the home of the deceased and that during the procession from the house of the deceased to the cemetery the mourners were to move quickly and silently. In several sessions the committee discussed appropriate behavior during celebrations, particularly weddings. They prohibited women from ululating in the streets and forbade the use of excessive lighting for outdoor celebrations at night. In the procession (*zafaf*) which accompanied the bride to the groom's home, the bride was forbidden to ride a horse although walking, riding a donkey, or being borne in a litter were permitted. The committee enjoined separation of the sexes in these events: the bride's guardian was prohibited from taking her into the women's gathering; and during the procession, women were not to leave the bride's house for that of the groom until the men had completed their journey. When it was reported that a prominent member of the community had failed to comply with the injunction against the bride being carried on a horse during the wedding procession and that others had then followed his example, the committee wrote the violator to complain about his behavior.[45]

Jam'iyat al-Haqq published what they called "compulsory" regulations in 1939, the elaboration of a set of regulations previously issued in 1933. They justified the regulations for both moral and economic reasons, and for both the private and the public good. The pamphlet averred that transgressors would be punished, although the mechanism for punishment was not specified. The sumptuary regulations issued by Jam'iyat al-Haqq in Tarim were extensive in coverage and precise in detail, in response to the flamboyance that had developed among the wealthy members of this community.

Tarim's reformers came up with an extensive list of goods and behaviors to prohibit or to limit: the great wealth acquired in the East Indies had led to the import of showy goods and fashions and to a competition in hospitality. Even the founding spirit and leader of this reform organization, the prominent Sayyid Abu Bakr b. Shaykh al-Kaf, used his great wealth not only in public largesse but also for constructing opulent homes filled with imported luxuries and modern conveniences, for importing splendid jewelry and clothing from Asia and Europe for the women in his family, and for lavishly entertaining visiting Europeans and local people. Still, his paramount position among the wealthiest and most generous families of Tarim provided him an impeccable position from which to oppose the acceleration of competition and his prominence and success protected him from the charges of envy that could potentially undo such a reformer.

The fifty-six articles of the organization's list of prohibited customs were divided into six sections: weddings; feasts; celebrations honoring births, circumcisions, deaths, and travelers; jewelry; clothing; home furnishings and appliances. The organization prohibited: ululation in ceremonies; use of pressurized white-gas lamps for nighttime outdoor wedding ceremonies (and limited the number of kerosene lamps to four); any special decoration or display on the donkey of a bride in procession. Some of the proscribed elements, such as ululation, were not related to monetary expenditure but simply to drawing the attention of the public to ceremonial events. The performance of a poem praising the groom and his family was forbidden, as was dancing by the women to a song in praise of the groom. More directly related to costs were the proscriptions on gifts. Certain gifts were prohibited: gifts of goats from the bride's to the groom's family; gifts of cookies and layer cakes to families of the bridal couple; and gifts to the groom from the bride's mother and grandmother. Other gifts were limited. Gifts to the bride while she was being made up were limited to five *riyals* from close relatives, one riyal from distant ones, and forbidden for others. Gifts presented as *shuna* from the groom to the mother of the bride were limited to ten *riyals* and to the grandmother, five *riyals*. Breakfast bread during the wedding had to be the usual whole wheat unleavened bread (*subuh*), not cakes or cookies. It was specified that when the bride was removed from among the women and taken to the groom, that it should be done by a woman with no male assistance. The feasts of the first night of the wedding were restricted to limited numbers of guests. Later feasts were also limited, while feasts for the celebration of the last day of the wedding and for parties in honor of the bridal couple held after the wedding were forbidden. When feasts were allowed, meat was to be prepared in a simple fashion, and the preparation of special foods for particular guests was prohibited.

Gifts for a birth were forbidden, except for a first birth, when they were limited to fifteen *riyals*. At the announcement of a first birth to the relatives, gifts were limited to a *riyal* for the mother and a token to the birth attendant. Feasts for births after the first were severely limited. Only close friends and relatives of a new mother might visit her to congratulate her, and only in the first week after a birth; the congratulatory party known as the *shamma* was prohibited. Similarly, the feast greeting a returning traveler was limited to close relatives and neighbors. Consolation visits to the family of departed travelers were limited to the first week after departure and welcoming visits for returned travelers to the first week after their return. Circumcision feasts were limited to 150 guests. Gifts to a circumcised boy were limited to one riyal; no clothes or food could be given. Women other than close relatives were forbidden to visit the house of a deceased person before the body was removed for burial. Visible symbols of mourning were prohibited more than three days after a death, except for the wife of the deceased. For social gatherings and visits in general, it was prohibited to serve the popular snacks of roasted chickpeas, fava beans, millet and pearl millet, peanuts, and roasted coffee beans, but it was permitted to serve coffee, tea, and *jifil*, a beverage brewed from roasted coffee husks. Hospitality to nighttime visitors during Ramadhan was limited to tea and coffee. Celebrations after completion of Qur'an recitation (*al-khitami*) during Ramadan were limited to one for young girls in the evening and one for young boys at night, and only roasted melon seeds and chickpeas could be served.

It was decreed that women be economical with their dresses. Some opulent dress styles were forbidden: *majuqat*, a dress with wide sleeves and long train; *jawiyat*, and *musadir sarum*, two sarong and blouse combinations; *til dhahabi*, a blouse with gold decorations; and all other decorated dresses. Pillows (*tuka'*) were limited to nine for a bride and groom, and were to be covered in *ghazal*, light woven cloth, rather than silk; all silk cushions were forbidden. The weight of the mattress given a bride was limited to fifty pounds and the stuffing had to be cotton. A *buqsh*, bag for holding clothes made of a colored scarf tied at the four corners, had to be made of cotton rather than silk.

This list of regulations did not prohibit any item of jewelry, but limited the number of items and the weight of each specific item that was permissible. This approach had resulted from resistance to earlier attempts at outright prohibition. The permissible number of *marari* or several-stranded "choker" necklaces was limited to three, weighing no more than five ounces. The necklace style *hurz ra'i* was limited to two ounces. The crescent-shaped necklace *ma'ana* was limited to four ounces, and the big medallion pendant called *shahr wa najm* was limited to six ounces. Bracelets could weigh no more than four ounces. The *maris*, thin ankle bracelet, could weigh only five and a half ounces. Earrings, *karabu*, had to be made of artificial stones (*brilyan*) rather than precious ones. Rings were limited to six. A gold buckle for a silver belt could weigh no more than three ounces. Wide bracelets could weigh no more than four ounces. A bride could wear her elaborate wedding headdress and chains in her hair for only four months after the wedding. Otherwise, silver and gold was prohibited in the hair except for earrings.

For visits, a woman could have one silk dress, while the other had to be made from ordinary woven fabrics. A bride could wear silk for four months. The *najm al-sabah* (morning star) style of dress with a highly decorated yoke was prohibited, as was any dress worth more than fifteen *riyal*s. The number of decorated and embroidered face covers (*niqab*) was limited to two.

With respect to houses and their furnishings, it was prohibited to furnish more than one house for a newly wed couple. Wall decorations were limited to six, including decorative mirrors and hanging pictures. No more than three decorative items could be put in the recessed ledges above windows, and those had to be made of glass, china, silver plate, or base metals, rather than precious materials. Dinner utensils and tea services also had to be made of ordinary materials. Tea-making equipment could not be included in the trousseau. Permitted items of coffee-making equipment were strictly specified and limited in number and displaying them in an open-shelf cabinet was prohibited. The number of jewelry boxes was limited to three and Indian-made kohl boxes to two. Clothing chests were limited to two. For social events and visits, women could only take one carrying case for cosmetics, changes of clothing, and jewelry.

The proclamation included a general principle for making choices in matters of consumption and hospitality: in case of any ambiguity, the correct choice was in the direction of the simpler and the less expensive. It included a warning as well: in the past some people had either accidentally or deliberately disobeyed earlier prohibitions without being punished, but in the future there would be no avoiding punishment for infractions. The extensive coverage, precise detail, and stringent warning in this proclamation indicated that the objects, occasions, and means of lavish display were on the increase in Tarim despite earlier attempts at regulation. The issuance of further announcements in subsequent years suggests that the inclination of the public to display and ostentation continued.[46]

In Say'un, a private organization known as the National Reform Council (Majlis al-Islah al-Watani) proclaimed a similar set of prohibitions, ratified by the sultan. The proclamation forbade all but specified items of jewelry, which were to be worn only singly. Silk dresses were allowed only for a few specified events or inside the home only when no women guests were present. Brides were allowed to wear silk dresses and their wedding jewelry only from their wedding until the first party the following week. Feasts were limited to a restricted number of close family members. Tea utensils and pressurized white-gas lamps were forbidden as part of the trousseau. The smaller number of items in Say'un's list of prohibitions indicated that the social competition had not reached the level of intensity of that of Tarim, with its higher level of wealth.

As time passed, the trend toward prohibition of ostentatious display continued and enforcement became more forthright. In one document, the names of girls who had been guilty of wearing ankle bracelets (*hujul*) were listed, identified by their father's names. Beside each name of girls (all from *sada* and *mashayikh* families) was listed the offense: wearing the hujul. The following page listed the fathers, stating that they were to take the ankle bracelets from their daughters. *Hujul* received special attention for two reasons. Traditionally ankle bracelets had been worn only by *badu* women and the style had only been adopted by other women in the twentieth century, so for settled women to wear them was an innovation and a sign of ostentation. Also, since ankle bracelets were audible even when all jewelry items were hidden by outer garments, they were considered a particularly brazen and obtrusive ornament for settled women to adopt. The *hujul* case exemplified both the association of women's ornamentation with sexuality and the resistance met by the reformers' attempts to regulate women's behavior.[47]

Media Discussion of Ostentation and Display

The handwritten journal *al-Tahdhib* (*Correction*), ten issues of which were published from December 1930 to September 1931, analyzed Hadhrami social issues and issued a call to bring progress by dealing with social ills. The editor, Muhammad Muhsin BaRaja, was the brother-in-law of the poet and social critic 'Ali Ahmad BaKathir, who at that time was serving as headmaster of al-Nahdha school. 'Ali Ahmad BaKathir was one of its most active and opinionated contributors and his older brother 'Umar Ahmad BaKathir, with whom 'Ali was very close, was also active in the production of the journal. Because of its sometimes contentious stand on social issues, this journal met with a great deal of opposition, and after ten issues, it ceased circulation. Years later, a volume of the collected issues of *al-Tahdhib* was published in Cairo, dedicated to Sayyid Abu Bakr b. Shaykh al-Kaf in recognition of his support for the journal.

Just as the reform groups and the government attempted to regulate and control consumption and social behavior, articles appearing in *al-Tahdhib* argued that social reform was necessary in order that Hadhramawt might return to a previous (idealized) state of greater social unity and solidarity. These articles advocated changes in the patterns of consumption and display that had developed, and particularly criticized goods and fashions imported from abroad. Several articles published by a pseudonymous author, using the byline "*mim sin*," focused on Hadhramawt's social problems. They depicted emigration as a symptom of Hadhramawt's stagnant economic and social condition and at the same time the cause of the persistence of that condition. The excessive concern of the populace with material goods and pleasures, particularly imported ones, embodied the problem, creating a drain on resources, diverting from local economic development, and necessitating further emigration. Like the sumptuary regulations, these critical articles focused on women and women's adornments as manifestations of society's errant materialist values.[48]

"Bad Customs and Their Effect on the Hadhrami People," dealt explicitly with the negative effect of "imported" customs on the society. The article stated that even though Hadhramis in the homeland and the *mahjar* had been discussing the negative effects of foreign customs on their culture for a quarter of a century, the customs continued unabated. It called Hadhramis' ready imitation of foreign ways a symptom of ignorance, and particularly criticized women for indulging in foreign luxuries. These included the imitation of the Indian custom of wearing of ankle bracelets and armloads of bangles; the Javan custom of wearing sarongs; the Najdi and Tihami customs of wearing chains (*silasil*), beads (*huruz*), and capacious garments of delicate fabrics; and the Asian custom of colored facial decorations.

Opposition to these customs was couched in socioeconomic terms: they encouraged the import of foreign goods and thereby discouraged local manufacturing, which ultimately increased the necessity for emigration. The author asserted that Europe and India were waging a war on Hadhramawt with shoddy goods that drained their resources, spoiled their morals, and caused men to emigrate, leaving their children. Hadhramawt was left with its houses empty, except for abandoned unhappy women. Another result of the influx of these goods was the spread of vain and prideful displays of material wealth that resulted in the poor falling into debt through their attempts to imitate the rich, which led to the debtors being forced to emigrate.[49]

Celebrations, Change, and Criticism

Celebrations of rites of passage, markers in the lives of individuals and families and displays of social group identity, took on a different meaning in the early twentieth century in Hadhramawt, as those celebrations became increasingly elaborate and the standards of display and hospitality were raised, raising of standards and expectations for the society as a whole. Social reformers initiated repeated attempts to regulate social display, concerned with the impact of innovations that upset the expected social order and disrupted the orderly enactments of social place. Changes in styles for women were of particular concern, since women's participation in rites of passage celebrations constituted their main involvement in public or community life. Despite arguments based on religion and modern notions of social progress, attempts to regulate festivities were continually subverted, as the public adopted new fashions and adapted traditional forms. These conflicts were more than just disagreements over fashion; they resulted from widespread consternation about the maintenance of social order. At the same time, debate took place in other aspects of the public arena, as innovations and reforms in social and educational institutions also provoked concern over the maintenance of social order.

6
Religious Belief, Practice, and Education: Tradition, Revival, and Critique

The fiercest critiques of Hadhrami society in this time of transition arose in the contention over changes in the practice of religion and the nature of religious education. While the religious identity and practices of the majority of the population during the late nineteenth and early twentieth centuries resembled those of their ancestors, the institutions of religious learning were changing. Religious practice and religious education became matters of contestation among social reformers and religious conservatives.

Religious Homogeneity and Diversity

Since Hadhramawt lacked a Jewish or Christian minority, its society appeared to be religiously homogeneous. It was a Sunni community that adhered to the Shafi'i *madhhab* (legal "school of thought") in legal matters and the Ash'ari school in theological issues. At the same time, the extreme reverence in which the *sada* held the family and descendants of the Prophet resembled that of Shi'is elsewhere. Additionally, while adherence to the Shafi'i *madhhab* in legal matters was the norm, a small minority rejected the Shafi'i *madhhab* and also the prevalent mystical tendency in religious belief and practice. But for the most part, the greatest difference among Hadhramis with respect to religion was the differences resulting from ascribed membership in either religiously prestigious or nonprestigious social groups, a factor which determined in large part the individual's degree of religious education and role in religious practices.

A Sunni Community, with Shi'i Influence?

Hadhramis retained their strong Sunni identity even though their migration in the Indian Ocean region exposed them to the beliefs and practices of Shi'is. The important nineteenth-century collection of *fatawa*, legal opinions, by Sayyid 'Abd al-Rahman b. Muhammad al-Mashhur, *Bughyat al-mustarshidin*, included questions about Shi'i practices such as the dramatic public displays of grief commemorating the martyrdom of Husayn. The *mufti*, the deliverer of formal legal opinions, counseled against such practices while asserting the special status of the descendants of the Prophet.[1]

The adherence of the 'Alawi *sada* to the ideal that descendants of the Prophet held spiritual authority and played a special role in the transmission of Sufi esoteric knowledge at times suggested Shi'i inclinations. Some *sada* espoused ideas which were *mutashi'*, or tending toward Shi'i belief. In a treatise published in 1909, Sayyid Muhammad b. 'Aqil Bin Yahya, a member of the Hadhrami community of Batavia, advocated hatred of Mu'awiya as a religious duty. He called for the name of Mu'awiya to be cursed, rather than eulogized through the honorific repeated after the name of the associates of the Prophet Muhammad. Some of his compatriots refuted Bin 'Aqil's view and, in response, he suggested that he was expressing a view which his ancestors had kept quiet, in a form of *taqiya* (legitimate dissimulation) within their Shafi'i milieu.[2]

Sayyid 'Abd al-Rahman Bin 'Ubaydillah al-Saqqaf, an individual who never shied from contention, expressed a similar controversial opinion in a treatise entitled *Nasim hajir*, about the nature of the Sufi *qutb*, the paramount spiritual leader of the Sufis of each generation. This spiritual leadership position, which he referred to as the hidden Caliphate, had passed from 'Ali b. Abi Talib through his sons to his grandson, Zayn al-'Abidin (the fourth Imam of the Shi'is), to the 'Alawi Sufis of Hadhramawt. He suggested that the ancestor of the 'Alawi *sada*, Ahmad b. 'Isa al-Muhajir, his followers, and his early descendants were Shi'is during their first two hundred years in Hadhramawt, when they lived only in small villages. He opined that when the *sada* families moved to Tarim, they struck a compromise with the *mashayikh* then holding spiritual authority, in which the *sada* agreed to adhere to the Shafi'i *madhhab* and Ash'ari belief, while the *mashayikh* in turn accepted the *sada* position that the Sufi *qutb* was inherited by the descendants of the Prophet.[3] Bin 'Ubaydillah's point of view on this matter was anathema to the majority, who were firmly attached to the notion of Sunni, Shafi'i, and Ash'ari identity as part of their past heritage as well as their present.

A Shafi'i Community, with Some Exceptions

Almost the entire population of Hadhramawt adhered to the Shafi'i *madhhab* and the *sada* considered their ancestors to have spread the Shafi'i approach to religious law in the *mahjar*. An exception existed in a small pocket of adherents to the Hanbali *madhhab*. Located east of Shibam, a community of Yafi'i *tulud* inclined toward the Wahhabi interpretation of Islam. In 1811, a Wahhabi force from the Najd had invaded Hadhramawt with the collusion of local leaders from the Tamimi and Yafi'i tribes. During this incursion, the zealous troops destroyed revered tombs and Sufi books and artifacts, burning them and dumping them down wells. Even after the force returned to Najd, their ideology persisted among a few supporters in Hadhramawt. Departing from their usual endogamous marriage practices, the leader of this Yafi'i community married his daughter to Bin Qumla, the leader of the Wahhabi troops.

Within that community, the jurists and scholars turned to the works of Ahmad b. Hanbal and Ibn Taymiyya for guidance in legal matters rather than following the Shafi'i *madhhab,* They also rejected the prevalent Sufi tendency, avoiding the practices of paying respect to spiritual leaders or visiting tombs, which they considered a form of *shirk,* dividing their allegiance to God. A tiny minority, this community guarded their differences of belief and practice. The only sign of their differing approach to religion was that in their territory stood no tombs of spiritual leaders such as those dotting the landscape elsewhere, and that they did not participate in visits to tombs nor in any ceremonies in which worshippers asked for intercession.[4]

Belief and Practice in a Diverse Society

The most pronounced difference among Hadhramis in terms of religious practice was between the members of the religiously prestigious groups, the *sada* and *mashayikh,* and the others. Some members of the religiously prestigious social groups served as religious leaders and spiritual guides for the wider society; the prestige of these individuals and their descendants often continued long after their deaths. The other groups, tribes and townspeople, looked to these religious leaders for moral, legal, and spiritual guidance and participated as their adherents in rituals and ceremonies, many of which centered around the tombs of departed spiritual leaders. Visits to these tombs were an important manifestation of collective spiritual practice, the largest of which was the annual visit to the tomb of the pre-Islamic Prophet Hud. New religious practices of a mystical nature were created by Sayyid 'Ali b. Muhammad al-Hibshi, leader of a religious revival in the late nineteenth and early twentieth centuries.

Mysticism: Sufi Seekers and Popular Practices

The Sufi path, or practice of a mystical nature, was widespread in Hadhramawt. Among the learned groups, their search for knowledge included not only the reading and study of Islamic sciences and law, but also esoteric knowledge that influenced their interpretation of texts and affected their private devotional practices and collective worship. The Sufis sought an intimate experience of closeness to God through personal dedication to worship, and they formed a community devoted to the esoteric knowledge passed from the Prophet to generations of seekers, communicated through a system of mystical symbols. Generations of spiritual mentors (*shuyukh,* sing. *shaykh*) passed their esoteric knowledge and devotional practices to seekers (*tulab al-'ilm,* sing. *talib*) who traveled within Hadhramawt and the wider Muslim world in order to benefit from the presence, influence, and teachings of different spiritual guides. The community formed a web extending over space and time, with prior generations of spiritual leaders commemorated in biographical collections and honored through respect for their tombs.

Sufism was introduced to Hadhramawt in the first half of the thirteenth century by Sayyid Muhammad b. Muhammad b. 'Ali Sahib Mirbat, known as "al-Faqih al-Muqaddam," who transmitted esoteric knowledge to his sons and other seekers.[5] The movement spread, with the 'Alawi *sada* claiming a special role in the transmission. Initiation into the mysteries of esoteric knowledge was not limited to *sada* and *mashayikh,* although most seekers came from these groups. The fifteenth-century agriculturist poet Sa'd al-Suwayni, for example, participated in the transmission of esoteric knowledge along with the most prominent *shuyukh* of his time.[6]

Although in some parts of the Muslim world, tension existed between those inclined toward the mystical path of Islam and those inclined toward the literal and legalistic point of view, this conflict was not found in Hadhramawt. The two tendencies were intertwined, with most of the religious specialists, *'ulama',* combining the search for mystical knowing with the study of Shafi'i jurisprudence and other Islamic sciences such as Qur'anic commentary, history, and grammar.[7] A typical biographical entry in a seventeenth-century collection described the studies of the subject with his mentor, a renowned Sufi, as including the Islamic sciences, especially jurisprudence and Sufism, and the same combination prevailed among the *'ulama* of the nineteenth and twentieth centuries.[8]

Those who dedicated themselves to the Sufi way did not renounce everyday life and business, but continued leading a normal life while devoting their free time to spiritual discipline. The mundane world and the spiritual world were not parallel to these seekers, but coterminous. Seekers sometimes traveled just to meet and study with a particular teacher, but they also took advantage of the opportunity to meet with renowned teachers while traveling for trade or family matters. The Hadhrami ports were staging points in the passage of travelers headed abroad and the *shuyukh* of those cities made them a "spiritual port" (*mina' ruhi*) at the same time.[9] For Hadhramis in the *mahjar,* particularly those of the religiously prestigious groups, Hadhramawt formed a spiritual as well as a geographical homeland. Accounts of their travels to the homeland focused on their meetings with *shuyukh* and other seekers of knowledge rather than on mundane scenes and events of travel and destination.[10]

When a seeker of knowledge met with a *shaykh,* the *shaykh* shared his knowledge of the esoteric readings of texts and supererogatory worship activities, often consisting of extended repetitions of devotional phrases. The *shaykh* recognized accomplishments of the seeker of knowledge through the ceremonial blessing and granting of a skullcap (*qalansuwa*) or other item of clothing that represented initiation into the spiritual lineage and through the granting of *ijaza*s or certificates that recorded connection with the lineage. These *ijaza*s recognized the achievement of seekers' obedience and devotion in worship, study, and good works.[11]

The seeker of knowledge embodied the spiritual quest through a sober discipline that valued abstemiousness in personal life and diligence in religious practice. In addition to the prayers and fasting incumbent upon all believers, the seeker of knowledge performed additional practices. During Ramadhan, devout seekers spent the nights in extended worship, which included prayers with a total of forty-one prostrations interspersed with Qur'anic recitation throughout the entire night. Seekers daily performed *rawatib* (special prayers and invocations) and *awrad* (periods of private worship and contemplation).

In Hadhramawt, *dhikr,* worship through the repetition of religious phrases and invocations, was not accompanied by the movement, dancing, or music that characterized some Sufi practices elsewhere. Simple recitations, sometimes with chanting and drumming, focused the consciousness of the seeker on God. A fifteenth-century *shaykha* of al-Ghurfa was remembered for repeating "God is one" a thousand times daily, reciting the Qur'anic verse *Ayat al-kursi* thirty-six hundred times, and for fasting during Rajab and Sha'ban as well as Ramadhan. *Shuyukh* prescribed patterns for the repetition of invocations, Qur'anic verses, and other religious texts for the seekers to employ during periods of private worship. When the seeker accomplished the task, the *shaykh* granted an *ijaza.*[12]

While the brotherhood of mystical seekers was a network rather than an institutionalized hierarchy, its worldview included different roles for people. For the masses, spiritual fulfillment was achieved by following the guidance of more advanced spiritual leaders. Among the more advanced, a few noteworthy individuals who fulfilled their role as guide and mentor to others while pursuing a life of devotion to God achieved the status of *wali,* friend of God, one who through purity and virtue remained always in the presence of God.[13]

While the majority of people lacked access to religious learning and the means to devote themselves to study and devotion, they paid their respects to popular spiritual leaders considered near God by virtue of their piety. The ritual life of the community focused around a spiritual leader and often around the memory of a previous spiritual leader as objectified in tombs and symbols of spiritual authority such as flags or ceremonial caps. The masses followed their spiritual leaders in processions and chanting. While the question of intercession was a matter of contention among '*ulama*' throughout the Islamic world, to the common folk of Hadhramawt intercession seemed obvious and necessary. Most people struggled to provide a living for themselves and their families and felt that those who devoted their lives to religious learning and worship had attained a greater proximity to God, which enabled them to intercede. The power of the pious to provide a connection to God was believed even greater after death, when they were with God. Through collective rituals led by spiritual guides and through appeals to respected spiritual leaders living and dead, ordinary people connected with the spiritual tradition of the seekers of knowledge.[14]

The ordinary people of Hadhramawt for the most part did not question the rituals focused on pious individuals, living and dead, even though there were a few,

Figure 6.1 Tomb of Saʿd al-Suwayni, patron of farmers

including the tiny Hanbali-oriented minority, who opposed such practices. Still, the fact that '*ulama*' defended intercession suggests that it received some criticism. For example, Sayyid 'Abd al-Rahman b. Muhammad al-Mashhur's collection of legal pronouncements, *Bughyat al-mustarshidin,* included a section entitled "Intercession by means of the favored ones, the response to those condemning it, and the verdict as to the miraculous."[15]

The Ziyara

Rituals in search of intercession centered on the tombs of departed spiritual leaders. Throughout Hadhramawt stood whitewashed domed tombs of individuals revered for their piety. At the beginning of the 'Id al-Fitr and 'Id al-Adhha holidays, people visited these tombs, where they offered greetings to the spirit of the deceased and prayed to God, asking for blessings and forgiveness for the living and the dead. At other times, people visited these tombs individually in order to pray from a sanctified site. Many towns and villages performed an annual collective ritual visit, a *ziyara,* to a local or nearby tomb. The revered person buried in the tomb was a spiritual leader whose pious attributes had been great enough and whose descendants or students had been active enough to create a tradition of continued respect around the deceased. These individuals were usually men from the *sada* or the *mashayikh,* although there were exceptions such as the fifteenth-century agriculturalist and poet Sa'd al-Suwayni, whose tomb was visited by farmers, and a few pious women such as Shaykha 'A'isha bint Ahmad BaJamal and Shaykha Sultana bint 'Ali al-Zubaydi.

On the evening of the fourteenth of Sha'ban, the city of Shibam held a *ziyara.* The ritual practiced exemplified the way that spiritual authorities, living and dead, formed the focus for local practice all over Hadhramawt. It also exemplified the competition between families, and between *sada* and *mashayikh* over local spiritual authority, which ebbed and flowed with time. In Shibam the *munsib* led a procession to visit the tombs of long-departed but still-venerated religious leaders, which included *mashayikh* from the Ba'Abbad family and *sada* from the Bin Sumayt. First they visited the tomb of the Shaykh 'Abdallah b. Muhammad Ba'Abbad (d. 1288), a Sufi who had trained with al-Faqih al-Muqaddam and who had instituted in Shibam a *ribat,* or center for seekers of spiritual wisdom. The annual visit to the tomb of 'Abdallah b. 'Umar Ba'Abbad was of great age, as indicated by its mention in the fifteenth-century Yemeni biographical collection, *Tabaqat al-khawass.* The procession then passed on to the tomb of Muhammad b. Abu Bakr Ba'Abbad (d. 1398/1399), who had revived Shibam as a center of Islamic learning and Sufi practice. They went finally to the tomb of the ancestors of the *munsib,* Sayyid Muhammad b. Zayn Bin Sumayt (d. 1758) and his three brothers. Sayyid Muhammad b. Zayn had come to Shibam from Tarim in 1722 at the request of his spiritual guide, the eminent Sayyid 'Abdallah b. 'Alawi al-Haddad, to revitalize religious learning, spiritual practice, and moral standards.[16]

The *ziyara* was a splendid occasion, with the community massed behind the *munsib,* accompanied by the sound of drums and a flute. Alongside the *munsib* walked the bearer of a tall wooden staff topped by a conical standard of green satin, the symbol of the spiritual authority of the Bin Sumayt. The green satin enveloped the *qub',* a cone-shaped cap which had been ceremonially bestowed on Sayyid Muhammad b. Zayn Bin Sumayt by his spiritual guide. At the tombs, the crowd recited the Qur'anic passages Ya Sin and the Fatiha. The visiting of the Ba'Abbad tombs following the standard of the Bin Sumayt showed that while the earlier spiritual authority of the Ba'Abbad had been superceded by that of the Bin Sumayt, the importance and power of the earlier spiritual leaders had not been totally eclipsed. Instead, it remained part of the system of collective religious observance.[17]

The Ziyara *to the Tomb of Prophet Hud*

While many popular local *ziyaras* drew participants from a wider hinterland, one *ziyara* was unique in its geographic and temporal scope. The *ziyara* to the tomb of Prophet Hud in far eastern Wadi Hadhramawt drew people from as far as neighboring Mahra and Zufar. The *ziyara* to Prophet Hud's tomb was unusual in that the honored deceased was not a local figure, but a pre-Islamic prophet whose story was related in the Qur'an among the tales of the ancient prophets of monotheism. To Hadhramis, the practice was connected with the heritage of ancient ancestors, the legendary people of 'Ad, and at the same time was part of the Islamic heritage of the Qur'an. Another *ziyara* associated with a pre-Islamic figure took place at the tomb of Prophet Salih in Wadi Khunab northwest of Shibam, but its practice was limited to *badu* of the surrounding sparsely populated area.[18]

The story of Hud and his people, the people of 'Ad, was recounted in the Qur'an in several locations: chapter 11, "Hud;" chapter 7, "al-A'raf" verses 65–72; and chapter 46, "al-Ahqaf" verses 21–26. Hud, who lived a few generations after Noah, was a prophet of the same type as Noah, a "warner." He told his people the message of the one God, and warned them that God would punish them if they continued their polytheism, but they persisted in their idolatry and were destroyed.[19]

The people of Hadhramawt believed that their ancestors had visited the tomb of Prophet Hud since time immemorial, and that great men such as the Prophet Solomon and Alexander the Great had also visited. Biographical notices of prominent Hadhrami scholars and spiritual leaders mention their participation in the *ziyara.* Shaykh 'Abdallah b. Muhammad Ba'Abbad, known as "the Ancient," is noted in *Tabaqat al-khawass* to have led a crowd of fifteen thousand on the *ziyara* in the thirteenth century. In al-Shilli's biographical collection, *al-Mashra' al-rawi,* prominent *sada* of the seventeenth century and earlier were noted as having taken part in this *ziyara.* The tomb played a role in the political legitimacy of the sixteenth-century Kathiri ruler known as "Abu Tuwayriq:" early in his rule some prominent *sada* traveled to the tomb of Prophet Hud, where they received confirmation that Abu Tuwayriq was a direct descendant of Prophet Hud and prayed for God's aid for the sultan's rule.[20]

The different social groups played different roles in the *ziyara*. The Ba'Abbad family (*mashayikh*) was responsible for the condition of the roadway, the site, and its facilities. They maintained the tomb and the mosque and granted permission for building houses in the town at the site of the *ziyara*. *Sada* served as leaders of the different groups participating, with different families of *sada* having a specified time to perform the ritual, accompanied by crowds of followers. Townsmen and tribesmen followed the spiritual leaders through the ritual; they also performed dances, chants, and songs and tribesmen fired their weapons afterward. While not occupied in the solemn practice of the ritual, the ordinary folk engaged in dance and poetry competitions and various forms of play to celebrate the occasion and to honor their spiritual leaders. Members of the religiously prestigious groups, particularly the Sufi seekers, spent their time in religious discussion and worship.

Local communities traveled collectively to the tomb site, each following its spiritual leader. As the pilgrims left town, women stood by the roadways and on the rooftops, adding the sound of their ululations to the men's drumming and chanting. The travelers visited tombs of various revered figures along the way. They made an impressive display, approaching the tombs in procession, with standards held aloft. Their progress resembled a moving festival. Camels and donkeys were stained with henna and bore special decorative saddles. The communities stayed largely within their own groups, which encouraged continuous intergroup rivalries. The rival quarters of Say'un traveled separately and traded insults as they traveled.

At the town surrounding the tomb of Prophet Hud, the spiritual leaders, other members of spiritually prestigious families, and wealthy merchants stayed in houses called *khadur* (sing. *khadr*). These tall stately houses were only occupied during the time of the *ziyara* and stood empty the rest of the year. Ordinary pilgrims camped under the cliff side of the wadi and on the banks of the river that rose as if by miracle from an underground river not far from the tomb.[21]

Each community and each of the major *sada* families had an appointed time for the ritual visit. Each group gathered with its leader at the appointed time beside the river, at a point marked by a white pillar of stone called the stone of 'Umar al-Mihdhar, after the fifteenth-century *sayyid*. After bathing in the river, the participants made a prayer of two prostrations and then walked in procession to the well of greeting (Bir al-Taslum). There they offered greetings to the souls of departed prophets and pious persons, which they believed to reside—or at least be easily contacted—at that site. First they wished peace upon Muhammad and then greeted a number of prophets and pious figures: Adam and his wife Hawwa' (Eve); Alexander the Great; Muhammad's wives and his daughter Fatima; and the angels Jibra'il (Gabriel), Israfil, and others. They praised Hud, Muhammad, and all pious believers of the past.

Figure 6.2 Town at Prophet Hud's tomb site, occupied only during annual ritual visit

Each group followed its leader to Hud's tomb, where they repeated the greetings and then recited the chapter "Hud" and the Fatiha. Their leader then asked for intercession, blessings, and forgiveness. Then the group moved to the large stone near Hud's tomb, believed to be Hud's she-camel that had turned into stone upon his death. There they recited the story of the birth of Muhammad and praised Muhammad and all the prophets. Individuals took turns touching, kissing, and putting oil on a crevice at the base of the stone, worn smooth from centuries of such attention.

While the stages of the ritual were reverent and dignified, the processions between the different stages were colorful and exciting, with the group leaders accompanied by flying banners and drumming while the crowds chanted and danced. The procession accompanying the *sayyid* family of Shaykh Abu Bakr b. Salim of 'Aynat was the most dramatic and drew the largest crowds. The last day of the visit included the tribesmen of Hadhramawt and Mahra territory, all of whom entered under the leadership of a *sayyid* from the al-Hamid family of 'Aynat.

On the eleventh of Sha'ban, the groups began to return home, carrying small gifts purchased from the market that took place during the *ziyara*. These were valued due to their association with the sacred location and event, even though they consisted of ordinary items available in any market and tooth-cleaning sticks from the roots of a plant abundant in the eastern wadi. The returning men were enthusiastically greeted by their families and communities. Each community celebrated the returnees with a day of processions, dancing, chanting, and poetry, with Tarim holding camel races. In this way, the whole community, including women and children, shared in the blessings and joy associated with the ritual at Hud's tomb.[22]

A Twentieth-Century Spiritual Leader: Sayyid 'Ali b. Muhammad al-Hibshi

In the late nineteenth and early twentieth century, Say'un was the center of a popular religious revival due to the creativity, energy, and charisma of the celebrated Sayyid 'Ali b. Muhammad al-Hibshi. A devout and pious Sufi, he created worship services that drew great crowds from all over. He was born in the village of Qasam in 1843. His father was Mufti of Mecca, and in 1860, Sayyid 'Ali b. Muhammad went to Mecca for the Hajj and remained for two years to study. When he returned to Say'un, he devoted himself to worship and teaching, developing a growing coterie of adherents. He taught grammar, jurisprudence, and mysticism to growing numbers of students at the Hanbal mosque near his home until establishing Say'un's *ribat*, in 1878 or 1879. In 1885 or 1886, he established the Riyadh mosque nearby. Seekers of knowledge of all ages came to study with Sayyid 'Ali b. Muhammad al-Hibshi. People from all walks of life, including the unlettered, flocked to the lessons and worship services he organized. An accomplished poet, he created new devotional services and rituals that were aesthetically satisfying to the participants. A charismatic speaker, he wept while preaching and his listeners wept with him.[23]

Figure 6.3 Processional line dance in Say'un, after the visit to Prophet Hud's tomb

Sayyid 'Ali b. Muhammad al-Hibshi created weekly public gatherings at the ribat tat included: a weekly commemoration of the birth of the Prophet; a Monday morning recitation from Bukhari's collection of *hadith;* and a Monday evening *hadhra,* or worship observance, with chanting and drumming. He also organized an annual *mawlid,* or commemoration of the birth of the Prophet, for which people came from as far as the coast. On the last Thursday of Rabi'a al-awwal, crowds gathered at a date orchard on the edge of the town, where, with incense burning, al-Hibshi recited the Fatiha and then recited *Sumt al-durur,* a poetic prayer of his own composition. After drumming and chanting, a recitation included miracles of the Prophet's childhood, the revelation of the Qur'an, and the Prophet's night journey to Jerusalem and ascension to heaven. He also organized special observances for the tenth of Muharram to commemorate the death of the Prophet's nephew, Husayn b. 'Ali b. Abi Talib, which the Hadhrami *sada,* their identity strongly tied to their status as descendants of the prophet naturally mourned. These observances consisted of prayers and chants and did not resemble those in the Shi'i world in which people rent their clothing and flagellated themselves.[24]

While al-Hibshi's purpose was to edify and stimulate people's spiritual lives, his activities and charisma led to the development of a popular cult centered on his person. The crowds of people who flocked to his lessons and devotional services began to swarm around him as he walked or rode his mule through the streets of Say'un. Feeling that this pious figure was imbued with *baraka,* or blessings from God, people tried to kiss his hand or touch his hair or clothing, some even going so far as to pluck at his hair and garments. Although he did not approve this devotion to his person, he was unable to quell the excessive expressions of admiration from those he inspired.[25]

When Sayyid 'Ali b. Muhammad al-Hibshi died in 1915, a huge outpouring of grief took place among the masses and the Sufi brotherhood. Thousands of mourners flocked to his home for prayers and recitation of the Qur'an. Some said that not a drop of the water used to wash the body touched the ground, since people took the water to drink or wash themselves.[26] The year after his death, large numbers came to visit his tomb and the traditions of an annual *ziyara* began to be elaborated, under the supervision of his heirs. On the tenth of Rabi'a al-thani, the faithful began to gather at the al-Hibshi home and neighboring Riyadh mosque, where they recited the Qur'an and prayed. The crowds built daily until the eighteenth of the month. Some years after his death, the custom developed of the *tilbis,* in which a procession accompanied the *mahmal,* or wooden frame that bore a new embroidered cloth cover for the tomb. In this procession, the culmination of days of prayer and worship and commemoration of the cherished spiritual leader, crowds passed through the street from the al-Hibshi home to his tomb, to the sound of chanting, drumming, and the ululation of women.[27]

Modes and Institutions of Religious Learning

Traditionally, religious learning was limited to men and women of the religiously prestigious social groups. The late nineteenth century saw a revival of religious learning, when wealthy Hadhramis of the *mahjar* began to fund new institutions of religious learning and mystical practice. In the ensuing decades, more new institutions were founded, innovations took place within those institutions, and the first secular schools were founded. The gradual transformation of the educational system was at the core of the social controversy over religion that was expressed through critiques and debates in public forums.

Women, Religion, and Learning

Women's participation in communal religious life took place primarily among other women and within their families. If women visited a tomb, they usually did so with members of their family in a private visit, rather than during a public communal ritual visits. When processions were held, women watched from vantage points such as rooftops so they could maintain their privacy.[28] While men participated in collective prayers in the mosques, women prayed at home, often collectively, although a few mosques had attached areas for women's prayers.[29] While men attended *mawlid* celebrations, commemorating Muhammad's birth, in Sufi centers and in mosques, women gathered in courtyards and homes for their observations. While men took part in prayers and Qur'anic recitation at the neighborhood mosque after the death of a man or at the home after the death of a woman, women gathered in the home of the deceased for prayers and recitation in either case. Their contributions to communal religious activity, while private, were important to the community. For example, during the forty-day mourning period after a death, women gathered in the home of the deceased for prayers and recitation every Friday.

In keeping with the privacy of their religious observation, most women learned about religion from their families—the obligatory prayers, requirements of fasting, and regulations of purity. At the same time, some women of the *sada* and *mashayikh* were known for religious learning and piety.[30] Women seekers were recognized as links in the chains of transmission of religious knowledge, both legalistic and mystical, which they passed along to children, to other women, and to male scholars, especially of their families. Often, these noted women were relatives of men known for their piety. Hadhrami biographical collections include notices of several *sada* women from the seventeenth century: Sharifa Khadija, sister of Sayyid Abu Bakr al-'Aydarus; Sharifa Fatima, daughter of Sayyid 'Umar "al-Mihdhar" al-Saqqaf; and Zaynab bint Muhammad al-Saqqaf. In the eighteenth century, Salma, the daughter of Sayyid Ahmad b. Zayn al-Hibshi, was noted for the transmission of esoteric religious knowledge acquired from her father. Noted women from the *mashayikh* included the fifteenth-century Shaykha 'A'isha bint

Ahmad BaJamal, famed for her zeal in devotional practice, and the sixteenth-century Shaykha Fatima bint Muhammad BaJamal, known both as the wife of a prominent Sufi and as a pious person in her own right. In the seventeenth century, Fatima bint Muhammad BaSharahil was counted among those advanced in mystical understanding.[31]

The most famous of the historic pious women was the fourteenth-century Shaykha Sultana bint 'Ali al-Zubaydi. Shaykha Sultana bint 'Ali al-Zubaydi was born in 1378/1379 in the tiny village of Qarat al-'Urr outside al-Maryama, east of Say'un. Under the tutelage of her teacher, Shaykh Muhammad b. 'Abdallah Ba'Abbad, she quickly advanced in her knowledge of the religious sciences, devotion, and mysticism, and she founded a *ribat* in which she and her teacher both taught. People from all walks of life came to visit her, including well-known religious authorities such as Sayyid 'Abd al-Rahman b. Muhammad al-Saqqaf of Tarim and his sons, 'Umar "al-Mihdhar" and Abu Bakr "al-Sakran" al-Saqqaf.

She was renowned for her poetry as well as her piety. According to popular lore, she was once challenged with the opening line of a couplet: "Can a female camel compete with a male?" She responded immediately in appropriate rhyme and meter: "She carries the same load, and in addition produces milk and offspring." Sayyid 'Abd al-Rahman b. Muhammad al-Saqqaf invited her to participate in the Sufi worship sessions held twice weekly in Tarim. Although she did not attend, the seekers began to open the sessions by reciting three poems composed by her, as they have continued to do until the present. After her death in 1443, Qarat al-'Urr became a *hawta*, or sanctified space. Her tomb became the site of regular visits by men and women and the practice of an annual *ziyara* to her tomb developed soon after her death. Shaykha Sultana's transmission of esoteric knowledge was recorded in biographical collections, her name appearing in the biographical notices of those who studied with her. She was also recorded as having through visions confirmed the sanctity of pious individuals of her time.

During the late nineteenth and early twentieth century, a *munsib* descended from one of the *shaykha's* brothers, mediated local problems, oversaw the *ziyara*, and provided hospitality for visitors to her tomb. Men came from the surrounding region for commemorations in the mosque, Qur'an recitation at her tomb, and preaching. Visitors, including many women, came at other times, often on Mondays (the day of the *shaykha's* death). Visitors were hosted in houses of the village, with different homes responsible for particular social and tribal groups. All kinds of people made the visit, from simple farmers and laborers and their wives to prominent persons including Sayyid 'Ali b. Muhammad al-Hibshi.[32]

In the nineteenth and twentieth centuries, some women continued to participate in religious learning, as the biographies of leaders in religious education indicate. Sayyid 'Ali b. Muhammad al-Hibshi's mother, born in 1824 or 1825, had learned the Qur'an and religious texts from a prominent *shaykh* during her childhood. In the early twentieth century, the Sharifa Khadija, Sayyid 'Ali b. Muhammad al-Hibshi's daughter, was recognized as brilliant, and demonstrated her abilities by joining her father in extemporaneous composition and recitation of collo-quial verse. Two years before her father's death in 1915, he composed for her a po-etic *ijaza* certifying the merit of her learning and a *wasiyya* (bequest) bequeathing her the legacy of his chain of transmission of learning and piety.[33]

The biography of the prominent *shaykh* Sayyid 'Alawi b. 'Abd al-Rahman al-Mashhur includes women of his family among his teachers and students. Women in this family acquired religious knowledge; those mentioned were notable in their piety and participated as links in the chains of transmission of mystical knowledge. Sayyid 'Alawi's *shuyukh* included his mother, who died in 1873 or 1874, among whose honorifics was al-Qanita, or "One devoted to God." Her in-tellectual and aesthetic capabilities had flourished under the religious training of her father and she was known for her piety and deep religious understanding, which she passed on to her sons.[34]

Among those who gained knowledge and received *ijaza*s from Sayyid 'Alawi was his wife, his paternal cousin. From childhood she had studied the Qur'an, *fiqh*, the biography of the Prophet, and had been guided in mystical practice by her fa-ther and grandfather. The three daughters of this pious couple learned to recite the Qur'an, and learned *fiqh* from family members. After one daughter was widowed young, her father frequently visited to contribute to the religious education and to guide the mystical practice of her and her daughter. The granddaughter, Sharifa Shaykha bint Ahmad BilFaqih, benefited from her grandfather's instruction and was recognized for her learning by the nickname "Faqiha" (one who knows *fiqh*). Another woman noted is Sayyid 'Alawi's niece, who studied with her uncle and other *shuyukh*.[35] While the experiences of these women cannot be considered com-mon to all women of Hadhramawt, they indicate that women of the *sada* and *mashayikh* participated in the networks of religious learning.

The Traditions of Religious Education

Access to traditional religious education was not available to most people. Knowledge was largely in the hands of the elite who had the means and leisure to aspire to higher study. The majority of the population learned the basics of reli-gion from relatives, and relied on those with education to counsel them in the cor-rect way to perform religious obligations. Most youth not from the *sada* or *mashayikh* devoted their time acquiring skills through working alongside family members to be able to make a living in crafts or commerce. In the case of laboring groups like farmers, builders, and fishermen, even minimal education for the young was a luxury they could not afford. The labor of farming was so great and the rewards so meager that a farm family could not afford to have a member con-sume without contributing to the collective effort to survive.[36]

Badu living outside the towns and villages had little exposure to religious or other knowledge, despite a few "missionary" teachers who traveled among the *badu* in the attempt to counteract their religious ignorance and reliance on tribal traditions and tribal law rather than *shari'a*. Even among settled tribesmen, there was little participation in formal education.[37]

Formal education was devoted not to transmitting skills, but to conveying knowledge of religious duties and to fostering moral development. Early education in Hadhramawt took place in traditional Qur'anic schools called the *katatib* (sing. *kuttab*) or *'ulam* (sing. *'ulma*). In each village or neighborhood, the Imam of the mosque taught young boys sitting on the floor in the mosque, in the Imam's house, or outdoors under a tree. In addition to arithmetic, reading, and writing, students learned the essentials of religion: the five pillars of Islam, the names of the prophets and angels, the requirements of ritual ablutions and prayers. They also learned the chants used in rituals and ceremonies.[38]

School supplies were simple. For writing practice, a board was covered with whitewash and students wrote in homemade ink; other times, a board was dyed with ink and students wrote with pieces of limestone. On the coast, students made their ink by burning fish oil in clay pots and collecting the soot, which they mixed with oil and water.

The paramount subject was recitation of the Qur'an. In every lesson, the students recited verses in chorus and each boy recited a few verses. Students memorized the entire Qur'an, often in the course of a year. Since only a few outstanding individuals managed to remember the whole Qur'an at once, most students recited segments over a period of time until they had recited the whole thing. The completion of a child's recitation was an occasion of pride for his family and of celebration for the community. After several students had completed the Qur'an, a ceremony commemorated the event.[39]

Completing the recitation of the Qur'an marked the end of formal education for most students. Some pursued further education, which was defined in spiritual and moral terms. One Hadhrami scholar described the search for knowledge as the worship of God, the purification of the soul through the sublimation of human desires by noble moral deeds. A scholar acquired knowledge to be able to advise others as to proper behavior and teach God's will.

A scholar did not necessarily gain employment or business opportunities as a result of studying, although some benefited materially from their educated status. A few scholars were employed by the government as judges or supported themselves as jurisconsults, but most had to rely on support from income from agricultural production on family lands or from family businesses in the *mahjar*.[40]

Students who were able to continue their studies participated in study circles (*halaqat*, sing. *halaqa*) which took place in mosques, in the homes of teachers, and in study centers known as *zawaya* (sing. *zawiya*). After learning from the teachers in his community, a seeker of knowledge traveled in search of the opportunity of learning from notable teachers. In Tarim, before the establishment of the *ribat* in 1886, instruction took place at seven mosques and *zawiya*s, each with a scholar who oversaw the study circles, and with some scholars teaching in more than one place.[41]

The curriculum of this traditional system included: Qur'anic exegesis, accounts of the Prophet and his companions, legal foundations, logical exposition, religious duties, grammar, astronomy, and timekeeping. All subjects were oriented toward religious purposes. The study of Arabic language and rhetoric was to understand the Qur'an and its commentators. The study of logic and law was to determine God's will for the ordering of human life. The studies of astronomy and timekeeping were to determine the correct timing of religious ritual obligations.

Books used included: Qur'anic commentaries by al-Tabari and Ibn Kathir; *hadith* collections, particularly that of al-Bukhari; geographies of al-Qazwini and Yaqut; biographical collections such as *Tabaqat al-kabir* of Ibn Sa'd and *Tabaqat al-Shafi'iyya al-kubra*; legal treatises of al-Shafi'i and commentaries on them by al-Nawawi, al-Rumli, and Ibn Hajar al-Haythami; and legal commentaries by Maliki and Hanafi jurists. Some students also read *Nayl al-awtar* by al-Shawkani, the Yemeni Zaydi scholar and jurist. Students studied collections of legal opinions by Shafi'i jurists including Ibn Hajar and Abu Ishaq al-Shirazi as well as those of Hadrami jurists such as BaMakhrama, BaShakil, and Bin Qadhi. Works by al-Ghazzali were popular among the students and advanced Sufi seekers read Ibn 'Arabi.[42]

The program and time periods of study for a scholar were flexible. The seeker of knowledge chose either to study a particular book with a scholar or to attend talks given by a scholar on a particular subject. The time required depended on the ability of the student and the judgment of the scholar. There were no examinations, but when a work or a subject had been covered to the satisfaction of teacher and students, the teacher might issue an *ijaza*, or certificate of accomplishment. If the seeker of knowledge had attended public talks by a *shaykh,* he received a general certificate (*ijaza 'ama*). If he had undertaken intensive study under a *shaykh's* supervision, he received a special certificate (*ijaza khassa*). In the case of Sufi seekers, their studies included the performance of special acts of worship for which they might receive an *ijaza.* For the opportunity to learn and collect certificates from the most noted *shuyukh* of their time, seekers traveled from place to place, visiting centers of scholarship in Hadhramawt and abroad.[43]

Study circles usually took place after morning and sunset prayers or after morning and afternoon prayers. The students gathered in front of the instructor in a line or semicircle, each student holding a copy of the text. A student offered an invocation before reciting a few sentences from his text, while the others followed along. The teacher then explained the passage, pointing out different interpretations and indicating which he thought correct. The teacher might cite commentaries or other works on the subject for clarification. The duration of the session depended on how long it took to complete a segment of the text.[44]

The efficacy of this system varied. Often, students of different levels of knowledge were thrown together, as were students studying different texts, even on widely disparate subjects. The efficacy of instruction depended on the skill of the *shaykh.* The most renowned teachers clarified the material and inspired the students in their efforts. Lesser talents often expounded on material without enlightening their listeners and often confusing them. A waggish student joked that he always got stuck between the rock (*al-hajar*) and the sandy spot (*al-rumli*), playing on the words of a typical uninspired teacher who repeatedly droned "and Ibn Hajar said . . ." and "and al-Rumli said . . ." while presenting commentaries of Shafi'i jurisprudence to a group of uncomprehending students.[45]

Revival and Reform of Education

The establishment of some new educational institutions in Hadhramawt enhanced the prior system of decentralized study circles, which also continued to take place in mosques and teachers' homes. There had been a decrease in the participation of students in higher learning, with more seekers of knowledge leaving to study abroad. With the support of Hadhramis in the *mahjar*, new *ribats*, study centers based on Sufi practice, were established, reinvigorating religious study at the higher levels. Providing instruction by several teachers in one location with boarding facilities, they simplified the task of the seekers of knowledge. They served the needs of the scions of Hadhramis of the *mahjar* as well as of those living outside the main towns. Unlike the *zawiyas* which charged fees, the *ribats* offered support to students in residence, which enabled more individuals to pursue higher studies. These institutions rejuvenated the spirit of the search for knowledge and devotion to God among the youth and throughout the community.

The *ribat* of Say'un founded by Sayyid 'Ali b. Muhammad al-Hibshi in late 1878 or 1879 was the first of the new institutions.[46] This popular spiritual leader, beloved for his inspiring use of language in devotional poetry was also respected for his instructional ability in the fields of *hadith* and Islamic jurisprudence. Just as his creation of new devotional forms had drawn large crowds to worship services, his clear and animating presentation drew large numbers of observers to his public lectures and study circles. The *ribat* and the neighboring Riyadh mosque were built with the financial support of a number of contributors, who paid stipends to students in addition to endowing construction of the buildings. The donors were men of wealth, including Sayyid Ahmad b. Muhammad Bin Shihab and Sayyid 'Abdallah b. Sa'id BaSalama, who both had fortunes acquired in Batavia. The former endowed a *waqf* with a value of four thousand riyals to support the Say'un *ribat*.[47]

A few years later, the *ribat* of Tarim was established with the support of wealthy Hadhrami *sada* in the *mahjar* and in Tarim. Pious endowments, including valuable real estate in Singapore, were established to fund the institution. In 1886, building began for the boarding school. The teachers were drawn from scholars who had previously been teaching in study circles at other venues. There was an attempt to implement more systematic instruction, with some division of students according to ability and with particular subjects being taught at fixed times so that people other than resident students might attend.[48] Students from the Hadhrami communities of the East Indies, East Africa, and India came to study in the *ribat*s of Say'un and Tarim, as did students from the coastal towns. In 1902/1903, a similar institution was founded at Ghayl BaWazir, which enabled students from the coastal region to study without traveling to the interior.[49]

Steps toward Secularization of Education

The first schools with a more secular orientation to curriculum appeared in the second decade of the twentieth century, shortly after similar schools for youth of Hadhrami origin were established in the East Indies. These schools departed from the traditional schools by emphasizing secular knowledge and skills in addition to religion. But the social ideal persisted that education was for individual and collective moral improvement. Another departure was that the civil schools were open to a wider population; more students from the other social groups aspired to study in the new schools. Some schools even served previously unserved populations, such as women and slaves. While the new schools were welcomed by the communities they served, they often became foci of ideological and even political contention.

The first modern school in Tarim, Madrasat Jam'iyat al-Haqq, opened in February 1916. It had a modern administration and calendar, and the curriculum included practical subjects while retaining a religious orientation. It was established by Jam'iyat al-Haqq, a community reform organization, which hired the principal and three teachers. The league's president, al-Sayyid 'Abd al-Rahman b. Shaykh al-Kaf, and three other officials served as school inspectors. The opening ceremony consisted of the recitation of the story of the birth of the Prophet, the reading of the school's charter, and speeches by the league president and by Sayyid 'Abd al-Rahman b. 'Ubaydillah al-Saqqaf.

The school's charter stated that the purpose of the school was to teach Arabic, math, morals, and ethics. Parents were urged to encourage their children's attendance and obedience to regulations and teachers. Class periods consisted of three hours in the morning, a half-hour break, and a further hour and a half in the afternoon, with no school on Thursday afternoons or Fridays.

In meetings of the league's executive committee, school matters were regularly discussed. These included: curriculum; the establishment of a library; protocols of discipline; and collecting school fees from the parents.[50] In 1929 a similar school, Madrasat Jam'iyat al-Ikhwa wa al-Mu'awana (School of the League of Brotherhood and Assistance), was founded in Tarim by another reform organization.

In December 1918, Madrasat Makarim al-Akhlaq (School of Noble Characteristics) was opened in al-Shihr under the supervision of Sayyid 'Alawi b. 'Abd al-Rahman al-Mashhur with the support of Sultan Ghalib b. 'Awadh al-Qu'ayti. The sultan granted the use of a large government building in the northeast corner of al-Shihr. The religiously prestigious families of al-Shihr, including the 'Aydarus *sada* and the BaFadhl *mashayikh,* supported the preparation of the building and acquisition of books and school supplies. Sayyid 'Alawi b. Abd al-Rahman al-Mashhur brought teachers from Tarim and his two sons, Muhammad and 'Umar, taught the advanced classes in religious subjects. Notably, the teachers included two young scholars of simple background from the small agricultural village of Tubbala. These two men, Salimin b. Sa'id Bin Surur and Mubarik b. 'Awadh BaRashid, had surprised the people of al-Shihr in the previous year with their outstanding performance in a public competition of knowledge of *fiqh*, the biography of the Prophet, and recitation of the Qur'an.

While this school focused on religious sciences, it included a more modern curriculum, offering geography, natural sciences, and history. The school was divided into ten levels, according to the age and knowledge of the students, with higher levels of study including only religious subjects. This institution greatly improved the standard of religious instruction at the same time that it introduced modern secular subjects and was much appreciated by the entire community.[51]

In 1920, 'Ali b. Salah al-Qu'ayti founded Madrasat al-Hudan (Guidance School) in al-Qatn. This school was the first to include a section for girls.[52] In the same year Madrasat al-Nahdha al-'Ilmiyya (Renaissance of Learning School) opened in Say'un. In the late 1920s and early 1930s, under the directorship of the iconoclastic 'Ali b. Ahmad BaKathir, this school became the focus of ideological contention. Students, teachers, other members of the *'ulama'* and the wider community engaged in public debate as to the goals of education, selection of texts, and methodology of teaching and study.

In 1930 or 1931, Madrasat al-Falah (Salvation School) was established in al-Mukalla by political exiles from the Hijaz, and initially had Qu'ayti support. This school had a highly organized curriculum and system of instruction. One of the founders of the school, Husayn al-Dibagh, who was also an administrator and instructor, had been a supporter of Sharif Husayn in the Hijaz and maintained connections with King Faysal b. Husayn of Iraq. The sultan began to suspect that the school and its supporters might be involved in political machinations and first withdrew his support from the school and later closed it down. The students were dismayed because they had appreciated the quality of the education, but the sultan's suspicions proved justified, as al-Dibagh was later to open a school in Aden of a distinctly nationalist character and also became involved in political agitation among the tribes of Southern Arabia and Yemen.[53]

Even before the sultan closed down Madrasat al-Falah, some of the teachers left the school and started another, Madrasat al-Haqq al-Salaffiyya (School of the Truth of the Pious Ancestors), supported financially by the sultan. In 1938, some of the *sada* of al-Mukalla who were former students and strong supporters of Madrasat al-Falah founded al-Madrasa al-Hashimiyya al-Ahliyya (Hashemite Civil School).[54]

Before his death in 1935, Sultan 'Umar b. 'Awadh al-Qu'ayti set up a school for the children of the slave soldiers of his armed forces. It later became a government public school, known as al-Madrasa al-Khayriyya al-Sultaniyya (Sultanic

Charitable School), which eventually absorbed Madrasat al-Haqq al-Salaffiyya. In 1937 in Ghayl BaWazir, 'Ali b. Salah al-Qu'ayti founded Madrasat Ghayl on the model of the Madarasat Makarim al-Akhlaq in al-Shihr.[55]

Despite the aspirations of the founders of these schools, all faced problems, including lack of funds and lack of trained educators and administrators. Disputes frequently arose with respect to curriculum planning, teaching methodology, and administrative matters. The teachers and administrators, while highly respected for their learning, had studied in the study circle system and had taught in that system before beginning to teach in the new schools. So it is not surprising that the changeover to a new system was difficult and contentious.[56]

Changing Access to Learning

Despite the fact that the *ribat* of Tarim did not generally serve students from among the craftsmen and farmers, by 1922 it included among its teachers an exceptional young man from a farming background. While previous teachers included *sada* and *mashayikh* from the BaFadhl and al-Khatib families, which had held religious prestige in Tarim for centuries, Salim b. Sa'id Bukayr Baghayshan was a unique addition to the faculty. As the son of farmers, he had been an unlikely candidate to participate in education.

When he was ten, Salim b. Sa'id began attending classes at the new Madrasat Jam'iyat al-Haqq, not as an official student but as a companion for a young *sayyid*. After school, he helped his father at the hard labor of raising water for irrigation. Although he proved a remarkably capable student, his father was not enthusiastic about the boy's education, feeling that the family needed his labor for its survival. However, his teacher, Sayyid Ahmad b. 'Umar al-Shatiri, perceived his ability and persuaded the father to allow him to devote himself to study. Sayyid Ahmad took the youngster into his home and provided for him for two years. The boy studied diligently under the supervision of various teachers, attending study circles at mosques, *zawiyas*, and at the *ribat* and devoting all of his free time to learning. His high level of ability, indicated by his memorization of the Qur'an within three months, gained him the respect of the *'ulama'* of Tarim.

In 1922 Salim b. Sa'id Bukayr began teaching *fiqh* at the *ribat* and later he also taught at an institute of *fiqh*. He eventually became well known as a *mufti* and was for a time head of the council of *mufti*s in Tarim. While his anomalous social background made him vulnerable to criticism when his decisions contradicted the interests of the powerful, the scope of his knowledge earned him the respect of the public and of the learned. It was said that the renowned Sayyid 'Abd al-Rahman 'Alawi al-Mashhur, who had been his teacher, once encountered him walking along a path and the *sayyid* dismounted his donkey to greet the much younger man in respect for his learning.[57]

Despite the presence of teachers of a simple background in Madrasat Makarim al-Akhlaq and even the remarkable success of Salim b. Sa'id Bukayr in

Tarim, participating in education was a difficult process for students from families other than the religiously prestigious. Also, as the system of modern civil schools expanded and their goals became more widely known, some students were frustrated when the local educational institutions did not measure up to their expectations. For example, Muhammad b. Sa'id BaYa'shut, from a farming background, had begun his education in Madrasat al-Falah in al-Mukalla. He thrived in that school and was studying and serving as a teaching assistant when the school was closed by Sultan 'Umar b. 'Awadh in 1934. He briefly attended other civil schools in al-Mukalla but was not satisfied. After trying unsuccessfully to enroll in one of the English schools in Aden, in 1937 he went to Tarim to further his education at the *ribat*. Perhaps because he had experienced a more modern style of education and had aspired to pursue further studies in that style, he was disappointed at the *ribat*'s reliance on older styles of teaching. He also deplored the condescension and neglect that he suffered, which he felt was the lot of the poorer students and outsiders. After less than three months, he left the *ribat*. He ended up returning to Aden, where he began teaching in one of the civil schools there, Madrasat al-Falah, the nationalist institution founded by his former mentor Husayn al-Dibagh in Aden.[58]

Critiques of Religion and Education

Although most people in Hadhramawt carried on in the same religious practices as had their ancestors, changes were taking place in religious practice and religious education. In periodicals and public speeches a debate over reform evolved, in which the necessity for change in traditional religious practices and education was proposed and contested.

A major forum for debate over religion and education was the handwritten journal *al-Tahdhib* (*Correction*). Its critiques of religion and education drew the approbation of conservative defenders of the social domination of the traditionally educated members of the religious elites. Another cause for opposition was its espousal of the ideas of those Islamic modernist thinkers who were making an impact in the wider Muslim world, particularly Muhammad 'Abdu. The journal met with considerable opposition, with opponents mocking it by calling it *al-Ta'dhib* (*Torture*).[59]

In the fourth issue of *al-Tahdhib*, the lead article entitled "The Verse of Correction" (Ayat al-tahdhib) and attributed to the byline Nasir al-'Ilm (Defender of Knowledge), 'Ali b. Ahmad BaKathir espoused the ideology of social reform prevalent in that journal. Reflecting on the Qur'an's injunction to encourage virtue and discourage vice, the article expanded the conventional meaning of these concepts. Virtue, the source of a people's wealth and strength, was described as their morals and understanding; it was encouraged by the establishment of mosques and religious institutions and the education of the ignorant. It was also encouraged by social acts including the establishment of security and order in the homeland; the advancement of industry, agriculture, and commerce; the establishment of schools, hospitals, and facilities for the infirm; and the spread of media that would provide enlightened and rational thinking. Virtue was exemplified as social service.

With respect to the discouragement of vice, this article focused on customary practices in Hadhramawt which in the opinion of the author were a degradation of genuine religious practice. It defined as vices those practices that had become institutionalized in local custom and had spread, with the *'ulama'* tolerating or ignoring them. Errant practices had thus become transformed into beliefs which people felt obligated to obey. Eventually people came to consider any departure from these customs as innovation departing from the will of God (*bid'*), or even apostasy.[60]

In the fifth issue of *al-Tahdhib*, BaKathir more explicitly addressed "vice" embodied in socially institutionalized religious practice in a critical article on the topic of tomb visiting and on the related issue of intercession. He characterized them as misguided forms of religious expression that required correction through the process of social and religious reform. In the article entitled "al-Tadhkir," (Reminding) 'Ali b. Ahmad BaKathir, again writing as Nasir al-'Ilm (Defender of Knowledge), commenced by stating the necessity of reminding people of their religion. His goal was to correct their beliefs from stains (*lawthat*) and delusions (*al-awham*) and to cleanse them from heretical tendencies (*niz'at al-ahwa'*). This was necessary because people employed their emotions rather than their intellect when trying to distinguish between the true and the false, the beneficial and the harmful. He questioned whether the religion that people were following was actually the religion brought by Muhammad and quoted the Islamic modernist thinker 'Abd al-Qadir al-Maghrabi saying that Muslims, by departing from true Islam, had become the same as non-Muslims.

His arguments followed the line of earlier and contemporary Islamic modernists. In the face of the political decline of the Islamic world in modern times, he wondered how it was that Muslims had reached such depths of defeat. He proposed two possible causes for the decline of the Muslim community. One possibility was that the Muslims were living according to the will of God, but had been deceived by God by false promises. The other possibility was that God's message was true, but the Muslims were not following their religion properly nor living as God willed, for which they were suffering. He pressed his readers to face the problem, examine their practice of religion, and reform their society.

After this preface, he strongly criticized people's participating in misguided un-Islamic superstitions and propagating them. He criticized the practice of people visiting tomb-sites, seeking intercession and making offerings, which he likened to the practices of the pre-Islamic Age of Ignorance. He criticized the *'ulama'* for failing to prevent these practices. He concluded by asserting that continuing such practices would impede progress, condemning the people of Hadhramawt to continue suffering the tortures of ignorance, decline, corruption of morals, loss of respect from other nations, and loss of their own independence, as well as torture in the afterlife.[61] As embellishment of ʿAli b. Ahmad BaKathir's point, below the initials of his pseudonymous byline, appeared bits of editorial "filler:" a quote from *hadith*, headed "Freedom of Opinion" (*Huriyat al-raʾi*) which stated that a man should not fear speaking the truth and a poetic excerpt entitled "The Intellect Is Fire" (*al-ʿAql nar*).[62]

The article received an outraged response from the *ʿulamaʾ* of Hadhramawt, who tried to suppress circulation of the journal; some of BaKathir's colleagues at al-Nahdha al-ʿIlmiyya school were among the outraged readers. An editorial entitled "*Hawla maqal al-tadhkir*" (About the Essay 'Reminding') reiterated the author's argument, stating that corrupted religious practices and superstitions led people to seek the intercession of the dead in defense against imperialist encroachment, when it was the responsibility of the living to defend their lands. It criticized the *ʿulamaʾ* for their criticism and attempts at suppression, and it asked: if this is how the seekers of knowledge reacted, how would seekers of ossification have reacted? But the editor of *al-Tahdhib* pronounced that Hadhramawt was not yet ready for such material to appear and he refused to print any further writings on the subject, leaving the author without a means of public response to his critics.[63]

Four months after the original article appeared, ʿAli b. Ahmad BaKathir finally had the opportunity to respond. His response, "My Beliefs on Visiting Tombs, and on Intercession," was conciliatory. While he denied that he was contradicting earlier views, he moderated his original stance on tomb visiting and intercession, as a result of the intense pressure brought to bear upon him both publicly and privately. In this long-delayed response, he justified the previous article. He reiterated his belief that the Muslim world would not rise again from the depths of decay in which it was currently sunk nor recover its former greatness, but would remain bound by the chains of occupation under the imperial powers until the Muslims corrected their errant beliefs and behaviors. Thus it was necessary that they be "reminded" of their true religion. He claimed that the tremendous outrage that his expression of this opinion had inspired and the harsh attacks he had suffered were the result of misunderstanding of his views. He had endured the pain of suffering attacks in silence, having been warned that the public, unaccustomed even to the existence of the press, was not yet ready for the ideas he had attempted to advance. But rumors that he had claimed that visiting tombs was impermissible and that intercession was forbidden in Islam forced him to further explain his beliefs. With respect to the religious aspect of these issues, he conceded that visiting tombs was proper if done correctly and quoted a hadith in which the Prophet condoned visiting grave sites if it was done to remind the visitor of the reality of death. Regarding intercession, he stated that it was permissible to ask for intermediation with God, particularly from the Prophet, his Companions, and their followers; he singled out the descendants of the Prophet as means of intermediation. (This is of interest since many of his critics were *sada*.) He appeared to have made a strategic withdrawal from his previous stance. But he further stipulated that the *ʿulamaʾ* needed to steer people from excess in the search for intercession, in order to keep them within the boundaries of the core belief of monotheism, tawhid or the oneness of God.

At the same time, with respect to the social aspects of these practices, 'Ali b. Ahmad BaKathir maintained his earlier stance. He cited Jamal al-Din al-Afghani and Muhammad 'Abdu as precedents in his opinion that the decline of the Muslim world and the loss of hegemony over the Muslim lands to unbelieving imperialists were due to dependence on the intercession of the dead to help the Muslims with their problems. But he conceded to his critics that other parts of the Muslim world were more inclined to "delusions and superstitions" than Hadhramawt, giving examples of popular religious practices in Egypt and India. These cases might otherwise have served as evidence for his argument correlating the decline of the Muslim world and capitulation to Western imperialism with the prevalence of misguided religious beliefs and practices. Yet he used them here—at least on the surface—to capitulate to his critics' claims that Hadhramawt was not to be singled out as the site of egregiously misguided beliefs and practices.[64]

Regardless of his apparent capitulation in this piece, after 'Ali b. Ahmad BaKathir had left Hadhramawt, he returned to the topic of tomb visiting and intercession in his play *Humam*, no longer pulling his punches. In the introduction, he referred to tomb visiting as *bid'* (an un-Islamic element introduced into religious practice) and enumerated it in a list including bad customs (*al-'adat al-say'*) and superstitions (*khurafat*). The play ridiculed the participants in a *ziyara* for gullibly seeking intercession and assistance with their problems from the visit, while the merchants and the custodians of the tomb were enriched by the participants' purchases and offerings.[65]

In the midst of the controversy about tomb visiting and intercession, 'Ali b. Ahmad BaKathir wrote an ostensibly noncontroversial article on the annual observance of the birth of the Prophet. Focusing on a topic of common interest—the reverence of all Muslims for the memory of the Prophet—the author highlighted existing ideological differences. With respect to the observation of the Prophet's birth, he pointed out that there was no difference between enlightened and rigid Muslims, between the reform-minded and the tradition-bound, defining a polarity underlying even apparent unity of belief. BaKathir did not explicitly make the argument here that the weakness of the contemporary Islamic community was a result of the community's straying from proper belief and practice, as he had previously. But he noted that evil was running rampant at the time God revealed his message to Muhammad, and that revelation resulted in the purification of belief, which ultimately led to the Muslims' gaining control of the Byzantine and Persian territories. This historical allegory combined with allusions to the rigid and the tradition-bound must have reminded his readers of his earlier articles and speeches and the controversy they provoked.[66]

The journal *al-Tahdhib* and 'Ali b. Ahmad BaKathir provoked dispute even on matters less obviously controversial than tomb visiting and intercession. Contention over the nature and practice of communal gatherings for the recitation of religious texts extended throughout the life span of the journal, from December 1930 through September 1931. The first issue of *al-Tahdhib* included a simple news announcement of the annual reading of the *hadith* collection *Sahih al-Bukhari*, which had taken place in a Say'un mosque on the fifteenth of Rajab. The announcement mentioned that the respected scholar Sayyid Salih al-Hamid had presented a poem in honor of the event and noting the large crowds that packed the mosque.[67] In the same issue appeared an article under the byline Nasir al-'Ilm entitled "Recitation of al-Bukhari in the Month of Rajab." The essayist, 'Ali b. Ahmad BaKathir, criticized the practice and offered suggestions of modifications that would make it more beneficial to the populace. Clarifying that he was not condemning the practice but merely suggesting improvements, the author suggested that people would benefit more from an extensive reading, study, and discussion of the material than from the rapid ritualistic recitation during Rajab. He suggested that other collections of *hadith* merited study, proposing that in some years people might benefit from exposure to *Sahih Muslim* or *Sahih Ibn Da'ud* instead of always *Sahih al-Bukhari*. He suggested similar communal performances of other Islamic sciences, proposing that Qur'anic commentaries be recited in the mosques during Ramadhan nights and extensive coverage of the sources and branches of Islamic jurisprudence be recited during the rest of the year.[68]

While apparently positive, practical, and innocuous, these suggestions for the enhancement of a public religious performance led to a debate in the pages of the journal and among those members of the populace concerned with religious dissemination. In the third issue of *al-Tahdhib*, a reader who signed his response Mulahiz (an Observer) responded to this article. This respondent indicated that concerned youth had been upset by Nasir al-'Ilm's critique and expressed his disagreement. He stated that the customary recitation of *Sahih al-Bukhari* during Rajab was an appropriate way to honor that holy month, and that the brevity and rapidity of the recitation had the benefit of not tiring or boring people. As to the suggestion that in some years other collections of *hadith* might be read, the respondent rejected it with the argument that people were not familiar with other works, so they would be unclear, boring, and could not be completed as quickly. He opined it was sufficient for *'ulama'* to study other collections, without presenting them as an event for the public. Furthermore, he rejected Nasir al-'Ilm's argument that scholars needed to do a deeper study of Islamic jurisprudence. He claimed that when people were busy with the modern sciences and no longer had sufficient interest to carry out in-depth studies of Islamic sciences, it was simply to be hoped that the system would produce people knowledgeable enough to issue legal opinions. He added that *ijtihad*, or independent legal reasoning, had become more difficult than it had been in previous times.[69]

In a later issue, the "Defender of Knowledge" responded with the wish that the "Observer" had employed logic in his purported attempt to soothe those youth who had become agitated by criticism of the Rajab event. Noting that people tended to preserve the status quo regardless of what would be most beneficial to society, he pointed out that he had not disputed that people benefited from the recitation, but merely had made suggestions for changes to further benefit the public. With respect to the argument that current practice had the advantage of being familiar and therefore fast, clearly comprehensible, and not boring for the audience, which encouraged workers and tradesmen to attend, Nasir al-'Ilm countered that people would also attend recitations of other collections and that the unfamiliarity and lack of immediate comprehensibility of these texts actually argued in favor of their presentation, not against it. Concerning the matter of the necessity for in-depth study of Islamic jurisprudence, Nasir al-'Ilm questioned the counterargument that people were currently too concerned with modern natural sciences to make in-depth studies of the traditional Islamic sciences. He pointed out that since in Hadhramawt there was a total failure to study the modern sciences, any lack of interest in the principles of Islamic law could not be attributed to that factor. At the same time, other Islamic countries such as Egypt, Iraq, and Syria, all of which enjoyed a flourishing interest in the modern natural sciences, also demonstrated a resurgence of study and interest in Islamic law. He also contended that if Hadhramawt lacked scholars qualified to make legal pronouncements, it was due to the lack of proper education and not to any trend toward modern science. He added that surely independent legal reasoning was easier than it had been in the past, due to the increased dissemination of knowledge made possible by the printing press.[70] The attention to the Rajab recitation of *Sahih al-Bukhari* exemplified *al-Tahdhib*'s goal of bettering the moral development of Hadhrami society through increased dissemination of religious knowledge and better understanding. While the tone of the article was conciliatory and appeared to be more in the spirit of helpfulness than criticism, its suggestions were met with a defensive response. In the end, even the good intentions and the logic of the reformers were not able to prevail over established custom and its proponents.

As the disputation in *al-Tahdhib* over the recitation of *Sahih al-Bukhari* indicated, there was no topic more contentious than that of change in educational institutions, whether in traditional schools or the new civil schools, which were still imbued with the traditional system of learning. Social conservatives and some of the *'ulama'* defended the continued transmission of learning in the accustomed style while social critics argued for a greater emphasis on secular subjects and called for a renewal of Islam in the spirit of the Islamic modernists exemplified by Muhammad 'Abdu and Rashid Ridha.

One of the earliest critics of educational change in Hadhramawt, Sayyid Hasan b. 'Alawi Bin Shihab, an early teachers in the *ribat* of Tarim, was dissatisfied with the methods and goals of instruction in the *ribat*. After leaving his post in 1902 and moving to Singapore, where he published articles on social reform directed toward the Arabic-speaking community there as well as publishing articles in the modernist Egyptian journal *al-Manar*. He also wrote a pamphlet entitled *Nihlat al-watan*, expressing his vision of educational reform. In it, he criticized the mode of instruction prevalent in Hadhramawt, urging that education relate to practical matters (*dunya*) as well as religion (*din*). He described the traditional system as one in which the scholar sat in the mosque nearest his house, repeating what he had learned to whoever came, randomly grouped in study circles with no regard to their level of knowledge, with all of the students simultaneously reading about different, wildly unrelated topics. He argued for a more modern type of curriculum, in which the students all studied the same book at the same time. He also criticized the traditional educational establishment for limiting the population that it served, deploring the fact that market people, farmers, slaves, and other members of lower-status groups lacked the opportunity to gain learning. He found this shameful in both social and religious terms. His treatise was later countered by Sayyid 'Alawi b. 'Abd al-Rahman al-Mashhur, his former colleague at the *ribat* and founder of Madrasat Makarim al-Ahlaq in al-Shihr.[71]

'Ali Ahmad BaKathir was also heavily involved in the debate, as exemplified in the speech that he had delivered on the first anniversary fete of Madrasat al-Nahdha al-'Ilmiyya school, the text of which was printed in three installments of *al-Tahdhib*. The speech, which had been considered radical to the point of outrage at the time of its delivery, provoked adamant responses again when it appeared in print, leading to a long delay between the printing of the early installments and the conclusion. While the first two installments appeared in the first two issues, the final installment did not appear until the tenth and final edition of the journal.

In the beginning of the speech, 'Ali b. Ahmad BaKathir addressed critics who had charged that the tone of the school was foreign. He responded that this was not the case, since Islam shared roots with the Judeo-Christian tradition and since Islam had preserved the great classical texts of antiquity through translations made during the Golden Age of Islam. He argued that the foundations of modern scientific thought and modern education were not foreign to Islam but rather were an integral part of its heritage.

What followed was more contentious. He enumerated what he saw as ills besetting the mental life of the society, specifically the maladies of intellectual rigidity (*da' al-jamud*), blind obedience to traditional precedents (*da' al-taqlid*), and the tendency to rush to judgment without understanding or knowledge (*da' al-tasarru'*). He blamed these intellectual ills within Hadhrami society on deficiencies in the way Islam had been studied. He asserted that a fuller study of Islamic history, literature, and law was needed to bring about a higher level of understanding than currently prevailed.

Finally, 'Ali b. Ahmad BaKathir extolled the value of literature, defending it against those who criticized "literature" in thinly veiled criticism of BaKathir himself, his work, belief system, and ideas about education and social reform. He responded to those who called literature inconsistent with true piety and worshipfulness by citing the devotional poetry and expressions of worship created by Hadhramawt's beloved spiritual leaders, Sayyid 'Abdallah b. Ahmad al-Haddad and Sayyid 'Ali b. Muhammad al-Hibshi.

He argued that there was no contradiction between progress and true Islam. In a stirring passage, he asserted that the spirit of Islam was a spirit of life and understanding, a spirit of effort and labor, a spirit of renewal and progress, a spirit of movement and continuation, with nothing of rigidity and immobility in it.

To compound the offense he caused his ideological opponents, 'Ali b. Ahmad BaKathir then suggested Muhammad 'Abdu as an example of the spirit of progress in Islam. He deplored the fact that while those in Hadhramawt knew who 'Abdu was, they were not familiar with his works. He considered it unfortunate that Hadramis knew the works of this great Islamic reformer only through the words of critics accusing him of sacrilegious innovation. He asked his audience repeatedly why they did not read the works of Muhammad 'Abdu rather than rigidly adhering to the opinion of his critics. Although he apologized if he had offended anyone, those words could not mollify those who saw in his progressive ideals and his advocacy of Muhammad 'Abdu's ideas a threat to Hadhrami society.[72] The vehement response of critics to this speech was later fictionally reflected in a scene in 'Ali b. Ahmad BaKathir's play *Humam*. In the play, the school anniversary speech concluded with the *'ulama'* shouting that the speaker (the fictional Humam) was trying to introduce a new religion and called him a Wahhabi and a Mu'tazali.[73]

Other writers sharing 'Ali b. Ahmad BaKathir's reformist zeal, including his brother 'Umar, wrote articles in *al-Tahdhib* criticizing the educational system. An article entitled "On the Education of Girls" proposed fostering girls' education and changing men's condescending attitude toward women in order to benefit society. The author noted that the issue of girl's education had previously been discussed without any constructive result, but he hoped that readers would be more responsive to the issue.

He wrote that the rigid nature of Hadhrami society meant that a Hadhrami woman was not able to understand her own affairs, and hardly knew how to manage her home, raise her children, and make a comfortable life for herself, her husband, and her family. She knew only the minimum requirements of her religious duties. He blamed that deplorable situation on Hadhrami men, who did not value women enough, regarding them with disdain and contempt, exemplified in a Hadhrami colloquial expression suggesting that women were "the lowest of the low" (*dhillan madhlulan 'azzak Allah*). The author asked how his readers could disrespect women since God's will made women and men equal and made it incumbent on women to attain knowledge and wisdom.

'Umar b. Ahmad BaKathir clarified that he was not suggesting that women be educated in order to become judges, open shops, or do "men's work." Rather he stressed the need for women to be taught the principles of religion and morality, her marital rights, and how to raise morally upright children. He quoted lines from a poem by 'Ali b. Ahmad BaKathir on the subject of the necessity of fostering the moral development of women. The poem said that "the mother was the stone forming a foundation, good or bad . . ." and "the source of everything under the sun which took place in the affairs of men . . ."[74]

In another article in the same issue, 'Umar b. Muhammad BaKathir, 'Ali b. Ahmad BaKathir's cousin and close friend, made a trenchant criticism of the *'ulama'* of Hadhramawt and the system of learning through which they claimed their legitimacy. In an article entitled "Correctness of Interpretation," 'Umar b. Muhammad BaKathir pointed out that while there were plenty of people called *'ulama'*, there actually were few qualified to interpret scholarly materials and misinterpretations were passed on from generation to generation. He attributed the problem to four causes. The first cause was that the scholars limited themselves to repeatedly reading a small number of weak and rigid texts. The second was scholars' failure to use the new print media to understand contemporary realities and to disseminate their own work. The third was the scholars' blind following of their teachers and peers. The fourth was the scholars' failure to edify themselves by enjoying works of inspirational poetry that would enrich their speech and writings. He quoted al-Ghazzali on the ideal confluence of eloquence, interpretation, and learning as a contrast to the example of what he called rigid and tradition-bound Hadhrami scholars.[75]

In another article in *al-Tahdhib*, Sayyid Muhammad b. Ahmad Bin Yahya also criticized the educational system. In "The Sciences and Our Schools," he enumerated various facets of education in religion, Arabic language, and math, asserting that education in Hadhramawt was currently in a state of deterioration. He felt that the schools focused on jurisprudence and grammar to the detriment of other critical areas of knowledge and that the schools merely taught texts rather than inculcating knowledge. Lacking knowledge, the students ended up rigidly fixated on interpretations they had learned of a few books.[76]

Along with other articles that carried out the stated mission of the journal by explicitly criticizing Hadhrami society, those articles which castigated the *'ulama'* with respect to the education of students and the moral guidance of the public drew scathing responses. These responses took the form of letters to *al-Tahdhib* and articles in other journals.[77] Since a significant segment of the journal's social critique focused on weaknesses in the educational system and in religious scholarship, it is not surprising that the dialogue was carried out in part in the schools. The eighth issue included a letter signed by "a pupil who loves learning," which praised the journal and expressed regret that the teachers regarded the newspapers with displeasure and forbade students to read them.[78]

Largely due to opposition based on its contentious stand on issues of religion and education, the journal *al-Tahdhib* ceased publication in 1932. The concerted responses to his social and religious criticism, even that which he expressed in the most tactful and conciliatory terms, along with tragedies in his personal life, led to 'Ali b. Ahmad BaKathir's departure from Hadhramawt the following year. That same year in exile in the Hijaz, he wrote his three-act play in free verse, *Hu-*

mam, aw fi 'asimat al-Ahqaf, which delivered a stringent commentary on social and religious issues in Hadhramawt.[79]

Change in Religious and Educational Institutions

During the late nineteenth and early twentieth century, traditional religious structures persisted and people continued to take part in the communal practices of their ancestors, with most people's level and role of participation in religious education and activities defined by their social group identity. This was far from a period of stagnation, however. Supported by concerned emigrants, new institutions of religious education were founded and new methods of education were attempted. Religious education became a possibility for a wider range of the population than previously and leaders such as Sayyid 'Ali b. Muhammad al-Hibshi and Sayyid 'Abd al-Rahman b. 'Alawi al-Mashhur helped to elevate the standard of religious knowledge of the public. Change in religious education was highly contested, with disputes taking place not only between modernizers and conservatives, but also among the modernizers themselves. 'Ali b. Ahmad BaKathir, in his speeches and writings, exemplified the arguments of those who, influenced by Islamic modernism, urged reform both of religious practice and education. Within all the contestation, perhaps the most controversial aspect of religious reform was its challenge to the social domination of the *sada,* long maintained through their monopoly of education and through their control of the rituals associated with the *ziyara.* In a time of political turmoil in the Kathiri and Qu'ayti sultanates—resulting from internal rivalries and conflicts and from the threat of external domination—concern about reformist ideology and its challenges to the social and political order increasingly affected the ongoing contests over power and politics.

PART FOUR
Politics, Power, and Conflict

7
The Two Sultanates: Rivals from Inception to Union (1880s to 1918)

The 1880s marked a transition in the development of political structures in Hadhramawt in which the foundation was set for the two sultanates that ruled Hadhramawt for subsequent decades. While the preceding decades had been a time of struggle for territory and power among a number of competitors, the 1880s began a period of consolidation of territory and power and the building of the states of the Kathiri and Qu'ayti sultanates. This period of consolidation and state building was not accomplished without conflict; both sultanates faced challenges from within their own ranks and from recalcitrant tribes that objected to the extension of state control over what they considered their traditional domains. At the end of this time period, the international conflict of World War I and the demise of the Ottoman Empire had local reverberations in Hadhramawt, in which conflicts over power briefly appeared to take on international significance.

Kathiri and Qu'ayti Prevail among Rivals

The years between 1880 and 1936 were a period of stability and development compared with preceding decades. Hadhramawt had not experienced unified rule since the sixteenth century, when the great Sultan, Badr "Abu Tuwayriq" al-Kathiri consolidated power over both the coast and interior, and even his claim to rule was challenged by rivals. Even at the time of Abu Tuwayriq's success, the seeds of the challenges to Kathiri rule had been sown. The Yafi'i tribesmen he brought to Hadhramawt to serve as his armed forces and provide the military administration for his rule eventually developed their own bases of power and in later generations resisted the authority of central Kathiri rule. The Yafi'is, who had settled on lands which they purchased or were granted as estates by Abu Tuwayriq in exchange for their service, eventually became a network of local strongmen interspersed among the Hadhrami tribes, holding hegemony over distinct small domains where they offered protection to the settled population in exchange for a portion of production.

In the early nineteenth century, two branches of the Kathiri dynasty ruled small areas in the interior of Hadhramawt, while various branches of Yafi'i tribes ruled the coast and much of the interior. The coast was controlled by two powerful families of the Yafi'i: the Bin Birayk in al-Shihr and the Kasadi in al-Mukalla

and in the coastal towns of al-Hami and al-Dis. Later in that century, the balance
of power was disrupted by three new contenders, all of whom had acquired wealth,
arms, and military prowess through service as *jamaʿdar*s (commanders) in the Arab
army of the Nizam of Hyderabad. Of these three, Ghalib b. Muhsin al-Kathiri of
the Al ʿAbdallah branch of the Kathiri tribe, ʿUmar b. ʿAwadh al-Quʿayti, and ʿAbdallah b. ʿAli al-ʿAwlaqi, only the latter was not of Hadhrami origin, being from
farther west in Southern Arabia.

In 1844, Ghalib b. Muhsin al-Kathiri purchased a village in the interior (reports of its price vary from 1,500 to 5,000 *riyals*) and he built a fort nearby from
which he began to reclaim the surrounding lands from various Yafiʿi strongmen.
With the financial and military support of the ʿAwlaqi *jamaʿdar* in Hyderabad and
his representatives in Hadhramawt, he managed to take territory which the Yafiʿis
had claimed or, in some cases, forced them to sell territory to him. Ghalib also attempted to take al-Shihr from its Yafiʿi ruler, Bin Birayk, but failed in the effort.
In addition to challenging the various Yafiʿi strongholds, Ghalib challenged his distant relative from the Al ʿIsa b. Badr branch of the Kathiri tribe, who, surrounded
by Yafiʿi-held territory, still ruled the important market center of Shibam.

Weakened by feuding with Ghalib b. Muhsin of the Al ʿAbdallah Kathiri
and without the advantage of money and arms available to the emigrant soldiers
serving in Hyderabad, Sultan Mansur of the Al ʿIsa b. Badr Kathiri was forced to
sell half of Shibam to the family of a powerful *jamaʿdar* from the Nizam's army,
ʿUmar b. ʿAwadh al-Quʿayti. Then ʿUmar b. ʿAwadh, who had acquired great
wealth and extensive estates in Hyderabad, purchased the town of al-Qatn, west of
Shibam, and sent four of his sons, ʿAli, Muhammad, ʿAwadh, and ʿAbdallah there.
He and another son Salih remained in Hyderabad, where they masterminded and
funded the struggle for power in Hadhramawt. By 1859, after protracted fighting,
assassinations, and assassination attempts, the Quʿayti prevailed and ejected the Al
ʿIsa b. Badr Kathiri ruler from Shibam. In 1849, the Quʿayti had tried to capture
Say'un, which had been taken over from its Yafiʿi overlords by Ghalib b. Muhsin
of the Al ʿAbdallah Kathiri; in 1869 he repeated the attempt with the assistance of
the Kasadi Naqib, then ruler of al-Mukalla. Unlike his kinsman Mansur of the Al
ʿIsa b. Badr Kathiri, Ghalib with wealth, military prowess, and power acquired in
Hyderabad was able to hold the Quʿayti at bay and retain a core of territory in the
center of his tribal homeland. Ghalib's success in retaining Say'un, which became
the capital of his tiny sultanate, prevented the Quʿayti from attaining his goal of
uniting all Hadhramawt under his rule.

In 1867, Ghalib al-Kathiri captured the important port town of al-Shihr after first taking its water supply in the inland town of Baqarayn from the ruling Bin
Birayk branch of the Yafiʿi. He then attempted to take the other port of al-Mukalla,
but was prevented from doing so by its ruler, the Kasadi Naqib. ʿAwadh b. ʿUmar
al-Quʿayti, aided by the Kasadi, then ejected the Kathiri from al-Shihr and repelled
his efforts to retake the port, despite the appearance of an Ottoman warship in support of the Kathiri. The Quʿayti did not return al-Shihr to Bin Birayk; instead, he

made it the first capital of the Qu'ayti domain. Given the military and economic dependence of the Qu'ayti on his family seat in the adopted homeland of Hyderabad, acquisition of a port was of critical importance.

As Qu'ayti power grew, he was opposed by an alliance consisting of his former ally the Kasadi Naqib of al-Mukalla, the Kathiri, and the third Hyderabad-based aspirant to power in Hadhramawt, 'Abdallah b. 'Ali al-'Awlaqi, whose ambitions were carried on by his son Muhsin b. 'Abdallah. Although the homeland of this *jama'dar* lay to the west (about halfway between al-Mukalla and Aden), in 1863 he had purchased from Bin Birayk the village of Sida' between al-Shihr and Ghayl BaWazir and built a magnificent fortress there, from which he had prepared to amass power and territory. But the greater strength of the Qu'ayti prevailed, and by 1876 he had not only retained his base in al-Shihr but had taken Ghayl BaWazir from the Kathiri and Sida' from the 'Awlaqi.

Besides dispensing with his 'Awlaqi rival and surrounding the Kathiri in a small landlocked territory, the Qu'ayti also dealt with his erstwhile ally, the Kasadi Naqib. When Naqib Salih al-Kasadi had joined with the Qu'ayti for the failed attack on the Kathiri seat of Say'un in 1869, he had borrowed money from the Qu'ayti in order to purchase arms and pay his troops. In 1873, 'Awadh b. 'Umar al-Qu'ayti demanded repayment of 160,000 *riyals* from 'Umar b. Salih al-Kasadi after his father's death. Unable to pay and facing Qu'ayti troops in al-Mukalla, the Kasadi sold half of al-Mukalla and Burum to the Qu'ayti for 240,000 *riyals*, which consisted of a payment of 80,000 *riyals* and forgiveness of the prior debt. Claiming that the sale was made under duress, the Kasadi then sought support from the British, the Ottomans, and the sultan of Musqat and Zanzibar, to no avail. In late 1881, supported politically and militarily by the British, the Qu'ayti took possession of al-Mukalla in its entirety, paying another 100,000 *riyals* to the disgruntled Kasadi Naqib, who went into exile in Zanzibar.

Thus ended the years of rivalry and shifting alliances among previous Yafi'i and Al 'Isa b. Badr Kathiri rulers of Hadhramawt and the three new aspirants to power from Hyderabad, the Qu'ayti, Al 'Abdallah Kathiri, and 'Awlaqi. By 1882, when the Qu'ayti signed a Treaty of Friendship with the British, of his rivals, only Al 'Abdallah al-Kathiri remained in power, with the small territory ruled by 'Ali b. al-Mansur surrounded and landlocked by Qu'ayti domains. Even though the rivalry between these two powers continued, the cessation of the continual warfare of the earlier decades allowed the Qu'ayti rulers to consolidate and build their state.[1] The Kathiri rulers, on the other hand, frustrated in their landlocked position, did little in the way of state building. The attention of the Kathiri rulers remained focused on attempting, albeit unsuccessfully, to break out of their disadvantageous position of being landlocked and surrounded by the more powerful Qu'ayti state. However, the 1882 Qu'ayti Treaty of Friendship with the British supported Qu'ayti rule of the coast and solidified the shifting power dynamics of the region. In late 1883, 'Abdallah b. Salih al-Kathiri visited the Aden Residency on behalf of Sultan Ghalib b. Muhsin al-Kathiri, in order to ascertain the British response in the case of a Kathiri attack on the Qu'ayti-held ports of al-Shihr and al-Mukalla. He also traveled to Zanzibar in an attempt to enlist the support of the exiled Kasadi Naqib. The Kasadi was not interested and the British government, cognizant of their engagement with the Qu'ayti, warned the Kathiri against carrying out his plan and pledged to send a gunboat to support the Qu'ayti in the event of such an attack.[2]

Foundations of the Qu'ayti State

The founder of the Qu'ayti state, Jam'adar 'Umar b. 'Awadh al-Qu'ayti, and his third son Salih remained in Hyderabad, from which they financed and directed the operations of establishing Qu'ayti rule in Hadhramawt carried out by 'Umar's other sons, 'Ali, Muhammad, 'Abdallah, and 'Awadh. In Jam'adar 'Umar's will of 1872, he bequeathed property and left instructions for the maintenance of Qu'ayti dominions in Hadhramawt. He left one-third of all his considerable wealth, including assets in Arabia and India amounting to several million rupees, in a trust for administering Qu'ayti possessions in Hadhramawt and establishing security and prosperity there. Money from the trust was to be spent on the needs of towns and cities under Qu'ayti rule and for providing the fortifications, arms, and troops necessary to provide security for the state and its subjects.[3]

While Jam'adar 'Umar's will provided a mandate for his heirs and successors, the Qu'ayti state also began to participate in international agreements. In 1873, the rulers of the coastal towns renewed the anti-slave-trade agreements of 1863 with the British. While the 1863 anti-slave-trade agreements had been contracted with the Kasadi Naqib of al-Mukalla and Bin Birayk of al-Shihr, the 1873 agreements were signed by the Kasadi Naqib of al-Mukalla and 'Abdallah b. 'Umar and 'Awadh b. 'Umar al-Qu'ayti of al-Shihr.[4] In 1882, 'Abdallah b. 'Umar al-Qu'ayti, acting on behalf of himself and his brother 'Awadh, signed the Treaty of Friendship with the British as *jama'dar* of al-Mukalla and al-Shihr. In this treaty, the British recognized the Qu'ayti takeover of the territory previously ruled by the Kasadi and promised a salary of 360 *riyals* annually to the brothers and their successors. The Qu'ayti agreed not to sell, mortgage, or cede territory to anyone other than the British and to abide by British advice in dealing with surrounding tribal leaders and with foreign powers. In 1888, 'Abdallah b. 'Umar al-Qu'ayti on behalf of himself and his brother 'Awadh signed a full Protectorate Treaty with the British.[5]

Later in that same year, 'Abdallah b. 'Umar died. 'Awadh b. 'Umar was then the sole remaining director of their father 'Umar b. 'Awadh's trust, Salih b. 'Umar having died in Hyderabad in 1877. 'Awadh b. 'Umar became ruler of the Qu'ayti state and was recognized as such by the British. During 'Awadh's rule, his succession was challenged by his nephews Munassir and Husayn, the sons of 'Abdallah b. 'Umar, who wanted Qu'ayti territory to be divided in order that they could inherit what they considered to be their father's share of the family estates. Perhaps because of this conflict, 'Awadh b. 'Umar left in his will of 1898 further instructions for succession to rule and management of the trust bequeathed by his father 'Umar b. 'Awadh.

'Awadh b. 'Umar's 1898 will determined that the succession alternate between his two sons and their descendants. It named his son Ghalib b. 'Awadh as his successor; next in line was his other son 'Umar b. 'Awadh; next was his grandson Ghalib b. 'Umar's son Salih b. Ghalib; next was the son of 'Umar b. Ghalib, if one was born. Succession was to continue to alternate from among the descendants of Ghalib b. 'Awadh and 'Umar b. 'Awadh.

The will included further instructions intended to foster cooperation rather than conflict among 'Awadh b. 'Umar's heirs. It specified that if a future ruler resided in al-Shihr, his designated successor should officiate at al-Mukalla on his behalf; if the ruler resided in al-Mukalla, his successor should officiate at al-Shihr in his behalf. The successor was to be named Chief Official superintending all goods, properties, and revenues of the country, under the command of the ruler. If the successor was in India, his heir should act on his behalf in Hadhramawt; if the successor was in Hadhramawt, his heir should act on his behalf in India. The successor was to be under the orders of the ruler and the heir to the successor under the orders of the successor. The ruler was to provide an allowance to his successor and to all the descendants of 'Awadh b. 'Umar. In addition, the ruler was to provide an allowance to any heirs of the founder 'Umar b. 'Awadh, for which in turn they were to loyally obey, assist, and support the ruler. The will ordained that the ruler held the power to appoint and dismiss government representatives in the cities and towns in Qu'ayti territory. In this way, 'Awadh b. 'Umar attempted to assure that his heirs and successors would function jointly as a strong dynasty supporting a single ruler over an undivided Qu'ayti dominion.[6]

In 1902, the British government dropped the title "Jama'dar" and began to use the title "Sultan" in their communications with 'Awadh b. 'Umar al-Qu'ayti; he was the first of the Southern Arabian rulers to be granted this title and to be referred to as "His Highness." He also was unique among the Southern Arabian rulers in being entitled to a twelve-gun salute. While the Kathiri in the interior resented and resisted the intrusion of this newer, more powerful, and expanding sultanate on the coast, with its foreign alliances, the Qu'ayti continued aspiring to incorporate the Kathiri domains.[7]

Consolidation and Expansion of Territory under Qu'ayti Rule

After the Qu'ayti had prevailed over the Kathiri, Kasadi, and others and gained control of the coast of Hadhramawt and Shibam in the interior, the next step was the consolidation of these territories under Qu'ayti rule by establishing the administrative presence of the state there. This process sometimes involved sending administrators to new territories, but it often consisted of appointing local notables to serve in the name of the Qu'ayti state. At the same time, a further step was the expansion of Qu'ayti control into adjacent territories, including Wadi Du'an and Wadi Hajr, ruled by local strongmen, either by absorbing them into the administration or by conquest.

To establish Qu'ayti administration, governors and deputies were sent to the various outposts of the state. The capital of al-Shihr was governed first by Jama'dar 'Abdallah b. 'Umar al-Qu'ayti, and after his death by his son Husayn. In 1888, Jama'dar 'Abdallah b. 'Umar began construction of the first Qu'ayti palace in al-Shihr and completed the building of the highly fortified wall around al-Shihr, which he had begun in 1867. The wall and fortifications provided an unprecedented degree of security from tribal incursions, which stimulated commercial activity of the port, then the most active on the coast. The state encouraged trade, and commercial activity flourished as import-export agencies set up within the port city.

The key cities of al-Shihr, al-Mukalla, and Shibam were all governed by members of the ruling family, appointed by the head of state, Jama'dar 'Awadh b. Umar. Other towns and cities were governed by appointed members of the extended Qu'ayti family, by loyal lieutenants of the Qu'ayti from their Yafi'i supporters and from the slave troops, or by prominent local leaders, often also from families of Yafi'i origin.[8]

For example, the town of al-Hami on the coast east of al-Shihr was governed by the local notables of the Kasadi family, members of the Yafi'i *tulud* family who had remained when their kinsman, the Kasadi Naqib, the previous ruler of the coast, the Kasadi Naqib, went into exile in Zanzibar. Although the family had lost its dominion over al-Mukalla and the rest of the coast, it retained its local prestige and extensive landholdings in the fertile environs of al-Hami. 'Abdallah Sa'id al-Kasadi, who governed al-Hami after the Naqib fled, assisted the Qu'ayti in making treaties with the intransigent tribes of the hinterlands surrounding al-Hami. Eventually, the influence of 'Abdallah Sa'id al-Kasadi was perceived as a threat to Qu'ayti rule and he was assassinated in the 1880s. Still, the Kasadi family maintained its local prominence and the governorship passed to Mahfuz b. Ahmad al-Kasadi and then to his son Muhammad b. Mahfuz, who continued to be addressed by the traditional honorific, "Naqib."[9]

While the Kasadi family maintained, under Qu'ayti sovereignty, a sort of continuity of authority in a loyal corner of their former domain, they also served as governors in various outposts of the growing Qu'ayti state, including al-Dis al-Sharqiyya, east of al-Hami. In addition, a member of the Bin Birayk family, which had ruled al-Shihr until the Qu'ayti, Kathiri, and 'Awlaqi began their competition for power in the region, was an early governor of the Qu'ayti state in the small eastern port of al-Qusay'ar. The reputation and prestige of their families helped these governors to establish order and provide security on behalf of the Qu'ayti state.

The administration provided by these governors primarily consisted of collecting levies on production and extending the security of the Qu'ayti state to the settled populace. The process began with the construction of forts and *kuts*, or

guard towers. Towns were ringed with a series of fortifications and kuts that overlooked the houses and fields of their inhabitants. Roads between towns and the
watercourses running to al-Shihr from its sources of water supply in Tubbala and
Baqarayn were also paralleled by strings of forts and *kuts*, manned by Yafi'i and
slave soldiers.

The Qu'ayti state also appointed judges to serve in each town and village it
administered. Many of those appointed to official positions were local notables
who already served their communities in the shari'a courts. For example, the 'Aydid family continued in their traditional role as judges in the town of al-Hami.
Other judges appointed in Qu'ayti territories included members of the al-Hamid,
BaWazir, BaMakhrama, and BuNumay families, whose members had long been
respected as scholars and jurists.[10]

In addition to setting up administrators and garrisons throughout Qu'ayti
territory, the state was expanding into new territory through the time-honored
dual process of purchase and conquest. The most hotly contested area of expansion was in Wadi Du'an, which stretched from the west of the Qu'ayti stronghold
of Shibam in the interior to the west of the Qu'ayti base on the coast. Since this
wadi comprised the important western caravan route from the coastal cities of al-
Shihr and al-Mukalla to the market center of Shibam via Ghayl BaWazir, it was of
critical strategic and economic importance to the Qu'ayti state. Wadi Du'an and
its branches also produced rich crops of dates, grain, and vegetables through spate
agriculture.

At the time that Qu'ayti power was being consolidated elsewhere in the region, Wadi Du'an was not under any type of unified rule, although the Kasadi
Naqib Salah b. Muhammad and his successor 'Umar b. Salah had previously tried
to impose rule on the wadi with limited success. The towns were each under independent rule and the population lacked solidarity. In 1898, having consulted
with his supporters among the Yafi'i leaders about the possibility of taking over
Wadi Du'an, Jama'dar 'Awadh b. 'Umar sent a force of two hundred Yafi'i soldiers
under the leadership of 'Abd al-Khaliq Almas (the son of the trusted slave who had
been sent by Jama'dar 'Umar b. 'Awadh with his son Muhammad to purchase al-
Qatn in 1847). These troops were joined by an additional force of two hundred
soldiers sent from Shibam by the governor, Salah b. Muhammad al-Qu'ayti.

The Qu'ayti force was countered by the 'Amudi family, which held both political power and spiritual influence over the major tribes of Du'an. The 'Amudi
called up a thousand men from the Dayyin tribe and five hundred from the Qithim
tribe. When the two sides met near Khurayba, the Qu'ayti troops managed to occupy some forts, but were then surrounded by the 'Amudi's forces, who blockaded
them and cut off supplies of food and water. Fortunately for the troops perishing
from thirst in the forts, Salah b. Muhammad al-Qu'ayti sent two hundred additional Yafi'i from Shibam to Khurayba. Under fire from the 'Amudi troops, they
reached their besieged compatriots. In response, the 'Amudi sent for reinforce-
ments, calling in tribes from Wadi 'Amd and Wadi Rakhya. 'Abd al-Khaliq Almas,

the leader of the Qu'ayti troops, feared this escalation and 'Umar sent a force of five hundred more soldiers from al-Mukalla, which met the 'Amudi troops outside Khurayba. Even though the 'Amudi forces had greater numbers, eventually Qu'ayti forces prevailed and the 'Amudi's troops fled to the mountains and their tribal homelands, giving up the campaign against the Qu'ayti. These tribal troops, motivated at least as much by the prospect of plunder as by loyalty to the 'Amudi, lacked the cohesion of the Yafi'i troops comprising the Qu'ayti army. Another critical factor in the dispersal of the 'Amudi's tribal forces was the intervention of another powerful Du'ani tribe, the BaSurra, which turned heavy weapons against the 'Amudi's troops.

Having lost in his military effort, the 'Amudi attempted to negotiate with the Qu'ayti. The people of Khurayba and environs did not support the 'Amudi in his bid to maintain local power and sent their own representatives to meet with the Qu'ayti force. In this way, Khurayba and the rest of Du'an were incorporated into Qu'ayti territory, and the local power of the BaSurra family was enhanced by their association with the Qu'ayti state. The first governor was Salim b. 'Ali al-Dahri, a member of a Yafi'i family closely related to the Qu'ayti, and his second-in-command was 'Umar BaSurra. After two years, al-Dahri was replaced as governor by 'Abd al-Khaliq Almas, who died within a year. Some said that he committed suicide, while others considered his death to have been an assassination instigated by BaSurra, who then took over the position of governor of Du'an. The BaSurra family remained loyal supporters of Qu'ayti rule and continued to hold the governorship of Du'an. While the local power of the BaSurra was enhanced by its alliance with the Qu'ayti, the 'Amudi suffered from having initially opposed the Qu'ayti presence in Du'an. Still the 'Amudi maintained their position of spiritual influence over the tribes of Du'an and their material status as well, since the 'Amudi family, along with the 'Alawi *sada,* was exempted from the heavy taxation the BaSurra governor imposed on Du'an.[11]

While the BaSurra governor of Du'an was known for the heavy hand of his rule, he was appreciated as well as feared by the people for the stability his rule fostered. Shortly after the Qu'ayti occupation of Du'an, BaSurra wished to extend his influence over one of its subsidiaries, the fertile Wadi al-Aysar, where tribal fighting was taking place. Taking advantage of an incident in which some Yafi'is were killed by tribesmen, BaSurra requested support from the Qu'ayti for an incursion into al-Aysar. With the support of the Qu'ayti, BaSurra sent his tribal and Yafi'i troops against the tribes of al-Aysar. Although the 'Amudi held influence over the Aysar tribes, he refrained from involvement in this struggle, wary from his previous experience in attempting to rally the tribes of Du'an against Qu'ayti forces. After a year of fighting, BaSurra's troops prevailed over the tribes. He imposed on the tribes fines of thirty thousand *riyals* as reparations, which forced many to sell their land against their wishes and forced others into exile. The 'Amudi was rewarded by the Qu'ayti government for his nonintervention. He received a salary of three hundred *riyals* a year to fulfill his traditional role as mediator in tribal disputes, serving as a sort of subgovernor of al-Aysar under the BaSurra governor of Du'an.[12]

The other significant expansion during this period was the occupation of Wadi Hajr. Sultan 'Awadh b. 'Umar, through the agency of his son Ghalib, purchased a huge tract of land in the fertile Wadi Mayfa', the coastal delta formed by the water of Hadhramawt's only permanently flowing river, the spring-fed Hajr river.[13] Upstream from Wadi Mayfa' was the fertile Wadi Hajr, occupied by: arms-bearing tribesmen of the Nuwwah; the *mashayikh* family of BaRas who served as spiritual leaders for the Nuwwah; and the *subiyan* or "clients" who tilled the land. Like Du'an, the wadi lacked centralized political authority. Although a leader was chosen from the notables of the town of Hajr, he lacked authority outside the town, where might prevailed, making security precarious for the subiyan and other unarmed groups.

In 1899, Sultan 'Awadh sent a force of six hundred Yafi'i and Tamimi tribesmen to occupy Hajr. The tribesmen organized themselves to protect their homeland against the Qu'ayti forces. Tribal lore relates that some tribesmen met the Qu'ayti troops en route from al-Mukalla to Hajr, whereupon one of the Nuwwah tribesmen recited a poem:

Tell the Qu'ayti: so the *suq* [al-Mukalla] is not enough for you,
and now you want Hajr, the protected.
Tell him: it's impossible, the notion is rejected,
you Indian, we don't even understand your language.
The sun is eclipsed and the moon is strangled
and the mountains moan with pain.
I swear to God, if I could,
I would take al-Mukalla and its dirt and throw it into the ocean.

The tribesmen of Hajr gathered to prevent the passage of the Qu'ayti forces through the entrance to the wadi. After losing thirty-six men, the Qu'ayti forces retreated to al-Mukalla. The personal references to the "Indian" and his language indicated the hinterlands tribesmen's disdain for the Hyderabad influences displayed by the Qu'ayti rulers. The disparaging references to al-Mukalla reflected the fact that at this time Qu'ayti rule was transforming the quiet fishing and boat-repairing town of al-Mukalla into a commercial entrepôt second only to Aden on the Arabian Sea coast.

A year later, Sultan 'Awadh again tried to gain control of Hajr, this time sending his *wazir,* Husayn b. Hamid al-Mihdhar, there to buy land to be occupied by his supporters. This approach was more successful. With the mediation of the 'Attas *sada* and the BaRas *mashayikh,* al-Mihdhar eventually was able to broker agreements between the Qu'ayti and the tribes of Wadi Hajr and those living between Hajr and Wadi Mayfa'. The addition of Wadi Hajr and Wadi Du'an to Qu'ayti territory consolidated Qu'ayti control over the transportation routes to the interior and incorporated some of the most fertile and productive agricultural lands in the region.[14] In 1908, the Nuwwah from Du'an and Hajr carried out a brief but dramatic insurrection in Du'an against the Qu'ayti government and its BaSurra governors. But the representatives of the Qu'ayti government, the spiritual leaders from the BaRas *mashayikh,* and the Barr and 'Attas *sada* were able to make an agreement with the Nuwwah and settle the conflict.[15]

There were, however, limits on Qu'ayti expansion, in part because the British, wary of Qu'ayti territorial ambitions, supported neighboring powers that feared absorption. In 1878, the Qu'ayti attempted to purchase half of the port of Bi'r 'Ali, between the mouths of Wadi Hajr and Wadi Mayfa', from members of the 'Abd al-Wahid family. Other members of the 'Abd al-Wahid (also known as the Wahidi), who each ruled separate sections of the territory controlled by the family, became anxious about the possible involvement of the powerful Qu'ayti in their territory and appealed to the British for assistance. The British advised the owner of Bi'r 'Ali not to sell to the Qu'ayti. In 1902, the Qu'ayti attempted to buy part of the port of BalHaf in Wahidi territory from one of the Wahidi rulers, but the British once again opposed the act. In 1905, a Wahidi leader who sold his share of BalHaf was deposed in favor of his brother, who attacked and captured the Qu'ayti vessel carrying *riyals* intended for the purchase.

In 1916, the *wazir* Husayn b. Hamid al-Mihdhar traveled to Aden to discuss the prospective agreement between the Qu'ayti and Kathiri, the precursor of the one ultimately signed in Aden in 1918. He also brought a draft agreement concerning the future status and administration of BalHaf and other Wahidi territories which the Qu'ayti hoped to sign with the Wahidi leaders, pending British approval. The colonial government deferred judgment on both matters until the end of the war, at which time they refused to support Qu'ayti aspirations with respect to BalHaf.[16]

Still, the incorporation of adjacent territories in the eastern hinterland continued well into the twentieth century. The date-producing wadi of 'Idim, south of Tarim on the caravan route south to al-Shihr, was territory traditionally controlled by the Al Jabir tribe. This tribe, which had client tribes tending their lands, had long demanded tribute from the settled populace within their territory. Their demands grew increasingly burdensome and in the second decade of the twentieth century, the Al Jabir retaliated harshly against those who refused to submit to their demands, destroying crops, burning date orchards, plundering, and murdering. In 1913/1914, a delegation including men from the unarmed groups and from the other tribes in Wadi 'Idim traveled to al-Mukalla to appeal for the assistance of Sultan Ghalib b. 'Awadh, requesting that the area be incorporated into the Qu'ayti state. Sultan Ghalib sent Salim Ahmad al-Bakri with twenty-five Yafi'i soldiers to assert the security of the Qu'ayti state over Wadi 'Idim, putting an end to Al Jabir control. The Al Jabir tribe submitted to state authority, although in later decades they created problems for both the Qu'ayti and Kathiri states by attacking travelers on the transportation route from coast to interior that passed through their territory.[17]

Conflicts within Dynasties: Succession Disputes

Sultan 'Awadh b. 'Umar al-Qu'ayti became aware of the dangers of dispute over succession, as previously noted, when his nephews disputed his succession to sole rule over Qu'ayti territory after the death of his brother 'Abdallah b. 'Umar in 1888. For Sultan 'Awadh, the disputation was complicated by demands of his office as *jama'dar* of the Hyderabad Nizam's army of Arab irregulars and his position as trustee of the family estates, which required him to spend a great deal of time in India. He was in the process of pressing claims against the government of Hyderabad for money due him for his service and for land that had been granted the family and then was reclaimed by the government. He was also involved in legal disputes there with his brother 'Ali b. 'Umar and with his nephew Muhsin b. Salih. While their uncle was absent taking care of these matters, Munassir and Husayn were setting up their own bases for power in Hadhramawt, trying to consolidate their position internally with the people and externally with the British authorities.

After 'Abdallah's death, 'Awadh b. 'Umar directed that the annual stipend of 360 *riyals* due the Qu'ayti ruler from the British government be paid to Husayn as the senior of the *na'ibs* (vice-regents) of the Qu'ayti government, and the one on whom 'Awadh relied when away in Hyderabad. Munassir received a third of the joint revenues of al-Mukalla and al-Shihr to administer Shibam and the interior. While Husayn kept up the appearance of loyalty to his uncle's authority, Munassir, who reportedly loved the pomp and glory of rule, proceeded to invest himself with the symbols of sovereignty. In 1889, not long after his father's death, he began to mint copper coins with the legend "*al-dawla Munassir*" (Munassir is the state) and to overstamp other specie in circulation, such as the *riyal* and the rupee.

Busy with affairs in Hyderabad, 'Awadh b. 'Umar sent his eldest son Ghalib to Hadhramawt, where he was to marry his cousin Muzna, the sister of Munassir and Husayn. Ghalib was to remain in Shibam for a time to become acquainted with the interior and then serve for a period cogoverning al-Shihr with Husayn, after which he was to be appointed governor of al-Mukalla. The purpose of appointing Ghalib alongside Husayn was initially to provide him with experience of Hadhramawt and its administration. Still, the news that Ghalib was to be appointed governor of al-Mukalla was perceived as a threat to their aspirations by Husayn and Munassir. Munassir, encouraged by Husayn, made a preemptive strike, seizing first Ghayl BaWazir and then al-Mukalla.

When 'Awadh b. 'Umar in Hyderabad learned of these events from Ghalib, who had remained in al-Shihr with Husayn, he summoned his nephews to Bombay and then ordered Munassir to return to his post as governor of Shibam. After Munassir's refusal and a subsequent trip to Bombay, Husayn openly expressed his support for Munassir's rebellious stance against their uncle's authority. Back in Hadhramawt, the brothers attempted to rally the support of the notables and different Yafi'i leaders against their uncle; the soldiers of the Qu'ayti forces began to take sides.

In June 1896, 'Awadh b. 'Umar arrived in al-Mukalla from Hyderabad. Munassir at first thought to prevent him from disembarking, but found himself losing support due to 'Awadh's presence in the harbor and allowed him to land. 'Awadh asserted his authority according to the terms of his father's will and announced the positions his son and nephews were to fill in the Qu'ayti government. Husayn returned to his post in al-Shihr, Munassir went to Ghayl BaWazir, and Ghalib became governor of al-Mukalla. 'Awadh then returned to Hyderabad and not long after, the brothers once again rebelled. Ghalib was able to suppress their rebellion with the support of those loyal to his father; Husayn and Munassir were unable to prevail against their uncle's greater authority and stature.

Not included in the order of succession mandated by 'Awadh b. 'Umar's will of 1898, the brothers became desperate and armed conflict appeared to be imminent. Both sides agreed to seek arbitration from the *munsib* of Al Shaykh Abu Bakr b. Salim of 'Aynat, who held spiritual authority among the Yafi'is. After spending two years examining the case, the *munsib* awarded Husayn and Munassir their share of their grandfather's estate and a further cash allowance in compensation for their loss of political status. The brothers rejected the decision of the *munsib* and made another unsuccessful attempt at rebellion. The British colonial government in Aden supported 'Awadh b. 'Umar and urged the brothers to submit to the authority of their uncle and return to their positions in his government, with the British Resident trying in late 1901 and early 1902 to bring about a settlement. They refused to settle, instead going to Hyderabad where they filed lawsuits against 'Awadh b. 'Umar. The case had not been settled to their satisfaction when they died in Hyderabad, Munassir around 1906 and Husayn in 1925.[18] The Qu'ayti sultanate thus weathered this internal challenge, remaining intact. Even though there were disputes as to succession, for example after the death of Sultan Ghalib in 1921, the state remained undivided.

Within the Kathiri sultanate, this issue was decided in the opposite fashion, with the division of territory between heirs. Years after the death of Sultan Ghalib b. Muhsin al-Kathiri, founder of the modern Kathiri state, his sons divided the sultanate between themselves in 1916, with Say'un and environs governed by Mansur b. Ghalib and his heirs and Tarim and environs governed by Muhsin b. Ghalib and his heirs.[19] This division of the Kathiri sultanate ultimately weakened that political entity, in relation to the Qu'ayti state and also in relation to its own subjects.

Establishing Security: Conflict between Sultans and Tribes

Both the Qu'ayti and the Kathiri sultanates met challenges from tribes disputing their right to govern territories considered by the tribes to be under their own authority. While part of the process of consolidating power for rulers in this region was the forging of alliances with the different tribes, the tribes did not consider these treaties of alliance nor the concomitant payments of tribal leaders to abrogate what they considered their traditional rights within their tribal territory. In the resulting conflicts of interest, the tribes frequently expressed their opposition to state authority by attacks on road traffic, called road cutting (*qatʿ al-tariq*), which were considered more serious than simple banditry or murder. While both sultanates experienced such incidents, perhaps the most dramatic case was that of the extended conflict of the Hamum with the Quʿayti. Hamum rebellion flared in the early twentieth century and was quelled in 1919, to recrudesce in the mid-1920s.

Quʿayti consolidation of territory and expansion of state authority in the nineteenth century encroached on Hamum tribal territory and authority. Hamum traditional territory encompassed the small ports and fishing settlements east of al-Hami, their hinterlands, and the hinterlands of al-Mukalla and al-Shihr extending far into the highland reaches of the *jawl*. Hamum territory included the eastern trade routes from the ports to the interior, which were the fastest and most direct routes; the eastern routes required four days while the western routes required eight. The Hamum thus controlled the caravan trade to the interior, which provided their primary source of livelihood. They were also accustomed to levying several types of duties (*jibayat*) on production within their territory. These included: a duty (*khafara*) on the boats that harbored in the small ports of al-Hami, al-Qarn, and al-Qusayʿar; a measure of grain (*kayla*) from the harvests of summer and winter sorghum; a measure of dates (*shiraha*) from the date harvest; and a measure of fresh or dried fish (*juduh*). These duties were paid in exchange for the protection of the property from attack or theft; that is, for the security of boats and cargo, fields, and date orchards. The Hamum considered the levying of these duties to be their ancestral right; they had long been exacting them and had been allowed to continue to do so under Bin Birayk and Kasadi rule of the coast.[20]

The Quʿayti was aware of the potential threat of the Hamum to the process of state expansion. The Hamum had long had treaty relations with Kathiri rulers in the interior.[21] During the earlier period of warfare among rivals for control in Hadhramawt, the Hamum had occasionally backed the Kathiri against the Quʿayti. In the unsuccessful attempt by the Kathiri to take al-Shihr in 1867, the Hamum had joined the Kathiri in the land attack. After quelling that assault, the Quʿayti began to build the wall and gates that protected the town from threat from the hinterlands. During the following two years, when the Quʿayti was attempting to dislodge the Kathiri from his center in Sayʾun, Hamum attacks on Quʿayti forces in transit to the interior had contributed to the failure of the attempt and the stalemate between the two powers. In order for the Quʿayti to establish state control in his domains, it would be necessary to come to terms with this tribe.[22]

The Quʿayti was cognizant of the necessity for good relations with the Hamum, since their territory encompassed such a strategically important part of his domain. At the same time, he was unwilling to cede them virtual control over that territory through the right to exact duties on production in exchange for protection of the populace, as the Birayk and Kasadi states had done. In the 1880s, with the mediation of Sayyid Ahmad b. Husayn al-ʿAydarus, the *munsib* of the

Hamum, the Qu'ayti began to negotiate a series of treaties of peace and alliance with the Hamum.[23] In 1888, 'Abdallah b. 'Umar al-Qu'ayti made an agreement with the clan leaders of the Hamum to pay a monthly salary of forty *riyals* to the paramount leader (*za'im*) of the tribe. Through this arrangement, the Qu'ayti expected allegiance from the tribe, so that the expansion of state power through the hinterland could be carried on in peace.[24]

Part of the process of state building was establishing security and taxation as functions of the state. As the Qu'ayti administration became more organized, establishing al-Shihr as its commercial as well as governmental center, the state began deriving a portion of its income from customs duties and taxes on import-export trade. It also organized the carrying trade from the coast to the interior, which was carried out by the tribes through whose territories the caravan routes passed. The state thus derived income from the passage of goods from overseas to the interior and maintained a degree of control over commerce within the Kathiri sultanate. The Qu'ayti further benefited from controlling the ports and the interior transportation routes by preventing the passage of weapons to the Kathiri in the interior. In addition, when the Qu'ayti established his administration in the hinterlands, he levied a state tax on production.

Despite the treaties pledging allegiance by the tribe to Qu'ayti rule in which they recognized Qu'ayti authority (*sulta*), the Hamum proved unwilling to cede their right to collect protection levies from the farmers, fishermen, and villagers within their territories. Although their leader received the monthly payment intended to ensure the allegiance of the tribe, the clans did not feel that this abrogated their rights in their territory. They also resisted paying taxes themselves to the Qu'ayti, since they considered themselves to be rightful collectors not payers of duties.

As Qu'ayti rule brought stability to the area, commercial activity in al-Shihr increased. Since the Kathiri sultanate and its subjects were allowed to use the port and trade freely in all goods except military supplies, the interior of Hadhramawt continued to prosper from its traditional sources of wealth, emigration, and Indian Ocean trade. While the carrying trade to the interior by the eastern routes continued to be conducted by Hamum caravans, the Qu'ayti state organized, regulated, and levied a small duty on the business. Even though the Hamum benefited financially from the increase in trade, they resented the Qu'ayti exerting control over their business.

Periodically, the Hamum responded to the new realities of Qu'ayti rule by rebelling and creating instability in the settlements and transportation routes of the Qu'ayti hinterland. The Hamum considered attacks on caravans and on the persons, property, and means of livelihood of the settled populace as a way of striking at the Qu'ayti by showing the population his inability to protect them. Although al-Mukalla and al-Shihr were protected, the villages, farms, and fishermen of the hinterlands were vulnerable; outside of garrisoned areas, Qu'ayti troops were unable to prevent the Hamum depredations. At these times of instability, the gates of al-Shihr were closed to the Hamum, and caravans traveled to the interior by the longer western route via Ghayl BaWazir through Wadi Du'an. The Hamum were thus blocked from participating in the caravan trade and prevented from selling livestock and buying food and other necessities in the markets of al-Shihr. Despite Qu'ayti objections to the Kathiri, the Hamum sold their animals and animal products in Tarim and Say'un, adjacent to northern Hamum territory and purchased imported goods in Sayhut in Mahra territory. Even so, the Qu'ayti economic blockade of the Hamum resulted in suffering both among the tribe and among the populations of the import-dependent interior of Hadhramawt.

During the time when Husayn and Munassir, the sons of 'Abdallah b. 'Umar, were trying to consolidate power against their uncle 'Awadh b. 'Umar, the Hamum situation appeared to be resolved. In 1902 Husayn b. 'Abdallah, as governor of al-Shihr, made an agreement with the Hamum through the mediation of the 'Aydarus *munsib* that they might once more enter al-Shihr; that they might levy their customary imposts on the population within their territory; and that they would be exempt from taxes to the Qu'ayti. When Husayn was removed from his position and went to Hyderabad to pursue his case against his uncle there, he was replaced as governor of al-Shihr by Ghalib b. 'Awadh, who also served as regent in his father's absence while in Hyderabad. Ghalib followed the original policy of the Qu'ayti state, preventing the Hamum from levying imposts in Qu'ayti territory and expecting the Hamum to pay taxes to the state. The Hamum objected and returned to their attacks in the countryside and the Qu'ayti moved to suppress their disruptive activities once again through economic blockade. Ghalib closed the gates of al-Shihr to the Hamum and banned them from the carrying trade and the market.[25]

Hamum disruption of security within the Qu'ayti state reached a peak in the years 1914 to 1918, when Hamumi tribesmen regularly attacked villages and roads around al-Shihr, killing, robbing, and terrorizing the populace and travelers. In late 1918, aggression intensified. Tribesmen killed a guard at the north gate of al-Shihr and entered the town in a spree of destruction, even crippling by hamstringing the camels that powered the sesame oil presses. Others plundered a boat harbored in the port of al-Qarn at al-Dis, stealing the cargo including one thousand *riyals* belonging to a businessman of al-Mukalla. Others hijacked a caravan carrying goods for the al-Mukalla businessman Shaykh 'Abd al-Qadir BaSharahil on the road to Ghayl BaWazir, the beginning stage of the western route to the interior. The tribesmen deceived and killed the guard, then stole the sixty camels and the goods they were carrying, including five thousand *riyals* belonging to BaSharahil.

BaSharahil and other businessmen complained bitterly of government inaction in the face of terrorism to the governor of al-Shihr, Nasir b. Ahmad BuBak (from a subtribe of the Qu'ayti). Nasir b. Ahmad relayed the businessmen's distress to Sultan Ghalib b. 'Awadh, who by that time had moved the seat of government from al-Shihr to al-Mukalla. Accompanied only by the messenger sent to him by Nasir b. Ahmad, Sultan Ghalib immediately traveled to al-Shihr, where he met with the governor and BaSharahil and other local businessmen, who apprised him of the situation and the necessity for an immediate, strong government response. Agreeing that such disruption of critical transport routes could not be tolerated, Sultan Ghalib pledged a strong response and asked the businessmen to underwrite the operation, to which they readily assented. After a financing agreement was drawn up and signed, Sultan Ghalib left the matter in the hands of Nasir b. Ahmad and returned to al-Mukalla.

Nasir b. Ahmad contacted the intermediaries who customarily handled Hamum interactions with others: the *dallal al-suq* or general broker of the al-Shihr market from the Hummuda family; the *munsib* of the Al Shaykh Abu Bakr b. Salim; and the ʿAydarus *munsib*. Through these intermediaries, the government opened negotiations with the Hamum, but the tribe refused to turn in the raiders or their ill-gotten goods; instead, they demanded a pardon and further concessions from the state. The tribesmen carried on negotiations and commerce in al-Shihr while the governor prepared to retaliate.

On January 29, 1919, the government began a coordinated action against the Hamum. The garrisons of the small towns and ports of the hinterland along with the forces of al-Shihr captured six hundred of the tribesmen. The soldiers even took clan leaders who were in town for negotiations under the protection of the traditional mediators; among them was Salim Bin Habraysh, the leader of the powerful and rebellious Bayt ʿAli clan. Members of clans innocent of raiding were freed and four hundred men from guilty clans were imprisoned, their weapons and camels taken in compensation for Hamum crimes. Twenty-seven leaders of the guilty clans were executed and buried in a common grave outside the al-Shihr wall, their number equaling that of casualties in previous Hamum raids. Although the ʿAydarus *munsib* was angry that the sacred trust between tribe and *munsib* had been violated, the government justified its action as punishment necessary to establish security after negotiations had failed. When he returned from his engagement with the Kathiri following the Aden Agreement, the *wazir* Husayn b. Hamid al-Mihdhar tried to persuade Nasir b. Ahmad to release the Hamum prisoners. He even tried to get the support of prominent townspeople in order to release them himself, but the people, weary of the insecurity created by the Hamum, supported Nasir Ahmad's decision to hold the tribesmen in prison, and al-Mihdhar had to back down. The weakened and demoralized tribe withdrew to the highlands until their sudden reappearance on the coast in 1925. The population of countryside and town, particularly the merchants, rejoiced at the prospect of security of property and person and safety of travel.[26]

World War I: Sultans, Subjects, and Imperial Powers

While the Quʿayti state was expanding its territory into Wadi Duʿan and Wadi Hajr at the turn of the century and extending the authority of the state into the hinterlands, the development of the Kathiri state was stymied by its position, surrounded and landlocked by the Qu'ayti domains. Sultan al-Mansur b. Ghalib al-Kathiri, the son of Jama'dar Ghalib b. Muhsin al-Kathiri who founded the modern Kathiri state, chafed against this limitation for decades, maintaining his father's goal of acquiring one of the ports of Hadhramawt. He unsuccessfully sought assistance against his nemesis, the Qu'ayti, from Imam Yahya of Yemen, and then he attempted to internationalize the Qu'ayti-Kathiri rivalry by allying the Kathiri sultanate with the Ottomans, against the British protected Qu'ayti sultanate. He was encouraged in these attempts at alliance by Sayyid 'Abd al-Rahman b. 'Ubaydillah al-Saqqaf, a scholar, poet, and political activist known as the Mufti of Hadhramawt, who hoped that the situation of Hadhramawt would be improved by alliance with a larger Muslim power.

The Kathiri Sultan's moves toward alliance with the Ottomans created conflict of interests among different groups in Hadhramawt and the Hadhrami emigrant communities overseas. The Kathiri sultan was motivated primarily by his rivalry with the Qu'ayti and his interest in acquiring a port to link the Kathiri sultanate to the outside world, a critical issue given the importance of emigration and the dependence of economy on remittances and imported goods. His advisor Bin 'Ubaydillah was motivated by ideological reasons: he wanted to see Hadhramawt part of a Muslim Empire under the leadership of the Caliph. He firmly believed that only adherence to Islamic law would rescue Hadhramawt from chronic chaos and periodic famine. His ideological stance was consonant with his group interests and his personal interests in the issue. As a prominent member of the *'ulama'*, he had a greater stake in an Islamic political order than a European one, since European rule established legal and educational institutions that diminished the importance of the *'ulama'*. As a person of great intelligence, ability, and ambition, he had a potential future within the administrative institutions of the Ottoman Empire as well; the Ottomans promised him the position of Deputy (*mab'uth*) for Hadhramawt.

Most Kathiri subjects in Hadhramawt and the Hadhrami emigrant communities overseas opposed the choice of the sultan and Bin 'Ubaydillah and opted to support the Qu'ayti and the British. Their choice was not based on ideological or religious but on pragmatic reasons. The transportation and communications systems of the Indian Ocean region, controlled by European powers, were a lifeline of survival extending from the emigrants to their family at home. In the end, the identity of Hadhramawt as a dispersed community of emigrants that maintained their base in the homeland prevailed over its strong identity as a Muslim community.

Sayyid 'Abd al-Rahman b. 'Ubaydillah began his correspondence with Imam Yahya of Yemen in 1911. In that year, when he left Hadhramawt for the first time at the age of twenty-nine, Bin 'Ubaydillah, like many of his countrymen, was concerned at the deplorable condition of his country, which was suffering as it had so often in the past from famine. He attributed the problems of his country to moral and social decline. He felt that conflicts between tribes and classes had gotten out of control; that wealth was in the hands of people unwilling to spend it for the common weal; and that the people of Hadhramawt had drifted from the true path of their religion. He was particularly concerned at the deterioration in the character of the *sada* during his time; he felt that they were failing in their duty to set a high moral standard for the rest of the society.

Bin 'Ubaydillah considered it his responsibility to try to right the wrongs he saw in Hadhramawt and his leaving there in 1911 marked the beginning of a life of political activism. According to his account, as he pondered the solution to Hadhramawt's problems, he came across a chronicle of the intervention of the seventeenth-century Zaydi Imam Isma'il in Hadhramawt. Inspired by the narrative, he decided to request the assistance of the Imam of Yemen in righting the ills of Hadhramawt.

He had reason to admire and respect the Imam. Like Bin 'Ubaydillah, the Imam was a *sayyid,* or descendant of the Prophet. A strong ruler, he had staunchly defended his territories from interference by Europeans. At a time of increasing secularization of law and other social institutions throughout the Muslim world, the Imam excluded such change from Yemen. This gained the admiration of Bin 'Ubaydillah and others in Hadhramawt who deplored the inroads that foreign influence was making in Muslim lands. In addition, the Imam's territory was then the outpost of the Ottoman Empire nearest to Hadhramawt. Bin 'Ubaydillah had held high expectations of the Ottoman Empire since his childhood, following in the footsteps of his grandfather, Sayyid Muhsin b. 'Alawi al-Saqqaf, who along with other *sada* had in the nineteenth century appealed to the Ottomans to intervene in Hadhramawt. Even though those earlier attempts to bring the Ottomans into Hadhramawt in an attempt at moral and political reform had failed, Bin 'Ubaydillah was influenced by his grandfather's hope of reform through Ottoman intervention and carried on in his footsteps.

Stopping in Aden on his way to Yemen, Bin 'Ubaydillah wrote his first poem in praise of Imam Yahya, beginning a correspondence with the Imam that continued until at least the mid-1930s. Bin 'Ubaydillah did not travel onward to Yemen at that time, but wrote the Imam again in the following year from Singapore, at the encouragement of Sayyid Muhammad b. 'Aqil, who enjoyed connections with the Imam. Throughout World War I, Bin 'Ubaydillah corresponded with the Imam and with Ottoman authorities. He advised the Kathiri sultan and at times served as an intermediary between the sultan and the Ottomans, who were also in direct correspondence. In the early years of the war, he communicated with Mahmud Nadim Basha, the Ottoman governor of Yemen; the correspondence was conveyed by the *ashraf* of Mareb, the descendants of the Prophet who controlled the desert reaches between Hadhramawt and Yemen. After the Turkish Army occupied Lahej in July 1915, Bin 'Ubaydillah communicated with 'Ali Sa'id Basha, the Ottoman military commander of Lahej.

In his *Diwan* (collected poems and memoirs), Bin 'Ubaydillah related the passion of his commitment to the Ottoman cause. 'Ali Sa'id Basha once sent him a call to *jihad,* in which he described the bravery with which his soldiers had faced the enemy cannons. Bin 'Ubaydillah wrote to him for permission to join the armed struggle, after having asked his mother since he was her only son. His mother gave him permission but 'Ali Sa'id Basha answered that the best way for Bin 'Ubaydillah to serve Islam was for him to stay in Hadhramawt, in order to serve the cause through his influence as a respected social and religious leader throughout the war, which he did.[27]

Probably in response to the urging of his correspondents Bin 'Ubaydillah and Sayyid Muhammad b. 'Aqil, Imam Yahya first wrote to Sultan Mansur b. Ghalib al-Kathiri in February 1914, asking him to forget about earlier conflicts between them and urging him to remain aligned with Islam. Sultan Mansur welcomed the Imam's advances, hoping for support against the Qu'ayti.[28]

Correspondence continued between the two leaders, sometimes conveyed by the sovereign of Mareb, Sharif 'Abd al-Rahman b. Husayn. The Kathiri sultan appealed to the Imam for assistance against the Qu'ayti and the British. He stressed ties of affinity with the Imam by indicating the centrality in Hadhrami society of the *sada,* who shared with the Imam common descent from Fatima, daughter of the Prophet Muhammad. The sultan urged that by assisting the Kathiri against Qu'ayti and thereby British domination, the Imam would secure the future of his genealogical and spiritual kinsmen, the *sada* of Hadhramawt. At one point, the sultan planned to send a delegation of Hadhrami *sada* to discuss the matter with the Imam, although this did not take place.

The Kathiri sultan told the Imam that his country was being taken over. He recounted Qu'ayti attempts to encroach on his domains by winning over the tribes, making treaties of alliance (*ahlaf*) with them, and putting them under his protection (*himaya*), a traditional step, along with acquisition of land, in gathering power for the leaders in this region. He pointed out that while some of his subjects supported the Qu'ayti, others simply feared him due to his control over the ports, which he was able to maintain through British support ; the Kathiri then summoned the image of his ancestor Abu Tuwayriq to back his own claim to ancestral right over the ports. The Kathiri said that he had refrained from signing a treaty with the Qu'ayti, despite incessant pressure and the offer of a stipend, since he refused to enter into a treaty agreement under the flag of the *kufar,* unbelievers. Having thus established common cause in resistance to Western influence, he concluded with a request for the Imam to assist in reclaiming one of the ports from the Qu'ayti.[29]

Although the Kathiri sultan continued this refrain of opposition to foreign influence and alliance with the West in his correspondence with the Imam, his enemy was the Qu'ayti, not the *kufar.* While continuing his overtures to the Imam for assistance against the British-backed Qu'ayti, he hedged his bets by attempting to contact the British directly, bypassing the Qu'ayti. At the same time that he was corresponding with the Imam, he wrote to the 'Abdali sultan, whose territory of Lahej bordered the Crown Colony of Aden, complaining that his people were being oppressed by the Qu'ayti and the British. He asked the 'Abdali to employ his good relations with the British on behalf of himself and his subjects and to persuade the British to be fair and deal justly with the Kathiri in relation to the Qu'ayti. He strengthened his appeal with a guarded threat, indicating that he had "kings and leaders," presumably the Ottomans and the Imam, on his side. He claimed to have dismissed their offers of military assistance, hoping to avoid resort to warfare by British assurance of a more favorable balance of power between himself and the Qu'ayti.[30]

While the Kathiri sultan got no reply from the 'Abdali or the British, the Imam responded in August 1915 that he was delighted to hear that the Kathiri and his subjects were interested in being under his protection. He mentioned receiving a letter from a *sayyid* (probably 'Abd al-Rahman b. 'Ubaydillah al-Saqqaf) which detailed conditions in Hadhramawt; it may have been that letter that brought up the issue of Imamic protection. At any rate, the Imam pledged to become involved in the situation. This suggestion of Imamic protection went well beyond the relationship the Sultan had intended when he contacted the Imam and his appeals to the Imam ceased at this time.[31]

Shortly thereafter, Bin 'Ubaydillah began his correspondence with the Ottomans through 'Ali Sa'id Basha, the Ottoman military commander of Lahej. In January 1916, about six months after the Ottoman takeover of Lahej from the 'Abdali, Bin 'Ubaydillah composed and sent a poem of praise to 'Ali Sa'id Basha. With his response to Bin 'Ubaydillah, 'Ali Sa'id Basha included a proclamation for the people of Hadhramawt to sign, stating that they supported the Ottoman Empire and considered themselves under its protection. He urged Bin 'Ubaydillah to help collect signatures. He sent copies to other prominent members of the *sada,* for their assistance in gathering signatures.[32]

'Ali Sa'id Basha sent the Kathiri sultan two versions of the proclamation: one was to be signed by the top notables of the society and the other was to be read in public meetings and signed by other social leaders. Pressing the point most sensitive to the Kathiri, 'Ali Sa'id Basha said that the Qu'ayti had colluded with the British to claim the whole of Hadhramawt under British protection and had asked other European countries to sanction the move. He advised the Kathiri that the only way to rectify the situation was for the people of Hadhramawt to unify to reject British hegemony. To initiate the process, he suggested that the sultan convoke a meeting of *sada,* businessmen, and tribal leaders at which they would sign a copy of the notables' proclamation; the public proclamation was to be read in large gatherings, signed, and stamped with the official Kathiri stamp.

The drafts of the two versions of the proclamation were written in the handwriting of 'Ali Sa'id Basha's scribe. The one intended for the notables stated that the signers were the *sada* of Hadhramawt, the Kathiri ruling family, the tribes, and the merchants. By this proclamation, they would reject the British influence, and their treaties and protection. Instead, they recognized the Ottoman Empire and declared themselves among its subjects, prepared to obey its rules and answer its calls to war because of shared religious ties. Since the Caliph had declared the war against the British and their allies to be a *jihad,* these notables of Hadhramawt rejected any claims of the British over them and declared themselves to be the enemy of the enemies of the Ottoman state.[33]

The proclamation intended for the public was longer and more detailed than the other. Created to be read to crowds, its language was more impassioned and its contents more inflammatory. In an attack on the Qu'ayti, it castigated those Arabian rulers under the influence of foreigners and warned that they heed the example of India having fallen into the hands of the British. It gave examples of atrocities allegedly committed by the British in their colonies: mocking the *'ulama';* converting the children of Muslims to Christianity; encouraging Christian missionaries to curse Muslims in their preachings. It pointed out problems the Muslims in Russia and North Africa had experienced as a result of Christian domination. Quoting the Qur'an and *hadith,* it called for Muslims to unite under the Caliph to protect Islam and to expel nonbelievers from the peninsula. It called for a rejection of foreign influence and protection and ended with a summons to *jihad.*

In exchange for compliance, 'Ali Sa'id Basha promised the protection of the Ottoman Empire for Hadhramawt. At the same time, he warned of the penalty for noncompliance, threatening harm to any who challenged Ottoman suzerainty over the entire Arabian Peninsula or who accepted European protection. He warned that the Ottoman Empire was on the verge of victory in the war, and that they soon would send their armies to attack those states under European protection. He claimed that the other rulers of the peninsula had all accepted Ottoman suzerainty.[34]

These documents created conflict in Hadhramawt. A few were passionately in favor of the proclamation while most opposed it on practical grounds. Regardless of their strong Muslim identity, the people of Hadhramawt were dependent on the goodwill of the Qu'ayti and the Europeans. Besides owning considerable property in British-controlled areas, they relied on British-controlled transportation and communications systems to transfer money and goods back to the homeland. Additionally, imports critical to the survival of the Kathiri subjects had to pass through Qu'ayti territory. For most subjects of the Kathiri, these practical considerations overrode the affinity they might have felt with their coreligionists in the Ottoman Empire.

'Ali Said Basha's activities in the interior worried the British, who wanted to send a political officer or advisor to the Qu'ayti sultanate to combat Ottoman propaganda. Sultan Ghalib refused. His *wazir,* Husayn b. Hamid al-Mihdhar, traveled to Aden to explain that a foreign advisor was not necessary since the sultan was capable of countering propaganda and had a greater interest in doing so for the defense of his state than did any employee that would be sent to him.[35]

Bin 'Ubaydillah tried to convince the Kathiri, the *sada,* and the notables to sign the proclamation. His experiences were mixed. He related showing the document to Shaykh 'Abdallah b. 'Awadh Bin 'Abdat, who immediately asked for pen and ink to sign. Bin 'Ubaydillah told him to wait, to spend some time considering the implications of his signature. He warned that Bin 'Abdat would be putting his property, money, and family in Singapore, al-Mukalla, and Aden at risk if he signed. He did not want others to claim that it was his fault if Bin 'Abdat was harmed. But Bin 'Abdat responded passionately, trembling as he said, "This is the duty of my religion. Is the Caliph not the sultan of all the Muslims?" He swore, "By God, if someone were holding swords to the necks of my sons in front of me, I would still not hesitate to sign." A copy of the proclamation with only Bin 'Abdat's signature was later sent to 'Ali Sa'id Basha.[36]

But most people did not respond so positively to the proclamation. Bin 'Ubaydillah found that most people were against it and were unwilling to alienate the British and the British-supported Qu'ayti. They felt that supporting the Ottomans would endanger their property and the livelihoods of their families, which depended on the prosperity of the emigrant communities abroad. While 'Ali Sa'id Basha assured Bin 'Ubaydillah that the Ottomans would be able to protect their supporters' property in British-controlled areas, the people of Hadhramawt were not convinced that they would be able to do so.[37]

The sultan found himself in a dilemma: he wished to declare allegiance to the Ottomans to gain their support for his struggle against the Qu'ayti, but he had to keep it quiet in order not to alienate his subjects. His failure to announce the proclamation publicly and his delay in returning the document irritated 'Ali Sa'id Basha. At the same time, the British were angered when they heard about the document circulating in Hadhramawt. Through his vacillation, the sultan managed to alienate both sides.

Sultan Mansur wrote 'Ali Sa'id Basha in July 1916, explaining that he had kept the proclamation secret rather than publicly circulating it for fear of repercussions and indicating two areas of concern. His subjects as well as his own family owned extensive properties in Singapore, which would be vulnerable to confiscation by the British. In addition, since his country produced so little, it depended on imports from abroad through the ports controlled by the Qu'ayti; an embargo would threaten his people not only with poverty but starvation. The sultan stressed that it was only his need to protect his subjects that overcame his desire to obey and serve the Caliph. The sultan offered 'Ali Sa'id a compromise with respect to the proclamation: rather than announcing the proclamation to the public, he had produced a copy signed by himself, his brother the crown prince, Bin 'Ubaydillah, and the *qadhi* of Say'un. He suggested that for the time being the signatures of these few individuals should suffice for those of the public, since these were the leaders of the society and everyone else their followers. He delayed sending even this secretly signed copy.[38]

Meanwhile, 'Ali Sa'id Basha wrote to Bin 'Ubaydillah with both an assurance that the Ottoman state would be able to protect even property held in foreign countries and a reproach to the people of Hadhramawt for allowing material concerns to deter them from their holy duty of *jihad*. The sultan eventually sent the copy of the proclamation with the few signatures, saying that later he might be able to make a public announcement and obtain the signatures of the community leaders. He also brought up the point perennially of the greatest concern to him, saying that he had been happy to hear from Bin 'Ubaydillah that 'Ali Sa'id Basha would be sending an Ottoman force soon to drive out the Qu'ayti and requesting information as to troop movements.[39]

When 'Ali Sa'id responded, he deferred the matter of the Sultan's request for the Ottoman force to help destroy the Qu'ayti. He said that the Qu'ayti was the only leader on the Arabian Peninsula who had not aligned with the Ottomans, and so they would send a force to crush him in the near but indefinite future. While tantalizing the Kathiri sultan by encouraging him in his great desire to be the sole sultan of Hadhramawt, 'Ali Sa'id offered nothing tangible in the way of assistance. Still, he expressed his dissatisfaction with the sultan's handling of the proclamation. He requested further copies of the proclamation with signatures of public leaders, to be sent to the sultan and to the secretary of war in Istanbul. As for the sultan's assertion that the public leaders were merely followers, 'Ali Sa'id Basha counseled that the sultan needed to state his allegiance to the Ottomans firmly and publicly, in order to demonstrate that he did indeed have power and influence over his subjects.[40]

At the same time, 'Ali Sa'id Basha repeated the request to Bin 'Ubaydillah for more copies of the proclamation signed by public leaders, suggesting that the proclamation should be copied onto full-size paper rather than a small sheet like the earlier one. 'Ali Sa'id Basha perhaps feared that the frugality so highly valued in Hadhramawt might be misconstrued by the Porte as lack of enthusiasm. He urged Bin 'Ubaydillah to assure the sultan's obedience to the Caliph, in order to bring about the salvation of Hadhramawt. He promised that those who supported the Ottomans would benefit from Ottoman support in the future. On a more immediate level, he promised Bin 'Ubaydillah that the Porte would appoint him Deputy of the Ottoman Empire for Hadhramawt when it became a province of the Empire.[41]

Even though Bin 'Ubaydillah was sincerely interested in incorporating Hadhramawt into the Ottoman Empire and the Kathiri sultan wanted Ottoman assistance against the Qu'ayti, most of the Kathiri subjects thought that their interests were best served by good relations with the Qu'ayti and with the British Empire. The Kathiri sultan explained to 'Ali Sa'id Basha that he feared sending copies of the proclamation to him because of the danger of interference with their communications. Some of his subjects, including important supporters from the Kathiri tribe, had learned of the proclamation and the sultan's signing of the "secret" copy. They had objected and he suspected that someone had discussed the matter with the British. He suggested at one point that objections to his support of the proclamation were leading to rebellion among his subjects. So the sultan was unable to overtly pursue his interest of garnering support from the Ottomans against his Qu'ayti enemy, due to the opposition of his subjects, including a part

Figure 7.1 Kathiri Palace, Say'un

of his Kathiri tribal power base, who considered their interests compromised by this activity.[42]

'Ali Sa'id Basha continued to encourage the Kathiri to publicly ally his sultanate with the Ottoman Empire, even after he was able to hold out little in the way of promises of assistance against the Qu'ayti. At the end of 1917, Bin 'Ubaydillah traveled to see 'Ali Sa'id Basha in Lahej on behalf of the Kathiri sultan to request Ottoman support against the Qu'ayti. The conflict between the two sultans had worsened, and the Kathiri feared absorption of his realm into the Qu'ayti state. 'Ali Sa'id Basha affirmed the Kathiri's claim that this struggle was a *jihad*, or fight in the cause of Islam, since the Qu'ayti was allied with the British. However, the Ottomans had not been able to send the forces for which the Kathiri had been bargaining. 'Ali Sa'id Basha claimed that the Arab Revolt in the Hijaz had diverted an Ottoman force which had earlier been mobilized for the purpose of expelling the Qu'ayti from Southern Arabia. He claimed that the Arab rebellion had thwarted the Ottoman goal of freeing the Arabian Peninsula of European influence.

During this visit to Lahej, Bin 'Ubaydillah laid his personal concerns before 'Ali Sa'id Basha. The British had found out about the proclamation and Bin 'Ubaydillah's activities in promulgating it. Bin 'Ubaydillah had been told that the British had offered a reward for his assassination or capture. 'Ali Sa'id Basha, who had encouraged Bin 'Ubaydillah in his activism on behalf of the Ottoman Empire and had promised him a position as an official of the empire, sympathized but offered him nothing. He consoled Bin 'Ubaydillah by pointing out that the struggle against the Qu'ayti was a *jihad*, which meant that he would be honored if he met death in its service. He also promised that after the imminent victory of the Central Powers the Ottomans would come to the assistance of the Kathiri in expelling the Qu'ayti. For the first time, he pointed out that the struggle between Kathiri and Qu'ayti was just a tiny skirmish in the context of the world war.[43]

Toward a Tenuous Union: The 1918 Aden Agreement

The impending defeat of the Ottomans left the Kathiri with no outside support for his campaign against the Qu'ayti. In addition to being frustrated in his desire for a port, the Kathiri felt under an additional pressure of fear that his tiny land-locked sultanate was to be entirely subsumed into the Qu'ayti state. The Qu'ayti sultan felt that an agreement establishing sovereignty over all Hadhramawt was necessary for the further development of the country. Although the Kathiri not surprisingly disagreed, he found himself under increasing pressure from the Qu'ayti, the British, and his own subjects to agree to the incorporation of his sultanate into a larger entity under Qu'ayti suzerainty.

The British had restricted travel from the Hadhrami colonies in the East Indies to Hadhramawt as a wartime exigency, which made the transmission of remittances and goods to Hadhramawt more difficult. By the end of World War I, the economy of the interior was suffering due to this separation from the Far Eastern sources of much of its prosperity. Distrustful of the Qu'ayti, the Kathiri sultan wrote to a contact in good standing with the British, requesting British assistance in strengthening his position relative to the Qu'ayti. He reported that the Qu'ayti *wazir,* Husayn b. Hamid al-Mihdhar, was coming to the interior in order to negotiate a treaty. He further complained that the Qu'ayti was putting pressure on him, that he had stopped all imports coming into Kathiri territory from the coasts and Shibam as well as from the Hadhrami overseas community. He attributed the embargo to the Qu'ayti rather than the British, since the British had not even blockaded Lahej when it was occupied by the Ottomans. He hoped to send a delegation to the British, bypassing Qu'ayti influence, in order to obtain British aid to "open the road to [his] country with their help"—at least to break the Qu'ayti embargo and at best to gain control of a port. However, the British refused to negotiate with him.[44]

Even after the Kathiri had turned his hopes from Ottoman toward British assistance against his Qu'ayti rival, 'Ali Sa'id Basha warned the Kathiri and Bin 'Ubaydillah to beware the machinations of the *wazir* Husayn b. Hamid al-Mihdhar and his intentions to ensnare the Kathiri in British ties.[45] When al-Mihdhar came to negotiate, the Kathiri rejected the Qu'ayti plan for a unified state out of hand.

The Qu'ayti sent an army of Yafi'i and slave soldiers to Shibam and fighting commenced between the Kathiri and Qu'ayti forces. Qu'ayti forces blocked travel between the coast and the interior and the flow of goods to the interior was stopped. The Qu'ayti asked the British authorities in Aden to prevent money being transferred into Kathiri territory.

The Aden government, which agreed with the Qu'ayti that further political and economic development of Hadhramawt required unification, contacted influential members of the Kathiri tribe in the East Indies. They asked Salim b. Ja'far Bin Talib, leader of the Al 'Umar branch of the Kathiri tribe, Salim b. Muhammad Bin Talib, and Salih b.'Ubayd Bin 'Abdat to intervene with the Kathiri sultan, who depended on the support of the large and powerful Kathiri tribe. These men, who had a great deal of wealth and influence in the community of Hadhrami emigrants in the East Indies as well as in their homeland, traveled to Aden in order to participate in the negotiations.

At the same time that the Qu'ayti sent the Kathiri notification that 'Ali Sa'id Basha had left Lahej in the hands of the 'Abdali sultan, he invited the Kathiri to come to Aden for negotiations between the two sultanates.[46] Although Sultan al-Mansur b. Ghalib al-Kathiri remained against the idea of the negotiations, he sent his son and successor 'Ali b. Mansur to represent him. 'Ali b. Mansur al-Kathiri traveled to al-Mukalla where he was formally and splendidly welcomed as a monarch by Sultan Ghalib b. 'Awadh al-Qu'ayti. Crown Prince 'Ali b. Mansur, Sultan Ghalib b. 'Awadh, and Sayyid Husayn b. Hamid al-Mihdhar then traveled on a British steamer to Aden where the negotiations took place.

With the Kathiri unable to withstand the pressure on him from all sides, the treaty of eleven articles known as the Aden Agreement was signed in 1918. This treaty established Hadhramawt as a unified entity under Qu'ayti sovereignty, which placed the Kathiri sultanate under the 1888 Protection Agreement between the Qu'ayti and the British. It recognized the Al 'Abdallah Kathiri as sultans of the Shanafir tribal confederation, ruling Say'un, Tarim, Taris, al-Gharaf, Maryama, and al-Ghayl in the interior. The Qu'ayti recognized the absolute rule of the Kathiri in their territory, within which the Qu'ayti would not interfere. Likewise, the Kathiri recognized the suzerainty of the Qu'ayti in their territory, within which the Kathiri would not interfere. Both parties agreed to renounce all conflict between them, to enforce security on the roads, and to protect and defend each other's subjects within their territories. They pledged mutual assistance in any matter concerning the well-being and prosperity of Hadhramawt. If one of the sultans wished to visit the other, he had to give notice of his intention to do so and to visit with no more than fifty soldiers in his entourage. Commerce was to be free, with charges applied impartially to subjects of either sultanate. While the Kathiri was bound by the 1888 Protectorate Agreement with the British, any negotiations or correspondence that the Kathiri held with the British would be carried on through the mediation of the Qu'ayti. The British government agreed to attempt to settle differences between the two sultans through the intermediary of the governor of Aden.[47]

The treaty was signed by Sultan Ghalib b. 'Awadh al-Qu'ayti, Sultan al-Mansur b. Ghalib al-Kathiri, Muhsin b. Ghalib al-Kathiri, and witnessed by the Qu'ayti *wazir*, Husayn b. Hamid al-Mihdhar, and two leaders of the Kathiri tribe, Salim b. Ja'far Bin Talib and Nasr b. 'Umar Bin Talib. One of the other leaders of the Kathiri who had traveled from the East Indies to attend the negotiations, Salih b. 'Ubayd Bin 'Abdat, did not sign since he objected to the treaty. His objections led him to take repercussions against both sultans in the following decades.

The Kathiri sultan, who had entered the negotiations reluctantly and almost entirely without bargaining power, almost immediately rejected the treaty and its conditions. He objected to the subsumption of his sultanate under Qu'ayti sovereignty; to the fixing of the boundaries of the sultanates, which gave him no hope of ever acquiring a long-desired port; and to the condition that he conduct all correspondence with the British through the Qu'ayti. While the Kathiri retained power over his subjects within his limited territory, he no longer had any power to conduct external affairs.

Sultan al-Mansur b. Ghalib al-Kathiri announced his rejection of the treaty soon after the delegation had returned from Aden. In response, Sultan Ghalib sent his *wazir*, Husayn b. Hamid al-Mihdhar, to the interior with an escort of fifty Yafi'i soldiers, in accordance with the specifications of the treaty. The *wazir* met with Sultan al-Mansur in the village of Hawtat Ahmad b. Zayn al-Hibshi, between Shibam and Say'un. Their negotiations broke down in disagreement. Regardless of Hawta's history as a sanctuary, al-Mihdhar and his men were surrounded by hundreds of armed men from the Kathiri tribe. They managed to escape, purportedly by a ruse. According to this story, the *wazir* sent out for rice, other foodstuffs, and goats to slaughter in order to feed the Qu'ayti party. This fooled most of the Kathiri tribesmen into leaving their positions and returning to their own homes for the evening, which allowed al-Mihdhar and his soldiers to flee to the Qu'ayti stronghold of Shibam. Although Sultan al-Mansur objected vociferously to this treaty in later years, to the Qu'ayti, to the British, and to anyone else who would listen, he had no other recourse but to comply with it.[48]

After the rivalries for power over Hadhramawt in the mid-nineteenth century ended in a stalemate between the Kathiri and Qu'ayti, the two sultanates maintained a simmering rivalry which provided the backdrop to their efforts to consolidate power within their territories. With the Protectorate Agreement of 1888, Qu'ayti control of the coast was internationally recognized, to the chagrin of the Kathiri, who hoped to acquire control of a port. The Qu'ayti went on to expand their territory and institutionalize their rule while the Kathiri struggled against the limitations of their landlocked position. Despite Kathiri efforts to gain international support against the Qu'ayti during World War I, the 1918 Aden Agreement, which established Hadhramawt as a unified entity, placed the Kathiri sultanate under Qu'ayti sovereignty and British protection. It provided international recognition to the de facto situation that the Kathiri was surrounded and landlocked by his more powerful rival and thereby subject to Qu'ayti control over his dealings with the outside world. At the same time, both sultanates remained embroiled in internal conflicts and challenges, exacerbated by increasing demands by subjects for social and political reforms.

8

The Sultanates: Challengers and Reformers (1918 to 1936)

The Aden agreement of 1918 offered Hadhramawt a formal end to continuing mutual mistrust and greater unity between the two sultanates. Unfortunately, the resistance of influential Kathiri subjects to this union stymied its potential for enhancing the administrative organization and economic development of Kathiri territory. Both sultanates were hampered in their development efforts by the continued resistance to their rule of recalcitrant tribes asserting claims of territorial authority and by rivals attempting to set themselves up as rulers of competing states within the sultanates. Continuous military operations drained the sultanates' budgets, making them dependent upon wealthy subjects. At the same time, subjects of both governments began to demand reform from the sultanates, including a more formally consultative form of government, posing a new type of challenge to the power of the sultans. After the intentions of the would-be reformers foundered on disagreements resulting from distrust of *sada* domination of the process, the Qu'ayti sultan sought resolution of the challenges by bringing in a British Resident Advisor.

The Aden Agreement and the Kathiri Sultan's Dilemma

The Kathiri sultan signed the Aden Agreement and retained his sultanate under Qu'ayti sovereignty and British protection, having no other options left to him. His attempts to involve Imam Yahya, the Ottomans, and even the British in his quest for the acquisition of a Hadhrami port had all failed. The treaty officially acknowledged the reality that the Kathiri sultan and his subjects could not leave the Kathiri sultanate without passing through Qu'ayti jurisdiction. The Kathiri sultanate was home to some of the wealthiest of all Hadhramis of that era, including the al-Kaf of Tarim and the Bin 'Abdat and Bin Talib families of the Kathiri tribe, and the cities of the Kathiri sultanate were among the oldest and richest in Hadhramawt. Yet the Kathiri sultan was never able to prevail against Qu'ayti overrule.

Some Kathiri subjects welcomed the treaty. Bin 'Ubaydillah wrote a poem in praise of the Aden Agreement and al-Mihdhar's skill in negotiating it, which he recited before a gathering of fifteen hundred notables and tribal leaders at al-Mihdhar's home after the negotiations had been completed.[1] Because of the importance of the ports to the economy of the interior, many of the wealthy subjects of the Kathiri, whose wealth derived primarily from Southeast Asia, welcomed the treaty for the promise it offered of improved transportation and communications between the *mahjar* and the interior and for the general development of the interior. Perhaps the most enthusiastic was Salim b. Ja'far Bin Talib. This wealthy and prominent member of the Kathiri tribe had come from the East Indies to Aden at the behest of the governor of Aden and witnessed the signing of the Aden Agreement. He had encouraged the Kathiri ruler to assent to the agreement, feeling that this measure of unification afforded all of Hadhramawt the opportunity for greater political stability and economic development. Salih b. 'Ubayd Bin 'Abdat, another wealthy and prominent member of the Kathiri tribe who had traveled from the East Indies to Aden along with Bin Talib, objected to the terms of the agreement and did not participate in the signing. Salih b. 'Ubayd's brother, Umar b. 'Ubayd Bin 'Abdat, also objected to the agreement. They felt that the Kathiri territory was disadvantaged by subsumption under Qu'ayti sovereignty.[2]

Many of their compatriots in the Kathiri tribe shared their feelings. When some Kathiri tribesmen had surrounded al-Mihdhar and his troops in Hawtat Ahmad b. Zayn shortly after the Aden Agreement had been signed, the tribesmen most likely complied in the ruse through which their prey escaped to Qu'ayti territory. While the tribesmen did not wish to take on both the Qu'ayti government and the British, their temporary surrounding of al-Mihdhar and the Qu'ayti forces expressed their dissatisfaction with the agreement. They objected to the terms of the agreement because of the subordinate status it enforced on the Kathiri sultan and the Kathiri tribe with respect to the Qu'ayti sultan and his supporters from the Yafi'i, Tamimi, and other tribes.[3]

Soon after the Aden Agreement was signed, the Kathiri began to appeal for material assistance from the Aden government. Defying the treaty stipulation that all correspondence with the British was to be channeled through the Qu'ayti, the Kathiri requested arms and money directly from the Aden government. In April 1919, the Kathiri asked for five hundred rifles, 150,000 cartridges, two cannons with one thousand shells for the armed forces, and another hundred Mauser rifles with fifteen thousand cartridges for the ruling family and leaders of the branches of the Kathiri tribe. He reported that he needed at least sixty thousand rupees to provide a monthly salary for tribal leaders to assure their allegiance and diligence in protecting the security of the roads, and furthermore "to plant affection for the British government in the hearts of the people."[4]

A few months later, the Aden government rewarded Sultan al-Mansur b. Ghalib al-Kathiri, ruler of Say'un, and Sultan Muhsin b. Ghalib, ruler of Tarim, with three thousand rupees, twenty guns, and five thousand cartridges each; the Kathiri crown prince, 'Ali b. Mansur, received one thousand rupees. Both Husayn b. Hamid al-Mihdhar and Salim b. Ja'far Bin Talib also received gifts as a token of recognition for their assistance in the realization of the agreement. The reward to the Kathiri sultans fell far short of what Sultan al-Mansur expected.[5]

This exchange, which seemed appropriate to the Aden government but offensively inadequate to the Kathiri, set the tone for the relationship between the colonial government and the successive sultans for decades. The Kathiri complained continually to the British about the terms of the treaty, particularly the necessity of corresponding with the British through the Qu'ayti, a stricture the Kathiri continually attempted to evade. Other recurrent complaints were the financial burden of Qu'ayti customs tariffs and the need of the Kathiri for more weapons. The Kathiri was able to receive weapons, both those he purchased and those he was granted as gifts by the British, only with the approval of the Qu'ayti sultan. Sultan al-Mansur b. Ghalib al-Kathiri protested these issues until his death in 1929, and his successor Sultan 'Ali b. Mansur al-Kathiri continued the litany of protests.[6]

The Kathiri position with respect to the Qu'ayti had almost reached a nadir in 1923, due to the Kathiri inability to provide security within his domains, primarily because of lack of finances. After tribesmen in the interior had attacked with impunity a camel caravan belonging to Qu'ayti subjects, the Qu'ayti threatened a total embargo against the Kathiri unless he began to resolve the security problem. The *sada* of the Kathiri state and the *wazir* al-Mihdhar of the Qu'ayti state served as mediators in the issue.[7] The threat of embargo was a potent one, since the Kathiri sultanate and its subjects had suffered greatly from the Qu'ayti embargo imposed at the end of World War I. A new treaty was made between the Qu'ayti and the Kathiri in 1924, which unfortunately failed to increase cooperation between Kathiri and Qu'ayti.

The merchants of the Kathiri sultanate found little advantage to their immediate interests from the Aden Agreement. While Qu'ayti control of Kathiri correspondence and external affairs was of little import to them, they objected to the double fees on imported goods that came to the Kathiri sultanate via the ports of the Qu'ayti sultanate, since taxes were levied by the Qu'ayti on all incoming goods whether they were in transit or not. The Qu'ayti justified taxing goods which were to travel to the interior on the grounds of the necessity of providing security over the trade routes, the greatest extent of which lay within his domains, to the cities of the interior. Despite continued calls on the Qu'ayti to protect the trade routes, Kathiri subjects complained of double taxation on imports and the issue was later taken up by subjects demanding governmental reform.[8]

Sayyid Abu Bakr b. Shaykh al-Kaf objected repeatedly to the Qu'ayti surcharge on caravan traffic of a rupee per camel-load from the coast to the interior. He complained to the Qu'ayti sultan, to the Qu'ayti *wazir* al-Mihdhar, to the Kathiri sultan, and to other Hadhrami notables. In an uncharacteristically militant tone, he even suggested at one point to the Kathiri that the leaders of disputing factions of the Kathiri tribe ('Umar b. 'Ubayd Bin 'Abdat and Salim b. Ja'far Bin Talib) should set aside their continual conflicts in order to unite the entire tribe against this affront by the Qu'ayti against those in the interior.[9] Such complaints continued throughout the decades following the Aden Agreement. When Sir

Bernard Reilly, then governor of Aden, visited the Kathiri sultanate in 1934, he was greeted by a speech given by Sayyid 'Abd al-Rahman b. Shaykh al-Kaf, which complained that the Qu'ayti-Kathiri agreement failed to benefit the Kathiri government and its subjects.[10]

In 1936, when the Qu'ayti entered into the Advisory Agreement with the British, according to the terms of the 1918 Aden Agreement, the Kathiri sultanate was automatically included. The Kathiri sultan immediately wrote to the new Resident Advisor, Harold Ingrams, appealing for British sympathy for his position. The Kathiri asserted that the prior agreements between the Qu'ayti and Kathiri, which purported to bring prosperity to Hadhramawt, had failed to do so. Therefore, he proclaimed himself no longer obligated to abide by the agreements nor obligated to consider the Kathiri territories under Qu'ayti sovereignty. He announced his intention to send Sayyid Abu Bakr b. Shaykh al-Kaf to present the Kathiri case to Ingrams.[11]

Ingrams responded directly to Sayyid Abu Bakr b. Shaykh al-Kaf, urging him to persuade the Kathiri to organize and improve the administration of his existing sultanate, rather than strive to extend his authority. In response to the internal weakness of the Kathiri sultanate and its lack of institutionalization, Ingrams suggested that Sultan 'Ali b. al-Mansur appoint members of his family to serve as resident deputies in the outlying towns of the Kathiri sultanate (al-Ghurfa, Maryama, and Taris), so that they could learn to administer justly. By developing a group of people to serve as deputies and governors, the sultan would then be better able to strengthen and improve his sultanate. Ingrams urged that al-Kaf persuade the sultan "not to try to run and fly before he learned to walk."[12] Following the same line of thought, Ingrams also repeatedly encouraged the Kathiri to send his sons and nephews to the school for the sons of chiefs that had been set up in Aden to raise the educational standard of the next generation of Southern Arabian rulers. He argued that, thus educated, they might provide more able administration of the Kathiri state in the future.[13]

The Qu'ayti State: Peaceful Expansion and Tribal Rebellions

The Qu'ayti state continued to expand, consolidating the western reaches of the interior of Wadi Hadhramawt under Qu'ayti rule. The expansion of the Qu'ayti state into the arid area of Haynan, west of al-Qatn, took place peacefully at the request of some of the inhabitants, rather like the earlier expansion of Qu'ayti authority into Wadi 'Idim. A Yafi'i strongman, Salim b. 'Ali Bin Harhara, had gained control of Haynan in 1864/1865, after which he ruled it as a supporter of the Qu'ayti state. But Bin Harhara's failure to provide security for the unarmed settled population led a delegation of the notables of Haynan in 1922 or 1923 to request from the governor of Shibam, 'Ali b. Salah al-Qu'ayti, the incorporation of Haynan under direct Qu'ayti authority. The governor responded by dispatching a force of Yafi'i and *hashiya* led by the Yafi'i Muhammad b. Salih al-Lahmadi to bring the area under direct Qu'ayti authority.[14]

At the same time that the Qu'ayti state was peacefully expanding, it met challenges elsewhere. One such challenge was a tribal rebellion instigated in 1924 by the wealthy Sayyid Muhammad b. 'Umar Ba'Aqil in Wadi Du'an, which was also the ancestral homeland of the *wazir* al-Mihdhar. This conflict was fueled by personal rivalry between the two *sayyids*, Ba'Aqil and al-Mihdhar, with the former exploiting his considerable personal wealth and the latter exploiting his access to the resources and soldiery of the state. Ba'Aqil began instigating tribal unrest after the *wazir* al-Mihdhar had denied him privileges and exemptions from state authority which Ba'Aqil considered his due because of his status and social position in the area. Ba'Aqil enlisted in his cause the Dayyin tribe, the largest, most powerful, and most aggressive of the tribes of Du'an, which had suffered greatly from poverty caused by years of drought.

Ba'Aqil encouraged rebellious tribesmen to carry out the same tactics of resistance to the government that had earlier been used by the Hamum tribe around al-Shihr. Through the tribal leaders, he hired tribesmen to engage in raids on the settled populace and their flocks. In response to this challenge to the ability of the Qu'ayti state to provide security, the governor of Du'an was forced to send increasing numbers of soldiers to quell the banditry of the growing tribal force enlisted by Ba'Aqil. At one point the government appeared to have prevailed, when the governor forced Ba'Aqil to pay five hundred *riyals* in reparations for the banditry of his henchmen. But Ba'Aqil continued his resistance, angered at the humiliation of having been treated as a common criminal by Qu'ayti soldiers at the order of al-Mihdhar. He enlisted an even larger force of Dayyin tribesmen. The tribesmen attacked the government troops, killing a few soldiers, and accelerated their attacks on the populace, stealing goods, animals, and even burning date palm orchards. They kidnapped a young man from the prominent al-Barr family of *sada,* under the mistaken impression that he was the son of the *wazir* Husayn b. Hamid al-Mihdhar. With the Dayyin tribesmen stepping up their destruction, al-Mihdhar led a large force of Yafi'i soldiers against the tribal henchmen of his old rival Ba'Aqil. Despite a fierce effort by the Dayyin, the government forces prevailed. The tribe sent emissaries from the al-Barr and the al-'Attas families to mediate their surrender. Twenty-four of the Dayyin were imprisoned near the governor's house in Du'an, while Muhammad b. 'Umar Ba'Aqil was imprisoned in al-Mukalla. He was released after spending four years in prison and paying fifty thousand *riyals* in reparations to the government.[15]

Not long after the rebellion of the Dayyin was settled, the Hamum, after several years quiescence, returned to create havoc for Qu'ayti authority in their territory, which dominated the hinterlands north and northeast of al-Shihr, including the critical caravan route from al-Shihr to Tarim. The Hamum, considering themselves the traditional authorities in their homeland with power to exact tribute from the settled population and traveling caravans, had earlier challenged the authority of the Qu'ayti with attacks on settlements, harbored ships, and caravans. In order to provide the security of his state to the hinterlands and the transportation routes, the Qu'ayti government in 1919 had imprisoned a large number of tribesmen, including fifty chiefs. It also executed twenty-seven leaders of those clans of the Hamum that had participated in the attacks as revenge for the twenty-seven persons killed in the course of the Hamum attacks.

Immediately after the execution of the Hamum leaders, the Qu'ayti expected retaliation. The fortifications of al-Shihr and al-Hami and the small eastern ports of al-Qarn and al-Qusay'ar were reinforced and the troops were on alert, but there was no response from the Hamum. The Qu'ayti attempted to negotiate with the Hamum through the mediation of the 'Aydarus *munsib,* but they refused. During this time, the trade of al-Shihr was insecure, as all of the caravan routes passed at least partially through Hamum territory. While the eastern and more direct routes from al-Shihr to the interior lay largely in Hamum territory, even the western routes from al-Shihr to the interior via Wadi Du'an had to pass through a segment of the westernmost portion of Hamum lands.

The Qu'ayti *wazir,* Husayn b. Hamid al-Mihdhar, who had been dealing with Kathiri tribal opposition to the Aden Agreement at the time of Governor Nasir b. Ahmad BuBak's retaliation against the Hamum, had attempted unsuccessfully on his return to the coast in 1919 to gain the release of the Hamum prisoners.[16] The *wazir* al-Mihdhar was able to negotiate on behalf of the Qu'ayti government with some of the Hamum. Some of the Hamum, including one large clan, the Qirzat, had not taken part in any of the Hamum attacks and so had not been punished by the Qu'ayti. None of their leaders had been executed and none of their members were among the Hamum languishing in al-Shihr's prison. With the assistance of the general broker of the al-Shihr market who mediated for the Hamum, the *wazir* made an agreement with the Qirzat that they would handle the caravan trade from al-Shihr, using the western route through Wadi Du'an. This agreement, which took advantage of a rivalry over the carrying trade that had long prevailed between the Qirzat and Al 'Umar, allowed the caravan trade from al-Shihr to resume.

However, the Qu'ayti naturally remained concerned about the strained relations with the Hamum. He anticipated an act of revenge from the tribe and tried to stay prepared for such an eventuality. The *wazir* and the governor of al-Hami, Mahfuz b. Ahmad al-Kasadi, made an agreement with the BaHasan clan that granted to the tribe the tribute they expected from the farmers and the fishermen in exchange for tribal protection.

For most of the clans of the Hamum, the years after the loss of their leaders were extremely difficult. Some of their members were still imprisoned, and they were missing their most respected and most capable leaders and advisors. Many of the youth were clamoring for some kind of quick and violent retaliation in an attempt to force the government to release the prisoners.

When the remnants of a tribal council met after the executions, they elected as their paramount leader the forty-five-year-old 'Ali b. Salim Bin Habraysh of the Al 'Umar, whose father had previously held the position. According to the tribe members, this leadership position was not a hereditary post and 'Ali b. Salim was chosen for his communicative ability and his wisdom. He found himself faced with the task of uniting the different branches of the tribe, rebuilding the moral of the members, and devising an appropriate response to the humiliation they had suffered.

'Ali b. Salim Bin Habraysh counseled patience and discipline to his fellow tribesmen, until the time would be right to act. He organized a convocation (*mahrajan*) for the youth of the Bayt 'Ali, which included a ritual of atonement and a new circumcision ceremony. Similar convocations were held periodically among all the branches of the tribe in order to keep the memory of the tragedy alive among the youth and to build solidarity among them. This rebuilding process lasted for a period of seven years, during which time the number of the Hamum fighting men increased as the young men matured.

During this time, the tribe experienced a period of unprecedented unity among the branches of the Hamum. They followed the discipline imposed on them by their leader, who forbade them to interfere in any way with subjects of the Qu'ayti state or their property. They took the customary imposts from the farmers and fishermen of al-Hami that they had been allowed in the agreement negotiated by the *wazir* and Mahfuz b. 'Awadh al-Kasadi. At the same time, 'Ali b. Salim made agreements of alliance with different branches of the Kathiri tribe. 'Umar b. 'Ubayd Bin 'Abdat of the Al 'Amr branch of the Kathiri tribe, at that time proclaiming himself independent ruler of al-Ghurfa, made an alliance with the Hamum and provided them with money and weapons with which to pursue their goals.[17]

In late 1925, after seven years of quiet recovery and reorganization, the Hamum made their move. The prisoners were still in jail in al-Shihr. At that time, Sultan 'Umar was in Hyderabad getting money needed to repay his government's debts in Hadhramawt. The *wazir* al-Mihdhar was occupied in military action against the Dayyin tribe and his old rival Ba'Aqil in Wadi Du'an. According to one government official, before leaving for battle in Du'an, al-Mihdhar alerted the Hamum of the impending absence of the Qu'ayti forces, one of several acts of duplicity against Sultan 'Umar at that time. However he learned of the westward movement of the Qu'ayti troops, 'Ali b. Salim Bin Habraysh took advantage of the opportunity to mount a Hamum attack on the small town of al-Dis al-Sharqiyya, east of al-Hami.[18]

While the Hamum sent a small delegation to al-Shihr to negotiate with the government for the release of the prisoners, 350 men of the Bayt 'Ali hid in the wadis around al-Dis. When the people of al-Dis spotted them, they immediately closed the gates of the town, which was mainly occupied by fishermen, farmers, and others of the unarmed classes. The town did include some armed tribesmen, including members of local tribes, some members of the Kasadi, and some Tamimi who had moved from the interior to al-Dis after conflicting with the Kathiri. There were also armed Yafiʻi tribesmen, landowners and merchants in the import-export trade of al-Dis's subsidiary port of al-Qarn, who received a monthly salary from the Quʻayti to serve as a reserve military force. In addition, there were regular Quʻayti soldiers in a fort in the town.

According to the Hamum, there were three reasons for their choice to attack al-Dis. First, it was far from the Quʻayti center at al-Mukalla, and was in the opposite direction from Wadi Duʻan, where the Quʻayti troops were occupied fighting the Dayyin tribe. Second, the armed tribesmen of the town were from groups that had treaties of alliance with the Hamum and could thus be expected to remain neutral. The third and most important reason was the presence of a small number of Quʻayti soldiers in al-Dis. This action was intended as revenge specifically against the Quʻayti state and its forces for the 1919 execution of Hamum leaders.[19]

When news reached al-Shihr that the Hamum had been seen in the vicinity of al-Dis, the governor, Jamaʻdar Salim b. Ahmad al-Quʻayti, feared for the security of his city and its prison. With a large number of the Quʻayti forces engaged in Duʻan, only a minimal defense force remained in al-Shihr. The prison, a likely target for attack, had been left with only eighteen guards, all aged and infirm. The governor called for the townspeople to assist the few Yafiʻi and slave soldiers left in the town. Two hundred volunteered, one hundred and fifty young and fifty old men, but they had only twenty or twenty-five weapons among them. Some of the Yafiʻi merchants opened their warehouses and distributed rifles to the volunteers. This aging local militia was distributed among the forts and fortifications, with a large number guarding the prison. It was probably the mustering of this improvised defense force that limited the Hamum attack to al-Dis.[20]

The attack commenced with the Bayt Ghurab of the Hamum coming in large numbers to surround al-Dis, cutting off its communications. They captured messengers on their way to the Quʻayti governor in al-Shihr seeking help. They spread the rumor in al-Dis and in al-Shihr that the Kathiri sultan was supporting their action, hoping that the Quʻayti would waste time trying to raise a huge army and bringing troops from far Duʻan. They also attacked a camel caravan traveling from the port of al-Qarn to al-Dis, killing the soldiers of its guard.

After the Quʻayti government representative (*hakim*) of al-Dis failed in an attempt to negotiate with the Hamum, he ordered the people of the town to prepare for a siege. That night the Hamum attacked the town and by sunrise they had taken the entire town except the main fort, to which the Quʻayti soldiers had retreated. After four days under siege in the fort without food and water, the Quʻayti soldiers were forced to surrender. First, they attempted to seek refuge in the homes of a family of *sada*, which was supposed to be a *hawta*, or sanctuary. The Hamum attacked and captured them. The tribe then fled the town with twenty-nine soldiers as captives, ahead of the well-equipped force of one thousand Quʻayti soldiers that was coming from al-Mukalla. The tribe averred that they left the town, not out of fear of the oncoming troops, but because they had accomplished their mission of vengeance on the Qu'ayti and his soldiers.[21] According to an official of the Qu'ayti state involved in the later stages of the pursuit, the Qu'ayti forces action got off to a poor start which was later rectified, although they were never able to capture the Hamum. The force that marched from al-Mukalla toward al-Dis consisted of Yafi'i soldiers from the al-Mukalla garrison, *hashiya,* and others from the regular army, under the leadership of a Yafi'i. Their progress from al-Mukalla to al-Shihr was slow and they required the stimulus of an elderly man from al-Shihr, Sa'id b. Muhammad Mukharish, who rode out and met the troops, challenged their leader for their slowness, and led the troops on to al-Dis, which the Hamum had already fled. On their arrival the Yafi'i troops started looting the shops and warehouses of al-Dis, on the excuse that the populace had aided the Hamum. Discipline was imposed by the other troops, the slave soldiers and the Hadhrami-born Yafi'i, or *tulud,* and order was restored to the town.

In the meantime, the Hamum, who had fled to the east, laid siege to the small eastern port of al-Qusay'ar. The people and the Yafi'i troops there held fast for nearly a month against the siege of the Hamum, who were aided by 'Umar b. 'Ubayd Bin 'Abdat, the self-proclaimed independent ruler of al-Ghurfa. Finally giving up, the Hamum and Bin 'Abdat went on to attack the village of Raidat Al 'Abd al-Wadud. The overland route there was quite difficult and at the time of the attack on Raidat Al 'Abd al-Wadud the rough waters of the summer monsoon prevented sea travel, which made it difficult for the Qu'ayti force to reach them.

The situation was resolved when Sultan 'Umar returned from his trip to Hyderabad and decisively met the challenge raised by this rebellious tribe. He brought in Yafi'i troops who had served in the Aden army and sent them to al-Shihr, where they awaited the onset of smooth seas and sailable winds. When the seas calmed, the governor of al-Shihr sent by sea to al-Qusay'ar a force that included fifty natives of al-Shihr and 150 of the newly arrived Yafi'i troops; later he sent another force of two hundred. Sultan 'Umar sent a force of 150 Yafi'i troops and 150 of the Qu'ayti *hashiya.* When this large and well-armed force arrived at al-Qusay'ar, the attack was at first delayed by difficulty in coordinating so many different forces.

After the command problems were resolved, they attacked by land and by sea but were driven back from Qusay'ar by Bin Habraysh's men. They moved on to Raidat Al 'Abd al-Wadud, where they liberated the town from the Hamum and were given a hero's welcome by the populace. Following reports that the Hamum were taking dried fish from the tiny fishing hamlets along the coast, the force sailed eastward. At one point, a Qu'ayti ship was fired on by a Mauser (called Mayzar Jawi, since they were imported to Hadhramawt from the East Indies). Knowing that the only person with such a weapon was Bin Habraysh, the troops pursued the Hamum throughout the area until they escaped to the highlands. During the pursuit, the Qu'ayti soldiers captured by the Hamum were split among the different branches of the Hamum; some died but many escaped their captors and fled to the towns.

The events of the attack on al-Dis and the strong response of the Qu'ayti state has different meanings to the different parties to events. To the Hamum, the attack was a vindication of their tribal pride. By taking the town from Qu'ayti forces, even for a few days, and by taking hostages from the Qu'ayti soldiers, they felt that they had achieved the revenge to which the Qu'ayti execution of their leaders obligated them. They felt that their success at evading capture by the strong force sent after them by Sultan 'Umar was a sign that their tribe had recovered its strength after the tragedy.

From the Qu'ayti point of view, the Hamum had simply been continuing their usual practice of banditry and seasonal predation on the settled populace. The massive force sent after the Hamum, which expelled them from the settled land of the coast, had effectively proved both to the Hamum and to the populace that the security of the Qu'ayti state extended throughout the hinterlands. This established state security even over the territory which the Hamum had considered their traditional sphere of influence.[22]

Rival to the Sultans: Bin 'Abdat's Challenge

More than thirty years after the nineteenth-century struggles for power had been settled in the unequal stalemate between Qu'ayti and Kathiri leaders, some members of the Bin 'Abdat attempted to establish a rival power base in the interior of Hadhramawt. Led by 'Umar b. 'Ubayd Bin 'Abdat, this family from the Kathiri tribal confederation withdrew its traditional support from the Kathiri sultans and claimed the village of al-Ghurfa as an independent principality under Bin 'Abdat rule. This created a dual problem for the Kathiri: Bin 'Abdat's action fragmented his traditional tribal base of support at the same time that it chipped away at the Kathiri sultanate's already limited territory. Bin 'Abdat created problems for the Qu'ayti sultan as well, since the terms of the Aden Agreement required the Qu'ayti to support the Kathiri militarily when necessary. Eventually Bin 'Abdat began to interfere more directly with Qu'ayti authority, by supporting Hamum tribal opposition and encouraging their obstruction of the passage of official and commercial traffic passing through the Qu'ayti hinterlands. At the same time, Bin 'Abdat made life difficult for ordinary people of the area from many walks of life by disrupting travel and caravan trade from Shibam and the western routes from the coast into Say'un. The decades-long conflict between Bin 'Abdat and his opponents led to great hardship for the people of al-Ghurfa, who were forced to travel from the village to the fields through a fortified trench.[23]

The Bin 'Abdat attempt to establish an independent sultanate in al-Ghurfa lasted for decades. The village of al-Ghurfa, or Ghurfat Ba'Abbad, lay twenty miles west of the Kathiri capital of Say'un, dominating the road leading from the important market center of Shibam, under Qu'ayti rule. It was part of the territory traditionally controlled by the tribes of the Shanafir confederation, which led to its inclusion in Kathiri territory as defined in the British-brokered 1918 Aden Agreement between the Kathiri and Qu'ayti rulers. The village of al-Ghurfa was also a *hawta,* an area under the protection of a spiritual leader. The Ba'Abbad, a *mashayikh* family of great prestige, had held authority over the hamlet since the fourteenth century.

In the late nineteenth century, the spiritual authority of the Ba'Abbad family in al-Ghurfa was weakening, partly due to internal dissension within the family and partly due to opposition from the tribes under its authority. At the same time, the authority of the Ba'Abbad family was challenged by opposition from the nearby Ahmad b. Zayn branch of the al-Hibshi family of *sada,* which held authority over the village just west of al-Ghurfa known as Hawtat Ahmad b. Zayn. Feuding between the rival spiritually prestigious families continued until the early 1880s.

While the Ba'Abbad continued to hold spiritual prestige, they were not strong enough to protect the unarmed inhabitants of al-Ghurfa, *dhu'afa'* and *sada,* from the armed tribesmen of the area who ran roughshod over the rights of the villagers. At the same time, the Kathiri sultan's power was not sufficient to control the tribesmen, even though they were from branches of the Kathiri tribe. During disputes, the tribesmen would occupy al-Ghurfa and feed their fighters from its stores of produce. The inhabitants suffered greatly from the general lack of security.[24]

The Bin 'Abdat claim of sovereignty over al-Ghurfa grew out of a local conflict between members of rival branches of the Kathiri tribe, all of whom possessed great wealth acquired in the East Indies. In the course of a dispute with the BalFas family (of the Al Fahum section of the Al 'Umar clan of the Al Kathir) from east of al-Ghurfa, 'Umar b. 'Ubayd Bin 'Abdat (of the Al 'Amr clan of the Al Kathir) claimed the village of al-Ghurfa and began to fortify it. He built a fortified wall around the town and imported weapons and a contingent of African slave soldiers—according to one report—two hundred commandos. Following the usual pattern for amassing and consolidating power in this region, he placed imposts on the production of the townspeople in exchange for providing them with security and provided tribal leaders in the vicinity with salaries. He then used the newly fortified town as a base from which to attack the BalFas. Revenue from family properties in Batavia and Singapore financed Bin 'Abdat's operations. Eventually other members of the Al 'Umar became concerned about the hostilities, including members of the Al Talib clan, which also included families possessing great wealth from the East Indies.[25]

The Bin 'Abdat rebellion was rooted in the 1918 Aden Agreement between the Kathiri and Qu'ayti sultans. Before the agreement was signed, the Aden government contacted wealthy and influential members of the Kathiri tribe in Singapore and Java, requesting their support for the agreement. The delegation that traveled to al-Mukalla included Salim b. Ja'far Bin Talib and Salim b. Muhammad Bin Talib, and 'Umar b. 'Ubayd Bin 'Abdat's brother, Salih b. 'Ubayd.[26]

Several members of the Al Talib section of the Al 'Umar, including Salim b.

Ja'far Bin Talib, had signed the 1918 Aden Agreement as witnesses. This treaty established Kathiri autonomy regarding local affairs within territory controlled by the Shanafir confederation, including that controlled by the Al 'Umar and the Al 'Amr clans of the Kathiri, but otherwise subordinated the Kathiri state under Qu'ayti authority. Salih b. 'Ubayd Bin 'Abdat, however, did not participate in the agreement despite having traveled from the East Indies to Hadhramawt at the request of the British to represent the Kathiri tribe in the negotiations. 'Umar and Salih both considered the terms of the agreement disadvantageous to the Kathiri. Active supporters of the Irshad movement in the East Indies, they distrusted the influential Qu'ayti *wazir,* Sayyid Husayn b. Hamid al-Mihdhar, and the powerful *sada* of the Kathiri sultanate. Thus, they certainly would have rejected the inclusion of the phrase "respect for the 'Alawi *sada*" (*ihtiram al-sada al-'Alawiyya*) in Article Six. (In British official documents, this phrase was wrongly translated as "respect for the higher authority," which in Arabic would be "*ihtiram al-sulta al-'aliya.*")[27]

After 1918, the Bin 'Abdat brothers maintained their opposition to the Aden Agreement. The rift between the Al 'Umar and the Al 'Amr clans was exacerbated by their differing stances toward the Hadhrami sultans, their relations with the British, and the Aden Agreement. While Bin 'Abdat struggled against the authority of first the Kathiri and later the Qu'ayti sultanate, Salim b. Ja'far Bin Talib of the Al 'Umar cooperated with the Qu'ayti, the Kathiri, and the British authorities in Aden in efforts to bring stability to Hadhramawt. He vigorously urged them to suppress the activities of Bin 'Abdat.

The Qu'ayti *wazir,* Husayn b. Hamid al-Mihdhar, was concerned about the reaction of the Kathiri tribes after the 1918 Aden Agreement, particularly because of the great wealth in Singapore and Java controlled by Kathiri tribesmen. He feared that 'Umar b. 'Ubayd Bin 'Abdat was fomenting a conspiracy of opposition to the Aden Agreement and to Qu'ayti rule among powerful Kathiri tribesmen in Hadhramawt and in the diaspora and even among some Qu'ayti subjects. At one point, al-Mihdhar even traveled to Shibam in order to observe Bin 'Abdat's activities in al-Ghurfa. He feared that the ongoing conflict between the Al 'Umar and the Al 'Amr clans would foster tribal insurrection. When Salim b. Ja'far Bin Talib went to the Kathiri sultan complaining of Bin 'Abdat's activities in al-Ghurfa, the concerned Kathiri pleaded poverty and lack of weapons and sent him to al-Mihdhar. The *wazir* pledged Qu'ayti support for action by the Kathiri sultan and the Al 'Amr against Bin 'Abdat. He encouraged the Kathiri to present Bin 'Abdat with an ultimatum, to cease his hostile activities around al-Ghurfa or face retaliation.[28]

In 1924, the Qu'ayti and Kathiri sultans agreed to cooperate to settle tribal conflicts and to keep the roads secure within both of their territories. At the same time, the Bin 'Abdat brothers continued their claim of sovereignty over al-Ghurfa, where they were increasing their fortifications and digging an additional series of trenches around the village. During this time, their attempts to establish sovereignty included peaceful means, among them the circulation of coins minted in the name of their rule. A year after the Kathiri-Qu'ayti security accord, in March

1925, Sayyid Husayn b. Hamid al-Mihdhar signed an agreement with the Kathiri sultan and Salim b. Ja'far Bin Talib. This stated that al-Ghurfa should be taken from Bin 'Abdat and restored to state sovereignty through united action of the Kathiri tribes, with the Qu'ayti supplying arms and ammunition.[29]

In early 1926, incidents of Bin 'Abdat's interference with travel through his territory continued, which led to Qu'ayti complaints about Bin 'Abdat obstructing the passage of Qu'ayti subjects.[30] Finally, the *wazir* Husayn b. Hamid al-Mihdhar decided to take action. After he had suppressed the Dayyin rebellion fomented by Ba'Aqil in Du'an, he traveled to Shibam with a force of well-armed Yafi'i and slave soldiers, bringing with him an artillery piece. There he met with the Kathiri sultan and with representatives of the different branches of the Kathiri tribe, including Salim b. Ja'far Bin Talib of the Al 'Umar, and garnered their support for a joint attack on Bin 'Abdat. According to Salah al-Bakri, al-Mihdhar hoped that this alliance with the Al 'Umar would help him negotiate a settlement with the Hamum tribe (who were assisted by Bin 'Abdat), or at least help him to pressure the Kathiri sultan not to allow the Hamum tribe access to shelter and commerce within his territory.

In July 1926, the combined forces surrounded al-Ghurfa, with the artillery piece positioned across from the village. Despite their superior numbers and arms, these forces were unsuccessful in dislodging Bin 'Abdat, even after a month-long siege. While Bin 'Abdat kept his forces within trenches, they employed effective tactics such as raining sniper fire on his enemies when they ventured near the well that supplied their water. The different fighting units besieging al-Ghurfa lacked solidarity and organization and had little zeal for their task. In particular, the Kathiri tribesmen soon lost their enthusiasm for attacking tribal kinsmen and most of them quickly deserted the battle. The slave forces of the Kathiri sultan quickly followed in desertion, leaving only the Yafi'i and slave forces of the Qu'ayti, who soon withdrew to Shibam. The *wazir* Husayn b. Hamid al-Mihdhar returned to al-Mukalla claiming to be doing so in order to dispatch or return with more Yafi'i troops, but none came. Only some of the Al 'Umar remained, to continue their quarrel with Bin 'Abdat in a desultory fashion.[31]

After the failure of the joint Kathiri-Qu'ayti attack on Bin 'Abdat, both sides turned to negotiations mediated by Major Bernard Reilly, then Resident of Aden. In late September 1926, Major Reilly invited Sayyid Husayn b. Hamid al-Mihdhar, Salim b. Ja'far Bin Talib, and the Bin 'Abdat brothers to come to Aden for negotiations. Negotiations took place, although al-Mihdhar's participation was delayed due to illness. In late January 1927, Salim b. Ja'far Bin Talib wrote from Aden to the Kathiri sultan. He related that he and al-Mihdhar had submitted a four-page memorandum to the Aden government, while the Bin 'Abdat brothers had submitted a memorandum of fifty pages, drafted by a Singapore lawyer, documenting their claim to sovereignty of al-Ghurfa. Husayn b. Hamid al-Mihdhar enumerated for the Aden government the offenses of the Bin 'Abdat brothers: fighting with the other branches of the Kathiri tribe; occupying al-Ghurfa; assisting the Hamum tribe against the Qu'ayti; attempting to raise a rebellion against the Qu'ayti by Kathiri subjects; attempting to enlist the governor of Shibam in an assassination plot against al-Mihdhar; and firing on Qu'ayti troops and on the *wazir*'s brother, 'Abd al-Rahman b. Hamid al-Mihdhar. Bin Talib and al-Mihdhar told the Aden government that they could not recognize Bin 'Abdat as a third sultan in Hadhramawt, since to do so would be to encourage myriad others in Hadhramawt and in the Hadhrami diaspora to advance similar claims.[32]

At the same time, Bin 'Abdat's seizure of al-Ghurfa continued to be a thorn in the side of the Kathiri sultan and to exacerbate other problems that he was having maintaining order under his rule. While negotiations were taking place in Aden, rebellious slaves from the Kathiri military force created a disturbance in the eastern part of the sultanate. The slaves then fled with their families to refuge in al-Ghurfa, despite the sultan's protestations to Bin 'Abdat.[33]

Meanwhile, negotiations in Aden were coming to naught. Salim b. Ja'far Bin Talib had remained in Aden for more than three months, presenting the case of the Qu'ayti and Kathiri sultanates and the Al 'Umar against Bin 'Abdat's claims of sovereignty in al-Ghurfa. After spending much time and effort, Bin Talib was annoyed that the Aden government, after earlier assurances of support, was backing down in the face of Bin 'Abdat's intransigence. The Aden government finally told Bin Talib that the protection (*himaya*) of the British over the sultanates applied only to outside forces and not to internal problems. They claimed to be willing to intercede in conflicts between the two sultans, but stated that they were unwilling to intercede in affairs between the sultans and their subjects. Bin Talib considered the stance of the Aden government to be either stupidity or the result of bad advice. Rather than following Aden's advice for further negotiations between the sultanates and Bin 'Abdat, Bin Talib suggested that eventually it might be necessary to bypass the Aden government and pursue their claim to the government of India, which then administered Aden, or even to London.[34]

Bin Talib returned to Hadhramawt and the Al 'Umar clan continued sporadic skirmishes against Bin 'Abdat. In 1928, at the same time that Qu'ayti troops had forced the Hamum tribe to cease their resistance and enter a treaty agreement, Bin 'Abdat finally agreed to a cease-fire at al-Ghurfa. This time the Al 'Umar refused and the periodic warfare continued for years, to the detriment of security, stability, and progress of the Kathiri state.[35] In 1931, when the Qu'ayti government raised the surcharge on goods transported from coast to interior from one-half to one rupee per camel-load, Sayyid Abu Bakr b. Shaykh al-Kaf protested vociferously and attempted to persuade Sultan 'Umar to reduce the surcharge. At that time he criticized the Bin 'Abdat brothers and Salim b. Ja'far Bin Talib for their continued conflict, since it prevented the Kathiri tribe from presenting a united front supporting the interests of the Kathiri sultanate before the Qu'ayti.[36]

From spring 1932 through late 1933, repeated short-term agreements were made attempting to establish a peace settlement between the Al 'Umar and the Al 'Amr clans of the Kathiri tribe. While leaders of the different groups comprising the Kathiri tribe signed these agreements, they were unable to guarantee an effective peace. When Harold and Doreen Ingrams first traveled to the interior of Hadhramawt in 1934, the long-standing feud between the two clans continued in a state of stalemate punctuated by sporadic attacks. Partisans of Bin 'Abdat and BalFas carried out trench warfare in the plain between Bin 'Abdat's stronghold of al-Ghurfa and the nearby BalFas fortifications.[37]

With the encouragement of the British, the Kathiri urged settlement on Bin 'Abdat. In late 1936, when Harold Ingrams, on the request of Sultan Salih b. Ghalib al-Qu'ayti and Sayyid Abu Bakr b. Shaykh al-Kaf, began attempting to broker a three year's truce among all the tribes of Hadhramawt, he found Salim b. Ja'far Bin Talib a willing but pessimistic participant. Despite his pessimism, Bin Talib eventually was one of the five men appointed to the Peace Board as representatives of Sultan Salih b. Ghalib al-Qu'ayti and Sultan 'Ali b. Mansur al-Kathiri.[38]

The question of whether Bin 'Abdat would agree to the truce loomed large over the negotiations. BalFas had agreed to cease hostilities only on the condition that Bin 'Abdat did as well. Like Bin Talib, Bin 'Abdat expressed pessimism about the prospects of success for the cease-fire, but eventually agreed to sign. From then on, he loyally supported the cease-fire, and ceased all hostilities toward BalFas and other members of the Al 'Umar.[39]

Unfortunately, this improved circumstance did not last even until the end of the decade. 'Umar b. 'Ubayd Bin 'Abdat died in 1939; his brother Salih b. 'Ubayd had already died. The family tradition of resistance was carried on by Salih's b. 'Ubayd's son, 'Ubayd b. Salih Bin 'Abdat, who did not abide by his uncle's assent to the peace treaty. The British considered 'Ubayd b. Salih to be strange, suspicious, and fanatical. He carried a loaded revolver at all times and was fearful of being poisoned.[40] He continued claiming to rule al-Ghurfa and blocked traffic between Shibam and Say'un, even though his domain was so tiny that the same soldiers guarded the gates on both sides of al-Ghurfa. The situation continued until the British sent in a force of soldiers from Hyderabad to remove Bin 'Abdat, as a result of his interference with the transport of relief supplies to victims of the famine of 1943 to 1945.[41]

Conflict within the Qu'ayti Government

The turbulent events of the 1920s, such as the Dayyin and Hamum rebellions and the Bin 'Abdat insurrection, were at times exacerbated by conflict within the Qu'ayti government after the death of Sultan Ghalib b. 'Awadh. His son Salih b. Ghalib hoped to succeed his father, even though 'Umar b. 'Awadh was the crown prince and vice regent at the time of Ghalib b. 'Awadh's death and expected to succeed him. This breach in solidarity was later exacerbated by actions of the *wazir* Husayn b. Hamid al-Mihdhar that complicated Sultan 'Umar's problems with fractious tribes.

Figure 8.1 Quʿayti Palace, al-Mukalla

When Sultan Ghalib b. 'Awadh died in 1921, his son Salih was ready to succeed his father, even though the 1898 will of 'Awadh b. 'Umar specified that 'Umar b. 'Awad was to succeed Ghalib. After the burial of Sultan Ghalib in Hyderabad, Salih b. Ghalib returned to Hadhramawt via Bombay before 'Umar b. 'Awadh was prepared to travel. Both Salih and 'Umar tried to create personal bases of support from among the military forces and government employees, whose ranks were equally divided. Each tried to gain the support of the *wazir*, Husayn b. Hamid al-Mihdhar, against the other. The *wazir*, playing the role of elder statesman, the neutral and ever loyal retainer of the family and trusted servant of the state, gained power through his position as arbitrator. In the end, in the interest of the stability of the sultanate, the matter was settled strictly according to 'Awadh b. 'Umar's will. 'Umar b. 'Awadh succeeded his brother Ghalib, and Salih b. 'Ghalib was named crown prince, despite 'Umar's complaints that he had attempted insubordination.[42]

In the opinion of 'Abd al-Khaliq b. 'Abdalla al-Batati, who was in the employ of the Qu'ayti government at the time, al-Mihdhar did not always act in the best interests of the Qu'ayti state and sometimes colluded with the Hamum. At other times, the *wazir* opposed Sultan 'Umar b. 'Awadh, creating a rift among the sultan's supporters and exacerbating the already existing rivalry between Sultan 'Umar b. 'Awadh and the crown prince in order to maintain his personal position as arbitrator. In 1925, according to al-Batati, al-Mihdhar alerted the Hamum that he was taking the main body of the Qu'ayti forces west to Wadi Du'an where the Dayyin were rebelling. The following year, when al-Mihdhar went to al-Shihr, he enabled some of the Hamum prisoners to escape. That action led to a rift between Sultan 'Umar and al-Mihdhar that was reproduced in a rift within the forces supporting the Qu'ayti government. In his efforts to gain support among the soldiery, Sayyid Husayn emphasized his closeness with the deceased Sultan Ghalib and presented himself as acting in the interest of his son, Salih b. Ghalib. The Yafi'i *tulud* aligned themselves with Sultan 'Umar, while about half of the Yafi'i *ghurba* sided with the sultan and half sided with Husayn b. Hamid al-Mihdhar. Of the *hashiya*, those of al-Mukalla and al-Dis al-Sharqiyya sided with al-Mihdhar, while the rest sided with the sultan. A few skirmishes between the two factions took place, including an incident in the marketplace of al-Mukalla in July 1927.

Soon after, the *wazir*'s machinations led to a confrontation between Sultan 'Umar b. 'Awadh and his nephew Crown Prince Salih b. Ghalib. Sultan 'Umar's position was complicated by the necessity for him to spend a great deal of time in Hyderabad sorting out legal problems involving the Qu'ayti estates there. The British became involved in the matter when, at the request of al-Mihdhar, they arrested 'Ubayd b. Salih Bin 'Abdat in Aden for his activities in al-Ghurfa. The Aden government released Bin 'Abdat to the custody of a Hadhrami resident of Aden, Salih b. 'Abdalla BaRahim, which angered al-Mihdhar. He responded by imprisoning two of BaRahim's brothers in al-Mukalla. But the BaRahim brothers had been born in the mahjar, in Singapore, and thus held British passports. The Aden government ordered the release of the BaRahim brothers, at which point Sultan

'Umar told them that the arrest had been al-Mihdhar's doing, carried out during the sultan's absence and without his prior consent. The sultan and the *wazir* were summoned by the government to Aden to explain. The *wazir,* fearing for his political career, summoned Salih b. Ghalib al-Qu'ayti to Aden. Sultan 'Umar, Salih b. Ghalib, and the *wazir* were scheduled to meet with Reilly, the Aden Resident, but Sultan 'Umar forestalled the meeting by instigating a private meeting with his nephew. Arriving unexpectedly at the home of the Hadrami merchant BaSharahil where Salih b. Ghalib was staying, Sultan 'Umar asked what he wanted. When the embarrassed nephew replied that he wanted full political authority, Sultan 'Umar wrote a document granting Salih the right to act as ruler with no interference. Although within a year dissension flared between the two over the Singapore Conference, the immediate situation was defused. Salih b. Ghalib was prevented from seeking support against his uncle from the British; he had been prepared to offer to sever ties with the Nizam of Hyderabad if recognized as sultan. The *wazir* remained in position until his death in 1928. Sultan 'Umar eventually returned to Hadhramawt, where his base of support had remained strong in certain quarters, and in 1930 denounced all understandings entered into by his nephew. Sultan 'Umar b. 'Awadh made no attempt to interfere with the order of succession and when he died in 1935, 'Umar was succeded by Salih b. Ghalib.[43]

Later, the succession process of the Qu'ayti dynasty was altered by the wish of Sultan Salih b. Ghalib, with the cooperation of the British. According to Sultan 'Awadh b. 'Umar's 1898 will, Salih b. Ghalib was to be succeeded by 'Umar b. 'Awadh's heir, Muhammad b. 'Umar, who had been born late in his father's life and was considerably younger than Salih's son 'Awadh. Salih had had to wait until late in life to assume his position as sultan and he was unwilling for his own son to do so. Early in his reign, Sultan Salih tried to assure that his son 'Awadh b. Salih would have the opportunity to succeed him, rather than the younger Muhammad b. 'Umar. Sultan Salih had positive relations with Harold Ingrams that dated from Ingrams' arrival in Hadhramawt in 1934, since the two in many respects shared a vision of reform and progress for Hadhramawt. Sultan Salih previously had hesitated to accept a British advisor in his sultanate, even though the governor of Aden and the Colonial Office had proposed an advisory relationship resembling those in place with the sultans of Malaya. When the possibility of Ingrams serving as Resident Advisor was proposed, Sultan Salih was amenable to the notion. In 1937, Ingrams met Sultan Salih in Aden, where he was stopping on his way to England to attend the coronation of King George VI. The sultan expressed his trust that if Ingrams were to serve as advisor, he would not usurp the ruler's power. At the same time, he informed Ingrams of his wish to see his son 'Awadh's succession secured. While in London for the coronation, Sultan Salih b. Ghalib and his son 'Awadh, represented by the famed British barrister Walter Monckton, took their succession case to the British authorities while Muhammad b. 'Umar brought a young Indian barrister, 'Ali Akbar Khan, to argue his side. The Colonial Office ruled in favor of the succession of 'Awadh b. Salih, preferring the principle of primogeniture to the alternating succession called for by Sultan 'Awadh b. 'Umar's will. After the sultan's return from London, he signed an advisory agreement with the Aden government on August 13, 1937. By doing so, he agreed to take the Resident Advisor's advice in all matters except those dealing with religion. The treaty also recognized the right of the sultans to appoint their heirs and successors, subject to British approval. This treaty with the British superseded the 1898 will of 'Awadh b. 'Umar with respect to its instructions for succession, so that Sultan Salih was succeeded by his son 'Awadh in 1956 and 'Awadh was succeeded by his son Ghalib in 1966. In 1939, Sultan Ja'far b. al-Mansur al-Kathiri followed the lead of Sultan Salih and signed an advisory treaty with the same terms.[44]

The Sultanates and Growing Financial Problems

The challenges to the sultans by obstreperous tribes and rivals for power resulted in increasing indebtedness of the sultanates, which led to increasing financial dependency on their wealthier subjects. At the same time that the Kathiri and Qu'ayti sultans' rule over their respective territories was legitimized and institutionalized by the Aden Agreement of 1918, both sultans found their power eroded by increasing financial problems.

In 1918, the Qu'ayti state received loans from the merchants of al-Mukalla and al-Shihr to finance operations against the Hamum. Since the merchants' property and profits were especially vulnerable to tribal attacks on caravans, they were a natural source of financing for security operations. They had the money available to lend to the government and it was in their interest to do so. During the last four years of Sultan Ghalib b. 'Awadh's life, 1918 through 1922, the Qu'ayti state was in financial trouble with a debt of about three million *riyals*. With the government in arrears of its payments to its employees and security forces, Sultan Ghalib b. 'Awadh and Husayn b. Hamid al-Mihdhar traveled to Aden to request financial assistance from the British government, which refused it. Sultan Ghalib b. 'Awadh was in Hyderabad collecting money from the family estates to pay state expenses when he died in 1921.

After Sultan Ghalib's death, his successor Sultan 'Umar b. 'Awadh was able to bring money from Hyderabad to settle the government debts, which included payments of a half million *riyals* to Adeni merchants, a half million to Hadhrami merchants (most to the Bu Saba'a and BaSharahil families), a half million to other commercial moneylenders, and a half million to the government employees and security forces. At that same time, he commenced on building projects, which included a new customs center in al-Mukalla and an improved motor road between al-Mukalla and the agricultural exporting center of Ghayl BaWazir, which facilitated the collection of an annual revenue of 200,000 *riyals* a year. This was accomplished by "farming-out" to the wealthy merchant families the right to collect customs at the ports of Hadhramawt and duties on tobacco production in Ghayl

BaWazir. Sultan 'Umar b. 'Awadh balanced the budget with money from the family estates in Hyderabad until the rent payments from the merchants came through at the end of the year.[45]

Sultan 'Umar b. 'Awadh further organized the state budget, reforming the system of payment of the government employees and security forces. He abolished the previous system of allocating the pay to the armed services, in which the military leaders received the monthly salary for their troops in a lump sum and were in effect free to distribute it as they chose. Sometimes the commanders delayed turning over the salary to their troops or turned over only a portion of the salary. Under Sultan 'Umar's reforms, each soldier received his pay personally. A system of regular monthly payments to government employees and soldiers was implemented, with the sultan paying from private funds when government coffers were low. This new system prevented the government from falling into the extreme arrears it had before Sultan Ghalib's death in 1922.[46]

Demands for Reform in the Kathiri Sultanate

Within the Kathiri sultanate, demands for social reform came largely from civic organizations comprised of local notables. The progression of these demands differed in the two main Kathiri towns of Say'un and Tarim. In 1912, Sayyid 'Abd al-Rahman b. 'Ubaydillah al-Saqqaf and other notables of Say'un attempted to establish an organization called Jam'iyat al-Haqq. This league was created for the purpose of establishing justice, regulating the nations economic, political, and military affairs, advancing development, and improving communications, with the assistance of the government of the sultans Mansur and Muhsin b. Ghalib al-Kathiri. While the reasons for the organization's early demise are not clear, it seems likely that the relationship between civic and state power it attempted to implement was the reason.

Its constitution established that the organization's center be in Tarim or Say'un, with branches elsewhere, including Singapore, Java, Aden, al-Mukalla, and al-Shihr. It established regulations for election of officers, who were to be competent and decent people (*min ahl al-kafa'a wa al-liaqa*). The presidency was reserved for members of the sultan's family. The administration was to meet monthly with an annual general assembly for all dues-paying members in which they might examine the workings of the organization and make suggestions. Members and directors had to swear loyalty to the organization and pay dues (one *riyal* on joining, and one-fourth *riyal* monthly thereafter). This organization proposed an unusual relationship with the state, with an incipient system of checks and balances. To join the organization, an individual was to petition the president. Resolutions, which needed the agreement of a majority of the administration, were to be taken to the sultan for execution. Resolutions had to agree with treaties and tribal agreements already entered by the state. The members' right to alter the constitution was limited only with respect to the stipulation of a member of the sultan's family as president; that could not be changed even though other articles might be altered on the agreement of a set proportion of the dues-paying members. At the same time, the constitution stipulated that the sultan could not make international treaties (*mu'ahadat*) or agreements with tribes (*muhalifat*) except with the consensus of the organization. According to the final article of the constitution, the *hashiya* would remain in the sultan's ownership, but were under the orders of Jam'iyat al-Haqq, which also was responsible for their salary.[47]

This organization did not get off the ground, probably having overstepped its bounds with the Kathiri government. The final article in the organization's platform, stipulating control of the sultanate's military force, indicated the reason that the members of this league felt so empowered: they provided the sultan with the funds to pay his army. Yet in the end, despite his financial dependence, the sultan refrained from sharing power with the organization. In Say'un, Bin 'Ubaydillah and others remained active in social reform and later established an organization in Say'un called Majlis al-Islah (Reform Council). In 1913, a group of seventeen *sada* agreed to confer responsibility for moral guidance of the society upon six others, including Bin 'Ubaydillah, who were to act in concert on their behalf. The seventeen *sada* gave full responsibility and authority to these six representatives to oppose bad behavior and guide toward good. The six were to meet weekly and to confer on matters of public concern and were to follow the opinion of the majority among them. Later, a group of *sada* and *mashayikh* of Say'un, including Bin 'Ubaydillah, formed another reform organization with similar aims.[48]

According to Bin 'Ubaydillah's account, Say'un's reform organizations were fraught with opposition, both from within and from the authorities. In the first volume of his collected poems, Bin 'Ubaydillah included a poem about a reform organization founded in 1919, which he administered along with a board of advisors of six members of the *sada* and *mashayikh* of Say'un. He reported that although the Kathiri sultan had originally ratified the organization's charter, he eventually opposed it. Even the failure of the reform groups was later contested. The sultan blamed Say'un's notables for not having implemented reform; Bin 'Ubaydillah blamed the sultan for not having supported the reform groups; and critics blamed Bin 'Ubaydillah for having subverted the reform organizations by using them to advance his own purposes. Bin 'Ubaydillah vehemently defended himself against the charges, but considering his continual political intrigues during these years, the accusations are understandable whether or not they are true.[49]

This ill-fated Jam'iyat al-Haqq of Say'un was succeeded by another reform organization of the same name that was founded and chartered in 1915 in Tarim, where it remained active for decades. While this organization was not free from criticism and opposition, it enjoyed a degree of effectiveness unknown among the transitory reform organizations of Say'un. Jam'iyat al-Haqq, composed of prominent *mashayikh* and *sada* of Tarim, was active through the 1940s, virtually controlling civil affairs in the town for a number of years. Its accomplishments included establishing Madrasat Jamʿiyat al-Haqq, the town's first modern school. The organization benefited from a different relationship with the Kathiri state: while Sayʾun was the seat of the Kathiri sultanate, Tarim was of lesser political importance. After the 1916 division of authority within the Kathiri sultanate, the town of Tarim was delegated to the authority of Muhsin b. Ghalib and his heirs, while the capital remained in the hands of the reigning sultan, al-Mansur b. Ghalib al-Kathiri, and his heirs. The notables of Tarim who organized for social reform, including Abu Bakr and ʿAbd al-Rahman b. Shaykh al-Kaf, were not only influential but extremely wealthy and were able to come to an accommodation with the Kathiri authorities there. Jamʿiyat al-Haqq took over responsibility for the civil affairs of the town. In exchange, the Kathiri sultan received a monthly stipend from the al-Kaf family. When Sultan Muhsin b. Ghalib al-Kathiri died at the end of 1924, the power of the league increased, as his successor Sultan Salim never served as more than a figurehead. The league also paid the salaries of the *hashiya* posted in Tarim. Along with the expenses of the state, the league took over its tax revenues. One of the actions implemented by this league was the construction of a fortified city wall and a garrisoned guardhouse.

Even though the league succeeded in taking over civic affairs from the Kathiri sultanate, its experiment in governance was not without opposition. People of Tarim objected to the system of taxation, and the *hashiya* rebelled when their pay fell into arrears. The ʿAydarus *munsib*, who held spiritual authority over the powerful Al Tamim tribe which controlled territory almost surrounding Tarim, opposed the league's co-optation of power in Tarim. In 1926 to 1927, the Tamimi tribe, with the support of their *munsib*, surrounded the city. The league-financed army protected the city until the al-Kaf family called on the Quʿayti government for support. The Quʿayti sent sixty of his Yafiʿi troops, led by the *wazir* Sayyid Husayn b. Hamid al-Mihdhar. After destroying the guardhouse, Yafiʿi troops were posted to both Sayʾun and Tarim and took over the protection of the road between the two cities. After an incident in which Tamimi tribesmen obstructed the passage of a vehicle guarded by one of the Yafiʿi soldiers, which resulted in the deaths of the soldier and two tribesmen, Sultan ʿUmar withdrew his troops. This left the al-Kaf family and the Kathiri to negotiate a settlement with the Tamimi. The net result of the Tamim action and the Quʿayti response was to check the power and autonomy of the league. The tribe continued to threaten the town; in later years, the al-Kaf family spent as much as twelve thousand *riyals* in settling disputes with the Tamimis.[50] Even though the political power of Jamʿiyat al-Haqq was diminished in later years, the organization continued to run Madrasat Jamʿiyat al-Haqq and advocated social and moral reform, promulgating and enforcing "sumptuary laws" for the community in an attempt to reduce conspicuous consumption of luxury goods. The al-Kaf family also strongly advocated the reform conferences that subjects were urging on the Kathiri and Quʿayti sultans during the 1920s.

The Reform Conferences and Their Failure

After the incident in Aden when Sultan 'Umar b. 'Awadh al-Qu'ayti handed full authority over the state to his nephew, Crown Prince Salih b. Ghalib, the latter attempted to initiate the process of modernization he believed necessary to bring about the improvement of material and social conditions in Hadhramawt. In October 1927, then Sultan Salih b. Ghalib convened a meeting in al-Shihr with the intention of mobilizing the Qu'ayti and Kathiri sultanates, their subjects, and the overseas Hadhrami communities in a concerted effort toward modernization of Hadhramawt. Under the joint leadership of Salih b. Ghalib al-Qu'ayti and the Kathiri Crown Prince 'Ali b. al-Mansur, a committee of representatives and subjects of the two states, most from the *sada,* met and planned the convening of further meetings to include both Hadhramis in the homeland and in the *mahjar.*

The committee at the al-Shihr meeting recognized that a greater degree of cooperation among Hadhramis was a necessary condition for progress to take place. In spite of their history of strained relations, the two sultanates commenced the attempt toward greater unification by agreeing upon the Treaty of al-Shihr. This treaty was signed by Salih b. Ghalib al-Qu'ayti, 'Ali b. al-Mansur b. Ghalib al-Kathiri, and 'Abdalla b. Muhsin b. Ghalib al-Kathiri (the latter two representing both branches of the family sharing rule of Kathiri territory). The treaty renewed the Aden Agreement's pledge of mutual assistance in settling disturbances and the governments agreed to reciprocal responsibility in apprehending those who disturbed the peace in either state. The Qu'ayti government would maintain an army sufficient to provide security for both states. In accordance with an agreement made three weeks earlier in al-Mukalla, a new system of passports was to be implemented, pending the approval of Sultan al-Mansur b. Ghalib al-Kathiri, who remained in the interior during these discussions. A council of subjects, including Hadhramis of the *mahjar,* was to be created in order to express public opinion, while the governments were to consult with a council of representatives of the people.[51]

An official proclamation affirmed the unity of the two states and announced the establishment of Qu'ayti representatives at Say'un and Tarim and that of Kathiri representatives at al-Mukalla and al-Shihr.[52] The conference appointed an emissary, Shaykh Tayyib al-Sassi, to carry the announcement of Qu'ayti-Kathiri unity and the call to participate in the process of reform of Hadhramawt to the Hadhrami communities of the East Indies. Tayyib al-Sassi was not a Hadhrami, but an exile from Hijaz who as a partisan of Sharif Husayn had fled Mecca at the time of its takeover by 'Abd al-'Aziz Ibn Sa'ud and wound up in Hadhramawt where he was hosted and employed by the al-Kaf family.

The emissary carried copies of the treaty, proclamation, another proclamation from Sultan Salih b. Ghalib al-Qu'ayti directed to his subjects in "Java" and a similar one from 'Abdalla b. Muhsin and 'Ali b. Mansur al-Kathiri to their subjects. Sultan Salih b. Ghalib proclaimed the new agreement of unification and announced that delegations were traveling to the interior and to Java to involve his subjects in the reform process, which would require their cooperation. He emphasized the necessity for the spread of education and the establishment of cooperative ventures to develop agricultural projects. He made a special appeal to those who had benefited from exposure to new ideas in the cosmopolitan world of the *mahjar* (*alladhina tanawarat afkaruhum bi-ihtikakihim bi-al-ajanib,* "those whose thoughts had been enlightened by contact with foreigners"). He advocated the importance of education, not only in religious subjects, but also in practical subjects such as math, science, economics, politics, and medicine; he noted that the society needed engineers, doctors, and writers. He thought that studies of the physical geography of the region indicated that, despite Hadhramawt's aridity, there was adequate water and fertile enough soil for agriculture if the necessary technology for reservoirs and irrigation systems were employed. He encouraged the establishment of joint enterprises for development of agriculture, industry, and commerce and recognized that security had to be established in Hadhramawt for these kind of development enterprises to be successful.

'Abdalla b. Muhsin b. Ghalib and 'Ali b. al-Mansur al-Kathiri sent a similar missive to their subjects in the East Indies, informing them of the unification agreement between the two sultanates as a step toward the unity and cooperation necessary for reform. They invoked the country's need of men of "action and exertion" rather than "talk and criticism," and called for donations toward the effort. Both the letters from the Qu'ayti and from the Kathiri affirmed that Tayyib al-Sassi was their emissary.[53]

Tayyib al-Sassi set off for the Dutch East Indies, where Salih b. Ghalib had stated that the conference would take place, by way of Singapore. However, he never got to Java. In Singapore, he was generously hosted and feted by the al-Kaf family, and the *sada* and their allies there ended up taking charge of the conference, which was then held in Singapore. The wealthy and powerful Hadhrami community of Singapore felt that the reform process would benefit from taking place under their supervision, away from the fierce conflicts taking place in Java between the Irshad and those *sada* and their supporters who opposed the Irshad. But this curtailed the participation of representatives of the numerous and sizable communities of Hadhrami emigrants on Java and other islands of the archipelago. The net effect of the usurpation of the process by the Singapore Hadhrami community was that the conference was tainted by the appearance of partisanship.

In March 1928, invitations were sent to prominent individuals and seventeen organizations of the Hadhrami communities of Singapore and the Dutch East Indies, requesting their attendance at a conference to be held at the headquarters of the Arabic Literary Club in Singapore.[54] Although an invitation was sent to the Irshad in Java, they replied with a letter of protest, refusing to participate in the conference and objecting to the change of venue to Singapore in what they considered a partisan "hijacking" of the process. The three-hundred-member Yafi'i

League (Jam'iyat Abna' Yaf') of the Dutch East Indies, largely composed of members or sympathizers of Irshad, was not invited.[55]

The Islah conference was convened on April 17, 1928, at the Arabic Literary Club, attended almost exclusively by supporters of the 'Alawi cause. Attendees included: representatives of al-Rabita al-'Alawiyya of Batavia, Sayyid 'Alawi b. Tahir al-Haddad and Sayyid Abu Bakr b. 'Abdalla al-'Attas; representatives of Jam'iyat al-Khayr of Batavia; representatives of al-Jam'iya al-Khayriyya of Surabaya; several individuals from Dutch East Indies Hadhrami communities representing themselves; several individuals from the Singapore community, including Sayyid Abu Bakr b. Shaykh al-Kaf; 'Abdalla al-Maghrabi, a non-Hadhrami Arab of Islamic modernist tendency representing an organization called al-Islah al-Hadhrami; and Tayyib al-Sassi, representing the Qu'ayti and the Kathiri sultans. After the conference was convened, elections were held to choose the president and secretary of the conference, Sayyid Ibrahim b. 'Umar al-Saqqaf and Sayyid Abu Bakr b. Taha al-Saqqaf, respectively. The conference began with a speech by Tayyib al-Sassi, bringing the news of the affirmation of unity between the two sultanates and recent progress toward peace among the tribes.

Over a fifteen-day period, sixteen sessions were held during which discussions resulted in the production of twenty-three resolutions. A delegation was chosen to carry the resolutions to Hadhramawt to present to the people and to the two governments.[56] During the sessions, the delegates discussed administrative matters such as: formation of committees and delegations to Hadhramawt; the collection of subscriptions to contribute to the reform process; and the creation of a consultative body. They also discussed problems in their homeland such as: the lack of an education system, an unfair customs system, corruption in the judicial system, the lack of public security due to tribal conflicts, and the failure of the rulers to consult with their concerned subjects. At the same time, they discussed matters primarily of interest to the emigrant communities, such as: representation in consular matters; relation of the emigrants to the governments of the homeland; representation of the emigrant communities in the newly proposed consultative body; and the resolution of the conflict among different groups in the *mahjar* (i.e., the Irshad-'Alawi dispute).

The discussions led to proposed solutions to some of these problems, which were included in the resolutions of the conference. The delegates called for clear and consistent customs regulations. In case of a dispute over too-high valuation of goods, they suggested that the importer should be able to pay in kind with a 5 percent fee. Goods bound for the Kathiri sultanate should have an "in-transit" status in the Qu'ayti sultanate to prevent the payment of double duties by Kathiri subjects. To assist in economic development of the homeland, they proposed the creation of a national commercial enterprise to be based in al-Mukalla, and requested Sayyid 'Abd al-Rahman b. Shaykh al-Kaf to establish the venture and put out a call for shareholders. This venture would devote 5 percent of its profits to charity, supporting education, hospitals, and emergency housing for the displaced. He was granted the right to negotiate its relations with the governments and the preferential treatment it should receive from them. They called on the two governments to buy 5 percent of the shares.

They made proposals for the improvement of the national educational and judicial institutions. With respect to education, they called for the implementation of a centralized administration to improve the standard of existing schools, spread education to unserved areas, and to establish a standard curriculum. With respect to the judicial system, they called for an independent judiciary free from outside interference. They enjoined the governments to pay judges a monthly salary adequate to pay their necessary expenses and maintain an appropriate standard of hospitality. They suggested examining the use of witnesses in court and following Shafi'i doctrine regarding the assessment of trustworthiness of witnesses in order to preclude the practice of giving false testimony for money. They called for the regulation of the legal profession, requiring lawyers to be certified by a committee of scholars and judges and prohibiting government employees from serving as lawyers. They called for the organization of official jurisdictions in which judges would serve, and for records to be kept of the claims and decisions made.

Addressing the security crisis that had resulted from tribal conflicts, the conference called for a five-year nonaggression treaty (*sulh*) among the tribes. The subject of government punishment of tribes for infractions committed by their members was brought up in the conference by a delegate from a tribal background, Shaykh Sa'id b. 'Abdalla BaJari. The conclusion of the group was that if a tribe disowned members involved in crimes against the state, then the government had no right to punish the entire tribe for the crimes of a few, but the tribe would be obligated to assist the government in apprehending the miscreants.

With respect to the overseas Hadrami community concerns, the conference called for the governments to facilitate connections with their subjects abroad and to appoint an official to coordinate with British consulates to facilitate consular matters such as travel documents and powers of attorney.

The delegates recognized that reform in Hadramawt was not possible while the overseas Hadrami communities were disunited and in conflict, and discussed means of settling that problem. In a resolution, they called for the two governments to appoint a committee under the leadership of Salih b. Ghalib al-Qu'ayti, with a member from the *sada* and a member from the other social groups to examine the conflict among Hadramis in the *mahjar*. If this committee was unable to resolve the conflict, the matter would then be taken to court where both sides were to be represented. After both sides presented their case, the court would make a careful decision that would then be published. Those who attempted to undermine the decision would be punished. While the absence of Irshad partisans among the participants made consensus on this point possible, it mooted the relevancy of the decision made by the conference with respect to this conflict.

In two sessions of the conference, the delegates considered the budgets and financial accountability of the two sultanates. In discussion, one of the delegates suggested that *they* should devise the budgets for the sultanates. After lengthy discussion, the delegates decided to demand that the two governments present their annual budgets to a "National Council" (al-Jam'iya al-Wataniyya), the membership of which would include representatives from all social strata and representatives from all the various leagues of Hadhramis in the *mahjar*. That proposed inclusiveness, of course, belied the efforts made to limit the participants in this conference. The governments were expected to adjust their proposed budgets according to the opinion of this committee and to publish their budgets in order to inform the public. This demand was expressed prominently in article number three, the first substantive article of the resolutions.[57]

Despite the efforts of the delegates to implement the reform process and initiate a more consultative form of government in their Hadhramawt, the narrowness of their representation and their positions on the latter two issues ultimately led to the downfall of their efforts. The domination of the conference by *sada* and those who supported the *sada* in their claim to a special spiritual authority was opposed by many Hadhramis of the *mahjar* who had not participated in the conference. These included members of the Yafi'i League of the Dutch East Indies, who had been excluded from participation and disagreed with the decisions of the conference. These Yafi'i tribesmen of the *mahjar* wrote and telegraphed some of their kinsmen in Hadhramawt and in Hyderabad as well as their kinsman the Qu'ayti sultan.[58]

When Shaykh Tayyib al-Sassi arrived in Hadhramawt bearing the resolutions of the conference and related letters, he met an unexpected reception. He was detained by government authorities and banned from the country. Sayyid Muhammad b. 'Aqil Bin Yahya was sent into exile at the same time on suspicion of conspiracy against the government. Although Salih b. Ghalib, as acting sultan, had initiated the process that had led to the Singapore Conference, his uncle 'Umar b. 'Awadh responded to the result. For the benefit of the Hadhrami overseas community, Sultan 'Umar wrote a letter to the Egyptian newspaper *al-Ahram* disavowing the outcome of the Singapore Conference. His disclaimer focused on the ill-starred emissary Tayyib al-Sassi, characterizing him as a outsider (*rajul gharib*) lacking knowledge of the customs, traditions, and people of Hadhramawt, having spent only a brief time there. Sultan 'Umar did not criticize Salih b. Ghalib's convening of the conference in al-Shihr or the goals of that body, but he blamed Tayyib al-Sassi's ignorance of Hadhramawt for the deficiencies of the conference in Singapore. He asserted that when Tayyib al-Sassi issued the conference invitations to the heads of organizations and to individuals in the East Indies, wise people had declined, wanting not to be involved with this outsider, while only a few accepted the invitation and participated in the conference. The sultan dismissed those participants as operating to advance personal interests in the guise of seeking national reform. He rejected the resolutions of the conference as divisive and harmful to the country, although he went on to express his own determination to develop and advance the country with the support of those elements interested in "true [. . .] reform."[59]

By disavowing the results of the Singapore conference, Sultan 'Umar upheld the interest of his Yafi'i support base as well as other tribal, *mashayikh*, and non-*sada* elements who leaned toward the ideals represented by al-Irshad. His rejection may have been influenced by his having learned that the al-Kafs, to whom the customs of al-Shihr had been leased for twenty thousand *riyals* a year, had allowed arms to be smuggled through there for their purposes in Tarim and for Bin 'Abdat. Sultan 'Umar also had reason to be wary of the proposed national commercial enterprise: while it was to enjoy state protection and preferential treatment it would offer meager benefit to the state. These wealthy emigrants, astute businessmen, had an eye on their own financial interests as they planned the development of the homeland. Although he resented 'Umar b. 'Awadh's proprietary behavior, when Salih b. Ghalib learned about the usurpation of al-Sassi's mission on the way to Java, he accepted his uncle's decision. In the end, he concurred with him and the numerous Hadhramis in the *mahjar* and the homeland who rejected the Singapore Conference and its participants as unrepresentative of the overseas communities and of Hadhramawt as a whole.[60]

While defaming Tayyib al-Sassi served the sultan's purpose of rejecting the outcome of the Singapore Conference, the question remains as to of why Tayyib al-Sassi was chosen as emissary for the two sultanates in the first place. Pro-Irshad scholars have blamed the failure of the reform process initiated at al-Shihr in late 1927 on Tayyib al-Sassi for allowing the *sada* of Singapore to "hijack" the East Indies reform conference. Another Hadhrami scholar praised al-Sassi and portrayed him as simply a victim of Yafi'i machinations and of Sultan 'Umar's jealousy of the influence of Salih b. Ghalib. Confidential British consular reports of the time suggested that al-Sassi, as a partisan of Sharif Husayn of Mecca, was acting from the beginning as an agent of Sharifi forces. In this view, al-Sassi was colluding in a conspiracy of Hadhrami *sada*, including the al-Kaf family and Sayyid Muhammad b. 'Aqil Bin Yahya, to support Imam Yahya of Yemen against 'Abd al-'Aziz b. Sa'ud. A struggle for power among the Hadhrami *sada* families may have contributed to their involvement. The conspiracy was thought to be a manifestation of widespread pursuit of political power by the descendants of the Prophet, financed by the Sharifi government of Iraq. If this analysis had been passed on to Sultan 'Umar either directly or through the government of Aden, it would explain both the vehemence of his personal attack on al-Sassi and the concurrent exile of Sayyid Muhammad b. 'Aqil. Sultan 'Umar naturally would have perceived support for the Imam as a challenge to his own power.[61]

Tayyib al-Sassi's readiness to serve the interests of the Hadhrami *sada* was probably predetermined by his Sharifi loyalties, his connection with Sayyid Muhammad b. 'Aqil, and his dependence on the al-Kaf family. Perhaps the choice of a non-Hadhrami as emissary was an attempt to present the appearance of objectivity in the face of the seemingly intractable conflict between social groups in the *mahjar.* There is no reason to think that Salih b. Ghalib was more concerned with upholding 'Alawi interests in the East Indies conflict than with implementing the social and economic development in Hadhramawt. Nor is there reason to think that the Salih b. Ghalib or other participants in the conference at al-Shihr intended to sabotage the reform process by choosing an untenable representative. The delegates to the Singapore Conference addressed issues of genuine social concern such as inequities in the educational and judicial systems and economic underdevelopment in addition to pursuing their own interests. Presumably these same issues were of concern to those organizations that boycotted the conference and those that were not invited.

Despite the Singapore Conference having been deemed unlawful by the sultans and unacceptable by much of the non-*sada* populace of the *mahjar* and the homeland, the al-Kaf family continued their efforts to promote social and economic development of Hadhramawt. Abu Bakr b. Shaykh al-Kaf and 'Abd al-Rahman b. Shaykh al-Kaf met with Sultan 'Umar b. 'Awadh in 1931 and urged him to convene another reform conference. The sultan complied, calling for a conference to be held in al-Mukalla in May 1932, with the participation of the Kathiri rulers and notables of both the homeland and the *mahjar.* He said that decisions would be determined by majority vote and requested the attendance of a British representative. This upcoming conference was announced in a public proclamation in October 1931. The al-Kaf brothers were active in the process, urging the Kathiri to meet with the notables of the tribes and the towns of the Kathiri sultanate in preparation for the conference in al-Mukalla.[62]

In the end, this conference did not take place, although it was never officially canceled. Although the October 1931 proclamation had stated that the conference would take place in the Islamic month of Muharram 1351 h., which began on May 7, 1932, little more than a week before that date the sultans delayed the conference indefinitely. They notified the Aden Residency and posted announcements for their subjects.[63] By this time, the fragile unification of the two sultanates that had been proclaimed by the Aden Agreement of 1918 and reiterated by the al-Shihr conference of 1927 had once again deteriorated. In June 1931, preoccupied by his weakness relative to the Qu'ayti, Sultan 'Ali b. al-Mansur al-Kathiri had written to Aden in an attempt to rescind the Aden Agreement.[64]

The passive resistance of the sultans to the 1932 al-Mukalla conference was part of a larger shift in focus of reform activities in Hadhramawt at the time. In Say'un, public advocacy of reform diminished. The controversial journal *al-Tahdhib,* which had been supported financially by Abu Bakr b. Shaykh al-Kaf, printed its final issue in July 1931. Its dynamic and outspoken contributor, 'Ali Ahmad BaKathir, left Hadhramawt in 1932 in despair over the loss of his beloved wife and the personal and professional ridicule to which he had been subjected in response to his attempts to promote social reform.[65] The al-Kafs focused their philanthropic efforts to develop the infrastructure of the country on constructing the motor road from al-Shihr to Tarim, which was completed in July 1937. Their organization in

Tarim, Jam'iyat al-Haqq, largely directed its efforts toward social change through mandating behavior and prescribing limits on material luxury and display. With Sultan Salih b. Ghalib's accession to power after 'Umar b. 'Awadh's death in 1935 and the Residency Agreement with the British of August 1937, the Qu'ayti state began to exert greater efforts to modernize its administration and institutions. With the encouragement of Harold Ingrams, the first Resident Advisor, the Qu'ayti government and reform-minded subjects of the two sultanates found common cause in modernization efforts, although struggles for power, influence, and advantage within the society continued.[66]

CONCLUSION

This analysis of the society and history of Hadhramawt during the time of European expansion in the Indian Ocean is in part a response to Eric Wolf's mandate to "uncover the history of the 'people without history.'"[1] This case study of a non-Western society illustrates its internal complexity, its high degree of linkage within regional networks, and also the active involvement of its members in the historical process of European imperial expansion. By listening to voices that were previously unheard, it helps make visible in history that which was previously unseen.

The process of "uncovering" in this instance consisted of seeking out written and oral accounts produced by members of this society, interpreting them in ethnographic context, and using them to fashion a narrative grounded in the unique and complex local milieu during a critical period of its history. This process required focusing on this society both in its local aspects and as a nexus within larger networks of peoples interconnected economically through trade and emigration and culturally through religion. It also required examining the dynamics of the developing relationship between the society and the economic and political structures of European imperialism in the Indian Ocean. Interactions among the rulers and subjects of the Kathiri and Qu'ayti sultanates, the Hadhrami communities and their host communities in the mahjar, and British and Dutch colonial authorities in the homeland and the mahjar all influenced the gradual incorporation of Hadhramawt into the imperial sphere. Incorporation was more complex and nuanced than is suggested by the commonly used terms "imperial penetration" or "imperial domination," or even terms such as "collaboration" and "resistance," broadly applied. At the same time that the British pursued their strategic interests, the Hadhrami rulers and various sectors of Hadhrami society, particularly the elites, were pursuing their perceived interests.

This book's analysis of Hadhrami identity—as manifested in the late nineteenth and twentieth century—illustrates the multifaceted and mutable nature of identity and group association. Hadhramis held a shared identity based on a common notion of attachment to the geographic homeland and a common cultural memory based on a heritage that included mythic, ancient, and Islamic times. This identity was strong enough, in many albeit not all cases, to survive separation from the geographic homeland resulting from extensive emigration throughout the Indian Ocean region over the centuries. At the same time that they shared an identity, Hadhramis differentiated themselves into social groups according to a system believed to be age-old and purported to be the model of ideal social order, a system reflecting a shared notion of an ideal rather than describing an absolute real-

ity. Social rituals such as rites of passage and religious rituals such as *ziyaras* served
as enactments of social station and depictions of social ranking, bolstering the social group identity of the participants while reinforcing the hegemony of the system as a whole. The association of a particular birth status being associated with
spiritual prestige and access to religious education unavailable to others also served
this purpose. In this way, the social regulations that determined a person's status
in mundane and temporal society were lifted to the more elevated plane of the eternal cosmological order.

Hadhramis, born at home or in the *mahjar*, inherited a social status that to
some degree determined the parameters of possibility within which they lived their
lives. The roles available to individuals were largely determined by the group into
which they were born and the interactions between members of different social
groups were largely delineated by customary patterns of mutual obligations. But it
is clear from this narrative of a society in transition that the dynamics of interac-
tion among members of these groups did not comprise a stylized tableau of stereo-
typical actors. To the contrary, this time period was marked by continuous contention over various aspects of power both within social groups and between them.
Members of the ruling dynasties, the slave soldiery, the religiously prestigious
groups, tribes both settled and *badu,* and ordinary townspeople such as merchants,
artisans, and *ahl al-hara* all strove to promote their own interests. Only the productive sector, the hardworking farmers and fishermen of the *dhu'afa'*, preoccupied with the struggle for simple economic survival, failed to find a means to
negotiate toward their greater benefit within the shifting dynamics of power.

While this shared notional system of an ordered society divided into social
groups was maintained to varying degrees in Hadhrami communities of the *mahjar,* the immersion of the Hadhrami community in the culture of the host community tended to mitigate its influence. Thus, it was in the *mahjar* that contestation arose over the maintenance of the system of social group identities and the
concomitant delineation of social status and limitation of social, religious, and educational potential. (A fruitful arena for comparative work will be the study of the
dynamics of the system of social group identity among the Hadhrami communities in different parts of the *mahjar,* and the degree to which the system persisted
or eroded over time in the various communities.)

Despite the relative strength of shared Hadhrami identity and preservation
of ties with the homeland that characterized many of the East Indies Hadhrami
communities, it was within these communities that challenges to the maintenance
of the traditional Hadhrami social order arose, originating among those who had
prospered in the *mahjar.* Supporters of the Irshad movement resisted the reproduction of that aspect of the social system of Hadhramawt that delineated the in-
herent spiritual status of the individual. They particularly opposed the limitation
of access to education. The rulers supported the interests of those who wished to
maintain the status quo in the homeland and supported their efforts to keep Irshad influence out of the homeland. Even without an overt presence in the home-

land, the influence of the organization was felt; it provided a shadowy subtext to the debates about social, religious, and educational reform.

This contributed to the stalemate that took place between rulers and reformers in the early twentieth century, at the time of the failed Singapore Reform Conference and the aborted reform conferences in Hadhramawt. This stalemate had several causes. The rulers hesitated to increase the already considerable power and influence of their subjects in state affairs. The reformers disagreed among themselves about perceived challenges to the traditional social system, particularly those resulting from increasing access to religious education and from questioning the privileges of the religiously prestigious groups. The reformers also tended to conflate mechanisms for social reform with means of pursuing their personal interests, which made their urging of reform suspect to the rulers (as well as to other subjects). Ultimately, this contradiction led to the failure of reform efforts initiated locally and in the *mahjar* communities and to the rulers' need to turn to British advisers in the effort to implement social and economic reforms.

The social groups were defined by parameters including prestige and power, elements that were related but not equivalent. Power was marked by complex and fluid boundaries, which shifted in the continuous process of negotiation among various actors. The religiously prestigious groups controlled the communication of religious knowledge and spiritual traditions. They dominated religious discourse, serving as guides in spiritual practice, transmitters of religious learning, and jurists in legal matters. Members of these groups provided leadership in ritual practice in life, and in some cases, the focus for ritual practice after death. Religiously prestigious individuals also served as intermediaries and negotiators between tribes and rulers. Tribesmen, from both the "indigenous" tribes and those that had originated in Yafi', held political power due to their armed status and their ethos in which tribal identity was tied to control of territory. The sultans came from tribal backgrounds, the Kathiri from a powerful and widespread "indigenous" tribe and the Qu'ayti of Yafi'i origin, and the sultans derived critical support from alliances with tribes. Clearly, power and prestige were related in complicated ways and had different meanings in different cultural and political contexts.

While slaves are ordinarily thought of as intrinsically powerless, in Hadhramawt the *hashiya* slave soldiers held a degree of power, their military support being critical to the survival of the sultanates. They held governmental administrative positions just as did members of the ruling dynasties and other powerful tribes. At times they participated, along with members of the sultanic dynasties and their tribal supporters, in internecine struggles for power. The slave soldiers also held a degree of social power as a result of their armed status, the power they derived from their service on behalf of the sultans, and their resulting economic benefits. Slaves of dynasties no longer holding political power retained a certain degree of social importance deriving from the prestige of the families in whose service they remained and the trusted financial and administrative positions they held. The existence of documents containing "sumptuary laws" for slaves similar to those for free people indicates that slaves fell under the same pressure toward ostentation and display as members of other groups, and that reformers felt it necessary to reign in these trends among slaves. Perhaps the reformers found this particularly necessary due to the power arising from the slaves' armed status and their military and administrative positions, which gave them a degree of control over the unarmed sectors of society.

The townspeople, merchants and artisans, did not hold political power for the most part, although certain wealthy merchants provided the sultans with financial support, in order to assist them in the crucial function of providing security for business and commercial transport. And at the same time, in the highly organized marketplace, merchants and artisans participated in the systems through which commercial order was maintained. Although these systems fell under the authority of the state, they were independently functioning institutions that outlasted individual ruling regimes and dynasties. Certain participants in the marketplace, the (low-prestige) market brokers, held important roles as economic mediators between tribes and townsmen and between tribes and rulers. Another group, the providers of social services, while low in prestige and power, held tight control over their social domain, constraining the choices of even more powerful elements of society with respect to social services.

As this complex web of prestige and power relations suggests, political power within the sultanates was far from a simple top-down matter. The sultans, absolute rulers on the face of it, were dependent on their subjects in varying ways. While political power was centralized in the hands of rulers from two dynastic families, whose relationship varied over time with respect to rivalry versus cooperation, the sultans did not hold absolute power over their subjects. They acquired power over territory not by conquest of populations but by consolidating their authority through several means: the purchase of land, alliance with tribes claiming traditional authority or sometimes subjugation of them, and conquest or cooptation of local regimes. To maintain power, they relied on the support of the *sada*, whose religious prestige gave them great influence over other segments of the population and who, along with the other religiously prestigious group, the *mashayikh,* controlled the legal system. To provide security for the settled population, they relied on the support of armed groups: allied tribes, slave soldiery, and members of the armed branch of the *sada*.

While subjects had limited expectations of government services, they did expect the state to provide security for persons, property, and economic enterprises such as agriculture, fisheries, caravans, and markets. The sultans had to secure the cooperation of the *badu* by payment, threat, or force in order to prevent their predation on the settled populations and their economic interests. In order to secure the acquiesence of the settled population necessary to rule, the sultans had to respond to challenges to security posed by *badu* resistance to state authority and by rivals to power who exploited that resistance. Besides relying on the military support of the armed groups, they also depended on the assistance of traditional intermediaries, with different tribes associated with members of particular families of the *sada, mashayikh,* and the *masakin* market brokers.

The Qu'ayti sultans also depended on the administrative, political, and military support of successive generations of *wazirs* from the Mihdhar family, a powerful family from the minority of *sada* who were arms bearers. The sultans also relied on various arms-bearing groups, including the *hashiya* slave soldiers and allied tribes (with the Qu'ayti rulers being particularly reliant on the Yafi'i tribes). They relied on wealthy subjects, *sada, mashayikh, tribesmen,* and townsmen—particularly merchants—for the financial support of their administrations and military and security apparatuses.

In the twentieth century, the sultans' actions were increasingly constrained by the interests of their subjects, as was dramatically demonstrated by the Kathiri sultan's dilemma during World War I. His subjects' extensive financial interests within the British Empire prevented him from being able to follow the course of diplomatic action—alliance with the Ottomans—that he considered the most advantageous in his rivalry with the Qu'ayti. In the twentieth century, both Kathiri and Qu'ayti were drawn into the reform agendas of their subjects, sometimes more willingly than others. The more powerful Qu'ayti ruler was drawn increasingly into the sphere of the British Empire in order to be able to carry out some of the social and administrative changes that he wished to implement, and also to be able to secure succession to power within his family line. The weaker Kathiri was reluctantly pulled along with the Qu'ayti into the imperial sphere, simply in order to maintain his rule.

This diverse society found the process of incorporation into the European imperial world system to be far more complex than the simple forging of treaty agreements between the local rulers and imperial powers. Since new fashions, institutions, and ideas entered Hadhramawt largely by the agency of members of Hadhrami emigrant communities, they were filtered according to deeply held local values. Still, the response to the challenge of material and ideological change was not uniform, with contention over ideas and discord over material wealth creating new cleavages in an already fragmentary social order. As result of the particular timing and circumstances of Hadhramawt's exposure to Western institutions and ideology, it was also exposed to the ideology of Islamic modernism or revivalism that was being articulated as a response to the Western domination of the Islamic world. This call to strengthen the Islamic world through reform of religious and social institutions served to exacerbate the discord experienced by this divided society at a time of profound change.

The example of Hadhramawt in the late nineteenth and early twentieth centuries expands our perception of a precolonial Islamic society and its social institutions and illustrates the complex effects on such a society stemming from technological, political, and economic changes in the wider region implemented by Western imperialism. The case of Hadhramawt illuminates the complexity of social organization and institutions and the diversity of identity found even in a society which, being entirely Arab and Sunni Muslim and sharing a cultural heritage, might superficially be viewed as homogeneous. It also illustrates the degree to which a territory with only a marginal position in Western imperial structures was tied, through longstanding cultural and economic association, to the wider region, and the degree to which imperial domination of the wider region affected it through those longstanding connections. Finally, the Hadhrami case indicates the degree to which members of a precolonial society in transition responded to change actively rather than passively, adapting and contesting manifestations of political, economic, and social change.

APPENDIX A
Rulers of Hadhramawt, Late Nineteenth and Early Twentieth Centuries

Kathiri Sultans

Ghalib b. Muhsin b. Ahmad	1865	1870
al-Mansur b. Ghalib b. Muhsin	1870	1929
'Ali b. al-Mansur b. Ghalib	1929	1938
Ja'far b. al-Mansur b. Ghalib	1938	1948
al-Muhsin b. 'Ali b. al-Mansur	1948	1967 (deposed)

Qu'ayti Sultans

'Umar b. 'Awadh (founder, remained in Hyderabad)	1850	1865
'Awadh b. 'Umar b. 'Awadh	1865	1908
Ghalib b. 'Awadh b. 'Umar	1908	1921
'Umar b. 'Awadh b. 'Umar	1921	1935
Salih b. Ghalib b. 'Awadh	1935	1955
'Awadh b. Salih b. Ghalib	1955	1966
Ghalib b. 'Awadh b. Salih	1966	1967 (deposed)

Source: al-Kaf, *Hadhramawt,* pp. 65–67.

APPENDIX B
Qu'ayti-Kathiri Agreement of 1918
(the Aden Agreement)

Written on 27th Shaaban, 1336.

In the name of God, the Merciful, the Compassionate.

God has said in his Holy Book "Ye are the noblest people that have been brought forth for the world, that ye may enjoin the doing of kindnesses, forbid the commission of that which is unlawful and believe in God." Again he saith: "As for those who, when we have enabled them to do so, in the world, perform their prayers, give alms, enjoin the doing of kindnesses, and forbid the commission of that which is unlawful, behold the requital of all things is in the hands of God." Behold, praise be to God, we believe in Him, we follow the guidance of our Prophet (upon whom be blessing and peace) and we believe in (combination to effect) whatsover shall bring benefits to Moslems, the good of mankind and the country—desiring whatsoever may bring security and peace to the people and their well-being both within and without the country. For that reason, the noble Qaiti governments and the family of Abdalla have signed a treaty together in perpetuity until the raven shall turn white and the earth shall fade away—the two parties being the Sultan Sir el Ghalib bin Awab [sic] bin Omar and Omar bin Awad bin Omar el Qaiti—contracting on their own behalf and that of their heirs and successors, and of those who have commissioned them on the one hand; and the Sultans Mansur bin Ghalib, and Muhsin bin Ghalib of the family of Abdalla contracting on their own behalf and that of their heirs and successors and those who have commissioned them, on the other hand. The following are the conditions they have laid down:—

I. The Qaiti Sultan, lord of Al Shahr and Al Mukalla, and the Sultans of the family of Abdalla al Kathiri recognise that the province of Hadramaut shall be one province, the said province being an appanage of the British Empire under the Sultan of Al Shahr and Mukalla.

II. The Qaiti Sultan lord of Al Shahr and Al Mukalla acknowledges that the Sultans of the family of Abdalla are Sultans of Al Shanafir, but the family of Abdalla rule within Hadramaut over the towns and villages of Siwun, Terim, Teris, Al Gharaf, Mariana, and Al Gheil. It is acknowledged that the sub-tribes of Shanafir mentioned as follows shall be under the Sultan of the family of Abdalla: namely the tribes of Omar and Aamir; the sub-tribes of Al Kathiri, Al Awamir, Bag-iri and Gabiri and all that is within their boundaries, as is well known and recognized.

III. The Qaiti Sultan lord of Al Shahr and Al Mukalla contracts on his own behalf and of his heirs and successors on the one hand, that he acknowledges and recognizes the rights and suzerainty of the Sultans of the family of Abdalla and their heirs and successors over the said towns and villages as well as the sub-tribe of Shanafir aforenamed in Article II above; and also that he will not interfere with it in any matter whatsoever, and that he recognizes them as Sultans absolute in their own country as defined in Article II.

IV. The Sultans of the Abdalla family admit on their own behalf and that of their heirs and successors on the other hand, that they will not interfere in any way soever with the Government of Hadramaut, with the exception of the towns and villages aforenamed in Article II and likewise the sub-tribe named in the said Article; and agree that they have no power to interfere in any other places.

V. The Abdalla Sultans acknowledge and recognize that the treaty signed between the British government and the Qaiti government in 1888 is binding upon them, just as if they themselves made it, and they agree to conform to its conditions faithfully. They further recognize that all their negotiations and correspondence with the British government shall be carried on through the Qaiti Sultan lord of Al Shahr and Al Mukalla.

VI. Both parties agree to suppress disorders both now and in future, immediately; they agree to forgive and forget all that has passed and to renounce severally all vendetta or claims for compensation; they agree to preserve in future security on the roads existing within their well-known frontiers, to enforce justice according to the Sheria and respect for the higher authority, to succour the oppressed and to maintain the common law within the stated boundary.

VII. The aforesaid agree to give each other mutual assistance in case of any transgression committed by either of the two parties against their subjects or friends or any person connected with them, or against a sherif, a wayfarer or any defenseless person. They agree mutually to defend life and property, as well as their followers and subjects and any who seek their hospitality, as long as the boundaries named shall endure; they further agree to treat them with the same justice and equity that they show towards their friends.

VIII. The aforesaid agree that absolute commercial freedom shall prevail, and that tithes shall be collected to the amount fixed from all persons impartially who are subjects of the aforementioned Sultans.

IX. If either of the aforenamed Sultans desires to visit the other he must give notice of his intention, so that fitting preparations may be made to receive him; and in no case must the number of the soldiers exceed 50, so as to avoid the occurence of brawls between the soldiers.

X. The Qaiti Sultans and those of the Kathiri family alike agree to give mutual assistance in so far as in them lies in any organization which is directed to the promotion of the well-being and prosperity of Hadramaut.

XI. In order to promote the acceptance of the aforesaid conditions between the Sultan of Al Shahr and Mukalla and the Sultans of the family of Abdalla of the

Kathiri family, the British Government shall endeavor to settle all differences arising in future between the aforesaid, from the date of the signature of this treaty
through the intermediary of the Governor of Aden.

Al Mansur bin Ghalib bin Abdalla Al Kathiri

Muhsin bin Ghalib bin Muhsin bin Ahmed bin Abdalla Ghalib bin Awad

Note: The underlined portion of the text is that which differs in the English translation
from the Arabic version. In the official translation found in Aitchison's *Collection* (XI,
pp. 157–59) and in Colonial Office records (CO 725/5; CO 725/32), this phrase reads
"respect for the higher authority." The Arabic text reads "*ihtiram al-sada al-'Alawiyya*" or
"respect for the 'Alawi sada," rather than "*ihtiram al-sulta al-'aliya*" or "respect for the
higher authority" (SM I 72, draft; al-Bakri, *Tarikh Hadhramawt al-Siyasi* 2, pp. 38–43; al-
Mihdhar, *al-Za'im al-Mihdhar,* pp. 101–105). The discrepancy is pointed out in BaMatraf,
al-Iqta'iyun, p. 29.

NOTES

Introduction

1. CO 725/32 (v. III, p. 125)
2. Previous works in the historiography of the Arabian peninsula that present society, politics, and history from "within" are Ochsenwald, *Religion, Society, and the State,* and Al Rasheed, *Politics.*
3. al-Hamid, *Tarikh Hadhramawt;* al-Shatiri, *Adwar al-tarikh al-Hadhrami;* BaHanan, *Jawahir tarikh al-Ahqaf;* al-Bakri, *Tarikh Hadhramawt al-Siyasi* and *Fi janub al-jazira al-ʿArabiyya;* BaWazir, *Safahat min al-tarikh al-Hadhrami.* The social group identity of each of these historians affected to some degree their view of history: al-Hamid and al-Shatiri reflect the *sada* perspective; BaHanan that of the tribes; al-Bakri that of the Yafiʿi tribesmen; and BaWazir that of the *mashayikh.* BaWazir and al-Bakri also reflect the point of view of those reformists who opposed a position of social supremacy for the Hadhrami *sada.*
4. BaMatraf, *al-Iqtaʿiyun kanu huna* and *Fi sabil al-hukum,* among others.
5. BaKathir, *Rihlat al-ashwaq al-qawiyya;* Bin Sumayt, *al-Nafha al-shadhdhiyya;* Bin Hashim, *Rihla ila al-thagharayn;* al-Quʿayti, *al-Rihla al-sultaniyya.*
6. Mimeographed "people's poetry" collections are included in the last section of the bibliography; BaMatraf, *al-Muʿallim ʿAbd al-Haq* contextualizes the verse. Bin Shihab, *Diwan,* and al-Saqqaf, *Diwan,* are collections of poetry in the formal style, the latter incorporating memoir and history to contextualize the works.
7. Printed works include al-Shilli, *al-Mashraʿ al-rawi;* al-Mashhur, *Lawamiʿ al-nur;* al-ʿAttas, *Tarjimat al-Habib al-ʿAttas.*
8. al-Saqqaf, *Tarikh al-shuʿaraʾ al-Hadhramiyin;* BaMatraf, *al-Jamaʿ;* al-Mashhur, *Shams al-zahira;* BaWazir, *al-Fikr wa al-thaqafa.*
9. BuNumay, *Tashil al-daʿawa;* al-Khatib, *al-Fatawa al-nafiʿa;* al-Mashhur, *Bughyat al-mustarshidin.*
10. al-Batati, *Ithbat ma laysa mathbut;* al-Nakhibi, *Rihla ila Yafaʿ;* al-Mihdhar, *al-Zaʿim al-Mihdhar.* al-Saqqaf, *Badhaʾiʿ al-tabut,* the three volume history and memoir by the iconoclastic ʿAbd al-Rahman b. ʿUbaydillah al-Saqqaf, is currently available only in manuscript, but a printed version edited by ʿAbdallah al-Hibshi is forthcoming. Sultan Ghalib al-Quʾaiti's works, published and unpublished, are included in the Arabic and English bibliographies.
11. In this book, Sayʾun Museum documents are indentified SMA, followed by section number and item number. Mukalla Museum documents are identified MMA, followed by item number. Privately held documents are identified by the Hijra date of the document, followed by the name of their owner.

12. van den Berg, *Le Hadhramout.* J. R. Wellsted, *Travels* vol. 2; Bent, *Southern Arabia;* Stark, *A Winter in Arabia,* and *The Southern Gates of Arabia;* van der Meulen and von Wissman, *Hadramaut;* Ingrams, *Arabia and the Isles;* Ingrams, *A Time in Arabia.* The 1934 three-volume report on Hadhramawt, to which Doreen as well as Harold contributed, is Colonial Office document CO 725/32, found in the Public Record Office at Kew. It was later condensed, revised, and published as *A Report on the Social, Economic and Political Conditions of the Hadhramaut.*

13. These mimeographed studies include works on popular poetry by well-known local scholars such as 'Abd al-Rahman 'Abd al-Karim al-Mallahi, 'Abd al-Qadir Muhammad al-Sabban, and 'Abdallah Salim Bukayr.

14. Jan Vansina has made this point with respect to oral traditions in Africa (Vansina, *Oral Tradition,* pp. 193–199).

Chapter 1. Identity in Hadhrami Society

1. Anderson, *Imagined Communities,* p. 6.
2. Horowitz, "Ethnic Identity," pp. 112–113. 118; Tajfel, *Social Identity,* pp. 6–9.
3. Naval Intelligence Division, *Western Arabia,* pp. 4, 23, 31–32, 146–50.
4. van den Berg, *Le Hadhramout,* pp. 41–43; Ingrams, *Report,* pp. 11–12, 141.
5. al-Sabban, *Visits and Customs,* pp. 3–13.
6. Doe, *Southern Arabia,* pp. 30–32, 49–53, 97–100.
7. Schoff, trans., *Periplus;* pp. 3–16; Hourani, "Roman Competition," pp. 291–95.
8. Salih al-Hamid, *Tarikh Hadhramawt* 1, pp. 120–36; 146–57; al-Shilli, *al-Mashra' al-rawi* 1, p. 292; al-Shatiri, *Adwar al-tarikh al-Hadhrami,* pp. 87–99.
9. Horowitz, "Ethnic Identity," p. 120.
10. Bujra, *The Politics of Stratification;* al-Sabban, *'Adat wa taqalid.*
11. The practice of *kafa'a* is sanctioned by the Hanafi and Shafi'i *madhhabs.* See Ziadeh, "Equality (Kafa'ah)."
12. Camelin, "Social Stratification," pp. 147–56.
13. Ingrams, *Report,* p. 36.
14. Horowitz, "Ethnic Identity," p. 113.
15. Giddens, *Constitution of Society,* pp. 280–86.
16. al-Shatiri, *Adwar tarikh Hadhramawt* 1, p. 158; al-Shilli, *al-Mashra' al-rawi* 1, p. 229. Twentieth-century non-*sayyid* historians such as Sa'id 'Awadh BaWazir and Salah al-Bakri contested *sada* historiography, to which the *sayyid* scholars 'Abdallah Hasan BilFaqih and 'Alawi Tahir al-Haddad responded with counterarguments.
17. al-Sabban, *'Adat wa taqalid,* pp. 34–37. For the religious and educational activities of women among the *sada,* see chapter 6.
18. 'Abdillah bin Sumayt, *munsib* of Shibam, interview, July 7, 1993.
19. al-Sabban, *'Adat wa taqalid,* pp. 34–37; Ingrams, *Report,* pp. 36–40. When writing of the past, I use the term "*Sayyid*" as an honorific exclusively for members of this group, and similarly use "*Shaykh*" and "*Shaykha*" as honorifics when referring to members of the

mashayikh group. This indicates the identity-group membership of those individuals, which I do explicitly in the case of members of other groups.

20. Ahmad 'Awadh BaWazir, interview, August 10, 1993; Muhammad 'Abd al-Qadir al-Hibshi, interview, September 2, 1993.

21. Ingrams, *Survey,* p. 95. An example of the argument that these clothing items are restricted to *sada* is found in al-Mashhur, *Lawami' al-nur* 1, p. 107.

22. al-Shilli, *al-Mashra' al-rawi,* quoted in al-Mashhur, *Lawami' al-nur* 1, p. 106.

23. al-Mashhur, *Bughyat al-mustarshidin,* pp. 296–97.

24. al-Mashhur, *Lawami' al-nur* 1, pp. 102–107.

25. al-'Attas, *'Uqud al-almas,* attachment to p. 5.

26. These include Sayyid Muhammad b. Husayn al-Hibshi, Mufti of Mecca in the middle of the nineteenth century, and Sayyid Muhammad b. 'Alawi al-Saqqaf, a religious leader associated with Sharif Husayn of Mecca in the early twentieth century.

27. Contention over the proper position of the Hadhrami *sada* continues into the present and takes place outside Hadhramawt as well as within. See al-Kaf, *Dirasa,* pp. 5, 13–21.

28. Document dated *fatihat* Rajab 1347, Ja'far Muhammad al-Saqqaf.

29. Sabban, *'Adat wa taqalid,* pp. 35–36. Hartley combined *sada* and *mashayikh* in the group "holy men," following the usage of the Nahid, and ranked them lower than tribesmen (Hartley, "Political Organization," pp. 18–20). Camelin suggested that this ranking reflected the tribal value system, in which the ability to defend honor held a higher value than religious prestige (Camelin, "Social Stratification," p. 149). Bujra combined *mashayikh* and *qaba'il* (tribesmen) in one group with the former having higher status than the latter (Bujra, *Politics of Stratification,* pp. 13–18). al-Sabban ranked *mashayikh* as lower in status than *qaba'il* despite their religious prestige, since women from the *mashayikh* married men from the *qaba'il* while women from the *qaba'il* did not marry men from the *mashayikh* (al-Sabban, *'Adat wa taqalid,* pp. 40–41).

30. As a member of the *mashayikh,* this important religious figure merited the honorific "al-Shaykha," and her given name was Sultana. Sources include al-Hamid, *Tarikh Hadhramawt,* pp. 793–95, 748 and al-Saqqaf, "al-Shaykha Sultana"; she is noted in biographical notices of men whom she influenced in al-Shilli, *al-Mashra' al-rawi* 2, pp. 163, 347. See also chapter 6.

31. al-Sabban, *Visits and Customs,* pp. 22, 30.

32. al-Zabidi, *Tabaqat al-khawass,* pp. 145–46, 171–72, 176–77, 311–12. This important collection includes biographical notices of Hadhrami *mashayikh,* but not of Hadhrami *sada,* although the notice for 'Abdallah b. Muhammad Ba'Abbad cites al-Faqih al-Muqaddam (Muhammad b. 'Ali Ba'Alawi) as one of his spiritual mentors (p. 176). BaWazir, *al-Fiqr wa al-thaqafa,* includes numerous biographies of *mashayikh* Sufis and jurists.

33. al-Zabidi, *Tabaqat al-khawwas,* pp. 176–77; BaWazir, *al-Fikr wa al-thaqafa,* pp. 129–30, 133–34. 'Abdillah Bin Sumayt, interview, July 31, 1993; Salim b. 'Abd al-Rahman al-Hibshi, 'Ali Shaykh al-Hibshi, and Muhammad Shaykh al-Hibshi, interview, August 6, 1993.

34. Members of the *mashayikh* appear among the students and teachers of the subjects

of the biographical notices in al-Mashhur, *Lawami' al-nur*. In the late nineteenth and early twentieth century, *mashayikh* figured prominently among the judges of the Kathiri and Qu'ayti state, including members of the BaRaja, BaKathir, BaWazir, 'Amudi, and BuNumay families.

35. Knysh notes contrasting stances taken by the *mashayikh* with respect to reform and modernism in "The Cult of Saints and Religious Reformism," pp. 208–213.

36. al-Sabban, *'Adat wa taqalid,* p. 40. 'Abd al-Rahman Abd al-Karim al-Mallahi, historian of al-Shihr, August 17, 1993. Husayn Salim BaRas, Salim Abu Bakr 'Abdallah BaRas, and Hasan Salim BaRas, whose family holds spiritual prestige among the Nuwwah, interview, August 25, 1993.

37. Hartley, "Political Organization," pp. 56–59, 74–76.

38. Ingrams, *Report,* pp. 41–42; Salih Muhammad Bin Sa'iydan and other members of Al Jabir of Husn Bin Dhuban, interview, July 23, 1993; 'Abd al-Majid Salih al-Tamimi, interview, September 7, 1993.

39. al-Bakri, *Tarikh Hadhramawt al-siyasi 2,* p. 115.

40. Conversation with women of the 'Awamir, July 20, 1993.

41. 'Abd al-Majid Salih al-Tamimi, interview, September 7, 1993; Ingrams, "Hadhramaut: A Journey," p. 527.

42. SMA VIII 530, 800, 943, 947, 951. Among the wills I examined, these and others in private hands, men and women of the tribes most frequently left such bequests.

43. Salih Muhammad Bin Sa'iydan and other members of Al Jabir of Husn Bin Dhuban, interview, July 23, 1993; al-Mallahi and 'Ali, "al-Sira'a al-Hamumi - al-Qu'ayti," pp. 253–55.

44. al-Bakri, *Tarikh Hadhramawt al-siyasi* 2, p. 110. I interviewed an indigo dyer of the coastal region, who in his youth had regularly visited *badu* he knew through his trade. He reported having had sexual relations with young women of the *badu,* giving in exchange gifts of cloth for her and her family, which did not consider their honor compromised. Although this interview was not anonymous and indeed included observers, I leave the interviewee unnamed.

45. Bents, *Southern Arabia,* pp. 86, 95, 136; Stark, *Southern Gates of Arabia,* pp. 32, 52, 67; al-Bakri, *Tarikh Hadhramawt al-siyasi* 2, pp. 110–11; Muhammad Ahmad Jirwan, indigo dyer, interview, August 9, 1993.

46. Bents, *Southern Arabia,* p. 93; al-Bakri, *Tarikh Hadhramawt al-siyasi* 2, pp. 110–12; Husayn Salim al-Sa'di, silversmith, interview, August 20, 1993.

47. al-Shatiri, *Adwar al-tarikh al-Hadhrami* 2, pp. 376–378; Ingrams Report, p. 41.

48. al-Shatiri, *Adwar al-tarikh al-Hadhrami* 2, pp. 352–373.

49. CO 725/32 (v. 3, pp. 54–55); SMA I, 204; document dated *fatihat* dhu al-Hijja 1328 h., family of Hasan 'Abd al-Rahman al-Saqqaf.

50. Bin Hashim, *Tarikh al-dawla al-Kathiriyya,* pp. 40–41. Salim Muhammad Bin 'Ali Jabir, *shaykh* of Yafi'i tribes in Hadhramwt, interview, July 24, 1993.

51. Dr. 'Adil al-Kasadi and Muhammad Ahmad al-Kasadi, interview, March 5, 1994.

52. Saba'a, *Min yanabi' tarikhina,* pp. 101–103; al-Batati, *Ithbat ma laysa mathbut,* p. 91. Salim Muhammad Bin 'Ali Jabir, interview, September 10, 1993.

53. al-Saqqaf, *Badha'i' al-tabut* 2, p. 97 (sections 47, 48, 49, and 50 of this work deal with the Yafi'i in Hadhrami history), and BaMatraf, *al-Iqta'iyyun.*

54. van den Berg, *Le Hadhramout,* p. 39: al-Sabban, *'Adat wa taqalid,* pp. 41–42. al-Sabban considered *qarwan* as a distinct social group, the smallest of his eight groups and the least differentiated from others.

55. 'Abd al-Rahman 'Abd al-Karim al-Mallahi, interview, February 24, 1994; Dr. 'Adil al-Kasadi, sociologist, interview, March 5, 1994. Camelin, "Social Stratification," p. 155.

56. Muhammad Ahmad and 'Abdallah 'Ali al-Mahafiz, boat builders, interview, August 10, 1993; Muhammad Ahmad Jarwan and other indigo dyers, interview, August 19, 1993; Sa'id Abu Bakr al-Jaru, fish broker, interview, August 23, 1993.

57. Bent, *Southern Arabia,* pp. 95, 122–23. Muhammad Ahmad Jarwan, interview, August 19, 1993.

58. 'Ubayd Marduf Imbarik al-Ham, market broker of Shibam, interview, September 30, 1993; Sa'id Khayr Hummuda, market broker of al-Shihr, interview, August 23, 1993.

59. al-Shatiri, *Adwar al-tarikh al-Hadhrami* 1, pp. 283–84; Salim Karama Jabar, Salim Hadi BaZamul, leaders of al-Hawta quarter in Say'un, and Rabi' b. Ahmad Hubays of Say'un market, September 3, 1993.

60. In his study of Hurayda, Bujra uses the terms *masakin* and *dhuafa* interchangeably for his lowest social stratum, which includes *hirthan* agriculturalists, *akhdam* laborers and craftsmen, and *subiyan* providers of services, with the former occupational group of higher status (Bujra, *Politics of Stratification,* pp. 19–21). al-Sabban separates the *dhu'afa',* as the lowest of eight social strata (al-Sabban, *'Adat wa taqalid,* pp. 43–45). Dr. 'Adil al-Kasadi includes fishermen and farmers in the *hadhar,* at the same time considering them two discrete social categories within the larger group (al-Kasadi, untitled article, p. 2). Ingrams includes merchants, artificers, laborers, and servants among the townsmen, but does not mention agriculturalists (Ingrams, *Report,* pp. 36–44).

61. al-Sabban, *'Adat wa taqalid,* p. 43.

62. Ahmad 'Awadh BaWazir, interview, August 10, 1993; 'Abdallah Salim Ba'Atwa, interview, January 20, 1993.

63. Khamis 'Ali BaDhawi, farmer, interview, September 29, 1993; Brayk Salim Ba-Haritha, farmer, interview, September 15, 1993.

64. Khamis 'Ali BaDhawi, interview, September 29, 1993; Brayk Salim BaHaritha, interview, September 15, 1993.; Hasan 'Abdallah al-Diyaybi and 'Ubayd 'Awadh Sabti, farmers, August 24, 1993; Sa'id Faraj Bin 'Uwaysh and other fishermen, interview, August 20, 1993, Sa'id Abu Bakr al-Jaru, fish wholesaler, interview, August 22, 1993.

65. Aitchson, *Collection* 7, p. 308; Aitchison, *Collection* 11, pp. 31–32; Ingrams, *Arabia and the Isles,* p. 10.

66. al-Batati, *Ithbat ma laysa mathbut,* pp. 39–43, includes numerous instances of slaves serving as governors and administrators of the Qu'ayti state; Ingrams, *Report,* pp. 43–44.

67. SMA I 33, 39, 61.

68. Slaves owned by tribe members in interior, SMA VIII 513, 550, 559, 571, 910. Slaves owned by the Kasadi family, documents dated *munsif* al-Hijja 1270, 16 Safr 1313 h.,

5 Rabi'a al-akhir 1246 h., 4 Rabi'a al-awwal 1330 h., 18 dhu al-Hijja 1337 h., 22 Safr 1346, 22 Jumada al-akhir 1346, Kasadi family.

69. Slaves as buyers, SMA VIII 407, 801; slaves as sellers SMA VIII 403, 412, 459, 518, 521; slaves as heirs SMA VIII 805. Slaves as sellers of *'uhda* SMA VIII 513, 550, 810, Ja'far Muhammad al-Saqqaf documents dated Jumada al-akhir 1346, Jumada al-akhir 1347; slaves as buyers of *'uhda,* SMA VIII 513, 559, 513. For more about *'uhda* transactions, see Boxberger, "Avoiding Riba."

70. Yusur Faraj al-Numay and Sa'id Yadayn Sa'iyaba, descendants of slaves, interview, February 10, 1993.

71. 'Abdallah Salim Ba'Atwa, interview, July 21, 1993. Ingrams, *Report,* p. 44.

72. Husayn Salim BaRas, Salim Abu Bakr 'Abdallah BaRas, Hasan Salim BaRas, interview, August 25, 1993.

73. CO 725/32 (v. III, p. 25). In Bujra's study of al-Huraydha, he found the *subiyan* in 1962–1963 to be at the bottom of the social hierarchy, performing social services for pay which in earlier years that group had performed for families to whom they were attached (Bujra, *Politics of Stratification,* pp. 43–45). This group does not appear in al-Sabban's analysis as they were not found in the towns of the main wadi which were his focus.

Chapter 2. Hadhrami Emigration and the Mahjar

1. Abdalla Bujra used the phrase "culture of emigration" in the workshop "Hadhramaut and the Hadhrami Diaspora, late 18th Century to c. 1967" (SOAS, University of London, April 1995).

2. Bujra, SOAS workshop.

3. 'Abd al-Majid b. Salih al-Tamimi, interview, September 27, 1993. Born in Java at the turn of the twentieth century, his grandfather had emigrated from Hadhramawt in the early nineteenth century to escape a blood feud.

4. van den Berg, *Le Hadhramout,* p. 123.

5. van den Berg, *Le Hadhramout,* p. 126.

6. Proverb contributed by Muhammad 'Abdallah Jawwas, former emigrant to East Africa.

7. CO 725/32 (v. III, p. 125). Ingrams, "Peace in the Hadhramaut," p. 511.

8. CO 725/32 (v. III, pp. 127–28, 137). van den Berg, *Le Hadhramout,* p. 124.

9. *Kitab al-durr al yawaqit,* manuscript (collection of 'Abd al-Qadir Muhammad al-Sabban).

10. Proverbs collected by Hasan Ahmad Bin Talib.

11. Muhammad 'Abdallah Jawwas, former emigrant to East Africa, interview, July 9, 1993.

12. van den Berg, *Le Hadhramout,* p. 125. Muhammad 'Abdallah Jawwas, interview, July 9, 1993.

13. Ahmad Salih Muhammad BaHulaywa, former emigrant to Java, interview, September 16, 1993.

14. van den Berg, *Le Hadhramout,* p. 128. 'Abdallah Salim Ba'Atwa, former emigrant to East Africa, interview, February 19, 1993.

15. Villiers, *Sons of Sinbad,* p. 183.

16. al-Sabban, *al-Sha'r al-sha'bi,* poem by 'Ali BaGharib pp. 22–24, poem by 'Abd al-Rahman Muhammad Bin Shihab, pp. 27–35.

17. al-Mihdhar, *al-Haya al-sa'ida bi-Hadhramawt,* p. 25.

18. Ho, "Hadhramis Abroad," pp. 134–37.

19. Ho, "Hadhramis Abroad," pp. 131–46. 'Abdallah Salim Ba'Atwa, returned emigrant, and Ahmad Yahya al-Zubaydi, *muwallad,* interview, August 6, 1993.

20. LeGuennec-Coppens, "Changing Patterns," pp. 156–58, 164–67; Martin, "Arab Migrations," pp. 377–84. Miraculous feats attributed to Hadhrami *sada* by the people of Lamu are recounted in el-Zein, *The Sacred Meadows.*

21. 'Abdallah Salim Ba'Atwa and Ahmad Yahya al-Zubaydi, interview, August 6, 1993; Sa'id Muhammad al-Muqdi, Husayn Ahmad 'Aydid and Abu Bakr Ahmad Aydid, retired seamen, interview, August 21, 1993.

22. Ingrams, *Arabia and the Isles,* pp. 39, 43.

23. CO 725/32 (v. III, pp. 138–49).

24. CO 725/32 (v. III, pp. 153–54 and addendum).

25. Snouck Hurgronje, *Mekka,* pp. 185–186.

26. CO 725/32 (v. III, pp. 154–57); CO 725/23/17. Abubaker Bagader, personal communication, November 23, 1997.

27. Dale, "Hadhrami Diaspora," pp. 175–78.

28. Khalidi, "Hadhrami Role," pp. 68–78; al-Qu'ayti, "Relations."

29. CO 725/32 (v. III, p. 128).

30. van der Kroef, "Arabs in Indonesia," pp. 302–305; Yegar, *Islam in British Malaya,* pp. 5–8.

31. van den Berg, *Le Hadhramout,* pp. 105–10.

32. CO 725/32 (v. III, pp. 130–133).

33. van den Berg, *Le Hadhramout,* pp. 105–10, 147–50; CO 725/32 (v. III, pp. 133, 136); Warner, "Notes on the Hadhramaut," p. 220.

34. van den Berg, *Le Hadhramout,* pp. 125–30. CO 725/32 (v. III, p. 137). Snouck Hurgronje, *Muhammedanism,* pp. 54. He described Hadhrami tribes as a "secular nobility . . . who grudge each other their very lives and fight each other according to the rules of retaliation unmitigated by any more humane feelings," and described the *sada* as "arduous patrons of a most narrow-minded orthodoxy and of most bigoted fanatacism."

35. de Jonge, "Dutch Colonial Policy," pp. 97–101, 106–10.

36. van den Berg, *Le Hadhramout,* pp. 129, 185–191.

37. SMA III 23, a 1920 letter from a Hadhrami visitor to Java to Sultan 'Ali b. al-Mansur al-Kathiri.

38. Noer, *Modernist Movement,* pp. 28, 32, 56–57; Bluhm, "Preliminary Statement," pp. 35–42.

39. Manuscript of lecture on Arab Leagues and Organizations in Indonesia by 'Abd al-Rahman 'Abdallah BaRaja to the Say'un Branch of the Yemeni Writers' League, pp. 3–5; Mobini-Kesheh, *Hadhrami Awakening,* p. 55; al-Bakri, *Tarikh Hadhramawt al-siyasi* 2, pp. 255–56.

40. Bujra, "Political Conflict," pp. 356–58; *al-Manar* 8 (1905), pp. 215–18; *al-Manar*

8 (1905), pp. 580–88; *al-Manar* 8 (1905), pp. 955–957.; al-Bakri, *Tarikh Hadhramawt al-siyasi* 2, pp. 244–53.

41. al-Bakri, *Tarikh Hadhramawt al-siyasi* 2, 262–273; Bin Shihab, *Diwan,* pp. 107.

42. Mobini-Kesheh, "Islamic Modernism," pp. 232–36; al-Bakri, *Tarikh Hadhramawt al-siyasi* 2, pp. 257, 262; BaRaja lecture, pp. 5–6.

43. Mobini-Kesheh, "Islamic Modernism," p. 236.

44. BaRaja lecture, pp. 11–12.

45. al-Rabita al-'Alawiyya, Organizational charter (collection of 'Alawi Sahl al-Kaf). In subsequent discussion, I employ the term "'Alawi" to signify those *sada* who aligned themselves with this organization.

46. BaRaja lecture, pp. 18–25; al-Haddad's speech, *al-Rabita* 1 (1st issue, n.d.): pp. 34–39.

47. *al-Rabita* volumes 1 and 2.

48. "Khawatir saniha wa ara' nasiha," *al-Rabita* 2 (Rabi' al-thani 1348): pp. 259–63.

49. *al-Rabita* 1, (2d issue, n.d.), p. 99; *al-Rabita* 2 (Shawwal 1347): p. 40.

50. *al-Haqa'iq.*

51. SMA III 180; SMA II 20; FO 371/16849/E868; FO 371/15280/E4396.

52. BaRaja lecture, pp. 5–6.

53. BaRaja lecture, pp. 24–25;

54. BaRaja lecture, pp. 23–24, 27.

55. BaRaja lecture, pp. 16–17.

56. BaRaja lecture, pp. 25–26. SMA III 207, 386, Kathiri League documents. 'Abd al-Rahman 'Abdallah BaRaja, local historian and Irshad supporter, interview, January 5, 1994.

57. BaWazir, "'Ali Ahmad BaKathir," p. 57; BaKathir, *Humam,* introduction, pp. 14–15.

58. BaRaja lecture, p. 15; "Bisha'ir al-sulh bayna al-'Alawiyin wa al-Irshadiyin," *al-Rabita* 1 (dhu al-Hijja 1346); al-Saqqaf, *Badha'i' al-tabut* 1, pp. 242–91 (section 29); al-Saqqaf, *Diwan,* pp. 247–351.

59. For the Singapore Conference, see ch. 8.

60. 'Abd al-Majid Salih al-Tamimi, student and teacher in Irshad schools, interview, February 16, 1994; Ahmad Salih BaHulaywa, Irshad supporter, interview, July 31, 1993; 'Abd al-Rahman 'Abdallah BaRaja, interview, January 5, 1994.

61. The Singapore Arabic daily, *al-Huda* 90 (25 Shawwal 1351 / 20 February 1933), pp. 1–5.

62. FO 371/5236, FO 371/5237.

63. BaRaja lecture, pp. 12–13, 16–17. *Tarikh Hadhramawt al-siyasi* 2, pp. 285–86. In a letter to the al-Kaf brothers (SMA III 195), al-Mihdhar mentioned that he exerted pressure on the Yafi'i.

64. Freya Stark, *The Southern Gates of Arabia,* p. 242. SMA I 189, 205, 212; SMA III 437; SMA I 193, SMA III 195.

Chapter 3. Urban and Rural Life in the Interior

1. The population of Say'un was estimated at: 15,000 in 1885 (van den Berg, *Le Hadhramout*); between 12,000 and 15,000 in 1931 (van der Meulen and von Wissman, *Hadramaut,* p. 141).

2. al-Sabban, *al-Ta'rifat al-tarikhiyya*, pp. 10–14; al-Hibshi, *Qasr al-thawra*, pp. 2–4, 7–8. Ja'far Muhammad al-Saqqaf, interview, July 22, 1993.

3. al-Sabban, *al-Ta'rifat al-tarikhiyya*, pp. 10–14. Ja'far Muhammad al-Saqqaf, interview, July 22, 1993.

4. al-Sabban, *al-Ta'rifat al-tarikhiyya*, p. 13. Muhammad 'Abd al-Qadir al-Hibshi, interview, August 5, 1993.

5. al-Sabban, *al-Ta'rifat al-tarikhiyya*, p. 10. 'Abdallah Salim Ba'Atwa, interview, December 14, 1993; household of 'Abdallah Muhammad Jawwas, conversation during visit, March 12, 1993.

6. al-Shatiri, *Adwar al-tarikh al-Hadhrami* 2, p. 284. Salim Karama Jabar, Salim Hadi BaZamul, and Rabi' b. Ahmad Hubays, interview, September 3, 1993.

7. SMA VIII 898.

8. Salim Karama Jabar, Salim Hadi BaZamul, and Rabi' b. Ahmad Hubays, interview, September 3, 1993. Bin Hashim, *Rihla ila al-thagharayn*, pp. 58–59.

9. al-'Aydarus, *Tarikh al-nur al-safir*, pp. 73–77.

10. van den Berg, *Le Hadhramout*, p. 42; al-Mashhur, *Lawami' al-nur* 1, p. 170, 2, pp. 214. SMA III, 1.

11. The population of Tarim was estimated at 10,000 in 1885 (van den Berg, *Le Hadhramout*, pp. 41–42) and 12,000 in 1931 (van der Meulen and von Wissmann, *Hadramaut*, p. 141).

12. al-Shilli, *al-Mashra' al-rawi*, pp. 279, 283; Serjeant, "Cemeteries of Tarim," pp. 152–53; BaWazir, *al-Fikr wa al-thaqafa*, p. 136. Accounts of anecdotes are found in Snouck Hurgronje, "Sa'd es-Suweni." Salim b. Muhammad Bin 'Ali Jabir, interview, January 14, 1993.

13. al-Sabban, *al-Ta'rifat al-tarikhiyya*, p. 19; Damluji, *Valley*, p. 306, van der Meulen and von Wissman, *Hadramawt*, pp. 140–41; al-Mashhur, *Shams al-zahira* 1, pp. 160, 455–56.

14. Damluji, *Valley*, pp. 218–22; Serjeant, "Quarters of Tarim," pp. 277–78; Sulayman, *al-Tarbiya wa al-ta'lim* 1, p. 51. Household of Abu Bakr 'Ali al-Kaf, interview, January 20, 1993.

15. Serjeant, "Building and Builders," pp. 281–82.

16. al-Sabban, *al-Ta'rifat al-tarikhiyya*, pp. 15–17; Damluji, *Valley*, pp. 230–32, 325–26. Household of Abu Bakr 'Ali al-Kaf, interview, January 20, 1993.

17. The population of Shibam was estimated at 2,000 in 1885 (van den Berg, *Le Hadhramout*, pp. 41–42); 6,000 in 1894, by the Bents, who misnumbered the houses at 600 when there were in reality 500 (Bent, *Southern Arabia*, p. 148; van der Meulen and von Wissmann, *Hadramaut*, p. 116); and 8,000 in 1932 (van der Meulen and von Wissmann, *Hadramaut*, p. 116).

18. al-Sabban, *Shibam*, pp. 6; Lewcock, *Wadi Hadramawt*, pp. 71–85; Bent, *Southern Arabia*, pp. 142–148; van der Meulen and von Wissmann, *Hadramaut*, pp. 111–18. 'Abdillah Bin Sumayt, interview, July 31, 1993.

19. Jum'an Salim Khuraz and Sa'id 'Ali al-Nusayr, market brokers, February 21, 1994; 'Abdallah Faraj al-Nusayr, market broker, interview, July 28, 1993; 'Ubayd Marduf Ham, market broker, interview, September 30, 1993; Salim Muhammad Bin 'Ali Jabir, interview, September 10, 1993.

20. SMA VIII 658, 796.

21. al-Sabban, *al-Falahun,* pp. 22–25.

22. 'Abdallah Salim Ba'Atwa, interview, January 25, 1993.

23. 'Abdallah Salim Ba'Atwa, interview, April 16, 1993; Salim Muhammad Bin 'Ali Jabir, interview, February 18, 1994.

24. SMA VIII 832, 689.

25. Salim Muhammad Bin 'Ali Jabir, interview, February 18, 1994.

26. Little, *Makalla,* p. 17.

27. Reconstructed *sinawa* on display in Say'un Museum. Brik Salim BaHaritha, interview, September 15, 1993; Khamis 'Ali BaDhawi, interview, September 29, 1993; Salih Muhammad Bin Sa'iydan and other members of Al Jabir of Husn Bin Dhuban, interview, July 23, 1993.

28.   *Ya dhi al-sinawa, la yughbitun lis-sifar*
      Shifna 'ala sifra wa hubl kunbar
      Bayni wa bayna al-mawt saba'a ashbar
      La yughbit ila man khalahu lil-dar
      Yusbur 'ala kisrat wasim 'asir.

Poem on display in Say'un Museum. Serjeant, *Prose and Poetry,* pp. 161–66, gives another version.

29. Khamis 'Ali BaDhawi, interview, September 29, 1993; Salih Muhammad Bin Sa'iydan and other members of Al Jabir of Husn Bin Dhuban, interview, July 23, 1993.

30. SMA VIII 660, 661, agricultural agreements that state duties of women family members.

31. Khamis 'Ali BaDhawi, interview, September 29, 1993.

32. Sa'd al-'Amri, member of 'Awamir tribe, interview, June 2, 1993.

33. Brik Salim BaHaritha, interview, September 15, 1993; Khamis 'Ali BaDhawi, interview, September 29, 1993. SMA I, 93; SMA VIII 490, 782, 841, 845, 944, 1012.

34. al-Sabban, *al-Falahun,* p. 33; al-Saqqaf, "Adhwa," p. 24.

35. al-Sabban, *al-Falahun,* p. 34.

36. al-Sabban, *al-Falahun,* p. 37.

37. A fifty-eight-page *manzuma,* or treatise in verse, written in 1926 by a Hadhrami *qadhi,* al-Shaykh 'Ali b. 'Abd al-Rahman BaKathir, entitled *Kitab Tashil al-Mathakira bi-Ihkam al-Mukhabara* (roughly, *A Work to Clarify the Legal Standards for Agricultural Agreements of Various Types*) discusses these contracts (collection of Ja'far Muhammad al-Saqqaf).

38. Brik Salim BaHaritha, interview, September 15, 1993; Ahmad Salim BaHulaywa, interview, September 16, 1993.

39. SMA VIII 702, 989, 993.

40. SMA VIII 22, 830, 873.

41. SMA VIII 620, 630, 779. Khamis 'Ali BaDhawi, interview, September 29, 1993

42. Khamis 'Ali BaDhawi, interview, September 29, 1993; 'Abdallah Salim Ba'Atwa, interview, January 25, 1993.

43. SMA VIII 793, 829, 980.

44. Brik Salim BaHaritha, interview, September 15, 1993; Khamis 'Ali BaDhawi, interview, September 29, 1993.
45. SMA VIII 630.
46. SMA VIII 587, 593, 594, 1022.
47. SMA VIII 612, 613, 619. 675, 677, 697, 699, 703, 727, 745, 793, 823, 824, 837.
48.   *Qad qulta lak wa inta tashra' adhhan*
      la tundhur al-ma' wa inta batadayyin
al-Sabban, *al-Sha'r al-sha'abi,* pp. 7–8.
49. al-Sabban, *al-Sha'r al-sha'abi,* pp. 36–39.
50. al-Sabban, *al-Sha'r al-sha'abi,* pp. 9–10.
51. Ingrams, *Report,* p. 35.
52. al-Saqqaf, "Adhwa," p. 21; BaKathir, "Harakat al-makinat al-rafa'at lil-ma' bi-Hadhramawt." *al-Tahdhib* 7 (Safr 1350 h.), columns 1–7.
53. al-Saqqaf, "Adhwa," p. 21.
54. BaKathir, "Harakat al-makinat al-rafa'a lil-ma' bi-Hadhramawt," *al-Tahdhib* 7 (Safr 1350 h.), columns 1–7.
55. BaKathir, "Hadhramawt min al-nahiya al-iqtisadiyya," pp. 4–10.
56. Boustead, *Wind of Morning,* pp. 189–92.

Chapter 4. Urban and Rural Life on the Coast and Its Hinterland

1. Wellsted, *Travels* 2, p. 139; Little, *Makalla,* p. 5.
2. The population of al-Mukalla was estimated at 7,000 in 1835 (Wellsted, *Travels* 2, p. 139); 6,000 in 1885 (van den Berg, *Le Hadhramout,* p. 42); 10,000 in 1925 (Little, *Makalla,* p. 7); 15,000–16,000 in 1934 (CO 725/32, [v. III p. 64]); and 19,000 in 1936 (al-Bakri, *Tarikh Hadhramawt al-siyasi* 2, p. 139).
3. Salih 'Ali BaMatraf, businessman of al-Mukalla, interview, August 17, 1993.
4. 'Abd al-Rahman al-Mallahi, interview, February 27, 1994. Stark, *Southern Gates of Arabia,* p. 40.
5. 'Abd al-Rahman al-Mallahi, interview, February 27, 1994; Muhammad Ahmad Jirwan, interview, August 19, 1993.
6. van der Meulen and von Wissman, *Hadramaut,* pp. 16–17.
7. The tragic events that followed the separation of Bara' al-Sidda in the 1950s are recounted in Boxberger, "Hadhrami Politics."
8. CO 725/32 (v. III, p. 25).
9. 'Abd al-Rahman al-Mallahi, interview, August 21, 1993; Muhammad Ahmad and 'Abdallah 'Ali al-Mahafidh, interview, August 10, 1993. CO 725/32 (v. III, p. 58).
10. Ingrams, *Arabia and the Isles,* p. 140.
11. Wellsted, *Travels* 2, pp. 140–142; Bents, *Southern Arabia,* p. 75; Das Gupta and Pearson, *Indian Ocean,* pp. 140–141.
12. Ingrams, *Arabia and the Isles,* pp. 137–40; van der Meulen and von Wissman, *Hadramaut,* pp. 16–17; al-Bakri, *Tarikh Hadhramawt al-siyasi* 2, p. 139.

13. The population of al-Shihr was estimated at: 20,000 in the sixteenth century (Ba-Matraf, *al-Shuhada' al-saba'a,* p. 30); 12,000 in 1885 (van den Berg, *Le Hadhramout,* p. 42); and was noted to be declining relative to al-Mukalla in 1894 (Bents, *Southern Arabia,* p. 205).

14. van der Meulen, *Aden to the Hadhramaut,* pp. 30–31.

15. Although the official estimate was 9,000 in the 1930s, van der Meulen assessed it at not more than 6,000 (van der Meulen, *Aden to the Hadhramaut,* pp. 30–31); Ingrams estimated 6,000 to 10,000, but assessed the latter figure as too high (CO 725/32 [v. III, p. 56]). Seasonal variations in population probably account for the wide range of Ingrams's estimate.

16. 'Abd al-Rahman 'Abd al-Karim al-Mallahi, interview, August 18, 1993. al-Mallahi and 'Ali, "al-Sira'a al-Hamumi - al-Qu'ayti," pp. 225–26.

17. 'Abd al-Rahman 'Abd al-Karim al-Mallahi, interview, August 18, 1993; Sa'id Khayr Hummuda, interview, August 23, 1993.

18. al-Shatiri, *Adwar al-tarikh al-Hadhrami* 2, p. 284.

19. 'Abd al-Rahman 'Abd al-Karim al-Mallahi, interview, August 18, 1993. BaMatraf, *al-Shuhada' al-saba'a,* pp. 30–34.

20. 'Abd al-Rahman 'Abd al-Karim al-Mallahi, interview, August 18, 1993. al-Mashhur, *Lawami' al-nur,* pp. 69–70.

21. 'Abd al-Rahman 'Abd al-Karim al-Mallahi, interview, August 18, 1993. CO 725/32 (v. III, p. 58). BaMatraf, *al-Shuhada' al-saba',* pp. 30–34.

22. 'Abd al-Rahman 'Abd al-Karim al-Mallahi, interview, August 18, 1993.

23. Muhammad Ahmad and 'Abdallah 'Ali al-Mahafidh, interview, August 10, 1993. The larger ships are usually called dhows by Europeans.

24. Muhammad Ahmad and 'Abdallah 'Ali al-Mahafidh, interview, August 10, 1993.

25. Sa'id Faraj bin 'Uwaysh, master fisherman and other fishermen of al-Shihr, interview, August 20, 1993. The indebtedness of the fishermen to boat owners and wholesalers was confirmed by Sa'id Abu Bakr al-Jaru, retired fish broker, interview, August 22, 1993.

26. Habayshan, "Hakadha kuna," pp. 3–4.

27. 'Abd al-Rahman 'Abd al-Karim al-Mallahi, interview, August 20, 1993.

28. Sa'id Abu Bakr al-Jaru, interview, August 22, 1993; 'Abd al-Rahman 'Abd al-Karim al-Mallahi, interview, August 18, 1993.

29. Sa'id Abu Bakr al-Jaru, interview, August 22, 1993.

30. For example, in 1937 and 1938, 214 and 241 foreign dhows, respectively, entered the harbor of Mombasa, according to port records (Villiers, *Sons of Sinbad,* p. 189).

31. Habayshan, "Hakadha kuna," pp. 3–4. Sa'id Muhammad al-Muqdi, Husayn Ahmad 'Aydid, and Abu Bakr Ahmad 'Aydid, retired seamen, interview, August 21, 1993.

32. Abu Bakr Ahmad 'Aydid, interview, March 4, 1994.

33. Salim Faraj Miflah, retired *nakhuda,* interview, August 19, 1993. Alan Villiers observed that the crew of the Kuwaiti vessel on which he sailed in 1938 followed the same practice, each sailor carrying a chest of goods bought in Aden for sale on the African coast (Villiers, *Sons of Sinbad,* p. 33).

34. Salim Faraj Miflah, retired *nakhuda,* interview, August 19, 1993.

35. Abu Bakr Ahmad ʿAydid, interview, March 4, 1994.

36. Saʿid Muhammad al-Muqdi, Husayn Ahmad ʿAydid, and Abu Bakr Ahmad ʿAydid, interview, August 21, 1993.

37. Salim Faraj Miflah, interview, August 19, 1993.

38. Salim Faraj Miflah, interview, August 19, 1993. Alan Villiers reported the practice of selling old dates to Somalia by Kuwaiti ships in 1938 (Villiers, *Sons of Sinbad,* pp. 91, 104).

39. Salim Faraj Miflah, interview, August 19, 1993.

40. Salim Faraj Miflah, interview, August 19, 1993; Saʿid Muhammad al-Muqdi, Husayn Ahmad ʿAydid, and Abu Bakr Ahmad ʿAydid, interview, August 21, 1993.

41. Salim Faraj Miflah, interview, August 19, 1993. Alan Villiers described smuggling on his 1938 voyage on a Kuwaiti vessel (Villiers, *Sons of Sinbad,* pp. 138–143).

42. Proverb collected by Hasan Ahmad Bin Talib.

43. Saʿid Muhammad al-Muqdi, Husayn Ahmad ʿAydid, and Abu Bakr Ahmad ʿAydid, interview, August 21, 1993.

44. Salim Faraj Miflah, interview, August 19, 1993; Saʿid Muhammad al-Muqdi, Husayn Ahmad ʿAydid, and Abu Bakr Ahmad ʿAydid, interview, August 21, 1993. Villiers, *Sons of Sinbad,* p. 189.

45. Saʿid Muhammad al-Muqdi, Husayn Ahmad ʿAydid, and Abu Bakr Ahmad ʿAydid, interview, August 21, 1993.

46. ʿAdil al-Kasadi, "Namadhij min al-foklur al-bahri" *al-Saʿiya* 1 (March 1993), pp. 8–9.

47. Saʿid Khayr Hummuda, interview, August 23, 1993; Salih ʿAli BaMatraf, interview, August 17, 1993.

48. Saʿid Khayr Hummuda, interview, August 23, 1993.

49. Saʿid Khayr Hummuda, interview, August 23, 1993; Salih ʿAli BaMatraf, interview, August 17, 1993.

50. al-Mallahi and ʿAli, "al-Siraʿa al-Hamumi - al-Quʿayti," pp. 257–58. Saʿid Khayr Hummuda, interview, August 23, 1993.

51. BaWazir, *Safahat min al-tarikh al-Hadhrami,* p. 109.

52. Muhammad Ahmad BaWazir, interview, August 23, 1993. al-Quʿayti, "Résumé," pp. 5.

53. Muhammad Ahmad BaWazir, interview, August 23, 1993. Ingrams, *Arabia and the Isles,* pp. 146.

54. Muhammad Ahmad BaWazir, interview, August 23, 1993. Little, *Makalla,* pp. 55.

55. Muhammad Ahmad BaWazir, interview, August 23, 1993. Ingrams, *Arabia and the Isles,* pp. 146; van der Meulen, *Aden to the Hadhramaut,* pp. 27–28. CO 725/32 (v. III, p. 64).

56. al-Mihdhar, *al-Zaʿim al-Mihdhar,* pp. 80.

57. Husayn Ahmad ʿAydid and Muhammad ʿAwadh BaʿAbbad, interview, August 24, 1993.

58. ʿAbdallah ʿAbd al-Latif al-Kasadi, interview, March 5, 1994; Salim ʿAwadh Bin ʿUrwa, interview, August 24, 1993; Husayn Ahmad ʿAydid, interview, August 24, 1993.

59. 'Abd al-Karim Salih al-Kasadi, interview, March 5, 1994.

60. 'Ubayd 'Awadh Sabti, Ahmad 'Abd al-Rahim BaSharahil; Salim 'Awadh Bin 'Urwa, interview, August 24, 1993. Documents of the al-Kasadi family.

61. 'Ubayd 'Awadh Sabti, Ahmad 'Abd al-Rahim BaSharahil, and Hasan 'Abdallah al-Diyaybi, interview, August 24, 1993.

62. Husayn Salim BaRas, Salim Abu Bakr 'Abdallah BaRas, Hasan Salim BaRas, interview, August 25, 1993. Doreen Ingrams, "Excursion," pp. 128–129.

63. Doreen Ingrams, "Excursion," p. 127.

Chapter 5. Rites of Passage, Ceremonies, and Critique

1. Wikan, *Behind the Veil,* describes similar ceremonies in Sohar, Oman, as do other ethnographies and travel accounts of the Arabian peninsula.

2. "Models and metaphors" is used for the collective subjective understanding of group structures in Turner, *Dramas,* p. 44.

3. al-Sabban, *'Adat wa taqalid,* pp. 52, 60–61. I collapse and qualify al-Sabban's detailed descriptions, which emphasize distinctions based on social group at the expense of other variations in practice over time, in space, and according to particular circumstances. 'Abdallah Salim Ba'Atwa, interview, February 25, 1993; 'Abd al-Qadir 'Ali BaSharahil, interview, August 23, 1993.

4. al-Sabban, *'Adat wa taqalid,* pp. 51–55, 57. Abu Bakr 'Ali al-Kaf family, interview, October 14, 1993.

5. al-Sabban, *'Adat wa taqalid,* p. 57. 'Abdallah Salim Ba'Atwa, interview, February 25, 1993.

6. al-Sabban, *'Adat wa taqalid,* pp. 59–61. Abu Bakr 'Ali al-Kaf family, interview, October 14, 1993.

7. al-Sabban, *'Adat wa taqalid,* pp. 62–65. Abu Bakr 'Ali al-Kaf family, interview, October 14, 1993; Ja'far Muhammad al-Saqqaf, interview, September 3, 1993.

8. al-Sabban, *'Adat wa taqalid,* pp. 74–76. Muhammad 'Abdallah Jawwas, interview, July 9, 1993.

9. al-Sabban, *'Adat wa taqalid,* pp. 76–78. Abu Bakr 'Ali al-Kaf family, interview, October 14, 1993; Muhammad 'Abdallah Jawwas family, interview, August 5, 1993.

10. Proverb collected by Hasan Ahmad Bin talib.

11. al-Sabban, *'Adat wa taqalid,* pp. 82–83. Abu Bakr 'Ali al-Kaf family, interview, October 14, 1993; Muhammad 'Abdallah Jawwas family, interview, August 5, 1993. Wills mentioning owed mahr include document dated dhu al-Hijja 1246, al-Kasadi family, and document dated Rajab 1343, Ja'far Muhammad al-Saqqaf.

12. al-Sabban, *'Adat wa taqalid,* pp. 91–95. 'Abd al-Qadir 'Ali BaSharahil, interview, August 23, 1993; Jum'an Muhammad BaMatraf, talk at BaWazir cultural club, August 22, 1993.

13. al-Sabban, *'Adat wa taqalid,* pp. 87–89. Abu Bakr 'Ali al-Kaf family, interview, October 14, 1993; 'Abd al-Qadir 'Ali BaSharahil, interview, August 23, 1993.

14. al-Sabban, *'Adat wa taqalid,* p. 101. 'Abd al-Qadir 'Ali BaSharahil, interview, August 23, 1993.

15. al-Sabban, *'Adat wa taqalid,* p. 97. Abu Bakr 'Ali al-Kaf family, interview, October 14, 1993.

16. al-Sabban, *'Adat wa taqalid,* pp. 98–99. Abu Bakr 'Ali al-Kaf family, interview, October 14, 1993.

17. al-Sabban, *'Adat wa taqalid,* p. 103. Abu Bakr 'Ali al-Kaf family, interview, October 14, 1993; Muhammad 'Abdallah Jawwas, interview, July 9, 1993; he contributed the proverb. This society did not pressure the newly married couple toward immediate consummation as noted in Sohar, Oman, in Wikan, *Behind the Veil,* pp. 223–226.

18. Abu Bakr 'Ali al-Kaf family, interview, October 14, 1993; 'Abd al-Qadir 'Ali BaSharahil, interview, August 23, 1993.

19. SMA VIII 567, 814, 833, 846, 951, 964, 974.

20. *Kitab al-dirr al-yaqut.*

21. Abu Bakr 'Ali al-Kaf family, interview, October 14, 1993. SMA VIII 576, 648, 814, 833, 856, 867.

22. Abu Bakr 'Ali al-Kaf family, interview, October 14, 1993; 'Abd al-Qadir 'Ali BaSharahil, interview, August 23, 1993. SMA VIII 943.

23. 'Abdallah Salim Ba'Atwa, February 25, 1993; Muhammad 'Abd al-Qadir al-Hibshi, interview, August 5, 1993.

24. 'Abdillah bin Sumayt, interview, July 31, 1993.

25. Muhammad 'Abd al-Qadir al-Hibshi, interview, August 5, 1993.

26. Document dated Jumada al-akhira 1291, Kasadi family; document dated Rajab 1343, Ja'far Muhammad al-Saqqaf. SMA VIII 698, 724, 943.

27. SMA VIII 795.

28. Jum'an Salim Khuraz and Sa'id 'Ali al-Nusayr, interview, February 21, 1994.

29. Documents dated Rajab 1343, Jumada al-akhira 1347, Ja'far Muhammad al-Saqqaf; documents dated 4 Rabi' al-awal 1330, 12 Jumada al-akhira 1291, 3 dhu al-Qa'da 1324, dhu al-Hijja 1246, Kasadi family. SMA VIII 963, 698.

30. SMA VIII 963.

31. Document dated Rajab 1347, Ja'far Muhammad al-Saqqaf.

32. Ja'far Muhammad al-Saqqaf, interview, September 3, 1993. Snouck Hurgronje, *Mekka in the Latter Part of the 19th Century,* p. 31.

33. SMA VIII 888.

34. Documents dated dhu al-Hijja 1246, dhu al-Qa'da 1345, Kasadi family; documents dated Rajab 1343, Jumada al-akhira 1347, Ja'far Muhammad al-Saqqaf. SMA VIII 530, 678, 698, 814, 856, 867, 951.

35. Documents dated 4 Rabi' al-awwal 1330, 12 Jumada al-akhira 1291, Kasadi family. This retroactive freeing corresponds to the practice, common in Hadhramawt, of the *nadhr mu'allaq,* a "hanging" or "pending" pledge or gift, which might be considered a retroactive endowment. Property transfered by nadhr was not part of the estate and not subject to inheritance laws. So a *nadhr* had to be made before death. The pragmatic Hadhramis

wrote gifts by *nadhr* into their wills, specifying a retroactive donation to have taken place a specified period before their death. See al-Mashhur, *Bughyat al-mustarshidin,* p. 261.

36. Interview with 'Abdallah Salim Ba'Atwa family.

37. Ja'far Muhammad al-Saqqaf, interview, September 3, 1993; Abu Bakr 'Ali al-Kaf family, interview, October 14, 1993.

38. SMA IV 3, draft of sultanic proclamation.

39. SMA IV 5. In SMA IV 34, dated 1938, another *sayyid* recommended the prohibition of a recent custom that created an unreasonable expense for girls.

40. SMA IV 18.

41. SMA IV 20.

42. SMA IV 21 is the same as SMA IV 18, except that it is addressed specifically to an individual. SMA IV 6–14 are all documents confirming the receipt of a copy of the sultan's decree of prohibition of customs by influential members of the community. 'Ali Salim Bukayr, interview, September 28, 1993.

43. SMA IV 16, 17. Ja'far Muhammad al-Saqqaf, interview, September 3, 1993.

44. SMA IV 24.

45. Records of Jam'iyat al-Haqq, 21 dhu al-Qa'da 1333 through 22 Rajab 1334.

46. SMA VIII 39. Notices of Jam'iyat al-Haqq, 7 dhu al-Qa'da 1360 h., 3 dhu al-Qa'da 1359 h., 25 Rabi' al-awwal 1361 h, 'Alawi Sahl al-Kaf.

47. SMA VIII 48. Abu Bakr 'Ali al-Kaf family, interview, October 14, 1993.

48. "Mita ya'amr al-watan," *al-Tahdhib* 1 (Sha'ban 1349 h.), columns 6–10; "Ma hiya al-amradh al-ijtima'iyya?" *al-Tahdhib* 2 (Ramadan 1349 h.); al-Qawl qabla al-'amal," and "'Adat al-su'" *al-Tahdhib* 3 (Shawwal 1349 h.).

49. "'Adat al-su'" *al-Tahdhib* 3 (Shawwal 1349 h.),

Chapter 6. Religious Belief, Practice, and Education

1. al-Mashhur, *Bughyat al-mustarshidin,* pp. 296–98.

2. Ende, "Schiitische," pp. 81–85, 90–91; letters section, *al-Manar* 12 (1909), pp. 953–55.

3. BaWazir, *al-Fikr wa al-thaqafa,* pp. 101–102; al-Saqqaf, *Nasim hajir.* Bin 'Ubaydillah also connects the 'Alawi *sada* with the Shi'i Imamate in *Badha'i' al-tabut,* sections 28 and 44.

4. al-Saqqaf, *Bada'i' al-tabut* manuscript 2, pp. 116–130. Salim 'Abd al-Rahman al-Hibshi, 'Ali Shaykh al-Hibshi, and Muhammad Shaykh al-Hibshi, interview, August 6, 1993. Their family lost manuscripts by their ancestor Ahmad b. Zayn al-Hibshi (d. 1733) in the Wahhabi attack. Salim Muhammad Bin 'Ali Jabir, interview, January 14, 1993.

5. The fifteenth-century biographical collection of Yemeni Sufis, *Tabaqat al-khawass,* includes al-Faqih al-Muqaddam only in the entry on Shaykh 'Abdallah b. Muhammad Ba'Abbad. The Ba'Abbad entry names Muhammad b. 'Ali Ba'Alawi (al-Faqih al-Muqaddam) as Ba'Abbad's *shaykh* and spiritual mentor.

6. Muhammad 'Abd al-Qadir al-Hibshi, interview, September 2, 1993; BaWazir, *al-Fikr wa al-thaqafa,* pp. 136.

7. BaWazir, *al-Fikr wa al-thaqafa,* pp. 106–108; al-Hibshi, *al-Sufiyya,* pp. 23–24.

8. al-Shilli, *al-Mashra' al-rawi* 1, p. 324; al-Mashhur, *Lawami' al-nur* 1, p. 17. Training in both *fiqh* and Sufism is seen in entries in all the Hadhrami biographical collections.

9. al-Mashhur, *Lawami' al-nur* 1, pp. 68–69.

10. These accounts include *al-Nafha al-shadhdhiyya* by Sayyid 'Umar b. Ahmad Bin Sumayt, who traveled from the Comoros Islands and Zanzibar to Hadhramawt and the Hijaz in 1920 and *al-Rihlat al-ashwaq al-qawiyya* by Shaykh 'Abdallah b. Muhammad BaKathir, who traveled from Zanzibar to Hadhramawt in 1896. Eng Seng Ho, in "Hadhramis Abroad in Hadhramaut," considers the latter in his discussion of the moral meanings of journeys in Hadhrami literature.

11. BaWazir, *al-Fikr wa al-thaqafa,* pp. 109–110. Muhammad 'Abd al-Qadir al-Hibshi, interview, August 5, 1993. An example of this type of *ijaza* is in al-Mashhur, *Lawami' al-nur* 1, reproduction, p. 379; transcription, pp. 218–20.

12. Muhammad 'Abd al-Qadir al-Hibshi, interview, August 5, 1993. al-Hibshi, *Mu'jam al-nisa',* pp. 140. An example of this type of *ijaza* is in al-Mashhur, *Lawami' al-nur* 1, reproduction, p. 389; transcription, pp. 291–92.

13. BaWazir, *al-Fikr wa al-thaqafa,* pp. 109–10.

14. Muhammad 'Abd al-Qadir al-Hibshi, interview, August 5, 1993.

15. al-Mashhur, *Bughyat al-mustarshidin,* pp. 297–98.

16. al-Zabidi, *Tabaqat al-khawwas,* pp. 176–77; BaWazir, *al-Fikr wa al-thaqafa,* pp. 129–30, 133–34; al-Saqqaf, *Tarikh al-shu'ara'* 2, pp. 127–29.

17. 'Abdillah bin Sumayt, interview, July 31, 1993.

18. Ingrams, *Arabia and the Isles,* p. 184; Bent, *Southern Arabia,* pp. 133–34.

19. al-Sabban, *Visits and Customs,* pp. 3–7.

20. al-Zabidi, *Tabaqat al-khawwas,* pp. 176–77; al-Shilli, *al-Mashra' al-rawi* 2, pp. 73, 145, 201, 324, 332, 391, 397, 468, 539; Bin Hashim, *Tarikh al-dawla al-Kathiriyya,* p. 36.

21. al-Sabban, *Visits and Customs,* pp. 28–30. 'Abdillah Bin Sumayt, interview, July 31, 1993; Salim b. 'Abd al-Rahman al-Hibshi, 'Ali Shaykh al-Hibshi, and Muhammad Shaykh al-Hibshi, interview, August 6, 1993.

22. al-Sabban, *Visits and Customs,* pp. 30–34; *Kitab wasilat al-sabb,* the liturgical text handed out to participants in the *ziyara.* Personal observation of the 'Ulaywa family making a "private" *ziyara.*

23. al-Saqqaf, *Tarikh al-shu'ara'* 4, pp. 132–138. Muhammad 'Abd al-Qadir al-Hibshi, the grandson of this revered and beloved *sayyid,* pointed out inaccuracies in al-Saqqaf's biographical notice, which exaggerated the splendor of 'Ali b. Muhammad al-Hibshi's lifestyle. According to Muhammad 'Abd al-Qadir, 'Ali b. Muhammad had only one servant and one horse, and the indoor bathing pool was actually a small meter-square pool on an upper floor, to which water was lifted by ropes for al-Hibshi's ablutions during his infirm old age (Interview, July 14, 1993).

24. Muhammad 'Abd al-Qadir al-Hibshi, interview, July 14, 1993.

25. al-Saqqaf, *Tarikh al-shu'ara'* 4, p. 136; Muhammad 'Abd al-Qadir al-Hibshi, interview, July 14, 1993.

26. 'Abd al-Rahman b. 'Abdallah BaRaja, interview, July 7, 1993.

27. Muhammad 'Abd al-Qadir al-Hibshi, interview, July 14, 1993.

28. Household of 'Abdallah Salim Ba'Atwa, conversation during visit, July 20, 1993; household of Abu Bakr 'Ali al-Kaf, interview, January 23, 1993.

29. Endowment of a women's prayer area for a mosque by Sayyid 'Alawi b. 'Abd al-Rahman al-Mashhur is recorded in al-Mashhur, *Lawami' al-nur* 1, p. 64.

30. Household of 'Abdallah Salim Ba'Atwa, conversation during visit, July 20, 1993; household of Abu Bakr 'Ali al-Kaf, interview, January 23, 1993.

31. al-Hibshi, *Mu'jam al-nisa'*, pp. 67, 105, 116, 140, 148, 153, 157, 160.

32. al-Hamid, *Tarikh Hadhramawt*, pp. 793–95, 748; al-Saqqaf, unpublished article; al-Shilli, *al-Mashra' al-rawi* 2, pp. 163, 347. Fadhl Muhammad al-Zubaydi, interview, February 15, 1994.

33. al-Hibshi, *Mu'jam al-nisa*, p. 67; al-Mashhur, *Shams al-zahira* 2, p. 484; al-Hibshi, *Majmu' wasaya wa ijazat*, pp. 110–11.

34. al-Mashhur, *Lawami' al-nur* 1, pp. 171–72.

35. al-Mashhur, *Lawami' al-nur* 1, pp. 212–13, 217–221.

36. 'Ali Salim Bukayr, interview, September 28, 1993.

37. BaWazir, *al-Fikr wa al-thaqafa*, pp. 98–99; biography of 'Alawi 'Abd al-Rahman al-Mashhur in al-Saqqaf, Tar'ikh al-shu'ra' 4, pp. 201, 204; al-Sabban, *'Adat wa taqalid*, p. 40.

38. BaWazir, *al-Fikr wa al-thaqafa*, p. 89.

39. Husayn Ahmad al-'Aydid and 'Umar Salim al-Kasadi, interview, August 22, 1993.

40. BaWazir, *al-Fikr wa al-thaqafa*, pp. 91–93.

41. al-Mashhur, *Shams al-zahira* 1, pp. 32–33.

42. BaWazir, *al-Fikr wa al-thaqafa*, pp. 90–91; al-'Attas, *Tarjimat al-Habib Ahmad ibn Hasan*, pp. 15–16, 21–23. SMA 964, division of the estate of 'Ali b. Salim BaHumayd, including his books.

43. BaWazir, *al-Fikr wa al-thaqafa*, pp. 95–96. Muhammad 'Abd al-Qadir al-Hibshi, interview, August 5, 1993.

44. BaWazir, *al-Fikr wa al-thaqafa*, pp. 95–96.

45. al-Mashhur, *Shams al-zahira* 2, p. 35.

46. al-Hibshi, *Majmu' wasaya wa ijazat*, a collection of 'Ali b. Muhammad poetic endowments and *ijazas* printed by his descendants, in the frontspiece dates the foundation of the *ribat* as 1296 h. (15 December 1878–3 December 1879). I consider this the most reliable source, although some sources give other dates.

47. al-Saqqaf, *Tarikh al-shu'ra'* 5, pp. 129–32, 134, 141; al-Mashhur, *Shams al-zahira* 1, p. 160. While al-Saqqaf stated that the mosque and *ribat* had been built at the expense of Bin Shihab and that the student expenses were funded by BaSalama, according to Muhammad 'Abd al-Qadir al-Hibshi (interview, August 5, 1993), these two men were generous donors among a number of contributors who donated property to support construction and student expenses.

48. al-Mashhur, *Shams al-zahira* 2, pp. 455–56; Sulayman, *al-Tarbiya wa al-ta'lim* 1, pp. 54–56.

49. Sulayman, *al-Tarbiya wa al-ta'lim* 1, p. 54; BaWazir, *al-Fikr wa al-thaqafa*, pp. 166; BaWazir, *Safahat min al-tarikh al-Hadhrami*, pp. 206–208.

50. Records of Jam'iyat al-Haqq, 4 Rabi' al-akhir through 22 Rajab 1334; Qanun Madrasat Jam'iyat al-Haqq, collection of 'Alawi Sahl al-Kaf.

51. Sulayman, *al-Tarbiya wa al-ta'lim* 1, p. 73; al-Mashhur, *Lawami' al-nur*, pp. 69–71.

52. Sulayman, *al-Tarbiya wa al-ta'lim* 1, p. 74.

53. Sulayman, *al-Tarbiya wa al-ta'lim* 1, pp. 62–63. Manuscript memoirs of Muhammad b. Sa'id BaYa'shut, p. 22 (collection of Sanad Muhammad BaYa'shut).

54. Sulayman, *al-Tarbiya wa al-ta'lim* 1, pp. 63–64.

55. Sulayman, *al-Tarbiya wa al-ta'lim* 1, p. 74.

56. BaWazir, *al-Fikr wa al-thaqafa*, pp. 165–167.

57. Bukayr, Fath al-manan, pp. 7–11; al-Mashhur, *Lawami' al-nur* 1, pp. 35–36. Interview with 'Ali Salim Bukayr, September 28, 1993.

58. Manuscript memoirs of Muhammad b. Sa'id BaYa'shut, pp. 24–37 (collection of Sanad Muhammad BaYa'shut).

59. References to modernists, including Jamal al-Din al-Afghani, Muhammad 'Abdu, and Shakib Arslan, are found in *al-Tahdhib* 1 (Sha'ban 1349 h.), column 19; 3 (Shawwal 1349 h.), columns 46–49; 4 (dhu al-Qa'da 1349 h.), column 79; 8 (Rabi' al-awwal 1350 h.), columns 141–148; 154; 10 (Jumada al-awwal 1350 h.), columns 198–204.

60. "Ayat *al-Tahdhib*," *al-Tahdhib* 4 (dhu al-qa'da 1349 h.), columns 21–25.

61. "al-Tadhkir," *al-Tahdhib* 5 (dhu al-Hijja 1349 h.), columns 81–86.

62. "al-Tadhkir," *al-Tahdhib* 5 (dhu al-Hijja 1349 h.), columns 81–86.

63. "Hawla maqal al-tadhkir," *al-Tahdhib* 7 (Safr 1350 h.), columns 135–136.

64. "Madhhabi fi ziyarat al-qubur, wa fi tawassal," *al-Tahdhib* 9 (Rabi' al-thani 1350 h.), columns 161–67.

65. BaKathir, *Humam*, pp. 14, 46–52. In the first scene of Act II, Humam's friend Muhammad described the *ziyara* to the tomb of an 'Amudi *shaykh* in Qaydun, comparing the crowds converging on the site to ants and likening their circling of the tomb to the movements of donkeys. He contrasted the participant's hopes to gain intercession, blessings, and prosperity from their circling, chanting, and kissing the sarcophagus with the material benefits gained by the merchants and the custodians of the tomb who collected the offerings of money, dates, and grain. He reported that on hearing the local religious leader telling the participants that they all would be rewarded for their participation, he angrily thought of him as the enemy of God (*'aduw Allah*, in opposition to the usual formula of "friend of God," *wali Allah*, used to refer to the most pious of spiritual leaders).

66. "Dhikra al-mawlid al-nabawi," *al-Tahdhib* 8 (Rabi' al-awwal 1350 h.), columns 141–148.

67. "Khatim al-Bukhari al-sanawi," *al-Tahdhib* 1 (Sha'ban 1349 h.), column 15.

68. "Qira'at al-Bukhari fi Rajab," *al-Tahdhib* 1 (Sha'ban 1349 h.), columns 11–13.

69. "Hawla qira'at al-Bukhari fi Rajab," *al-Tahdhib* 3 (Shawwal 1349 h.), columns 50–53.

70. "Hawla qira'at al-Bukhari fi Rajab," *al-Tahdhib* 10 (Jumada al-awwal), columns 189–96.

71. Hasan 'Alawi Bin Shihab, *Nihlat al-watan*, Sulayman, *al-Tarbiya wa al-ta'lim* 1, p. 56; biography of Hasan b. 'Alawi in al-Saqqaf, *Tarikh al-shu'ra'* 5, pp. 23–25.

72. "Khutbat al-ihtifal al-sanawi li-madrasat al-nahdha al-'ilmiyya bi-Say'un," *al-Tahdhib* 1 (Sha'ban 1349 h.), columns 16–19; 2 (Ramadhan 1349 h.), columns 37–38; 10 (Jumada al-awwal 1350 h.), columns 198–204.

73. BaKathir, *Humam,* Act I Scene 2, pp. 30–33.

74. "Ta'lim al-binat," *al-Tahdhib* 6 (al-Muharram 1350 h.), columns 113–16.

75. "Husn al-ta'bir," *al-Tahdhib* 6 (al-Muharram 1350 h.), columns 110–12.

76. "al-'Ulum wa madarisna," *al-Tahdhib* 8 (Rabia' al-awwal 1350 h.), columns 149–52.

77. *al-Tahdhib* 2 (Ramadhan 1349 h.), column 32.

78. *al-Tahdhib* 8 (Rabia' al-awwal 1350 h.), columns 155–56.

79. Never performed, the play was first published in Egypt in 1934 and a later edition, retitled *Humam, aw fi bilad al-Ahqaf,* was issued in 1965 by Matba'at al-Sabban in Aden. Recent studies dealing with the play include Knysh, "The Cult of Saints," and Freitag, "Dying of Forced Spinsterhood." 'Ali Ahmad BaKathir was well known in his adopted homeland of Egypt for his numerous plays, historical novels, and collections of romantic poetry. *Humam* was the only one of his literary works that dealt with a Hadhrami theme.

Chapter 7. The Two Sultanates

1. al-Qu'aiti, "Résumé," pp. 1–5; al-Batati, *Ithbat ma laysa mathbut,* pp. 23–29; al-Nakhibi, *Rihla ila Yafa',* pp. 96–102; al-Bakri, *Tarikh Hadhramawt al-siyasi* 2, pp. 4–11; BaHanan, *Jawahir tarikh al-Ahqaf,* pp. 226–30. Other accounts of these nineteenth-century power struggles include: BaMatraf, *Fi Sibil al-Hukum;* 'Ukasha, *Qiyam al-Sultana al-Qu'aytiya;* al-Saqqaf, *Badha'i' al-tabut,* section 48. al-Mihdhar, *al-Za'im al-Mihdhar,* while sketchy, includes poetry commemorating the events. English-language sources include Ingrams, "Report on the Hadhramaut" (CO 725/32); Collins, *Hadramawt;* the chapter "The Hadhrami Sultanates 1800–1900" in Gavin, *Aden;* Hartwig, "Expansion " and Freitag, "Hadhramis" in Freitag and Clarence-Smith, eds., *Hadhrami Traders.*

2. Aitchison, *Collection* 11, pp. 30–31.

3. al-Qu'aiti, "Résumé," pp. 3–4. Will of 'Umar b. 'Awadh al-Qu'ayti dated Rajab 1279 h., Sultan Ghalib al-Qu'aiti.

4. Aitchison, *Treaties* 7, pp. 308–309; Hertslet, *Treaties* 14, pp. 2–3.

5. Aitchison, *Treaties* 11, pp. 160–63.

6. al-Qu'aiti, "Résumé," pp. 5–6. Will of 'Awadh b. 'Umar al-Qu'ayti dated 1 Sha'ban 1316 h. in al-Mihdhar, *al-Za'im al-Mihdhar,* pp. 54–59.

7. Hunter and Sealey, *Account,* p. 155; al-Nakhibi, *Rihla ila Yafa',* p. 133.

8. al-Batati, *Ithbat ma laysa mathbut,* pp. 39–43. 'Abd al-Rahman al-Mallahi, historian of al-Shihr, August 23, 1993.

9. al-Batati, *Ithbat ma laysa mathbut,* p. 39. Muhammad Ahmad and 'Umar Salim al-Kasadi, interview, August 25, 1993.

10. al-Batati, *Ithbat ma laysa mathbut,* pp. 39–43. 'Abd al-Rahman al-Mallahi, interview, August 25, 1993.

11. al-Bakri, *Tarikh Hadhramawt al-siyasi* 2, pp. 18–19.

12. al-Bakri, *Tarikh Hadhramawt al-siyasi* 2, pp. 21–24.

13. MMA 203 n.d., 204 (14 al-Muharram 1315).

14. al-Bakri, *Tarikh Hadhramawt al-siyasi* 2, pp. 20–23. Husayn Salim BaRas, Salim Abu Bakr ʿAbdallah BaRas, and Hasan Salim BaRas, from the *mashayikh* family respected for spiritual authority by the Nawwah tribe, interview, August 25, 1993.

15. al-ʿAttas, *Tarjimat al-Habib Ahmad ibn Hasan,* pp. 135–136.

16. Aitchison, *Collection* 11, pp. 28–30, 34–35. MMA 192 (22 Rabiʿ al-awwal 1323). Sultan Ghalib al-Quʾaiti, personal communication in letter, January 15, 1996.

17. al-Bakri, *Tarikh Hadhramawt al-siyasi* 2, p. 29.

18. Aitchison, *Collection* 12, pp. 33–34; al-Bakri, *Tarikh Hadhramawt al-siyasi* 2, pp. 22–23; al-Mihdhar, *al-Zaʿim al-Mihdhar,* pp. 11–13; al-Nakhibi, *Rihla ila Yafaʿ,* p. 138 (the latter erroneously gives an ending date of 1888 for the conflict between ʿAwadh b. ʿUmar and his nephews Munassir and Husayn); al-Saqqaf, *Badhaʾiʿ al-tabut* 2, pp. 257–73. ʿAbdallah Ahmad al-Nakhibi, personal communication conveyed through Sultan Ghalib al-Quʾaiti in letter, January 15, 1996. A coin minted by Munassir dated 1307 h. is on display in the Sayʾun Museum.

19. SMA I 67.

20. al-Mallahi and ʿAli, "al-Siraʿa al-Hamumi - al-Quʿayti," pp. 253–55. ʿAbd al-Rahman al-Mallahi, interview, August 23, 1993; Saʿid Khayr Humudda, market broker for the Hamum, interview, August 23, 1993.

21. SMA I 6.

22. al-Mallahi and ʿAli, "al-Siraʿa al-Hamumi - al-Quʿayti," pp. 226–27.

23. MMA 28 (Rajab 1298 h.); 48 (Rajab 1300 h.); 63 (1300 h.).

24. al-Mallahi and ʿAli, "al-Siraʿa al-Hamumi - al-Quʿayti," p. 228. These authors point out that Muhammad ʿUkasha reported erroneously in *Qiyam* that the Hamum had ceded land to the Quʿayti for a payment of forty riyals.

25. al-Mallahi and ʿAli, "al-Siraʿa al-Hamumi - al-Quʿayti," pp. 226–30.

26. al-Batati, *Ithbat ma laysa mathbut,* pp. 45–48; al-Bakri, *Tarikh Hadhramawt al-siyasi* 2, pp. 29–30; al-Mallahi and ʿAli, "al-Siraʿa al-Hamumi - al-Quʿayti," pp. 230–32. Saʿid Khayr Humudda, interview, January 25.

27. al-Saqqaf, *Diwan,* pp. 405–408, 415, 425, 438–41.

28. SMA I 42.

29. SMA I 44, draft; 45, draft.

30. SMA I 46, draft.

31. SMA I 47.

32. al-Saqqaf, *Diwan,* pp. 423. SMA I 57; SMA I 54. Others who received copies of the Proclamation were Sayyid Ahmad b.Hasan al-ʿAttas and Sayyid Salim b. Muhsin al-ʿAttas of Huraydha. Sayyid Ahmad b. Hasan spoke about the war to a group of scholars and notables of Tarim at the end of December 1915, presenting it as a war between Islam (the Ottoman Empire) and the enemies of Islam (Christian Europe) (al-ʿAttas, *Tarjimat al-Habib Ahmad ibn Hasan,* pp. 190–91).

33. SMA I 49, draft.

34. SMA I 52.

35. al-Mihdhar, *al-Za'im al-Mihdhar,* p. 99.
36. al-Saqqaf, *Diwan,* pp. 423. Document dated 21 Muharram 1335, family of Hasan 'Abd al-Rahman al-Saqqaf.
37. Document dated 6 Sha'ban 1334, family of Hasan 'Abd al-Rahman al-Saqqaf.
38. SMA I 56, draft.
39. Document dated 21 Safar 1336, family of Hasan 'Abd al-Rahman al-Saqqaf. SMA I, 55.
40. SMA I 58.
41. Document dated 14 dhu al-Qa'da 1334, family of Hasan 'Abd al-Rahman al-Saqqaf.
42. SMA I 55. Includes two drafts.
43. SMA I 63; al-Saqqaf, *Diwan,* pp. 423–35. Document dated 21 Safar 1336, family of Hasan 'Abd al-Rahman al-Saqqaf.
44. SMA I 25.
45. SMA I 65, 69, 71. Document dated 6 Shawwal 1336, family of Hasan 'Abd al-Rahman al-Saqqaf.
46. SMA I 74.
47. SMA I 72, draft; al-Mihdhar, *al-Za'im al-Mihdhar,* pp. 101–105.
48. al-Bakri, *Tarikh Hadhramawt al-siyasi* 2, pp. 42–43; al-Mihdhar, *al-Za'im al-Mihdhar,* p. 116.

Chapter 8. The Sultanates

1. al-Mihdhar, *al-Za'im al-Mihdhar,* pp. 106–107. Additional poems of praise by Bin 'Ubaydillah honoring this event are in al-Saqqaf, *Diwan,* pp. 432–37.
2. al-Bakri, *Tarikh Hadhramawt al-siyasi* 2, p. 38.
3. al-Mihdhar, *al-Za'im al-Mihdhar,* pp. 114–116.
4. SMA II 4, 5.
5. SMA II 6.
6. SMA II 18, 19, 22, 25, 38, 42, 43, 46, 51.
7. SMA II 105, 106.
8. al-Bakri, *Tarikh Hadhramawt al-siyasi* 2 p. 68.
9. SMA II 99, 100, 101, 102, 115.
10. SMA II 33.
11. SMA II 63.
12. SMA II 65.
13. SMA II 40, 45, 50, 52, 54, 55.
14. al-Bakri, *Tarikh Hadhramawt al-siyasi* 2, p. 46.
15. al-Bakri, *Tarikh Hadhramawt al-siyasi* 2, pp. 47–48; al-Batati, *Ithbat ma laysa mathbut,* p. 53. Sultan Ghalib al-Qu'aiti, personal communication in letter, March 12, 1996.
16. al-Mallahi and 'Ali, "al-Sira'a al-Hamumi - al-Qu'ayti," pp. 235–36; al-Batati, *Ithbat ma laysa mathbut,* p. 49.
17. al-Mallahi and 'Ali, "al-Sira'a al-Hamumi - al-Qu'ayti," pp. 236–38.

18. al-Batati, *Ithbat ma laysa mathbut,* pp. 53–54.

19. al-Mallahi and 'Ali, "al-Sira'a al-Hamumi - al-Qu'ayti," pp. 239–40.

20. al-Batati, *Ithbat ma laysa mathbut,* pp. 53–54.

21. al-Mallahi and 'Ali, "al-Sira'a al-Hamumi - al-Qu'ayti," pp. 239–43; al-Batati, *Ithbat ma laysa mathbut,* pp. 53–55. Salim Faraj al-Miflah of al-Dis al-Sharqiyya, interview, March 19, 1993.

22. al-Batati, *Ithbat ma laysa mathbut,* pp. 55–62; al-Mallahi and 'Ali, "al-Sira'a al-Hamumi - al-Qu'ayti," pp. 242–243.

23. Ingrams, *Arabia and the Isles,* p. 241.

24. BaMatraf, *al-Iqta'iyun kanu huna,* pp. 28–29; al-Bakri, *Tarikh Hadhramawt al-siyasi* 2, pp. 49–51.

25. BaMatraf, *al-Iqta'iyun kanu huna,* pp. 28–29; CO 725/32 (v. III, pp. 106–108); al-Mihdhar, *al-Za'im al-Mihdhar,* p. 116; Salim Muhammad Bin 'Ali Jabir, interview, January 14, 1993.

26. al-Bakri, *Tarikh Hadhramawt al-siyasi* 2, pp. 37–43.

27. BaMatraf, *al-Iqta'iyun kanu huna,* p. 29. See Appendix B.

28. al-Mihdhar, *al-Za'im al-Mihdhar,* pp. 114–18.

29. SMA I 113, 118. The Say'un Museum collection of southern Arabian coins includes examples of coins minted by Salih b. 'Ubayd Bin 'Abdat dated 1344 h. (1925 A.D.). According to Sultan Ghalib al-Qu'aiti, these were either struck in Singapore or acquired there (personal communication in letter, March 12, 1996).

30. SMA I 126.

31. al-Batati, *Ithbat ma laysa mathbut,* pp. 63–65; al-Bakri, *Tarikh Hadhramawt al-siyasi* 2, pp. 51–52.

32. SMA III 50, 52, 54; SMA I 131.

33. SMA III 55, 56.

34. SMA III 57.

35. SMA I 145.

36. SMA III 99.

37. SMA I 183, 189; Ingrams, *Arabia and the Isles,* pp. 178, 241.

38. SMA I 265; Ingrams, *Arabia and the Isles,* pp. 245–46, 250–52.

39. Ingrams, *Arabia and the Isles,* pp. 269–71.

40. Ingrams, *Arabia and the Isles,* pp. 271, 298, 352–53.

41. Ingrams, *Arabia and the Isles,* pp. 271, 298, 352–53; BaMatraf, *al-Iqta'iyun kanu huna,* pp. 29–31; al-Batati, *Ithbat ma laysa mathbut,* pp. 66–68.

42. al-Mihdhar, *al-Za'im al-Mihdhar,* pp. 83–87; al-Batati, *Ithbat ma laysa mathbut,* p. 50. Personal communication, Sultan Ghalib al-Qu'aiti.

43. al-Batati, *Ithbat ma laysa mathbut,* pp. 53–54, 65–68, 75; al-Mihdhar, *al-Za'im al Mihdhar,* p. 85. Sultan Ghalib al-Qu'aiti, personal communication by letter, March 12, 1996

44. Ingrams, *Arabia and the Isles,* xx, xxiv, xxvii; al-Mihdhar, *al-Za'im al Mihdhar,* pp. 85–88. Sultan Ghalib al-Qu'aiti, personal communication by letter, March 12, 1996.

45. al-Batati, *Ithbat ma laysa mathbut,* pp. 45–46, 50–52.

46. al-Mihdhar, *al-Za'im al Mihdhar*, pp. 8–81.

47. SMA III 2.

48. Document dated 29 Jumada al-awwal 1331 h.; and undated document, family of Hasan 'Abd al-Rahman al-Saqqaf.

49. al-Saqqaf, *Diwan*, p. 271.

50. SMA I 67. al-Bakri, *Tarikh Hadhramawt al-siyasi* 2, pp. 54–55; CO 725/32 (v. III, p. 40). Ja'far Muhammad al-Saqqaf, interview, January 4, 1994.

51. Translations of the al-Shihr treaty and the al-Mukalla agreement on internal security and passports are in the confidential report from Crosby, the British Consul-General in Batavia, FO 371/13005.

52. al-Bakri, *Tarikh Hadhramawt al-siyasi* 2, pp. 56–57.

53. al-Bakri, *Tarikh Hadhramawt al-siyasi* 2, pp. 57–62.

54. English translation of invitation is found in the attachments to the confidential report from Crosby, the British consul-general in Batavia, FO 371/13005.

55. al-Bakri, *Tarikh Hadhramawt al-siyasi* 2, pp. 61–62. Handwritten text of lecture on the Singapore Conference by 'Abd al-Rahman 'Abdallah BaRaja to the Say'un Branch of the Yemeni Writers' League.

56. In the end, this delegation consisted of: Sayyid 'Abd al-Rahman b. Shaykh al-Kaf, Sayyid Abu Bakr b. 'Abdallah al-'Attas, Shaykh Sa'id b. 'Abdallah BaJri, and Shaykh Abu Bakr b. Muhammad al-Tawi. Other delegates considered were Sayyid 'Alawi b. Tahir al-Haddad and Shaykh 'Abd al-Rahman b. 'Umar Jawwas.

57. Records of Islah Conference and Conference Resolutions, 'Alawi Sahl al-Kaf. al-Bakri, *Tarikh Hadhramawt al-siyasi* 2, pp. 66–75.

58. al-Bakri, *Tarikh Hadhramawt al-siyasi* 2, p. 63; al-Saqqaf, "Tarikh al-harakat al-sha'biyya al-islahiyya," pp. 28, 30.

59. al-Bakri, *Tarikh Hadhramawt al-siyasi* 2, pp. 64–65.

60. Personal communication from Sultan Ghalib al-Qu'ayti, who discussed these matters with Shaykh 'Abdallah al-Nakhibi, an official of the Qu'ayti government at the time who knew both Sultan 'Umar and Sultan Salih well.

61. The pro-Irshad scholars noted are Salah al-Bakri and the late 'Abd al-Rahman 'Abdallah BaRaja, both cited above. al-Saqqaf, "Ta'rikh al-harakat al-sha'biyya al-islahiyya," pp. 30–31. British consular reports: FO 371/13003, FO 371/13005, and FO 967/17.

62. SMA I 178; also SMA III 112; SMA II 17; SMA III 116.

63. SMA II 17.

64. SMA II 18.

65. BaWazir, "'Ali Ahmad BaKathir," pp. 51–59.

66. Ingrams, *Arabia and the Isles*, pp. 297–99.

Conclusion

1. Wolf, *Europe and the People Without History*, p. xvi (page 2 of the preface to the 1982 edition).

SELECTED BIBLIOGRAPHY

English and European Languages

Aitchison, C.U. *A Collection of Treaties, Engagements and Sanads Relating to India and Neighbouring Countries.* 5th ed. Vol. 7, 11, 12. Delhi: Government of India, 1933.

Anderson, Benedict. *Imagined Communities: Reflections on the Origin and Spread of Nationalism.* 2d ed. London: Verso, 1991.

Bent, J. Theodore, and Mable Bent. *Southern Arabia.* London: Smith, Elder, 1900.

van den Berg, L. W. C. *Le Hadhramout et les Colonies Arabes dans L'Archipel Indien.* Batavia: Imprimerie du gouvernement, 1886.

Bluhm, Jutta. "A Preliminary Statement on the Dialogue Established Between the Reform Magazine *al-Manar* and the Malay-Indonesian World." *Indonesia Circle* 32 (1983): 35–42.

Boustead, Hugh. *The Wind of Morning.* London: Chatto and Windus, 1971.

Boxberger, Linda. "Avoiding Riba: Credit and Custodianship in Nineteenth- and Early Twentieth- Century Hadhramawt." *Islamic Law and Society* 5 (July 1998): 196–213.

———. "Hadrami Politics 1888–1967: Conflicts of Identity and Interest." In *Hadhami Traders, Scholars, and Statesmen in the Indian Ocean, 1750s–1960s,* edited by Ulrike Freitag and W. G. Clarence-Smith, 51–66. Leiden: E. J. Brill, 1997.

———. "Conflicts of Identity and Interests in Hadramawt during World War I." Paper presented at the SOAS Conference "Hadhramaut and the Hadhrami Diaspora, Late Eighteenth Century to c. 1967," London, 1995.

Bujra, Abdalla S. "Political Conflict and Stratification in Hadramaut-I." *Middle Eastern Studies* 3 (July 1967): 355–75.

———. *The Politics of Stratification: A Study of Political Change in a South Arabian Town.* Oxford: Clarendon, 1971.

Camelin, Sylvaine. "Reflections on the System of Social Stratification in Hadhramaut." In *Hadhami Traders, Scholars, and Statesmen in the Indian Ocean, 1750s–1960s,* edited by Ulrike Freitag and W. G. Clarence-Smith, 147–156. Leiden: E. J. Brill, 1997.

Cochrane, R. A. "An Air Reconnaissance of the Hadhramaut." *Geographical Journal* 77 (1931): 209–22.

Collins, Brinston Brown. "Hadramawt: Crisis and Intervention 1866–1881." Ph.D. diss, Princeton University, 1969.

Dale, Stephen F. *Islamic Society on the South Asian Frontier: The Mappilas of Malabar 1498–1922.* Oxford: Clarendon, 1980.

———. "The Hadhrami Diaspora in South-Western India: The Role of the Sayyids of the Malabar Coast. In *Hadhami Traders, Scholars, and Statesmen in the Indian Ocean,*

1750s–1960s, edited by Ulrike Freitag and W. G. Clarence-Smith, 175–184. Leiden: E. J. Brill, 1997.

Damluji, Salma. *The Valley of Mud Brick Architecture: Shibam, Tarim and Wadi Hadramaut.* Reading: Garnet, 1992.

Das Gupta, Ashin, and M. N. Pearson. *India and the Indian Ocean 1500–1800.* Calcutta: Oxford University Press, 1987.

Doe, Brian. *Southern Arabia.* New York: McGraw-Hill, 1971.

Ende, Werner. "Schiitische Tendenzen bei sunnitischen Sayyids aus Hadramaut: Muhammad b. 'Aqil al-'Alawi (1863–1931)." *Der Islam* 50 (1973): 82–97.

Freitag, Ulrike. "A Poetic Exchange about Imperialism." In *Encounter of Words and Texts: Intercultural Studies in Honor of Stefan Wild on the Occasion of his 60th Birthday,* edited by Lutz Edzard and Christian Szyska, 203–14. New York: G. Olms, 1997.

————. "Hadhramis in International Politics c. 1750–1967." In *Hadhrami Traders, Scholars, and Statesmen in the Indian Ocean, 1750s–1960s,* edited by Ulrike Freitag and W. G. Clarence-Smith, 112–130. Leiden: E. J. Brill, 1997.

————. "Dying of Enforced Spinsterhood: Hadhramaut through the Eyes of 'Ali Ahmad BaKathir (1910–1969)." *Welt des Islams* 37 (1997): 2–27.

————, and W. G. Clarence-Smith, eds. *Hadhrami Traders, Scholars, and Statesmen in the Indian Ocean, 1750s–1960s.* Leiden: E. J. Brill, 1997.

Gavin, R. J. *Aden under British Rule 1839–1967.* London: C. Hurst, 1975.

Giddens, Anthony. *The Constitution of Society: Outline of the Theory of Structuration.* Berkeley: University of California Press, 1984.

Glazer, Nathan, and Daniel P. Moynihan, eds. *Ethnicity: Theory and Experience.* Cambridge: Harvard University Press, 1975.

Hamilton, R. A. B. "The Social Organization of the Tribes of the Aden Protectorate." *Journal of the Royal Central Asian Society* 30 (1943): 142–157.

Hartley, John. "The Political Organization of an Arab Tribe of the Hadramawt." Ph.D. diss., London University, 1961.

Hartwig, Friedhelm. "Expansion, State Foundation and Reform: the Contest for Power in Hadhramaut in the Nineteenth Century." In *Hadhami Traders, Scholars, and Statesmen in the Indian Ocean, 1750s–1960s,* edited by Ulrike Freitag and W. G. Clarence-Smith, 35–50. Leiden: E. J. Brill, 1997.

Hertslet's Commercial Treaties. Vol. 14. London: H.M. Stationer's Office, 1880.

Hirsch, Leo. *Reisen in Süd-Arabien, Mahra-land und Hadhramut.* Leiden: E. J. Brill, 1897.

Ho, Engseng. "Hadramis Abroad in Hadhramaut: The Muwalladin." In *Hadhami Traders, Scholars, and Statesmen in the Indian Ocean, 1750s–1960s,* edited by Ulrike Freitag and W. G. Clarence-Smith, 131–45. Leiden: E. J. Brill, 1997.

Horowitz, Donald. "Ethnic Identity." In *Ethnicity: Theory and Experience,* edited by Nathan Glazer and Daniel P. Moynihan, 111–40. Cambridge: Harvard University Press, 1975.

Hourani, George F. "Did Roman Commercial Competition Ruin South Arabia?" *Journal of Near Eastern Studies* 11 (October 1952): 291–95.

Hunter, F. M., and C. W. H. Sealey. *An Account of the Arab Tribes in the Vicinity of Aden.* 1909. Reprint, London: Darf, 1986.

Ingrams, Doreen. *A Survey of Social and Economic Conditions in the Aden Protectorate.* Eritrea: Government Printer, 1949.

———. "An Excursion into the Hajr Province of Hadhramaut." *Geographical Journal* 98 (September 1941): 9–134.

———. *A Time in Arabia.* London: John Murray, 1970.

Ingrams, W. H. *Arabia and the Isles.* 3d ed. New York: Frederick Praeger, 1966.

———. "Hadhramaut: A Journey to the Sei'ar Country and through the Wadi Maseila." *Geographical Journal* 88 (1936): 524–51.

———. "House Building in the Hadhramaut." *Geographical Journal* 85 (1935): 370–72.

———. "Peace in the Hadhramaut." *Journal of the Royal Central Asian Society* 25 (1938): 507–41.

———. "Political Development in the Hadhramaut," *International Affairs* 21 (1945): 236–52.

———. *A Report on the Social, Economic and Political Condition of the Hadhramaut.* London: His Majesty's Stationery Office, 1937.

Jonge, Huub de. "Dutch Colonial Policy Pertaining to Hadhrami Immigrants." In *Hadhrami Traders, Scholars, and Statesmen in the Indian Ocean, 1750s–1960s,* edited by Ulrike Freitag and W. G. Clarence-Smith, 94–111. Leiden: E. J. Brill, 1997.

Khalidi, Omar. "The Hadhrami Role in the Politics and Society of Colonial India, 1750s to 1950s." In *Hadhrami Traders, Scholars, and Statesmen in the Indian Ocean, 1750s–1960s,* edited by Ulrike Freitag and W. G. Clarence-Smith, 67–81. Leiden: E. J. Brill, 1997.

Knysh, Alexander. "The Cult of Saints and Religious Reformism in Hadhramaut." In *Hadhrami Traders, Scholars, and Statesmen in the Indian Ocean, 1750s–1960s,* edited by Ulrike Freitag and W. G. Clarence-Smith, 199–216. Leiden: E. J. Brill, 1997.

———. "The Cult of Saints in Hadhramawt: An Overview." *New Arabian Studies* 1, (1993): 137–52.

Kostiner, Joseph. "The Impact of the Hadrami Emigrants in the East Indies on Islamic Modernism and Social Change in the Hadramawt during the twentieth Century." In *Southeast and East Asia,* edited by Raphael Israeli and Anthony H. Johns, 206–37. Islam in Asia Series. Boulder: Westview, 1984.

van der Kroef, Justus M. "The Arabs in Indonesia," *Middle East Journal* 7 (1953): 300–23.

Le Guennec-Coppens, Francoise. "Changing Patterns of Hadhrami Migration and Social Integration in East Africa." In *Hadhami Traders, Scholars, and Statesmen in the Indian Ocean, 1750s–1960s,* edited by Ulrike Freitag and W. G. Clarence-Smith, 157–74. Leiden: E. J. Brill, 1997.

Lewcock, Ronald. *Wadi Hadramawt and the Walled City of Shibam.* Paris: UNESCO, 1986.

Little, O. H. *The Geography and Geology of Makalla (South Arabia).* Cairo: Government Press, 1925.

Martin, B. G. "Arab Migrations to East Africa in Medieval Times." *International Journal of African Historical Studies* 7 (1975): 367–90.

van der Meulen, Daniel. *Aden to the Hadhramaut: A Journey in South Arabia.* London: John Murray, 1947.

————. "A Journey in Hadramaut." *The Moslem World* 22 (1932): 378–92.

————, and Hermann von Wissman. *Hadramaut: Some of its Mysteries Unveiled.* Leiden: E. J. Brill, 1932.

Middleton, J. "The Towns of the Swahili Coast of East Africa." In *The Diversity of the Muslim Community: Anthropological Essays in Memory of Peter Lienhardt,* edited by Ahmed al-Shahi, 99–114. London: British Society for Middle Eastern Studies, 1987.

Mobini-Kesheh, Natalie. "Islamic Modernism in Colonial Java: the al-Irshad Movement." In *Hadhami Traders, Scholars, and Statesmen in the Indian Ocean, 1750s–1960s,* edited by Ulrike Freitag and W. G. Clarence-Smith, 231–248. Leiden: E. J. Brill, 1997.

————. *The Hadrami Awakening: Community and Identity in the Netherlands East Indies, 1900–1942.* Southeast Asia Program Publications. Ithaca: Cornell University Press, 1999.

Mollat, Michel. *Sociétés et compagnies de commerce en Orient et dans l' Ocean Indien.* Paris: SEVPEN, 1970.

Naval Intelligence Division. Western Arabia and the Red Sea. Geographical Handbook Series. Oxford: H. M. Stationery Office, 1946.

Noer, Deliar. *The Modernist Muslim Movement in Indonesia 1900–1942.* London: Oxford University Press, 1973.

Ochsenwald, William. *Religion, Society and the State in Arabia: The Hijaz under Ottoman Control, 1840–1908.* Columbus: Ohio State University Press, 1984.

al-Qu'aiti, Sultan Ghalib. "Relations Between the Arabian Peninsula and the Deccan (Southern India)."

————. "A Résumé of the History of the Qu'aiti Dynasty of Hadhramaut."

————, translator and editor. "Basic Constitutional Principles for the Establishment and Administration of the Qu'aiti Possessions in Arabia and India: Extracts from the Will of 'Omar bin 'Awadh al-Qu'aiti of 1st Rajab 1279 H and the Will of 'Awadh bin 'Omar al-Qu'aiti of 1st Sha'baan 1316 H."

Al-Rasheed, Madawi. *Politics in an Arabian Oasis Town: The Rashidi Tribal Dynasty.* London: I. B. Tauris, 1991.

Reid, Anthony. "Nineteenth Century Pan-Islam in Indonesia and Malaysia." *Journal of Asian Studies* 26 (1967): 267–83.

Reilly, Bernard. "The Aden Protectorate." *Journal of the Royal Central Asia Society* 28 (1941): 132–45.

al-Sabban, 'Abd al-Qadir Muhammad. *Visits and Customs: The Visit to the Tomb of Prophet Hud.* Edited by Linda Boxberger. Translated by Linda Boxberger and Awad Abdelrahim Abu Hulayqa. Ardmore, Pa.: American Institute for Yemeni Studies, 1999.

al-Saqqaf, Ja'far Muhammad. "A Legal Document from Saywun relating to Vessels, House and Carriages owned by a Saqqaf Sayyid in 19th Century Java." *New Arabian Studies* 1 (1993): 189–202.

Schoff, Wilfred, trans. *The Periplus of the Erythraean Sea: Travel and Trade in the Indian Ocean by a Merchant of the First Century.* London: Longmans, Green, 1912.

Serjeant, R. B. "Building and Builders in Hadramawt (Sacrificial Rites and Trade Guilds)." *Muséon* 62 (1949): 275–84.

———. "The Cemeteries of Tarim (Hadramawt) (with notes on sepulture)." *Muséon* 62 (1949): 151–60.

———. "Customary Law among the Fishermen of al-Shihr." *Middle East Studies and Libraries: A Felicitation Volume for Professor J. D. Pearson,* edited by B. C. Bloomfiedl, 193–203. London: Mansell, 1980.

———. *Farmers and Fishermen in Arabia: Studies in Customary Law and Practice,* edited by G. Rex Smith. Brookfield, Vt.: Variorum Reprints, 1995.

———. "Historians and Historiography of Hadramawt." *Journal of the British Society for Oriental and African Studies* 25 (1962): 239–61.

———. *Prose and Poetry of Hadramawt.* London: Taylor's Foreign Press, 1951.

———. "The Quarters of Tarim and Their Tansurahs." *Muséon* 63 (1950): 277–84.

Shafie, Ibrahim. "The Social Conflict In and Out of Hadramaut." *Islamiyat* 5 (1983): 15–29.

Snouck Hurgronje, Christian. *Mekka in the Latter Part of the Nineteenth Century.* Translated by J. H. Monahan. Leiden: E. J. Brill, 1931.

———. *Mohammedanism.* New York: G. B. Putnam's Sons, 1916.

———. "Sa'd es-Suweni, ein selsamer Wali in Hadhramot." *Zeitschrift für Assyriologie und vorderasiastische Archaeologie* 26 (1912): 221–39.

Stark, Freya. *The Southern Gates of Arabia: A Journey in the Hadhramaut.* London: John Murray, 1936.

———. *A Winter in Arabia.* London: John Murray, 1940.

Tajfel, Henri, ed. *Social Identity and Intergroup Relations.* Cambridge: Cambridge University Press, 1982,

Turner, Victor. *Dramas, Fields, and Metaphors: Symbolic Action in Human Society.* Symbol, Myth, and Ritual Series. Ithaca: Cornell University Press, 1974.

Vansina, Jan. *Oral Tradition as History.* Madison: University of Wisconsin Press, 1985.

Villiers, Alan. "Some Aspects of the Arab Dhow Trade." *Middle East Journal* 2 (1948): 399–416.

———. *Sons of Sinbad.* New York: Charles Scribner's Sons, 1969.

Warner, W. H. Lee. "Notes on the Hadhramaut." *Geographical Journal* 77 (1931): 217–22.

Wellsted, J. R. *Travels to the City of the Caliphs Along the Shores of the Persian Gulf and the Mediterranean including a Voyage to the Coast of Arabia and a Tour on the Island of Socotra.* Vol. 2. London: Henry Colburn, 1840.

Wikan, Unni. *Behind the Veil in Arabia: Women in Oman.* Chicago: University of Chicago Press, 1982.

Wolf, Eric. *Europe and the People Without History.* 2d ed. Berkeley: University of California Press, 1997.

Yegar, Moshe. *Islam and Islamic Institutions in British Malaya: Policies and Implementation.* Jerusalem: Magnes, 1979.

el-Zein, Abdul Hamid. *The Sacred Meadows: A Structural Analysis of Religious Symbolism in an East African Town.* Evanston, Ill.: Northwestern University Press, 1974.

Ziadeh, Farhat J. "Equality (Kafa'ah) in the Muslim Law of Marriage," *American Journal of Comparative Law* 6 (1957): 503–17.

SELECTED BIBLIOGRAPHY

Arabic Language

Books and Articles

al-ʿAṭṭās, Aḥmad Ḥasan. *ʿUqūd al-almās*. Compiled by ʿAlawī Ṭahir al-Ḥaddād. 2 vols. Singapore: al-Aḥmadiyya, 1949–1950.

al-ʿAṭṭās, ʿAlī Aḥmad. *Tarjimat al-Ḥabīb Aḥmad ibn Ḥasan ibn ʿAbdallāh al-ʿAṭṭās*. N.p., 1959.

al-ʿAydarūs, ʿAbd al-Qādir Shaykh. *Tārīkh al-nūr al-sāfir ʿan akhbār al-qarn al-ʿāshir*. 2d ed. Beirut: Dār al-Kutub al-ʿIlmiyya, 1985.

BāHanān, Muḥammad ʿAlī. *Jawāhir tārīkh al-Aḥqāf*. Mecca: Maṭbaʿat al-Fajāla al-Jadīda, 1963.

BāKathīr, ʿAbdallāh Muḥammad. *Riḥlat al-ashwaq al-qawiyya ilā muwāṭin al-sāda al-ʿAlawiyya*. Edited by ʿAbdallāh Muḥammad al-Saqqāf. Cairo: n.p., 1985.

BāKathīr, ʿAlī Aḥmad. *Ḥumām . . . aw fī bilād al-Aḥqāf*. 2d ed. Aden: Manshūrāt al-Ṣabbān, 1965 (1st ed. [Cairo, 1934] was entitled *Ḥumām . . . aw fī ʿāṣimat al-Aḥqāf*).

———. *Haḍramawt min al-nāḥiya al-iqtiṣādiya*. Cairo, n.p., n.d.

al-Bakrī, Ṣalāḥ. *Fī janūb al-jazīra al-ʿArabiyya*. Cairo: Maṭbaʿat Muṣṭafā al-Bābī al-Ḥalabī, 1949.

———. *Tārīkh Haḍramawt al-siyāsī*. 2 vols. Cairo: Maṭbaʿat Muṣṭafā al-Bābī al-Ḥalabī, 1936.

———. *Tārīkh al-Irshād fī Indūnīsiyā*. Jakarta: Jamʿīyat al-Irshād al-Islāmīya, 1992.

BāMaṭraf, Muḥammad ʿAbd al-Qādir. *Fī sabīl al-ḥukum*. Aden: Dār al-Ḥamdānī, 1982.

———. *al-Iqṭāʿīyūn kānū hūnā*. Aden: Dār al-Ḥamdānī, 1985.

———. *al-Jāmaʿ*. 4 vols. Aden: Dār al-Hamdānī, 1984.

———. "Kayfa kūnā wa kayfa aṣbaḥnā." Transcript and tape of lecture delivered in al-Shiḥr, 1977.

———. *al-Muʿallim ʿAbd al-Ḥaq*. Aden: Dār al-Ḥamdānī, 1983.

———. *al-Rafīq al-nāfiʿ ʿalā durūb manẓūmatay al-mallāḥ BāṬāyiʿ*. Aden: Maṭbaʿat al-Salām, 1972.

———. *al-Shuhadāʾ al-sabaʿa*. Baghdad: Maṭbaʿat al-Jumhūriyya, 1974.

BāRajā, Muḥammad Muḥsin, ed. *al-Tahdhīb* (collected issues). Cairo: al-Maṭbaʿa al-Salafiyya, n.d.

BāṢurra, Ṣaliḥ ʿAlī and Muḥammad Saʿīd Dāʿūd. *Wathāʾiq al-nadwa al-ʿilmiyya al-tārīkhiyya hawla al-muqāwma al-shaʿbiyya fī Haḍramawt 1900–1963*. Aden: Jamaʿat ʿAdan, 1989.

al-Baṭāṭī, ʿAbd al-Khāliq ʿAbdallāh. *Ithbāt mā laysa mathbūt min tārikh Ḥaḍramawt.* Jedda: Dār al-Bilād, 1989.

BāWazīr, Aḥmad ʿAwaḍ. "ʿAlī Aḥmad BāKathīr: Sanawāt fī Jāwa wa Ḥaḍramawt 1910–1932." In *Watha'iq mahrajān BāKathīr,* edited by Ittiḥād al-Udabā' wa al-Kuttāb al-Yamanīyīn, 51–59. Beirut: Dār al-Ḥadātha, 1988.

BāWazīr, Saʿid ʿawaḍ. *Ma'ālim tārīkh al-jazīra al-ʿArabiyya.* Aden: Manshūrāt Mu'assasat al-Ṣabbān, 1966.

———. *al-Fikr wa al-thaqāfa fī al-tārīkh al-Ḥaḍramī.* Cairo: Dār al-Ṭibāʿa al-Ḥadītha, 1961.

———. *Ṣafaḥāt min al-tārīkh al-Ḥaḍramī.* Cairo: al-Maṭbaʿa al-salafiyya, 1958.

BilFaqih, ʿAbdallāh Ḥasan. *Istidrākāt wa taḥarrīyāt ʿalā "Tārīkh Ḥaḍramawt fī shakhṣīyāt."* Aden: al-Maṭbaʿa al-Tijāriyya, 1956.

———. *Tadhkirat al-bāḥith al-muḥtāṭ fī shuʿūn wa tārīkh al-Ribāt.* Aden: Maṭbaʿat al-Fajā la al-Jadīda, 1961.

Bin ʿAqīl, ʿAbd al-ʿAzīz. "Hawṭa . . . fī ṭawr al-ta'sīs." *Afāq* 10 (n.d.): 27–40.

Bin Hāshim, Muḥammad. *Tārīkh al-dawla al-Kathīriyya.* Cairo: n.p., 1948.

———. *Riḥla ilā al-thagharayn al-Shiḥr wa al-Mukallā.* Cairo: Maṭbaʿat al-Ḥijāzī, 1932.

Bin Shihāb, Abū Bakr ʿAbd al-Raḥman. *Dīwān Ibn Shihāb.* 2d ed. Dār al-turāth al-Yamanī, 1996.

Bin Shihāb, Hasan. *Niḥlat al-waṭan.* N.p., n.d.

Bin Sumayṭ, ʿUmar Aḥmad. *al-Nafḥa al-shadhdhiyya min al-diyār al-Ḥaḍramiyya.* Aden: Dār al-Janūb, [1954?].

Bukayr, ʿAbd al-Raḥmanʿ Abdallāh. *Bay' al-ʿuhda bayna mu'īdiyya wa ma'āriḍiyya.* Baghdad: Dār al-Ḥurriya, 1988.

Bukayr, Sālim Saʿīd. *Fatḥ al-āla al-manān.* Jedda: ʿĀlim al-Maʿrif, 1988.

BūNamay, Muḥsin Jaʿfar. *Tashīl al-daʿāwī fī raf'i al-shakāwī.* al-Mukalla: Maṭbaʿat al-Akhbār al-Ḥukūmiyya, 1954.

Habāyshan, Saʿīd Sālim. "Hākadhā kunā." *al-Sā'iya* 3 (1993): 3–4 (mimeographed periodical from al-Ḥāmī).

al-Ḥaddād, ʿAlawī Ṭāhir. *Janī al-shamārīkh: Jawāb as'ila fī al-tārīkh.* Aden: Maṭbaʿat al-Waʿtaniyya, 1950.

———. *al-Qawl al-faṣl fī-mā li-banī Hāshim.* 2 vols. Cheribon, Java: Maṭbaʿat Arshīvāl, 1926.

al-Ḥāmid, Ṣāliḥ. *Tārīkh Ḥaḍramawt.* Jedda: Maktabat al-Irshād, 1968.

al-Ḥibshī, ʿAbdallāh Muḥammad. *Mu'jam al-nisā' al-Yamanīyāt.* Sanaʿa': Dār al-Ḥikma al-Yamaniyya, 1998.

———. *al-Ṣufiyya wa al-fuquhā fī al-Yaman.* Sanaʿa': Maktabat al-Jīl al-Jadīd, 1976.

al-Ḥibshī, ʿAlī Muḥammad. *Majmūʿ waṣāyā wa ijāzāt.* Edited by Aḥmad ʿAlawī al-Ḥibshī. Singapore: Maṭbaʿat Karājī, 1990.

Ittiḥād al-Udabā' wa al-Kuttāb al-Yamanīyīn. ed. *Wathā'iq mahrajān BāKathīr.* Beirut: Dār al-Ḥadātha, 1988.

al-Kāf, Saqqāf ʿAlī. *Dirāsa fī nasab al-sāda banī ʿAlawī: Dhurriyat al-Imām al-Muhājir Aḥmad ibn ʿĪsā.* Madina: Maṭābiʿ al-Mukhṭar al-Islāmī, 1989.

———. *Ḥaḍramawt ʿabra arbaʿat ʿashir qarnan.* Beirut: Maktabat Usāma, 1990.

al-Kasādī, 'Ādil. "Namādhij min al-foklūr al-baḥrī." *al-Sā'iya* 1 (March 1993): 8–9 (mimeographed publication from al-Ḥāmī).

———. Untitled, unpublished article on the changing structure of the Ḥaḍramī family, n.d.

al-Khaṭīb, Abū Bakr Aḥmad. *al-Fatāwā al-nāfi' fī masā'il al-aḥwāl al-wāqi'a.* Cairo: Maṭba'at Muṣṭafā al-Bābī al-Ḥalabī, 1960.

Kitāb wasīlat al-ṣabb al-wadūd ilā al-ilāh al-ma'būd. n.p.: Mu'assasat al-jazīra, n.d.

al-Mallāḥī, 'Abd al-Raḥman 'Abd al-Karīm and 'Alī Ḥasan 'Alī. "al-Ṣirā' al-Ḥamūmī-al-Qu'ayṭī wa Duwāfi'hu 1867–1967." In *Wathā'iq al-nadwa al-'ilmiyya al-tārīkhiyya hawla al-muqāwma al-sha'biyya fī Ḥaḍramawt 1900–1963,* edited by Ṣāliḥ 'Alī Bā Ṣurra and Muḥammad Sa'īd Dā'ūd, 179–201. Aden: Jāma'at 'Adan, 1989.

al-Mashhūr, 'Abd al-Raḥman Muḥammad. *Shams al-ẓahīra fī nasab ahl al-bayt min Banī 'Alawī.* 2d ed. 2 vols. Jedda: 'Ālam al-ma'rifa, 1984.

———. *Bughyat al-mustarshidīn.* Cairo: Dār al-Fikr, n.d.

al-Mashhūr, Abū Bakr. *Lawāmi' al-nūr: Najba min a'lām Ḥaḍramawt.* 2 vols. Sana'a': Dār al-Muhājir, n.d.

al-Miḥḍār, Muṣṭafā Aḥmad. *al-Ḥayā al-sa'īda bi-Ḥaḍramawt.* N.p., 1953.

al-Miḥḍār, Ḥāmid Abī Bakr. *al-Za'īm al-Sayyid al-Ḥabīb Ḥusayn ibn Ḥāmid al-Miḥḍār wa al-Sultana al-Qu'ayṭiyya.* Jedda: 'Ālim al-Ma'rifa, 1983.

al-Nākhibī, 'Abdallāh Aḥmad. *Riḥla ilā Yāfa' fī adwār al-tārīkh.* Jedda: Dār al-'Ilm, 1990.

al-Qu'ayṭī, al-Sulṭān Ṣāliiḥ. *Al-Riḥla al-sulṭāniyya ilā al-jiha al-gharbiyya min al-mamlika al-Qu'ayṭiyya.* Cheribon, Java: al-Maṭba'a al-Miṣriyya, 1950–1951.

———. *Ta'ammulāt 'an tārīkh Ḥaḍramawt.* N.p., 1996.

al-Rābiṭa, al-'Alawiyya. *Ḥaqā'iq.* Batavia: Maṭba'at Jam'iyat Khayr, 1931.

Rif'at Bāshā, Ibrāhīm. *Mirāt al-Ḥaramayn.* 2 vols. Beirut: Dār al-Ma'rifa, 1925.

Saba'a, Naṣr Ṣāliḥ. *Min yanābī' tārīkhinā al-Yamānī wa ash'ār Rājiḥ Ḥaytham Saba'a al-Yāfa'ī.* Damascus: Muṭba'at al-Kātib al-'Arabī, 1994.

al-Saqqāf, 'Abdallāh Muḥammad. *Tārīkh al-shu'arā' al-Ḥaḍramīyīn.* 5 vols. Cairo: Maṭba'at al-Ḥijāzī, 1934–1943.

al-Saqqāf, 'Abd al-Raḥman Bin 'Ubaydillāh. *Dīwān.* Cairo: Maṭba'at Lajnat al-Bayān al-'Arabī, n.d. (Later volumes of the Dīwān are available only in manuscript.)

———. "Badā'i' al-tābūt fī akhbār Ḥaḍramawt." 3 vols.

———. *Nasīm ḥajir fī ta'iyyīd qawlī 'an madhhab al-muhājir.* Maṭba'at al-Nahḍa al-Yamaniyya, 1948.

al-Saqqāf, Ḥasan 'Abd al-Raḥman. *Fihrist Badā'i' al-tābūt.* Aden: Fatāt al-Jazīra, n.d.

al-Saqqāf, Ja'far Muḥammad. "Aḍwā' 'alā tārīkh Wādī Ḥaḍramawt al-zirā'ī." *al-Turāth* 5 (April–June 1992): 17–26.

———. "Min tārīkh al-ḥarakāt al-sha'biyya al-iṣlāḥiyya fī Ḥaḍramawt (al-mu'tamar al-iṣlā ḥī fī Singhāfūra)." In *Wathā'iq al-nadwa al-'ilmiyya al-tārīkhiyya hawla al-muqāwma al-sha'biyya fī Ḥaḍramawt 1900–1963,* edited by Ṣāliḥ 'Alī BāṢurra and Muḥammad Sa'īd Dā'ūd, 25–34. Aden: Jāma'at 'Adan, 1989.

———, comp. "Tarjimat al-Shaykha al-'ārifat bi-llāh Sulṭāna bint 'Alī al-Zubaydī."

286 Selected Bibliography, Arabic Language

al-Shāṭirī, Muḥammad Aḥmad. *Adwār al-tarīkh al-Ḥaḍramī.* 2d ed. 2 vols. Jedda: ʿĀlam al-Maʿrifa, 1983.

al-Shillī, Muḥammad Abī Bakr. *al-Mashraʿ al-rawī fī manaāqib al-sāda al-kirām abī ʿAlawī.* 2 vols. N.p., 1982.

Sulayman, Karāma Mubārak. *al-Tarbiya wa al-taʿlīm fī al-shaṭr al-janūbī min al-Yaman.* 2 vols. Sanaʾa: Markaz Dirāsāt wa al-Buḥūth al-Yamanī, 1994.

Surkattī, Aḥmad Muḥammad. *Masāʾil al-thalāth.* Cairo: Dār al-ʿUlūm, 1977.

ʿUkāsha, Muḥammad ʿAbd al-Karīm. *Qiyām al-Sulṭana al-Quʿayṭiyya wa al-taghalghal al-istiʿmārī fī Ḥaḍramawt 1839–1918.* Amman: Dār Ibn Rashad, 1985.

al-Zabīdī, Aḥmad al-Sharjī. *Ṭabaqāt al-khawāṣṣ ahl al-ṣidq wa al-khalāṣ.* Sanaʾa: al-Dār al-Yamaniyya, 1986.

Mimeographed Booklets Printed by the Bureau of Culture and Information, People's Democratic Republic of Yemen

BāMaṭraf, Muḥammad ʿAbd al-Qādir. "Sūr al-Shiḥr." 1977.

Bukayr, ʿAlī Sālim. "Baḥth fī muṣādir al-tārīkh al-Ḥaḍramī." 1979.

———. "Shuʿarāʾ Tarīm fī al-qarn al-rābiʿ ʿashar al-hijrī." 1989.

al-Ḥibshī, Muḥhammad ʿAbd al-Qādir. "Qaṣr al-thawra." 1985.

al-Mallahī, ʿAbd al-Raḥman ʿAbd al-Karīm. "Dirasāt shiʿr al-mallāḥīn wa al-ṣayyādīn: Shiʿruhum wa ʿadātuhum al-mihniyya." Illustrated by Anwar ʿAbdallāh ʿAbd al-ʿAzīz.

al-Ṣabbān, ʿAbd al-Qādir Muḥammad. "al-Shiʿr al-shaʿbī maʿa al-mazāraʿīn", 1987.

———. "al-Falāḥūn wa ʿādatuhum al-mihniyya." 1983.

———. "Baḥth ʿan al-shaʿr al-shaʿbī aw ... shaʿr al-jumhūr."

———. "Dalīl mathaf al-ʿādāt wa al-taqālīd al-shaʿbiyya bi-mudīriyyat Sayʾūn." 1986.

———. "Madīnat Shibām fī suṭūr." 1981.

———. "al-Taʿrīfāt al-tārīkhiyya ʿan Wādī Ḥaḍramawt."

———. "ʿĀdāt wa taqālīd bil-Ahqaf."

———. "Ziyarāt wa ʿādāt."

INDEX

mediation *(continued)*
  shari'a court, 85, 87; by spiritual au-
    thorities, 20, 25, 119, 163, 190–192,
    194–198, 215–216; in water disputes,
    87; by *wazir,* 211–212
al-Mihdhar, Husayn b. Hamid; and Aden
  Agreement, 208–213; and 'Alawi-Irshad
  conflict, 59, 62; and Bin 'Abdat rebellion, 222–224; and Hajr, 189; and succession disputes, 225–228; and tribal rebellions, 196, 215–217, 225–227, 229
al-Muhajir, ancestor of Hadhrami *sada,* 19,
  22
Muhammad b. 'Ali b. Muhammad Sahib
  Mirbat. *See* al-Faqih al-Muqaddam
*munsib*s (spiritual authorities): arbitration
  of, 189–191, 194–198; political activity of, 232; role and position of, 20, 25,
  81, 130, 134–135, 155–156; tribes
  and, 27, 119
mystical practice. *See* Sufism

N
Nahid tribe, 29–30, 51
*nakhuda*s, 109–114
Nuwwah tribe, 29–30, 50, 119–120,
  191–192

O
Ottomans, 185, 199–208

P
palaces, 69, 77, 79, 99, 117, 204, 24
Periplus of the Erythraean Sea, 15, 49
population figures, 14; emigrants and emigrant communities, 41, 47–48, 50;
  Ghayl BaWazir, 117; al-Mukalla, 98;
  Say'un, 69; Shibam, 78; al-Shihr, 102;
  Tarim, 75
pregnancy, 124. *See also* women and birth
Prophet Hud, 14–15, 24, 73, 156–159,
  160
proverbs, 41–43, 112, 128, 132

Q
quarter system, 32, 67, 72–74, 81,
  99–100, 105, 118, 263n; of Dutch
  East Indies, 51–52
al-Qu'ayti, 'Abdalla b. 'Umar, 103,
  185–188, 193
al-Qu'ayti, 'Awadh b. 'Umar, 247; state-
  building, 116, 186–192; in succession
  dispute, 193–194; will of, in succession
  dispute, 227–228
al-Qu'ayti, Ghalib b. 'Awadh, 247; and
  agriculture, 92; and education, 168;
  state-building, 192–194, 197–198,
  208–210, 229–230, 232; succession
  dispute after death of, 225–227
al-Qu'ayti, Salih b. Ghalib, 187, 225,
  227–229, 233, 240, 247
al-Qu'ayti, 'Umar b. 'Awadh (1850–1865),
  184, 186–187, 247
al-Qu'ayti, 'Umar b. 'Awadh (1921–1935),
  247; and agriculture, 116; construction
  of palaces, 99, 117; and education,
  169; and Hamum rebellion, 219–220;
  and Jam'iyat al-Haqq, 230; and reform
  conferences, 237–240; resolution of
  budget problems, 229–230; in succession dispute, 225–229

R
al-Rabita al-'Alawiyya, 56–62, 235–239
al-Rabita journal, 5, 56–58
Reilly, Bernard, 213–214, 223, 228
ribat. See Sufism, centers of learning
ridda rebellions, 15–17, 74–75
Ridha, Rashid, 3, 53, 55

S
sailing vessels, 106–107, 109, 118. *See also*
  sea trade
al-Saqqaf, 'Abd al-Rahman b. 'Ubaydillah:
  and Aden Agreement, 211–212; and
  'Alawi-Irshad conflict, 60; and reform
  organizations, 230–231; works of, 5,
  150, 168, 201, 231; and World War I,
  199–207